CLA

53°

New Quay
Abbey
reehy
ughmanna
Turlogh

Kilkeady

Kilneboy
Crusheen
Feacle

gh
CUROFIN
Inchicronane
Moynoe
Ruan
Tomgraney
Feacle
Dysert
SCARIFF
Templemaly
Kilraghtis
Tomaraney
Kilnoe
Ogonniloe

Dromcliffe
TULLAGH
ENNIS
Downie Clonie
Callaghans Hills Killuran
Kilmaly Clare Abbey
Quin
Clare
Clonlea
Broadford
KILLALOE
Kilkishen
Killone
Killmurrynegaul Killeily
Killogennedy
Tomfinlough
Kilnasoolagh
NEWMARKET
Killinaghty
Bridge Town
Clondegad
Kilmaleere
Finogh
SIX MILE BRIDGE
Kilchrist
Droniline
Deer
Clonlognan
Kiltonanlea
Kilconry
Kilfentinane
Doonass
Bunratty
Healick
Killeliy
Kilquane

50°

40°

SCALE of IRISH MILES
0   5   10

SCALE of ENGLISH MILES
0   5   10

The
Strangers
Gaze

Also published by CLASP PRESS

County Clare: A History and Topography
by Samuel Lewis.

Poverty Before the Famine: County Clare 1835;
first report from His Majesty's commissioners
for inquiring into the condition
of the poorer classes in Ireland

Two Months at Kilkee
by Mary John Knott.
(originally published 1836)

The Antiquities of County Clare;
letters containing information relative to the
Antiquities of the County of Clare
collected during the progress of
the Ordnance Survey in 1839
& letters and extracts relative to
Ancient Territories in Thomond, 1841
by John O'Donovan and Eugene O'Curry

Kilrush Union Minute Books, 1849.

A Handbook to Lisdoonvarna and its vicinity
giving a detailed account of its
curative waters, and tours to
the principal places of interest
in the County Clare
by P. D.   (originally published 1876)

Sable Wings Over the Land;
Ennis, County Clare, and its wider community
during the Great Famine
by Ciarán Ó Murchadha

The Strangers Gaze

Travels in County Clare
1534-1950

Edited by

Brian Ó Dálaigh

CLASP PRESS

Published by
CLASP PRESS, 1998.

© CLASP PRESS, 1998.

ISBN 1 900545 08 x

Brian Ó Dálaigh is hereby identified
as editor of this work

Text prepared by
Margaret Clancy, Catriona Malone, Joanne Considine, Emer Kinsella, Áine Clune,
Siobhán Murphy, Maria Meaney, Lorna Downes, Tracey Hayes, Katie Kearney,
Joyce Cronin, Michelle Moroney, Siobhán Dunne, Siobhán Kenny, Linda Burke,
Paulette O'Mahony, Ollie Carmody, Shay Dunphy, Georgina Belmour,
Gráinne Kinnane, Linda McMahon, Niamh Brennan, JP Considine, Brendan Daly,
Mary McNamara, Michelle Hansen, Noleen Corry, Conor Quinn, Marie McNamara,
Regina Eustace, Sharon Considine & Jackie Dermody.

Designed by
Anthony Edwards

Index & Layout by
Maureen Comber

Cover design: A. Edwards & M. Comber
Cover layout: A. Edwards & S. McCooey

Printed by Colour Books, Dublin

CLASP PRESS,
Clare County Library Headquarters,
Mill Road, Ennis, Co. Clare.

Chairman of Clare County Council

Tá áthas an domhain orm toisc go bhfuil mo Chómhairle páirteach I bhfoilsiú an leabhair seo. Cuirfidh sé go mór le tuiscint fás and forbairt an Chontae, agus a mhuintir leis, le ceithre céad blian anuas. *The Strangers Gaze* allows us to taste the atmosphere of times gone by while also allowing us to peep through the window of time as witnesses to change. The reader will have a far greater appreciation of life in Clare through the centuries.

It is a brave gesture to hold ourselves up so that others can comment on our lovely county and its wonderful people. We Dalcassians are a proud people and are conscious of our achievements. This book is testimony to the great survival instincts of the people of Clare and of what we have achieved. My Council, in no small way, has played a major role in the development of the county over the past 100 years and I congratulate my current colleagues and acknowledge our great indebtedness to all former elected representatives. I would also like to take this opportunity to express my thanks to all present and past staff of Clare County Council.

This work contains almost seventy descriptions of County Clare by a variety of individuals, including newspaper reporters, clergymen, judges, soldiers, etc. who came here from many different countries and indeed for many different reasons. Many historic events are described giving us invaluable first hand accounts of great events e.g. the Cromwellian conquest.

Some of the more well known works were not selected in order to facilitate the inclusion of many sources unfamiliar to the general reader. The material not included e.g. *Lloyd's Tour of Clare*, Mr. and Mrs. Hall's travels, *Dutton's Statistical Survey*, etc. are already readily available in other sources. A number of accounts are published here for the first time.

To celebrate the centenary of the establishment of Clare County Council, there was a temptation to commission a history of the Council and its activities over the past 100 years. However, one has only to travel throughout the county to see the results of our work, and I am unashamedly proud of our record through the years. The history of our work does not need to be written as it is all etched on our landscape - a landscape that continues to attract and fascinate people from every corner of the globe.

Rath Dé ar a léitheoirí, *Pádraig Ó Ceallaigh*

Clare County Manager

Clare County Council was anxious to mark the centenary of Local Government in County Clare and, as County Manager, I was delighted to recommend to my Council that sponsorship of the publication of *The Strangers Gaze* would be a unique way to celebrate one hundred years of Local Government in the county. This excellent and imaginative work holds a mirror up to the face of Clare allowing us to see ourselves as others saw us. When this is done over a period of four centuries, not alone does it give the visitors reaction to us, but also shows the development of our county. The various descriptions of the journeys described stretching from 1534 to 1950 enable us to open the covers of the book and, in almost time capsule fashion, travel backwards in time while listening to a contemporary commentary. These commentaries are all the more valuable through the scholarly introductions to each extract by Editor Brian Ó Dálaigh, which not alone give relevant biographical details of the narrator, but also place each piece in context.

We learn that the professional travel writers of the 18th Century avoided County Clare and concentrated on well known places like the Giant's Causeway and Killarney. This, of course, makes the extracts unearthed by the editor all the more valuable. Charles Bowden in *A Tour of Ireland* (1791) says that "the roads in this county are extremely bad". Now, where did I hear that comment before? History indeed has a habit of repeating itself. The cry "our roads are in a shocking state" has been heard by me many times over the last decade.

Some of the early accounts portray a harrowing picture of the poor people living with great hardships. Indeed the Rev. George Whitefield, Methodist Evangelist, whose ship suffered severe storm damage and was lucky to make landfall on the coast off west Clare, records in the year 1738 , "if my parishioners at Georgia complain to me of hardships, I must tell them how the Irish live; for their habitations are far more despicable". However, he also concedes that "content dwells in many of these low huts", showing that despite poor conditions, people looked contented. We in the Clare County Council can look back in pride at the great improvements visited on the county through the hard work and dedication of both elected representatives and staff over the past one hundred years. We face the new millennium and our second centenary with great confidence and enthusiasm for the future. We will stay astride of the Celtic Tiger and continue to improve the foundations built by our predecessors.

Willie Moloney

Chairman of CLASP

From its humble beginnings in May 1995, Clare Local Studies Project (CLASP) has grown in reputation with every activity and publication. *The Strangers Gaze*, our eighth formal publication, continues the standard of our previous titles. Our formal partnership with FÁS continues to be our major asset and indeed without FÁS our work would not be possible.

We have had very important informal links, from the start of our project, with Clare County Council and are delighted to join with the Council to produce this excellent work. Without the financial help of the Council, this publication would not be possible, and I sincerely believe that this book will hold pride of place in the bookshelves of everyone with a love of County Clare. The county holds a great fascination for people all over the world, and modern visitors can now match their memories with those who came over the centuries and recorded their thoughts.

Many people continue to play an active part in ensuring the continued success of our projects. The talents of our FÁS trainees, now under the leadership of Martina Crowley-Hayes and Linda Burke, is evident in everything we achieve. To the editor of the publication, Brian Ó Dálaigh, I say well done, it has been a pleasure to work with you again. Brian is a true Clareman, with a burning desire to ensure that the history of his county is accurately recorded. This present publication will further enhance his reputation as a historian and chronicler.

The back room team have, as always, been magnificent, giving so unselfishly of their time and expertise. Ted Finn continues to keep the ship afloat with his steady hand on the rudder. Maureen Comber is, as ever, totally professional in her editorial duties and her involvement ensures excellence. Designer, Anthony Edwards, lives with every project with the passion of a parent and demands commitment and excellence from everyone involved. External Director, Gerry Collison, continues to assist and support the work of the overall project in every way. Any words I might write could not adequately describe the debt we all owe to this team who are slowly but surely creating a "Clare Bookshelf" - a shelf that will be unique. Finally, I would like to thank the County Manager, Willie Moloney and Chairman of Clare County Council, P.J. Kelly, for their encouragement and support.

Noel Crowley

Acknowledgements

This book could not have been completed without the advice and assistance of a number of colleagues and friends. It was conceived a number of years ago when I first became aware of the wealth of material relating to County Clare contained in travel books. Most of the travel books, however, were long out of print and only available to specialists in the copyright libraries of Ireland or England. My idea in publishing travellers' accounts of Clare was firstly to make the travel writings of the county more accessible to the general reader, and secondly to illustrate the potential and value of travel writing for the purposes of historical research.

My first debt is to Noel Crowley, Clare County Librarian, who responded immediately to my proposal and placed the resources of the county library and of CLASP at my disposal. Few people have done more to encourage the study of local history in Clare than Noel. When he first became county librarian over twenty years ago there were only two works of note on the 'Clare shelf', Frost's *History and Topography of County Clare* and Fr. White's *History of the Dalcassian Clans*, both published over a hundred years ago. Since then, with the setting up of the Clare Local Studies Centre and more recently CLASP, there has been a virtual explosion in the number of books on the history of Clare. Old books, long out of print, have been reprinted and new works commissioned.

My greatest debt, however, is to Maureen Comber, who has toiled ceaselessly since the work began. Maureen corresponded with the deposit libraries of Dublin, Belfast, Edinburgh and London and tracked down the obscure publications necessary for our project. The Clare sections were then input and proofed by CLASP trainees under the able direction of Martina Crowley-Hayes and Linda Burke. Again in the final stages of production Maureen Comber and Ted Finn brought their formidable proof-reading skills to bear on the texts before the work was despatched to the printers, while Anthony Edwards was responsible for the overall design, illustrations and book cover. To all of them my sincere thanks.

I am also indebted to Dr. Christopher Woods of Maynooth who provided me with his invaluable catalogue of Irish tours and travel books. Dr. Woods had spent a number of years compiling his bibliography which will undoubtedly become the definite guide to Irish travel literature. May I express the hope that it will not be too long until we see the fruits of his labours in print. My special thanks are due to colleagues who suggested sources and provided books including Sean Spellissy, Martin Breen, Ciarán Ó Murchadha, Raymond Gillespie, Bernadette Cunningham, and the members of the Local History Group in St. Patrick's College Maynooth. Not-withstanding the contributions of others, the errors in this book are my responsibility alone.

Finally my most grateful appreciation is to my family who have long endured my physical and mental absences and especially my wife Assumpta, who has been my greatest support and to whom this work is dedicated.

The permission to reproduce extracts from the following manuscript material is hereby acknowledged:
The Board of Trinity College Dublin for TCD MSS 883/1 folio 227 & MS 4029 ;
Petworth House Archives for MS 9342.

Lá na Naomh Uile, 1998   *Brian Ó Dálaigh.*

Editorial Note

Generally speaking those descriptions most illustrative of the county's history and topography, were prepared for publication. Accounts of Clare pre 1800 are relatively rare and thus almost all early accounts were included. However, after 1800 when tours became common, it was possible to be more selective. Only accounts which were written directly from the observation or experience of the writer were included. Thus topographical dictionaries, guide books and books with secondary reports were excluded. Autobiographies and memoirs were excluded on the basis that the accounts were written many years after the events described. Some reports ran to over seventy pages and it was necessary to reduce them to more manageable proportions. Generally pseudo-historical matter, descriptions of picturesque scenery and information derived from secondary sources was excluded. An ellipse (three dots) indicates in the text where sentences have been deleted; material deleted at the end of paragraphs is indicated by an ellipse and a full stop. Words occurring within square brackets were inserted by the editor. Capitalisation was normalised, ancient spelling modernised and misprints, spelling errors etc. silently corrected. Names of people and places appear as in the original accounts.

Maidir leis an gcúntas a scríobh Peadar Ó hAnnracháin ar chondae an Chláir sa bhlian 1909, is sa seanchló Gaelach a foilsíodh é i 1937. Cuireadh cruth nua-aoiseach air don leabhar seo, ach ceapadh go mba cheart gan rialaca an chaighdeáin a chur i bhfeidhm go docht ar an téasc.

Illustrations

Contents

Introduction

Travel writing is a historical source of high quality. The best writers record their own observations and ignore second hand reports and hearsay. Being strangers their accounts are rarely contaminated by local loyalties or party politics. Travellers bring a fresh eye to the local scene and are able to appreciate differences not immediately apparent to the native inhabitant. It is this ability to compare and contrast that is perhaps their greatest advantage. That is not to say that their accounts are without fault. Obviously travellers are often unfamiliar with the scenes they describe and they are all too often governed by their own prejudices and loyalties. Indeed some writers pretend to give a full account of the country after spending only a few short weeks passing through it. The informed reader, however, can quickly spot such defects and make allowances for them. Traveller accounts attract because people have always been curious to know what others think of them; and because they entertain and provide so many different points of view they are an interesting and pleasurable way of exploring a country's past.

The accounts in these pages were written by visitors to County Clare over a period of four centuries. The writers journeyed through the county in many different capacities. They were military adventurers seeking land, surveyors attempting to map territory, evangelical clergy seeking converts, newspaper men in search of stories and travel writers in search of the picturesque. What they have in common for our purposes is that they all provide first hand accounts of what they observed and they all write directly out of their own experience. There is a wealth of factual information in their reports - on diet, clothing, places of abode, farming practice, religious customs, political allegiances and so forth. Moreover they provide special insights into the divisions that existed within Clare society: between the colonisers and the colonised, between Protestant and Catholic and between the landed classes and the landless. A persistent feature of the works, even when they are written by Irish people, is the sense that the writers were outsiders, even intruders on the local scene. The interaction between outsider and native was unequal. The local voice is heard only through the mediation of the stranger. This inequality of relationship creates a tension in the accounts which provides a fundamental dynamic of the works collected here.

Historically, Clare was a disadvantaged county on the western sea-board. A county of wet climate and poor soils it had little attraction for strangers. The county was never widely planted with settlers as happened in Ulster or in the rest of Munster. Surrounded on three sides by water, Clare remained isolated and its traditional Gaelic way of life persisted well into the eighteenth century. Indeed so widely was the county's isolation perceived to be that in 1721 an English writer, Peter Browne, published a volume entitled *A letter from Ireland giving an account of the taking of a great number of sea monsters at Monster Creek, in the county of Clare, Ireland.* The story concerns a ship's crew shipwrecked on the coast of Clare where they encounter many monsters. With the development of roads and the improvement of transport, the descriptions that were subsequently to appear, while less spectacular, were certainly better informed.

The first entry in the anthology is the letter of Connor O'Brien to the European Emperor Charles V in 1534. The letter was obviously not written by an outsider. Connor O'Brien was the last ruler of the independent lordship of Thomond. His letter is included here on the basis that it was written for the benefit of outsiders. By describing the military potential of his lordship O'Brien hoped to attract the armed intervention of the European emperor. Indeed almost all sixteenth century accounts were compiled with military intervention in mind.

Edmund Sexton's description of the Shannon estuary in the 1540s was designed to facilitate the subduing of Thomond by the English. Fr. Wolf's report in 1574 was written to encourage invasion of the country by the Spanish. Lughaidh Ó Cléirigh's account in 1599 glorified the plunder of Thomond by the Prince of the North, Hugh O Donnell. An exception is the entry written by the English Jesuit, Fr. Goode, for Camden's historical survey of Britain and Ireland in 1586. Goode provides a factual account of Thomond, (which had just recently been renamed County Clare) but like all English accounts of the period it is hostile to the native Irish.

The first four decades of the seventeenth century were relatively peaceful. Peaceful interludes clearly did not inspire traveller accounts and apart from Donough Mooney's *Franciscan Houses of Clare* it is not until war starts again in the 1640s that further descriptions of the county are produced. Three accounts of the Cromwellian conquest of Clare are reproduced in this anthology. All were compiled by military personnel, who participated in the war on the English side. The first is a diary kept by Sir William Penn, a sea captain, who foraged up and down the Shannon Estuary in 1646 to keep the Parliamentarian garrison at Bunratty supplied. The second, another diary, kept by an unidentified Parliamentarian officer at Limerick, describes the military incursions into County Clare in 1651. From a historical point of view diaries are particularly valuable, because being a daily record, they give a more accurate account of events. Of less value are the memoirs of General Ludlow. Written some years after his departure from Ireland, they are a selective account of the conflict in County Clare. Unfortunately we have no record of the war from the Irish point of view; it is only through English reports that we hear of the atrocities and appalling suffering inflicted on the population during those awful years. With the completion of the Cromwellian conquest the purely military inspired accounts come to an end. Subsequent descriptions of the county, when written, arose from entirely different motivations.

The Clare Franciscan, Fr. Anthony McBrody, writing from Prague, Czechoslovakia, in 1669 was concerned to take to task those English writers, who wrote 'false histories' and 'erred magnificently' about his native Thomond. McBrody praises the natural resources of Clare, its saints and holy wells and the nobility of the people. A different type of report is provided by the English traveller Thomas Dineley. Dineley came to Clare in 1681 to look over, as it were, the newly acquired territory, to see how best it could be managed and made to produce. He illustrates his travelogue profusely with drawings of the castles and houses of the newly arrived settlers.

Cartographers were to make a substantial contribution to the topographical writings of Clare. The Molyneux survey of 1682 set out to provide a topographical description of the counties of Ireland for a world atlas then in the process of being published in London. While the publishing scheme collapsed, two accounts of the county were compiled, one by Hugh Brigdall, an Ennis attorney, and the other by Robert Downing, a researcher for the project. They are the first 'scientific' accounts of Clare in that they attempt to describe the physical and human geography of the county and are generally free of bias. In 1703 another cartographer, Thomas Moland, surveyed the lands of the Thomond estate. The earl of Thomond, then an absentee living in England, ordered the mapping of his estates in Ireland so as to maximise his rental income. Moland produced a beautiful series of maps and in a survey of extraordinary detail provides the first accounts of some of the remotest parts of the county. Two further mapmakers in the eighteenth century contributed to the travel literature of Clare. The first, Col. William Roy, a military surveyor sent to Ireland in 1766 to report on the state of the country's defences, commented on military installations, the conditions of roads and the diet of the people. The second was the Rev. Augustus Beaufort, Rector of Navan. Beaufort initially set out to compile a detailed map of the diocesan boundaries of Ireland. Entering Clare from Galway in 1788 he travelled the length of the county in a horse drawn vehicle. The first of our travellers to achieve such a feat. Clearly roads and bridges had greatly improved from the days when only the pedestrian or mounted traveller could penetrate the most inaccessible parts. Beaufort's map of Ireland, the most accurate to appear before the Ordnance Survey maps of the 1840s, was published in 1793.

If one had to choose a theme that pervades the accounts across the centuries it would have to be the extreme poverty of the people. Visitors to Ireland were appalled at the poverty they encountered. In 1689 John Stevens, a Jacobite soldier and a friend of the people commented, 'the Irish live in hovels no better than pig-sties'. While passing through east Clare he thought the town of Killaloe 'the meanest I ever saw dignified with that character'. George Whitefield, a clergyman returned from missionary work among the Indians of North America in 1738, was astounded by 'the meaness of the poor people's living . . . If my parishioners at Georgia complain to me of hardships, I must tell them how the Irish live; for their habitations are far more despicable'. As the years passed and the population increased the situation worsened. In

1817 the pedestrian, Bernard Trotter, passing between Quin and Spancelhill commented 'the village near the Abbey is wretched, the cabins very poor . . . There is a great poverty in Clare and the miserable attempt to sell unlicensed spirits in their mud-cottages scarcely excited displeasure'. The German traveller Johann Kohl going from Ennis to Kilrush in 1842 'passed not a single village, nor a single hut fit for human habitation . . . nowhere else do we find human beings gnawing, from year's end to year's end at the same root, berry or weed. There are animals who do so, but human beings, nowhere except in Ireland'. Perhaps the worst excesses of poverty and deprivation were witnessed in the wake of the Great Famine in west Clare. The Rev. Sydney Osborne, when passing between Kilrush and Kildysart in 1849 observed the ruins of hundreds of houses, tumbled by landlords for non payment of rent. Amid the ruins of one he found a woman and her young children. 'The place was a mere pig sty, a lad of four feet could hardly have stood in the middle of it . . . here this poor creature had dwelt for weeks, with her three children; her stock of food was at her feet; a large bundle of corn-weed and nettles; she was positively naked to the waist but by hitching up some of her rags she extemporised a bodice'. It was only in the second half of the nineteenth century, following the drastic fall in population levels and the change in land ownership from landlord to tenant that living standards began slowly to rise.

In Ireland, as elsewhere, agriculture was the fundamental generator of wealth. Visitors keenly observed the farming practices of the country. Three individuals, whose primary interest was in agriculture, recorded their observations on the farming practices of County Clare. In 1776, Arthur Young, the foremost agriculturist of his age, gave an indepth account of the county's agriculture. His insights on farming and on its potential for development have rarely been equalled. In 1813, John Curwen, the Manx M.P., followed in Young's footsteps. He compared the state of contemporary agriculture with Young's observations and commented on how farming had developed over the intervening period. He particularly noted the huge increase in rents and farming incomes, brought about mainly through the demand created by the Napoleonic wars. Curwen was one of the few visitors to note the prosperity then being enjoyed by the people, a situation, which unfortunately proved to be short lived. The third agriculturist to visit the county was James Caird. Caird was sent by the British government in 1850 to assess the agricultural potential of the then near deserted farming lands of the county so that they could be advertised to investors in Britain.

If tourism is travel undertaken for pleasure, then the first tourist to leave an account of his travels in Clare was the Rev. Richard Pococke, the Protestant bishop of Ossory. In the eighteenth century only the rich and powerful travelled for pleasure. Pococke was unusual in that he visited the county twice, once in 1749 and again in 1752. Few roads could cope with wheeled traffic and so the bishop journeyed on horseback. There was still little incentive to visit County Clare where roads were poor, inns uncomfortable and transport inconvenient. Most visitors avoided the county altogether. In the two most popular tours of Ireland published in the eighteenth century, Richard Twiss' *A Tour of Ireland in 1775*, and Thomas Campbell's *A Philosophical Tour of the South of Ireland* (1788), Clare is not even mentioned. Most tourists came as far as Limerick and immediately turned south to savour the delights of the Lakes of Killarney. In 1791, Charles Bowden was the first to mention the county in a contemporarily published tour. Bowden journeyed on horseback up the west coast of Clare and complained 'the roads in this country are extremely bad and the accommodations they afford are worse'. In the nineteenth century as the wayside inns and the county's road network improved tourists became more common. Three tours were published in the second decade of the century: the first by William Reed who visited Kilrush in 1810; the second by Rev. James Hall, who toured the east of the county in 1812; and the third by the aptly named John Trotter who completed the first walking tour of Clare in 1817.

Some of the best travel accounts, however, were written in the years 1830-42. Indeed this period can be termed the golden age of Clare travel writing. In 1834 William Bilton produced his marvellous *Angler in Ireland*. In pursuit of good fishing Bilton described many areas of the county previously unvisited. In the same year Henry Inglis, foremost travel writer of the day, travelled on the stage coach to Ennis and gave a masterful account of the cases being tried at the Clare assizes. In the winter of 1835 the poor law commissioner Henry Binns journeyed up the west coast and experienced at first hand the tourist accommodation at Kilkee, Miltown Malbay and Lehinch. The novelist William Thackeray devoted a chapter of his *Irish Sketch Book* to the county in 1842. But perhaps the most outstanding contribution was made by the German travel writer Johann Kohl. Kohl, a perceptive traveller, filled his account with a wealth of descriptive detail. Being a well travelled individual, he could assess Irish conditions in the European context. His observations are excellent, his judgements fair and balanced. In short his description of pre-Famine Clare is unequalled.

Why did so many accounts of the county appear in the 1830s, when in the previous decade not a single tour was published? Improved communications across the Irish sea in the 1820s greatly increased the number of visitors to Ireland. The initiation of a regular stage coach service between Limerick, Ennis and Galway made the county much more accessible. As communication by road improved and as travel came within the means of more people, a demand for travel literature was created, which resulted in many new tours being published. But the event that most propelled the county into prominence was the election of Daniel O'Connell in 1828 and the achievement, subsequently, of Catholic emancipation. After that the county featured in the itinerary of most visitors to Ireland.

The type of visitors that came to Clare during and after the Great Famine were entirely different from those who had gone before. They were not tourists but rather individuals with strong religious or social convictions. Like the Quakers who distributed relief during the Famine or social reformers who advocated fundamental changes in land-ownership. Their accounts are free of the condescension and ridicule that characterise pre-Famine accounts. Men like the Scottish essayist and social critic Thomas Carlyle, who felt compelled to come to Ireland to witness the scenes of mass starvation for himself. Or the M.P. Poulet Scrope, who advocated agrarian reform, or the Rev. Sydney Osborne, whose harrowing accounts of the evictions in west Clare did so much to highlight the plight of the Irish tenant farmer in Britain. Accounts such as these continued up to 1862 when the newspaper columnist Henry Coulter carried out an extensive survey of the social conditions and the state of agriculture in the county. Thereafter with the threat of famine lifted commentators concentrated on the question of land reform. The Scottish activist, Jessie Craigen, reported on the struggle of the tenants in Bodyke against their landlord Col. O'Callaghan in 1880. Three further accounts concentrate on the land issue but from the landlord's point of view: Bernard Becker (1881), William Hurlbert (1888) and Robert Buckley (1893). Becker's account is of interest for his extensive report on the land reclamation project in the estuary of the Fergus. Hurlbert, a veteran of the American civil war, describes the predicament of the landlord Richard Stackpoole at Edenvale and Buckley, a journalist from Birmingham, returns to the situation in Bodyke and the heightened expectations of the tenants. By 1893 it was apparent that tenants would soon come into the ownership of their farms and that the focus of politics was about to shift from land reform to the national question.

The era of modern tourism in Clare begins with the opening of the railway line between Limerick and Ennis in 1859. Ironically the coming of the railway did not lead to an increase in travel literature but rather the reverse. By travelling at speed tourists saw less of the countryside so there was less need for tour books. In any event, travel had become so inexpensive, it was more interesting to travel oneself than to read the accounts of others. An exception to the trend was the Wexford author Thomas Lacy, who used the train extensively to collect material for his book *Sights and Scenes of our Fatherland*. Lacy, who had a penchant for architecture, wrote extraordinarily detailed accounts of the interiors of the newly constructed Catholic churches. As tourist numbers increased a steam ship operated between Galway and Ballyvaughan. The English pedestrian William Barry was among the early passengers to take advantage of the service, which greatly increased the number of visitors taking the spa waters at Lisdoonvarna. Hotel standards, however, still fell well below the expectations of continental visitors and the French author Marie de Bovet in 1890 was deeply critical of the standard of the hotel accommodation she encountered in Kilkee and Miltown Malbay. By 1909 the Irish language revival was in full sway. In his tour *as Gaeilge*, Peadar Ó hAnnracháin produced a most informative account of the county's Gaelic poets and the language as it was then spoken in north Clare.

Peadar has the distinction also of being the only traveller in this anthology to have toured the county by bicycle.

In the early twentieth century, despite a huge increase in the number of books, few tours of any quality were published. There appear to be no accounts associated with the War of Independence, which is strange, or perhaps such accounts were written but await discovery. In any event it was not until professional writers like Seán Ó Faoláin and Frank O'Connor published their travel books in the 1940s that quality accounts of the county again appear.

The coverage the different parts of the county receive in these accounts is uneven. While some areas have several reports devoted to them, other parts are hardly mentioned. There were three basic corridors in the county through which travellers moved. The first is the passage along the Shannon from Limerick to O'Brien's Bridge, Killaloe and Scarriff. John Stevens used this route on his march to Athlone in 1690, as did the French aristocrat, the Chevalier De Latocnaye, in 1797. With the completion of the Grand Canal to the Shannon in 1804, many travellers entered the county by boat through Lough Derg. This is how Johann Kohl entered Clare in 1842 as did the canal enthusiast, L.T.C. Rolt, in his voyage down the Shannon in 1946. The second corridor through the county was the central roadway connecting Gort with Ennis, Newmarket on Fergus, Sixmilebridge and Limerick. This became a tolled turnpike road as early as 1734. But it was the setting up of the regular stage coach service in the first decade of the nineteenth century that made it particularly attractive to travellers. Joseph Lancaster used it in 1812 as did Henry Inglis in 1834 and William Thackeray in 1842. Today it still remains the principal conduit for traffic through the county. The third corridor was along the west coast. From Kilrush to Kilkee, Miltown Malbay, Lehinch and Ballyvaughan. John Bowden was among the first to use this route in 1791. But it was the opening up of the steam boat service from Galway to Ballyvaughan in the 1860s that really made the route attractive. Travellers could land in north Clare, visit Lisdoonvarna, tour down along the west coast and take the boat at Kilrush for either Limerick or Tarbert.

The intermediate areas of the county are but poorly served. In east Clare, for instance, there is no account of the town of Tulla, or the villages of Kilkishen or O'Callaghan's Mills. Similarly with west Clare, the tract of territory from Kilmaley and Connolly to Kilmihil and Cooraclare receives not a single mention. Perhaps such areas will feature in future tours.

Although almost seventy accounts of Clare appear in this anthology, the collection is by no means exhaustive. Many more good tours await discovery. Some are still in manuscript form, others hidden in obscure journals or in appendices to larger printed works. In many ways the tours appearing here are the most obvious ones. At some future date, perhaps at the end of the next century, some individual may well undertake a similar project, publishing those tours yet to be discovered and the new ones to be written.

B. O'D.

Letter of Connor O'Brien to Charles V, 1534

In the 1530s the government of England under Henry VIII began to exert its authority in the remotest corners of Ireland. The ancient freedoms enjoyed by Irish lordships were threatened with extinction; Irish lords appealed to the Roman Emperor Charles V, England's main rival on the continent, to come to their assistance. The earl of Desmond had exchanged letters and envoys with Charles in 1529 but nothing came of the initiative. At the outbreak of the rebellion of Silken Thomas in 1534, Connor O'Brien of Thomond, a staunch ally of the house of Kildare, again appealed to the emperor; O'Brien offered allegiance to Charles V in return for military aid. O'Brien's letter is notable, not just for its anti English sentiment, but because its reveals how militarised society then was in County Clare and the determination of its inhabitants to retain their ancient rights and liberties.

To the most sacred and most invincible Cæsar, Charles Emperor of the Romans, most Catholic King of Spain, health with all submission. Most sacred Cæsar, lord most clement, we give your Majesty to know that our predecessors for a long time quietly and peacefully occupied Ireland, with constancy, force, and courage, and without rebellion. They possessed and governed this country in manner royal, as by our ancient chronicles doth plainly appear. Our said predecessors and ancestry did come from your Majesty's realm of Spain, where they were of the blood of a Spanish prince, and many kings of that lineage, in long succession, governed all Ireland happily, until it was conquered by the English. The last king of this land was of my blood and name; and ever since that time our ancestors, and we ourselves, have ceased not to oppose the English intruders; we have never been subject to English rule, or yielded up our ancient rights and liberties; and there is at this present, and for ever will be, perpetual discord between us, and we will harass them with continual war.

For this cause, we, who till this present, have sworn fealty to no man, submit ourselves, our lands, our families, our followers, to the protection and defence of your Majesty, and of free will and deliberate purpose we promise to obey your Majesty's orders and commands in all honest behests. We will serve your Majesty with all our force; that is to say, with 1,660 horse and 2,440 foot, equipped and armed. Further, we will levy and direct for your Majesty's use 13,000 men, well armed with harquebuss, bows, arrows, and swords. We will submit to your Majesty's will and jurisdiction more than a hundred castles, and they and all else shall be at your Majesty's disposition to be employed as you shall direct.

We can undertake also for the assistance and support of our good brother the earl of Desmond, whose cousin, the daughter of the late earl James, your Majesty's friend, is our wife.

Our further pleasure will be declared to you by our servants and friends, Robert and Dominic de Paul, to whom your Majesty will deign to give credence. May your Majesty be ever prosperous.

Written at our castle at Clare, witness, our daughter, July 21, 1534, by your humble servant and unfailing friend,

Connor O'Brien,
Prince of Ireland.

Taken from J. A. Froude (ed.) *The Pilgrim* (London 1861), pp 175-6

A Description of the Shannon Estuary
by Edmund Sexton *c.* 1540

Edmund Sexton, Mayor of Limerick, was one of the first converts to the Protestant religion in north Munster. He made several journeys to England and was an enthusiastic supporter of Henry VIII. Through his efforts the rebellion of Silken Thomas received no support in Limerick in 1535. For his services to the Crown he was rewarded with the confiscated properties of the Augustinian and Franciscan houses of the city. He clearly had sailed the Shannon estuary many times and had an intimate knowledge of its castles, bays and harbours; according to him the bay of Limerick stretched from Loop Head in the north to the Blaskets in the south. His account of the southwest coast of Ireland (from Limerick to Waterford) was intended as an aid to the English interest in their attempts to subdue the country.

Here follows the names of all the havens, rivers, creeks, places of importance, territories and lordships with the landlords of them and their commodities from Lupes Head which is the furthest land a seaboard by north the river of Limerick as also within the said river collected by Edmund Sexton one of the servers of King Henry VIII and found among old papers of his hand and written here from memory.

First there is an island eight miles within the head called Inish Scatty, where there are merchants of Limerick dwelling and having castles and stone houses of their own inheritance; where also there is great idolatry used to a saint called Shenand and also there is a *connerbe*, that is to say a priest or warden belonging to a great old church within that island where in went no woman since the death of the saint, which *connerbe*, as I am informed, may despend a hundred marks per year.

Also I cannot imagine in all the west of Ireland so good and meet a place for a fortress for the king, for the reformation of that country and that for divers considerations: first if the earl of Thomond with his alliance should rebel, and as yet these are not brought to any order, that fortress would be a death to them; also the earl of Desmond and the English men joining to the river with all the Irish men of that quarter would be in awe thereof; also with one ship of sixty tons and two or three galleys, it would cause all the Irish men from Waterford to Galway to be in great fear and the sooner would be brought to reform by the sea coast with the help of Galway and Limerick. . . .

Item within the great river is the river of Forragus where upon is situated the manor of Clare and the earl of Thomond's chief manor called Clounoude and a house of friars, which stands as yet, and also a great island Ileanvooragh with a castle and in the east side of that island a fair manor of the earl of Thomond's called Ballyconilleth [Dromoland].

Item there is an island called the Chanons Island between it and Bonratty where there is a house of canons with a castle, which were a meet house for subduing of those parts.

Item there dwells next the point of the lands called Lupes Head McMahuny in the west also next him McMahuny in whose country are two manors, the one called Ballyvercolloman and the other Clonideralagh which are the fairest houses in Ireland and situated upon the river of Limerick, the one three miles from the island and the other eight miles in the north side.

Item next that is a river called Owinogarny in McNamara's country running into the Shannon, the river of Limerick, where upon is seated the manor of Bonratty which is the king's by inheritance.

Item eight miles from that is Limerick.

Item in the south side of the river seven miles from Limerick there is a river called the Mag whereupon is situated the manor of Adair in which manor is three houses of friars. Also the manor of Cromie with diverse other manors of the king's [in the] country called Cosmay. . . .

Item next the river of Asketin, called the Dyle, is a manor of the earl of Desmonds whereupon is a house of friars and a leap of salmon.

Item next the river of Corgraige which is also a manor of the earl of Desmond in the comings in or entry whereof there is an island called Feneth [Foynes].

Item next that is a manor of the knight of the Glines called Glancorbry where is a bay and a good bed of oysters and mussels.

Item next that is a strong castle seated upon the river called Carigifoile and also a house of friars and a goodly bed of oysters.

Item next that there is a great bay with an island and a rock whereupon is built a pretty castle with a stone house called Likfewine where there is also a mine. . . .

Item next that the great bay of Trally where there is a house of friars. There is in the said bay a castle called Groors castle where there is two great beds of eels and when the gent of the castle list to kill any of the eels he sends one of his servants called Hussey.

Item next that is a haven called Smericke where dwells a gent called Senater, who is lord of the islands, where a great number of pissines [fish] be taken which islands be west the sound of Blaskyes.

Item next is Blaskey the head of the river of Limerick. . . .

Taken from British Museum Add. Ms 19865, ff 19-21 [N.L.I. mcf. p. 513]; transcript made by Sir William Betham from papers relating to the Sexton family of Limerick.

Ennis Assizes, 1570

By 1570 the English were in a position to hold their first courts of law in the territory of Thomond. The assizes were held in the dissolved Franciscan friary of Ennis because Connor O'Brien, earl of Thomond, refused to give the government possession of Clare Castle. O'Brien was dissatisfied because of the appointment of his arch rival Teige McMurrough O'Brien as sheriff. The appointment of a sheriff would lead inevitably to a serious diminution in the earl's authority, but the nomination of Teige McMurrough added insult to injured pride. O'Brien refused to co-operate with Edward Fitton, President of Connacht, and eventually drove him and the assize judges from his territory. The altercation is neatly summarised under the year 1570 in the *Annals of the Four Masters*; a more detailed version of events is provided by the President of Connacht, Edward Fitton, in his letter to the Lord Deputy in Dublin. Fitton's account provides interesting topographical detail: it appears, for instance, that no bridge spanned the Fergus at Clare Castle in 1570.

A proclamation for holding a court in the monastery of Ennis, in Thomond, was issued by the president of the province of Connaught, to the O'Briens and [the inhabitants of] upper Connaught. Teige, the son of Murrough O'Brien, who was at this time sheriff in the territory (and he was the first sheriff of Thomond), placed a quantity of food and liquors in the monastery of Ennis for the use of the president. The president arrived in the town about the festival of St Bridget. The earl of Thomond (Conor, the son of Donough, son of Conor O'Brien) was at this time at Clare, [and] the president on the third day dispatched a party of his guards, [consisting] of the chiefs of his people and his cavalry, to summon the earl. It was at the same hour of the day that these and Donnell, the son of Conor O'Brien, who was also coming to the earl, arrived at the gate of the town. The earl came to the resolution of making prisoners of Donnell and all those who were withinside the chain of the gate, and killing some of those who were outside. [This he did]. The rest of them [perceiving his intention] escaped, by swiftness of foot and the fleetness of their horses, to the president, to Ennis. On the following day the president departed, and the sons of Murrough, son of Turlough [O'Brien], i.e. Teige and Donough, conducted him out of the country, and guided him through the narrow passes and the wild and intricate ways. The earl followed in pursuit of them, and continued skirmishing with them until they arrived at Gort-innsi-Guaire on that night.

Taken from the *Annals of the Kingdom of Ireland by the Four Masters*, (ed.) John O'Donovan (Dublin 1851), v, *sub anno* 1570.

Letter from Edward Fitton, President of Connaght, to the Lord Deputy, Touching on the Disorder in Thomond, 1570

May it please your Lordship to understand the whole course of our journey since we wrote last from Clonferte, [20 January 1570]; we came that night to Logereagh [Loughrea], from thence the next day to O Shaughnessy and so upon Sunday, being the 22nd of the month, to Inishe [Ennis]; whither came to us that night Mr Apsley and under him forty of his band.

When we came, we neither found provision for man nor horse, saving a little that the sheriff [Teige McMorogh O'Brien] had brought in of his own charge, although both the earl [of Thomond] and a number of gentlemen that were at Galway before, were warned to levy and bring in both man's meat and horse meat. Neither heard we anything from the earl before three o'clock in the afternoon of yesterday, saving that a man of his named William Nailande came to us about a mile short of the Inishe, whom we committed for not providing horsemeat.

Upon the earl's coming we thought good to estrange ourselves from him because of his undutiful behaviour and because all the people under his rule in the country were fled away as though we were enemies. Nevertheless we gave him no evil words but thinking to reprehend him openly in the morning said we were busy and willed him to take his ease for that night.

The earl of Clanricarde being present with the earl, he neither seemed to excuse his doings nor talked one word with him of our being here. But when our message was brought to the earl, he said he would go to his next house [at Clare Castle], being but half a mile away, and come again in the morning; and sent word by William Martin to us that he might go home and fetch his English apparel. We answered him that in no case would we consent to his departing the town; nevertheless, despite all the persuasion my Lord Clanricarde could make upon him, he took his horse and went his way. We sent William Martin after him, commanding him upon his allegiance, that he should immediately come to us. Martin found him at his castle of Clare, and by occasion of the flood he could not get in till about midnight. Martin was well used at his hands and promised answer in the morning, which was, he was ashamed to tarry here [in Ennis], having no provision to bestow upon the soldiers. And also reciting the great injuries that Teige McMorogh, the sheriff, had done unto him, saying plainly that he would not be earl, if he were sheriff.

He concluded plainly that he would not come to us without protection and also that the earl of Clanricarde should meet him about a mile out of this town. We thought good to deny him and instead sent unto him the sergeant at arms with Mr Apsley and his band to guard the mace. And doubting that the earl would be in the ward of the castle, when the sergeant came, we sent Martin before them under the pretence of delivering an answer, that might justify the earl's presence at the same time. But the earl not only took Martin in hand and kept him, but also sending to Apsley to come in, promising him such cheer as was there, overcame the gentleman. (This was contrary to our precise command that none should enter the castle.) And a number of soldiers to the number of ten were enticed likewise to go in, whereof some were killed and some taken; amongst them that were slain was old John McRobin. Whereupon the sergeant and the rest of Apsley's company resorted hither to us safe again.

The news amazed us greatly and we resolved to go to the castle to speak to the earl, but coming thither and sending our trumpeter to the castle requiring the earl to come forth, we were answered that the earl was not there. And demanding where Apsley and Martin and the rest were, were answered that only the earl of Thomond could tell and that he would meet us tomorrow. But it is plainly judged that the earl hath both Apsley, Martin and the rest with him and is gone to Bonrattie.

The situation considered, together with our own strength, being now these twenty five of Apsley's, we have resolved to retire ourselves to Galway.

And thus we humbly take our leave: From Inishe, the 24th of January 1570.

Edward Fiton, R. Clanricarde, Rafe Rokey, Robert Dillon.

Taken from *The Halliday Papers, Fifteenth Report*, [Irish Council Book], Historical Manuscripts Commission (London 1897), pp 201-03. Abridged.

Fr Wolfe, Description of Thomond, 1574

The Jesuit Fr David Wolfe, a native of Limerick city, was appointed papal legate for Ireland in 1560. He was subsequently imprisoned, spending five years in the dungeons of Dublin castle, from where he eventually escaped in 1572. The following year he fled to the continent and spent the remaining years of his life promoting the cause of the Counter Reformation. Fr Wolfe's account of Thomond forms part of his *Description of Ireland*, which he wrote in 1574 shortly after his arrival in Spain, for the purpose of enabling the King of Spain to come to a decision in favour of armed intervention in Ireland.

The third part of Munster is called Thomond, and its lord up to our time is called O'Brien. . . In times past he was always king of all Munster and often monarch of the whole island. Not wishing to allow such a renowned name to continue in that country, Henry VIII, about the year 1540, called over to England him who was then O'Brien, and made him lay aside the name and called him earl of Thomond. To-day the lord of that country is Cornelius O'Brien, earl of Thomond, and he has a few lords in his country who obey him, but there are other nobles of the same nation who make continual war on him, and they are: Baron Inchiquin, the two MacNamaras who are great lords, and the two MacMahons also great lords.

There are O'Loughlin, O'Grady, O'Connor Corcomroe, Lord Donald O'Brien, and many other noble knights and gentlemen of Spanish descent, who have not the title of lord although they have large territories, castles, and towns, but the majority of these do not obey the earl, because he takes the side of the English and they do the opposite.

In Thomond there is no city, or even seaports, although the earl holds many beautiful castles near the river Shannon, where ships may have safe anchor in any storm, but there is no commerce with those castles or towns.

In Thomond are many mines of metal and silver, and so indeed in the whole island in abundance, and Earl Cornelius worked them with much profit, but the English do not allow him to work them any longer, and he was exiled from his country by Lady Elizabeth in the year 1571 but was afterwards received back into the Queen's favour through the intercession of the king of France, although he is none too secure in his dominion or safe from the wickedness and perfidy of Lady Elizabeth.

From Myles V. Ronan, *The Reformation in Ireland under Elizabeth* (Dublin 1930), p. 484.

William Goode, Account of County Clare taken from William Camden's *Britannia*, 1586

William Camden, English antiquary and pioneer of the historical method, was the author of *Britannia*, the first comprehensive historical and topographical survey of England, Scotland and Ireland. Camden graduated from Oxford in 1571 and, with no regular employment, devoted himself entirely to his historical researches. He learned Anglo Saxon and Welsh and was among the first to realise the importance of ancient languages in the study of placenames. After years of arduous labour *Britannia* was finally published in 1586. The book was a great success and ran to several editions. The Irish section was not however written by Camden but attributed by him in the 1607 edition to J. Goode. The individual in question was most likely the English Jesuit William Goode, the headmaster of Well's Grammar School during the reign of the Catholic Queen Mary but who withdrew from England after the accession of Queen Elizabeth. In 1562 he was admitted to the Society of Jesus. Later he was sent to Ireland with Richard Creagh of Limerick, the newly appointed Archbishop of Armagh, to further the cause of the counter reformation. Dr Creagh was arrested soon after his arrival and Goode, finding no one sympathetic to his mission at Armagh, retreated to Limerick, where he was employed as a teacher in Dr Creagh's former school. He taught for four years in Limerick before the school was compelled to close in 1568 following an attempt to impose the Protestant religion. Fr Goode was subsequently appointed confessor of the English college in Rome. His Irish narrative while accurate is unsympathetic. In outlook he was strongly pro-English and in favour of the reform of church and state in Ireland. It was Goode's claim that the Irish had been civilised through their contact with the English that motivated the Clare Franciscan, Anthony MacBrody, to write his major work *Propugnaculum Catholicae Veritatis* in 1669. The fact that Goode never returned to Ireland is perhaps an indication that his superiors felt him unsuited to further work in the Irish field. *Britannia* was first translated from Latin into English in 1610 by Philemon Holland under the supervision of William Camden; it is the account of County Clare from the 1610 edition that appears here. Spelling has been modernised and punctuation introduced.

Twomon or Twomond, which Giraldus called Thuetmonia, the Irish Twowoun, that is, the North-Mounster (which although it lies beyond the river Shannon yet was counted in times past part of Mounster, until Sir Henry Sidny lord deputy laid it unto Conaught) shoots out into the sea with a very great promontory growing by little and little thin and narrow. On the east and south sides it is so enclosed with the winding course of the river Shannon, which waxes bigger and bigger, like as on the west part with the open main sea, and on the northside confines so close upon the county Gallway, that there is no coming unto it by land, but through the Clan Ricard's territory. This is a country wherein a man would wish for nothing more, either from sea or soil; were but the industry of the inhabitants correspondent to the rest; which industry Sir Robert Muscegros an English nobleman, Richard Clare and Thomas Clare younger brethren of the stock of the Earls of Glocester (unto whom King Edward the first had granted this country) stirred up long since, by building towns and castles, and by alluring them to the fellowship of a civil conversation; of whose name the chief town Clare, now the dwelling place of the earl of Twomond, took denomination, as also the whole tract, of it called the county of Clare. The places of greater note and name than the rest, are Kilfennerag and Killaloe or *Laon*, the Bishop's seat. This in the Roman province is termed *Episcopatus Ladensis*, where there stands a rock in the mid channel of the river Shannon, from which the water rushes down a main with a great fall and noise, and by standing thus in the way as a bar hinders the river that it can carry vessels no further, which if it were cut down or a drain made about it, the river were able to bring up vessels much higher, to the great commodity of all the neighbour inhabitants.

Not far from the bank of Shannon, is seated Bunraty for which Sir Robert Muscegros obtained from King Henry the third the liberty of a market and fair, and when he had fortified it with a castle, gave it at length unto King Edward the first, who granted both this town and the whole territory unto Richard Clare aforesaid. And seven miles from thence, appears Clare the principal town, at a creek (flowing up out of Shannon) full of islands: and these two are the only market towns here, and those but small ones. Most of the English who were in times past brought hither to inhabit, are either rooted out, or become degenerate and grown Irish: but they who carry the whole sway here at this day, be of the Irish blood as Mac Nemors, Mac Mahon, O'loughton, and the mightiest by far of all other, the O'Briens, descended from the ancient potentates or kings of Conaught, or as themselves give it forth, from the monarchs of Ireland. Of these, Morogh O'Brien was the first earl of Twomond created by King Henry the eight for the term of life and after him to Donough his brother's son, and his heirs; who at the same time being made baron of Ibarcan, succeeded in the earldom and was slain by his brother Sir Donel, O'Brien. Connogher O'Brien, Donough's son, was the third earl, and father to Donaugh now the fourth earl, who has showed singular good proof of his faithful loyalty and courageous valour unto his prince and country in most dangerous times to his singular commendation.

Taken from William Camden, *Britannia sive . . . Angliae, Scotiae, Hiberniae chorographica descriptio* (London 1586, translated by Philemon Holland, 1610), pp 98-9.

Hugh O Donnell, Raid into Thomond, 1600

During the Nine Years War, 1594-1603, Donough O Brien, fourth earl of Thomond, a staunch supporter of the English interest, pursued the war against the Irish with great vigour. To weaken the O Brien power base, Hugh O Donnell of Tyrconnell conducted two raids on Thomond; the first in 1599 was confined to the Burren and the area about Corofin but the following year in a more ambitious incursion, O Donnell despoiled the territory from Ogonnelloe in the north east to Kilmurry Ibrickan in the south west. The account of O Donnell's exploits was written by Lughaidh Ó Cléirigh, a member of the famous literary family of County Donegal. Ó Cléirigh clearly had a detailed knowledge of Clare and may well have been an eyewitness to the events he describes; his brother Duibhgheann was killed during the Ulstermen's assault on Clare Castle. Ó Cléirigh's book was one of the sources used in the 1630s during the compilation of the *Annals of the Four Masters*

His troops were gathered together by O Domhnaill in the month of June precisely, and they crossed the Saimer, a stream rich in salmon, the Drowes, the Dubh, and the Sligeach, until they came to Ballymote, where the men of Connacht awaited him. After a while he marched with his forces by Corann, through Magh Aoi Findbendaigh, through Clann Chonnmhaigh, through the territory of Maine, son of Eochaidh, and through the plain of Clanrickard, without fight or conflict, without wounding or being meddled with during that time. He made a halt in western Clanrickard in Oireacht Réamoinn on the evening of Saturday, and this was the Saturday before St John's day, which was on the following Tuesday. Warning and report went before him to Thomond, but they thought O Domhnaill would not leave the place where he had stopped until Monday morning. This was not what he did at all, but he rose before the early dawn of the morning of Sunday, and after hearing Mass himself and the chiefs who were with him, he marched with his troops by Oireacht Réamoinn, by the mountain of Echtge, daughter of Urscothach, son of Tinne, to Cenél Aodha, to Cenél Dúnghaile, and by upper Glancullen, until he crossed the Fergus westwards before mid-day on Sunday, so that they made a halt on the north-western side of Clonroad and Ennis. Ennis was burned and preyed entirely and made bare by the army all but the monastery, for O Domhnaill ordered protection and kindliness to be given to it in honour of the Lord. There it happened to the earl of Thomond, Donncha, son of Conor, lord of Thomond, to be with a small force of not more than two hundred in number at Clonroad, a short distance to the west of Ennis, at the same time that O Domhnaill and his armies came into the country. When he heard the murmur of the great army and the shouts of the soldiers and the noise of the heavy troops and the loud report of the quick-firing from bright, sharp-sighted guns throughout his territory all about him, and the bright, wide-spread conflagrations which extended in every quarter and on every border all round, which he could not defend or protect, what he did was to march with a small body of troops secretly by the bank of the Fergus due west as securely as he could till he came to Clare. That town was one of his fortresses, and it was strong, impregnable, even if he had not the force he had defending it.

As for O Domhnaill, when he had reached Ennis, he sent skirmishers to cover the surrounding country. Far and wide, violently, aggressively, these quick active courageous bodies of men separated from each other, for they traversed and plundered before night from Craig Uí Chíordhubháin, in the lower part of the territory in the cantred of Islands, to Cathair Murcha in west Corco Baiscinn, to the gate of Cill Muire, and Cathair Ruis, and the plain of Uí Bracáin, to the gate of Baile Eóin Gabhainn in Corcomrua, and Boith Néill in Cenél Fermaic. There was many a 'time of plenty' for gentlemen, noblemen, and lords of territories with prey and cattle and every sort of spoil, in the hands of a company of four or five of O Domhnaill's people under the shelter of bush or thicket, rock or wood in Thomond that night, for they had to stay wherever the darkness of nightfall overtook them.

O Domhnaill encamped that night on the bank of the Fergus to the west of Clonroad. This was a famous castle and princely lodging for him who was chief of the country. The army arose (on Monday exactly) calmly and firmly from their tents and huts, and proceeded to march by the road diagonally across Thomond in a north-easterly direction straight through the east of Uí Cormaic and the plain of Cenél Fermaic and the speckled-hilled Boirenn, till they came at sunset to the monastery of Corcomrua and to Carcair na cCleireach. Those of the forces who were unoccupied throughout the day were traversing and patrolling the lands around, so that they did not leave a habitation or dwelling worth talking about unburnt or undestroyed that day. The troops arose at dawn on Tuesday. They set out with their spoils and preys towards Carcair, and though their march was severe and their pace slow, owing to the enormous amount of cattle and plunder, they left the cleft stone passes of white Boirenn behind. When they came to the dwellings of the smooth plain of Maree, they rested at Cnoc an Ghearráin, between Cill Colgáin and Galway. They divided the spoil between them after that, so that each body had its own share of the enemy's cattle, flocks, and booty, and they proceeded the next day to guide and drive their portion of the prey along the roads of the ancient province of Sreng, son of Sengan. The journey they made on that day was not long, for they were tired after the great toil in coming through the narrow mouthed roads of Boirenn; neither had they eaten or slept in comfort the night before, for they had thought the earl of Thomond would come with all his forces in pursuit of them and on their track to attack them, on the winding defiles through which they were marching, though he did not come at all. They made their camp in the neighbourhood that night, since they had banished their fear. They made neither huts nor buildings, owing to the heat of the summer weather, but they lighted bright, flaming fires, and their attendants and servers, their cooks and houseboys, their ostlers and their soldiers fell to butchering and killing, slaughtering and chopping the bones of the enemy's cattle to prepare their dinner for their chiefs and their nobles, till they consumed their feast and slept soundly, as they had cast aside their fear.

Taken from Lughaidh Ó Cléirigh, *Beatha Aodh Rua O Domhnaill*, Irish Texts Society (London 1948) i, pp 253-9.

Observations made by Sir John Davies, Attorney of Ireland, 4 May 1606.

Sir John Davies, Irish attorney general and author of *Discovery of the True Causes Why Ireland was Never Entirely Subdued until the Beginning of His Majesty's Reign*, was assize judge of the Munster circuit in 1606. Unusually the assizes were not held in the county town of Ennis, but, for convenience, on the Clare side of the river Shannon opposite Limerick city. Although the Anglicization process was well under way by the early seventeenth century, Davies, nevertheless, was struck at how Gaelic the inhabitants of Thomond still were in manner and custom.

At our entry into the town [of Limerick] we were met by the earl of Thomond, the Lord Burke and others; the earl having for our great ease prepared a commodious house, to sit in the county of Clare on the other side of the Shannon, which divides the county of Clare and Thomond from the county of Limerick; so that we still kept our residence and lodging in Limerick and yet performed the services of both counties. In the county of Clare which contains all Thomond, when I beheld the appearance and fashion of the people, I would I had been in Ulster again, for these are as mere Irish as they, and in their outward form not much unlike them, but when we came to despatch the business we found that many of them spake good English and understood the course of our proceedings well. For the justices of Munster were wont ever to visit this county, both before my Lord Thomond had the particular government thereof and since then. After the despatch of the gaol, which contained no extraordinary malefactor, our principal labours did consist in establishing sundry possessions of freeholders in that county, which had been disturbed in the time of rebellion, and had not been settled since then. The best freeholders next to the O'Briens are the McNamaras and the O'Laneyes. The chief of which families appeared in civil habit and fashion, the rest are not so reformed as the people of Munster. But it is hoped that the example of the earl, whose education and carriage your Lordship knows, and who indeed is served and waited upon very civilly and honourably, will within a few years alter the manner of this people and draw them to civility and religion both. We ended our business of the county of Clare somewhat sooner than we expected, and therefore we began the session of the county of Limerick, a day or two before my lord president arrived there.

Taken from *Calendar of State Papers Ireland 1603-06* (London 1872), p. 470.

Franciscan Houses of County Clare, 1616

The friaries of Ennis and Quin were officially suppressed in 1543 and their properties bestowed on the leading families of Thomond. However, while communal religious life ceased, individual friars continued to live in both monasteries. By 1616 the roofs of Quin friary had fallen in but Ennis friary was well preserved, due principally to the efforts of Donough O'Brien, fourth Earl of Thomond, whose predecessors, the first three earls of Thomond, had been laid to rest in the friary church. The descriptions of Ennis and Quin were written by Fr Donagh Mooney, Provincial of the Irish Franciscans, during his visitation of the Irish convents in 1616. Fr Mooney, after a short military career, joined the Franciscan Order in 1600. He became guardian of the new Irish College in Louvain in 1607 and was elected Irish Provincial in 1615. His original Latin manuscript is preserved in the Bibliotheque Royale, Brussels; his accounts of the Clare friaries are given below in translation.

The Convent of Quin

The convent of Quin is situated in that part of Thomond called Cloncullen in the County Clare, province of Connaught and diocese of Killaloe. It was founded by the Chieftain McNamara. The building is very striking, a type that is scarcely ever seen in other convents, all the walls being of dressed stone. All the roofs have fallen in with the exception of the choir and principal chapel. Two or three brothers of the community still live here; being old and disabled they are permitted to remain, but they have scarcely any knowledge of the state of the convent before the suppression. They did report to me however, as did many others, that when the suppression was impending, the brothers had their gold and silver vessels sent for safe keeping to McNamara in his castle at Knapogue. He is dead and his wife has not yet returned them. I even spoke to her myself, but she did not seem willing to admit even the possession of those things. I recorded them in the provincial register. The chief nobles of the territory are buried in this convent.

Convent of Ennis

This convent is also in Thomond and is only six miles from the former. It was founded by the ancestors of the earl of Thomond, through their chieftain Prince William O'Brien. It is a convent of passing beauty and entirely in good repair, thanks to the efforts of the forementioned earl who, at a favourable time, proclaimed himself a heretic and received the convent as a gift from the queen and established in it a court of justice for the county. He even brought the English there and placed the buildings at their disposal, and in them they were lodged and entertained. It was stipulated, however, that the forms of the buildings were not to be changed in any way but were to be preserved in their original state: as a result not a single cell is changed or destroyed, and that worldly creature who refuses openly to profess Christ is the effective means for preserving the convent for better days. All that family of the O'Briens are buried here.

The convent was much frequented by brothers, but only one of them now remains. He is allowed to live here in his robes among the English and he celebrates mass privately in his cubicle. This religious was most zealous, and in contradistinction to him was William Neylan who had been pseudo-bishop of Kildare, he who feigned heresy when the time was ripe for favours. This man made scant effort to become reconciled to God as death approached, but he took good care to build for himself a tomb beautifully wrought from polished stone in the church of the friars minors in Ennis, where his ancestors were buried. The brother of whom I write was at that time on a mission in another part of the province so that he could not (nor could he, indeed, if he were present) oppose, much less prevent, the erection of that tomb and the burial of a heretic in it. A few days after the burial of the pseudo-bishop the brother returned and was grief-stricken that a holy place had been defiled by such an unworthy corpse. He pretended otherwise however, as he dare not attempt to do openly what he had in mind. Taking a few companions more robust than himself, he came to the tomb by night and removing the stone they extracted the body and brought it outside the church, and even outside the whole town, to an obscure and filthy place where they covered it with earth lest it should become offensive to those who passed by. When it was noised abroad that a pseudo-bishop received an ass's burial, no one had enough sympathy to search for his bones again and bring them to a more respectable place. People jeered and commended the brother for his zeal.

Of all the noted men who had been to this convent, I could not get information on any save this one whom I must not neglect. There was in the convent about the year 1570 [*recte* 1496] a very pious and zealous brother named . . . . and at the same time lived Prince Conor O'Brien, nicknamed 'Nosey,' who was ruler of his people. He was a warlike man who had caused a lot of bloodshed and brought many misfortunes on his people so that he was known to all for his tyranny and cruelty. When death was nearing he began to have remorse of conscience for his evil deeds and eventually despaired of salvation. Nor did he make any effort to do penance as the devil prompted him to believe that his wickedness was beyond the goodness and mercy of God. When this was told to the brother he was stirred by Godly zeal and visited the prince in his castle at Clonroad, which was not far from the convent. He discovered, on enquiry, that the prince was completely without hope, and when he failed after much reasoning and persuasion to bring him from despair and make a confession, he said to him in zeal for his salvation: 'Prince, if it pleases you, I will take on myself all your sins and I grant you all my merits towards the future life, but on condition that you being sorry for your sins and resolving not to sin again if God spares you, say to me as best you can all the sins you have heaped upon me; I will even take responsibility for the sins you are forgetting, whatever they may be.' The prince was very consoled by those words and began to make a confession - something he had not done for years. As the brother listened, he continued his confession with difficulty, was absolved, received holy communion and was fortified by extreme unction. The brother returned to the convent and immediately went to his cell. He closed the door and began to pray. He remained in prayer for twenty-four hours until the following day. Then the prince died and the bell was rung calling the brothers together to say the divine office for the dead. It was only then he left his cell to join the others, remaining silent. At the same time there was in Lismore, in Munster, some fifty miles distant, a holy man reputed for his sanctity. This man at the same hour was saying mass in the presence of the earl of Desmond, and when he came to the commemoration of the dead he laughed aloud and for a long time could not contain himself. When mass ended the earl asked him why he laughed. He replied that at that same hour a certain brother in the convent at Ennis was so vehemently praying to God that if his prayer was channelled to the many souls in purgatory they would all, undoubtedly, be released: 'Such,' he said, 'was the force and efficacy of his prayer. He was praying, however,' he said, 'for the salvation and forgiveness of Prince Cornelius O'Brien who after a life of continuous evil-doing became intensely penitent and, helped and exhorted by that brother, made a confession and received the sacraments before his death: for him the brother had prayed for twenty-four hours.' When the earl heard this he immediately sent messengers to find out the truth as soon as possible. They discovered that everything had happened as was told and returned to the earl with the news. From these happenings the mercy of God and His regard for His saints was magnified among the people.

The gold and silver vessels and also the furniture of this convent were converted to his own use by the present earl, Lord Donogh O'Brien - perhaps some time, when peace returns to the church, he or his successors will make restitution.

Taken from the Rev Martin Ryan, 'The Franciscan Houses of Thomond in 1616' in *North Munster Antiquarian Journal* 10 (1967), pp 112-14.

William Penn,
Diary of an English Sea Captain, 1646

William Penn, admiral and general of the fleet, was born at Bristol in 1621. He was the father of William Penn, a prominent Quaker and founder of the state of Pennsylvania. Appointed captain of the *Fellowship*, a ship of twenty eight guns, by parliament in 1644, Penn was engaged in active service on the Irish coast until 1651. During the siege of Bunratty castle in 1646, Penn's mission was to keep the Parliamentarian garrison supplied by sea. He marauded up and down the Shannon estuary, burning houses, plundering villages and driving off cattle in a vain attempt to provide food for the besieged soldiers. Despite the spectacular failure at Bunratty, no blame was attached to Penn and he continued in his command. In 1648 he was taken into custody on suspicion of being engaged in the royalist interest. Suspicion soon passed and a month later he was made rear-admiral of the Irish fleet. He pursued the royalist fleet under Prince Rupert into the Mediterranean in 1652 and a year later fought with distinction against the Dutch at the Battle of Portland. As part of the Cromwellian settlement, Penn was awarded large estates in County Cork but being discontented with parliament was in regular communication with royalists. Appointed commander in chief of the fleet in 1654, he was directed to act against the Spanish West Indies where he captured the island of Jamaica in May 1665. Returning to England he was imprisoned for being absent from his post without leave. Released after a few weeks he retired to his estates in Ireland. On the restoration of King Charles II Penn was knighted and confirmed in his Irish estates. Appointed a commissioner in the navy, he fought against the Dutch at the battle of Lowestoft in 1665 where he incurred the censure of the admiralty and was not employed at sea again although he continued in the navy until his death in 1670.

In 1646 Bunratty castle was occupied by Barnabus O'Brien, sixth earl of Thomond. O'Brien had little in common with the native Irish, being born of an English mother, he was educated at Oxford, married an English wife and stood aloof from the people. The Thomond estate, which he had inherited from his brother Henry in 1639, was hopelessly in debt and unlikely to yield any income for many years. Rather than allow Bunratty to fall into the hands of the Irish Confederates, he surrendered it to the English Parliamentarians and retired to England. The castle was quickly besieged by the confederate forces under Muskery and fell to the Irish 14 July 1646. Penn's diary is a detailed day to day record of the events associated with the siege of Bunratty from 24 January to 16 August 1646; it illustrates the critical use made of shipping in supplying the land forces and the kind of warfare employed against the Irish population in the 1640s.

[25 January 1646].   At two in the afternoon [the ships] arrived in Cork bay.

27th.   The admiral and myself went in our pinnace [boat] up to Cork, to take advice of my Lord of Broghill, vice-president of the province of Munster, about the affairs of these parts; how and where we might do service to the state, in helping or encouraging our friends, or in weakening or disheartening our enemies, the merciless rebels in this kingdom. . . .

[11 March 1646].   I received order from my admiral to take charge and command of all the frigates in the fleet, and to dispose of all the soldiers and seamen. . .   Between six and seven we anchored near Bonratty, and sent a trumpeter to my Lord of Thomond, with a letter from my admiral and Lieutenant Colonel M`Adam; who received it kindly, embracing our motion, and promising to join with us; but not being well himself, would send a gentleman of his to treat in his behalf with the lieutenant-colonel and myself, the next day.

12th. We landed our forces, being about 700, upon an island close to Bonratty, where the gentleman of my lord's, Captain Huntley by name, came unto us, inviting us to my lord to confer with his honour, which we did.   Having dined with his lordship, we held consultation about the end of our coming hither, to see how his lordship stood affected to the parliament of England. . .   We found his lordship willing (as he said) in what he could to comply with us, only he feared we were not a party considerable (enough) to undergo so great a work.   We promised to do our best; and, God blessing our endeavours, we doubted not of success in so good and honest a design.   The soldiers marched over, and quartered in Bonratty this night.

14th.   About eleven at night my admiral went down from Bonratty in his barge, after all discourse ended with the Earl of Thomond.

15th.   We drew out our forces, marching to a place adjoining, called Smith's-Town, where we faced a part of the enemy, being gathered together into a body; but night coming on we were not able to do any good upon them, and so made our retreat.

23rd.   I dispatched away our carpenters on shore to Bonratty, for the service of the lieutenant-colonel. We put our men to half allowance, by reason of the scarcity of our provisions, together with the necessity of our continuance here; and agreed to give, one half provision, the other half money.   My men desiring fresh meat for their money, I promised to make what provision I could for them. . . .

[1 April 1646].   The lieutenant-colonel intended to beat up the enemy's quarters, and to see what strength their main body did consist of, but they saved us that labour; for, about five this morning, they having drawn up a party from Six-mile-bridge, to the number of 120 horse and 300 foot, came to fire Bonratty, with commission to kill man, woman, and child; and accordingly began at the end of the town, fired seven houses, killed some English, etc. The alarm being given, 25 of our horse issued out under the command of Captain Vauclier, charged the enemy, and by a fortunate shot wounding Captain M'Gragh, commander-in-chief of the horse, they were totally routed, and both horse and foot took flight. We followed the pursuit, slew 80 upon the place, took Captain M'Gragh alive, with his brother who came to his rescue; a lieutenant of foot, and another of horse; with about an 100 arms; not one man of ours being hurt. In the afternoon, our horse and foot being refreshed, we marched with two drakes, 600 foot, and 50 horse, to the rebels' camp at Six-mile-bridge, consisting of 1400 horse and foot; having fortified themselves with scarffes and counter-scarffes, etc. We set upon them, beat them out of their works, and, being hotly charged, they betook them to their heels. Our horse and foot pursued them two miles; yet little execution was done, by reason of the woods, and a river near hand. Having killed about 30, and taken five prisoners, we retreated to the town, possessed their strong works, lay therein that night, fired the town, excepting those houses wherein the provision was; and brought away 250 barrels of oatmeal, which served the soldiers six weeks for bread, our stores being much exhausted.

2nd. In the morning we marched from thence with 350 musqueteers to Bally-maguing, *alias* Smith's-Town, the place of their first in-camping. Our horse marched some six miles into the country, burned one of their grand store-houses of corn, with many other houses, did much spoil unto the rebels, and so marched, with what lumber we had gotten, to our garrison of Bonratty. Captain M'Gragh, with lieutenant of foot, died, being desperately shot.

3rd. Upon the request of Lieutenant Colonel M'Adam, I went up to him to Bonratty, to consult of the affairs that most concerned the benefit of the service. My minister gave a sermon to the soldiers, being suddenly to march abroad. Captain M'Gragh and the lieutenant were honourably buried, with three volleys of small shot. . . .

9th. I went on shore to M'Adam, about raising of works for the strengthening the garrison; so that having considered how and where to raise the works, the rest of the day was spent in pulling down walls, removing thatched houses out of the town, into a field near adjoining to the castle. I gave order for the making of a platform for a great gun in the pigeon-house. . . .

13th. I went from Finnis' Island to and again, about and upon several islands thereabouts, to see what cattle we could make purchase of. Upon one I found nothing but conies [rabbits]; another some deer, which if they had been killed had not been man's meat; only five horses of my Lord of Thomond, and a hay-rick; which the very first opportunity shall be fetched off, and carried to Enislow, which island I intend (God willing) to make the common receptacle for such cattle as can be possibly gleaned up for the relief of our shipping and garrison. . . .

16th. This morning I went, with our own and the *Ann Percy's* boats, unto the deer-island, where (after much time spent and labour had) we caught the five horses, none of them being, as was supposed, my lord's; three of which we transported to Enislow: the other two, not being worth the labour, we let alone. It being near the evening, I returned on board. Those which landed the horses brought me word, that the rebels had killed and carried away all the sheep, save half-a-score or thereabouts, on Enislow; which much grieved me to hear, having taken such care, and used such diligence, for the preservation thereof, night and day. But the extremity of the weather, together with the rebels' familiar acquaintance with these islands (being dry in some places at low water), did so disenable us, that all the art we had, or industry we could use, it seems could not possibly prevent them, they being both cunning and close in their roguery.

17th. Having consulted over-night with my guide, and finding it feasible, with his approbation, to gain some sheep and other cattle from off the island called Croneraughan [Kiladysert], in the possession of the rebels, half-musquet-shot from the main, where the rebels have a strong ward in a very good castle; I sent our own and Captain Smith's boats on shore, the tide falling very opportunely, to get what cattle they could, for the subsistence not only of the garrison but ourselves. . . About eight, a party issued out of the garrison [Enislow] to look for prey; took 200 cows, 250 sheep, 80 garrans; killed six rogues, summoned Ballinclay Castle, commanded by John M'Namara; who, professing friendship to the Earl of Thomond, and we not possessing engines to annoy the same, being (contrary to report) very strong, drew off and returned home. . . .

[3 May 1646]. About ten in the morning Captain Liston came down from Bonratty, with many passengers, both men, women, and children, to be transported to Kinsale or Cork. . . .

6th. About eleven, at noon, I went on shore, where I heard the rebels had summoned Cappah Castle, but were slightly answered by the commander, whereupon they retreated to their quarters at the bridge again. . .

7th. I sent a warrant directed to the commanders of the several frigates, to send half their men every day on shore, to work at the fort which we had concluded should be raised at the water-side for the security of our ships; provided always and by all means (no excuse to the contrary) they repaired on board every night. . . .

9th. Near upon eight in the morning, the Earl of Thomond came down from Bonratty, and went on board Captain Grigge to go for Cork: I went on board to wait upon his honour. About ten, Captain

Southwood weighed for the Blascoes. . . About two, my Lord of Thomond came on board our ship to dinner; I gave his lordship five guns at his entering. Not long after came down the lieutenant-colonel, with some of his commanders, to demand certain men which had an escape with my lord, but could by no means be spared. At his request I sent for them, and returned them up immediately to Bonratty in a boat. Having dispatched the present affairs, and dined, the lieutenant colonel and his company went up again; at whose departure I gave three guns. Not long after, my lord took leave, to whom I gave 9 guns.

10th, Sunday. At eight this morning came on board my lord's gentleman, and told me, 'twas his lordship's desire that my minister should preach before him; which I consented to, sent him on board, and after went myself; dined with his honour. . . .

13th. I went to the fort, to view the works, and hasten them on, for the more security of the shipping. After, I betook myself to the lieutenant-colonel, with whom I consulted about the present affairs; and hearing some shot made not far from Bonratty, we conceived the rebels were then assaulting of Cappah Castle, about two miles from us, where a ward of ours consisting of two files of musqueteers of the lieutenant-colonel's (of which one Serjeant Morgan had command), and some that formerly inhabited the castle or thereabouts. The rebels, having brought down their great guns, made 26 desperate shot, they within very gallantly maintaining it; but being much battered, with a breach made, and (as we heard after) being stormed by the rebels, our men, not able any longer to hold out, yielded upon quarter for their lives. Having entered the castle and taken our men prisoners, they marched from thence to a castle called Rossmonnahane, not a full mile from Bonratty, formerly commanded by one Hunt; which, but two days before, he quit, and was now with his wife and family in Bonratty Castle. This castle also they summoned, being kept by a file of our men; bringing Morgan with them, and using him as an instrument for the surrender. What he did, being compelled, or how the matter was ordered, is not yet known; but the castle was delivered up, without so much as a shot made: we believe the soldiers were hanged, as justly they deserve.

24th, Sunday. I received a letter from the lieutenant-colonel, requesting some minion shot, having spent what they had in this day's service. I sent up to Captain Brown, by his pinnace, a 100 shot, to be disposed of as the lieutenant-colonel adjudged fit. Many shot were made this day by our men against the rebels: our men sallied out, upon the intended design of surprising the enemy's guns, but were prevented, for they had drawn their artillery up the hill. However, our men set upon them, and, with the help of our seamen, beat them out of their works, killed divers of them, among the rest one principal commander; but their horse coming down, our men retreated. In this sally I had a man shot through the body, but not past hope. About twelve at night, Captain Smith's ten men came down, and eight of ours; one being hurt, the other stayed to look to him. . . .

29th. We first landed at the fort, to see what was yet wanting for their better subsistence; and having spent some time there in ordering their affairs, upon the request of the lieutenant-colonel we went on shore on that side, to him. With whom, after much debatement, we concluded of the necessity of transporting many women and children (burthen some to the garrison, in regard of the scarcity of provisions; a thing which I desired, and might with some ease, and greater advantage, have been done long since,) to Cork or Kinsale. Now, necessity forcing their departure, and in a greater number than can be imagined, the lieutenant-colonel supposing Liston's ship not capable of containing so many, desired Captain Smith might be ordered to transport one-half of them. But having no provisions to afford them out of the garrison, and Captain Smith very much straitened, he was not willing to take any of them on board. . . .

[4 June 1646] The lieutenant-colonel desired, that I would take down a 1000 lb. weight of lead, to cast into bullets for the use of our men; one quarter whereof was to be cast into pistol and cabine, which I took order with Captain Brown for. This day many shot were made between us and the rebels, some of which came into the castle, but did no harm. They have brought down two guns, which shoot directly down the river, and will much annoy us in our making to the castle. We unhappily lost, this morning early, about 80 mares and colts, being feeding over in the marshes, the guard whereof being too soon drawn off; at the loss of which we had some bickering with them; lost about two men, but could do no good. Having dispatched with the lieutenant-colonel, I came on board our ship.

9th. Our men, digging a trench to secure the corkasse, were set upon by the rebels, intending to beat them from their works; but, with the loss of 15 men, shamefully retreated. I considered the want of wood in the garrison, and took order for a timely supply. It growing late, and the lieutenant-colonel having business to do, I took leave of him, and went on board *Darce*, quartering there this night. . . .

10th. This day the hoy went down near so low as Enniscattery, and the next tide came up again; in which passage, up and down, they discovered not many cattle; yet where that small number was, upon their approach to the shore, the rebels drove them up into the country; so that I fear we shall do little good this way. . . .

17th. The barge came down according to my order yesterday, by which I sent up an 100 minion shot to M'Adam: our boats likewise carried up 60 soldiers to Bonratty, brought by Captain Coachman; which, with those that came with Liston, make up an 100 good proper men to look upon. God grant they may prove truer to their cause and colours than the Welsh have done. . . .

24th. Between one and two in the morning I received three letters from M'Adam: one for ten barrels of powder, (I sent order to Captain Winnall to spare so many of the *Globe's* store which he had on board); another, desiring the assistance of what men and arms we could possibly spare, in regard of the intelligence he received of the rebels' intention (this day being a festival with them) to storm all our works together; which I forthwith performed, sending up between 30 and 40 men out of our three ships here, besides them already there, and took order with the ships aloft to do the like: the third was concerning the sheep-skins, etc. With these letters from M'Adam, came one likewise from Captain Brown, by which I had notice of a sally made yesterday by our men upon the enemy; but being much engaged, and not able to make retreat, after some execution done upon the rogues, had near on thirty of our men killed and wounded. . . .

[1 July 1646]. Early this morning I received a letter from the lieutenant-colonel, certifying me, that in regard he hourly expected the enemy to make an assault . . . [I] went to Bonratty, where I found him and his officers at a council of war: in which I desired not to interpose, as not willing to engage myself in the shore-affairs, otherwise than I might with freedom perform my duty in my proper sphere; and so, walked about the works till the council was concluded and the assembly dissolved; I mean, from serious matters, but again convened to dinner. At which the lieutenant-colonel sitting, the rebels made divers shots at Jefford's house; which they had often attempted to gain, but as yet could not. He (hearing them shoot so thick, and ply their guns so hard,) rose from the table, went to the house to see what breaches were made, and to encourage his men; where being entered, a shot was made, by which the lieutenant-colonel, John M'Adam, was most unhappily slain, to the general lamentation of us all. Upon which I, being there by, hearing a muttering among the common soldiers about some money that M'Adam had found in the castle, out of which they desired some part of their pay, I willed them to put a guard upon his chamber that night. As also, some differences among the officers being risen, I endeavoured the allaying thereof for the present, and moved that every one might be appointed his post, and charged carefully to attend it; lest any Welshman, or other, running away, should inform the enemy of the death of the lieutenant-colonel, and so encourage them to make an assault. . .

2nd. This morning, very early, I went on shore into the castle, where I found some of the officers in M'Adam's chamber, having there 18 bags of money, and some plate, before them, which, with two more formerly disposed of, were found by the lieutenant-colonel in the castle. I, perceiving them to be resolute in sharing the money among them, willed them to consider, that money is the nerves and sinews of war, which being spent, the strength of that side must needs be weakened and abated; and therefore desired, that look, whatsoever they disposed of, yet a sufficient stock should be left as a reserve for the future, which would much encourage the common solider. But, what power my poor rhetoric to this purpose had, you may easily guess, if ever you saw or heard it practised on a covetous miser. They kept on their course, and would not be dissuaded. . . .

3rd. I was informed, that the guns the rebels shot were at Jefford's house; and that another Welshman, running away the last night, told the enemy of the death of the lieutenant-colonel; who called to our men, and bid them 'get a better commander', when they had not such a one among them: I would also such rogues might be hanged, for example's sake. The rebels intend this night an assault for the gaining of the corkasse, but I hope they will come short of it.

8th. Captain Line and myself went up to Bonratty to take some order with the major about the transport of the lame and wounded soldiers, together with such women and children as remained in the garrison. Captain Coachman, the hoy, and barge, came up again; having gotten from the enemy 40 steers and milch cows, 30 sheep, besides what cattle the soldiers had; all which I resolved for the present relief of the garrison, the enemy being set down so close that they must now look to be plyed hard; and therefore ordered the hoy to carry up part of the cattle to Bonratty. . . .

9th. I sent up 20 cattle more by the hoy to the garrison. Captain Line and Captain Coachman coming on board, we consulted about a conveniency of dispatching the maimed soldiers, women and children, so soon as they should be ready. The enemy plyed very hard at one Keeme's house (which is within the house which Captain Jefford maintained so long), killed one man, hurt two; a great part of the house being battered down. A Frenchman, a trooper of ours, ran away to the rogues, with his horse, pistols, and carbine. The enemy got a gun down this day into the corkasse, which flanks all our works, and will thereby do us very much damage. . . .

11th. There was not one great gun or musquet discharged on either side the last night, nor as yet this morning. About eleven of the clock, Captain Dechicke and Lieutenant Gibbon, bringing with them a captain of the rebels, came on board the *Peter* frigate, where I was, to give me notice of the present condition of the garrison; that they had not above 300 serviceable men among them, the rest being either killed or maimed, and so not able to make their conditions, and so required my advice. I desired to know upon what terms, and to see their propositions; which were - having quarter, with a convoy to march to Cork by land, to quit the garrison with bag and baggage, their artillery and horse, drums beating, colours flying, and musquet-bullet in their mouths; with the rest that were hurt, to be transported by the shipping to Cork or Kinsale. I could not dislike the propositions, if granted by the rebels; but yet was more willing to have the garrison maintained, expecting daily to hear some comfortable news from my Lord of Broghill. Notwithstanding, they, concluding it could not be, departed. For my part, I could say nothing to, nor would determine anything further therein, because I saw how they in the castle stood affected. . . .

14th. About seven this morning came down a boat from the rebels, with a captain of theirs, a lieutenant and ensign of ours, with certain articles of agreement (interchangeably signed, by the Lord Muskerry on their part, and the major and officers on ours) for the surrender of the castle. The conditions were so mean, and so far beneath the honour of a solider, that I should never have consented thereunto. Yet, things past cure ought to be past care: I performed my part therein, which is, to send up Captain Fitz-Gerald to the garrison, with boats to bring off our seamen and soldiers, upon such conditions as per copy of the articles appears. . . About nine, the hoy, with all our boats, returned from Bonratty, as full of soldiers and inhabitants, men, women, and children, as they could thrust, which put me to no small trouble to dispose of; yet, so conveniently as the present opportunity would give leave, I shipped them on board our several ships.

15th. The rest of the inhabitants, with the commanders, came down, having quit the garrison, and the rebels taken possession of it; which did not a little grieve me, after all the care and pains which I had taken, night and day; but it was not in my power to work a remedy. I ordered these, with as much accommodation both for themselves and our seamen as the accommodation both for themselves and our seamen as the time (being night) would permit.

16th. We weighed from Beth-road [Bonratty], and came down to Enniscattery. In the afternoon I caused all the soldiers on board our ships to be landed on the island, mustered them there, taking also the number of the passengers, that so we might be able to distribute to every ship a proportionable number, according to her burthen and convenience of stowage; putting the sick, lame, and wounded, together into one ship, that so the whole and healthy might not be prejudiced by an intermixture. . . Our proportion of beer being small, our company great, and numbers many, we were constrained to make a more plentiful provision of water; which proved very scarce here, and not to be supplied on any of the adjacent islands; yet here we filled, and got on board, what we could. The wind S. and S. by E.; a hand some gale, and fair weather.

Extracts taken from Granville Penn, *Memorials of the Life and Times of Sir William Penn,* 1644-70, 2 vols (London 1833), i, pp 159-211.

Diary of the Parliamentary Forces
in County Clare, 1651

By June of 1651 the army of the Parliament of England under Henry Ireton, son in law of Oliver Cromwell, prepared to lay siege to Limerick. Parliamentarian ships in the Shannon estuary had landed a small force which captured Carrigaholt castle and possibly also the McMahon castle at Clonderalaw. To prevent the Cromwellians from crossing the Shannon the Irish army under Lord Castlehaven was stationed at Killaloe and O'Brien's Bridge. However, Castlehaven, receiving reports that the English and Scottish army under Charles Coote were marching into east Galway, withdrew suddenly from Killaloe and allowed the Parliamentarian army to cross the river unopposed. Ireton and his men marched unhindered to the outskirts of Limerick and took up positions opposite Thomond bridge on the Clare side of the river. Following the Killaloe debacle, the Irish commanders in Clare, Col. David Roche and Col. Murtagh O'Brien, retook Carrigaholt castle and attempted to join up with the Irish army in Connacht in a forlorn attempt to raise the siege of Limerick. The progress of the siege and the excursions of Ireton and his deputy, Edmund Ludlow, into County Clare are recounted by an anonymous Cromwellian officer who kept a detailed diary of events during the summer and autumn of 1651.

Friday, 18 July 1651. By the last intercepted letters out of Limerick, the enemy in Conaught being invited to a speedy conjunction for relieving of that place; and David Roch and Murtogh O'Brien, with their forces in Thomond, having taken our garrison of Carrigahilt, proceeding to attempt on the rest of our garrisons in the county of Clare, there being no considerable party of ours in that county for opposing them; therefore was it resolved at a council of war this day that a considerable party should be sent speedily into the county of Clare for dispersing those there in a body; and for preventing that conjunction with Ferrall and the rest out of Conaught on which the besieged so much depend and for securing those of our garrisons in that county.

Saturday, 19 July 1651. His excellency [Henry Ireton] with the Lieutenant General [Edmund Ludlow] marched from the league with about 2,000 foot and 12 troops of horse and 8 troops of dragoons, into the county of Clare, according to the resolution the day before taken. The Major General commanded here. This day we heard of a party of Ulster men [under Ferrall] coming into the county of Clare for joining with Roch and Bryan. . . .

Tuesday, 22 July 1651. His Excellency returned to head quarters with some horse and foot, leaving the Lord General in Thomond with

7 troops of horse and 8 of dragoons and 1,200 foot, for attending the enemies motions, and for securing our remote garrisons.

Wednesday, 23 July 1651. The enemy in Limerick sallied with some horse and foot, but they were beaten back, ours both horse and foot, readily answering the alarm. Herein by the blessing of God his Excellency escaped narrowly. We heard that the enemy in Thomond had on the Lieutenant General's advancing burnt Carrigahilt, and that they were gathering their party to engage the Lieutenant General.

Friday, 25 July 1651. The Lieutenant General returned to the head quarters, of whom we had these particulars: that he relieved the garrison of Carrigahilt besieged by the enemy and finding it a place within the land and remote and not easily to be relieved, he drew up the garrison and blew up the castle. That in his return, hearing of the enemy drawing together at a pass near Ennis, he fell into their quarters, killed many, took some prisoners and pursued the rest 3 or 4 miles. Among others was there slain Connor O'Brien of Lymenaugh in the county of Clare, a colonel of horse, the most considerable person in the county, although not acting in chief, he was much lamented in the country, and his cutting off gave a stop to the proceeding of the enemy and did break that regiment of horse commanded by him.

Saturday, 26 July 1651. A woman was taken this night endeavouring to go into Limerick on the Thomond side, she being at the fort there and supposing it belonged to her party. She desired to be admitted to the governor's presence, Major General O Neal, and being brought into the fort and finding her error, she laboured to recall herself; but fearing torture (there threatened) she confessed she was sent the day before from Quin in the county of Clare by Col. Roch to tell the governor of Limerick that on the 27th a party should be about six-mile-bridge (six miles from Limerick) desiring instruction how to order the relief there attending him, and ordering her if she could not pass into Limerick, to return with what intelligence she observed. (This spy was hanged for fear of giving further intelligence.). . .

Lord's Day, 27 July 1651. This being the day appointed by Roch and his party for being at six-mile-bridge, his Excellency commanded out a party of sixty horse for discovering them, but there was nothing heard of them. . . .

Tuesday, 29 July 1651. Orders were sent to Sir Theo. Jones that he should hinder all he might Ferrall's conjunction and his Ulster forces with the forces of the County Clare, that thereby neither his Excellency before Limerick, nor the Lord President before Galloway should be disturbed in their work, and to that end his residence at Loughreagh was thought convenient as answering the enemy's motions either way, that if Ferrall were passed by already into the county of Clare and if the Lord President could not spare any considerable forces, then Sir

Theo. Jones should march to Thomond side of Killaloe and from there to expect further orders from his Excellency.

Friday, 1 August 1651. We heard that Sir Theo. Jones with 12 troops of horse and dragoons was there falling into the county of Clare, following David Roch and his party; that Ferrall was governor of the Ulster army and Philip Mac Hugh O Rely assisted him.

Lord's Day, 3 August 1651. Some of the inhabitants out of Limerick to escape ferried out on Thomond side; some were slain and the rest back. This day his Excellency by a dispatch to the Lord President of Conaught certified him what by intelligence he understood of the enemy's designs, that they intended the sending 500 horse to join with the Clare forces, who were about 2,000 foot, that by them intending the relief of Limerick and that the forces of Conaught were principally designed for engaging him the Lord President.

Monday, 4 August 1651. We intercepted letters from Limerick desiring supplies; also some going into Limerick from Col. Roch to the Governor promising within 5 nights to be near with relief. This letter was dated July 31st, and that the same night there should be a sign given by him from Glanne grosse, a mountain in Thomond towards Limerick. We thereupon strengthened our guards towards Foybee passe with more horse and dragoons. . . .

Thursday, 7 August 1651. By some out of Limerick we heard of the sickness there increasing, 24 buried in a morning; that they wanted great shot, and for the supplying of small shot they had untiled the Earl of Thomond's house. Out of Thomond we heard that on the 5th instant Col. David Roch and Murtough O Bryan with their forces about 2,500, marched from Ennis to Downemoyhill between the two counties of Clare and Galloway. . . .

September 1651. This day a party of horse and dragoons in our new garrison of Clonrone on the other side of Clare Castle appearing before Clare, the enemy sallied in number about 150, ours retiring for advantage, and the enemy pursuing, we charged them and killed and took about 40, among whom was Capt. Lalor, who charged Col. White, (late governor of Clare) for conferring with his Excellency on August 25th. In this the castle of Clare found what they might after expect of those our new garrisons, their neighbours. . . .

Friday, 5 September 1651. In this expedition [into Clare] was our party before Limerick secured from the attempts of the enemy, and the hopes of the besieged at present disappointed as to supplies from theirs on this side; thereby was the enemy in County Clare dispersed, and many persons therein considerable brought under contribution who till then held out, and either would not or durst not by reason of the enemy's power submit to us; and by it had we the advantage of placing convenient garrisons in that county, where was laid a force of about 500 horse and dragoons, and as many foot, for answering all motions of the enemy there, and for repressing the oppression of the country by those in Clare Castle. . . .

Monday, 8 September 1651.   His Excellency went this day to Bunratty, belonging to the Earl of Thomond, which lying on the Shannon was conceived fit to be fortified.   There was laid Captain Preston with his troop of horse and foot company.   This place was very convenient for baking and making and laying up provisions for the army and other garrisons thereabout.   Some labouring to pass out of Limerick were by our guards on Thomond side met withall and put to the sword. . . .

Tuesday, 28 October 1651.   Out of the county of Clare was thus certified that Col. Murtough O'Brien and Col. Bourke lay at Balliturry, that their forces were 1600 foot and 250 horse and that we had garrisoned the town of Inchinglin in Thomond.   At a council of war it was this day debated and voted that part of the army should march into the county of Clare to fortify the town of Enis, and thence to march to Gallway. . . .

Wednesday, 29 October 1651. [Fall of Limerick]   This day the enemy marched out of Limerick about 1200 [men], and, according as their interests led them, some went into the county of Clare, some towards Muskery [in Munster] and others towards their party in the county of Tipperary. . . .

Thursday, 30 October 1651.   Col. Warden with 6 troops was sent from us to Enis in the county of Clare there to attend the coming thither of the army and to assay what might be done by treaty for gaining the strong castle of Clare. . . .

Saturday, 1 November 1651.   The Lieutenant General marched with the army into the county of Clare.

Lord's Day, 2 November 1651.   Col. Warden (sent before into the county of Clare) this day summoned the castle of Clare.   Hereunto was the following answer returned:

Sir, I can hardly believe that the Governor of Limerick was brought to such low conditions as you make mention of in your letter. Howsoever, the officers here desire a respite of time until Monday next, seeing our Governor is not in place, and in the interim we may send him notice of the contents of your letter, and then resolve you; wherein we desire a speedy answer and rest your servant, W. Butler. Clare Castle, 1 November 1651. . . .

Tuesday, 4 November 1651.   The Lieutenant General coming before Clare Castle, it was at a council of war debated whether it had been advisable to summon or attempt the strong castle of Clare.   The strength of it would make a siege or a storm equally dangerous, considering the time of the year and the strength of the place, not short of any of that we had to deal with, all appearing by description of the place and the map of it before given.   A refusal on a summons would be tending to Carigaholt in the county of Clare on the Shannon, which was to be now looked after, and the place had been already summoned by Col. Warden, and the time passed wherein an answer should have been given as if not inclining to surrender. In this difference of opinions it pleased God to incline us to a second summons from the Lieutenant General, which was this day sent, and God thereupon ordered the delivering of the place contrary to our expectation or hopes.

The conditions of surrender are as follows:

Articles of agreement by and between Lt. Gen. Ludlow on the behalf of the lord deputy General of the one part and Capt. William Butler and Capt. Donogh O Connor on the behalf of Col. McEgan of the other, touching the surrender of Clare for the use of the Parliament and Commonwealth of England, dated the 4th November, 1651.

1. That the castle and all places of strength within the same with all the arms, ammunition, stores, and other utensils of war (except hereafter excepted) shall be delivered up to such as shall be appointed to receive the same without embezzlement or spoil by 8 of the clock tomorrow morning, being the 5 of November.

2. In consideration whereof all the officers and soldiers shall have free liberty to march away with their arms, bag and baggage, drum beating, colours flying, muskets loaden, matches lighted, bullets in pouch.

3. That all persons of what degree and quality soever shall have liberty to march away with bag and baggage, chattel of all sorts.

4. That all persons (except Romish priests, Jesuits and friars) who desire to live in protection shall have liberty so to do, submitting themselves to all acts and ordinances of parliament.

5. That convoys and passes shall be allowed to such of them as desire the same.

6. That Col. Stephen White shall have the benefit of these articles in case he accepts of it within twelve days.

7. Each musketeer shall carry with him half a pound of powder with bullet and match proportionable.

8. That none shall suffer for another man's default in breaking of the articles.

9. That two hostages be forthwith given by the Lieutenant Colonel for the performance of these articles.

In testimony whereof we have hereunto set our hands the day and year within written.

Edmund Ludlow.   William Butler,   Donogh O Connor.

This day the place was delivered according to the articles and committed to Col. Sadler's government, and in his absence to Lt. Col. Fowkes of his regiments. There marched away of the enemy about 230. We found there 8 barrels of powder, 70 bundles of match, 2 barrels of bullets, some old unfixed arms, with provision of meal and corn etc. also a small iron piece mounted on the works, and here we recovered our mortar piece and shells (about 23) and our two guns (one a cannon of 7, the other a demi cannon) with their shot, about 60, which had been lost as is before mentioned, July 5.

Extracts taken from 'Diary of Parliamentary Forces' in J. T. Gilbert (ed.) *A Contemporary History of Affairs in Ireland, from A. D. 1641 to 1652*, 3 vols, (Dublin 1879), iii, pp 244-63.

Edmund Ludlow, The War in County Clare, 1651.

Edmund Ludlow came to Ireland with the army of the commonwealth in 1649. Originally a graduate of Trinity College, Oxford, he represented the county of Wiltshire in parliament. A man of extreme views, he was one of the individuals who signed the death warrant of King Charles I. In Ireland he acted as second in command to Henry Ireton with authority to replace him in case of death or illness. By act of parliament he was appointed one of the four civil governors of Ireland and on Cromwell's orders commissioned lieutenant general of the horse in Ireland. On the death of Ireton, November 1651, Ludlow assumed command of the army until October 1652. He accepted the surrender of Clare Castle in November 1651 and Galway in April 1652, after which the war was virtually at an end. As commander of the army he presided over some of the worst excesses of the war, as the Cromwellians sought to quieten the countryside following the capture of the urban centres. He thoroughly approved of the policy of transportation of the Irish landowners into Connacht. Even among his own party Ludlow was difficult and uncompromising; he refused to accept Cromwell's authority as lawful, after he expelled the rump of the Long Parliament in 1653. In 1655 he was removed from office when it was found he was circulating pamphlets hostile to the government. On the restoration of the monarchy in 1660 he was compelled on fear of his life to flee to the continent. He established himself eventually in Switzerland, being granted an act of protection by the government of Bern in April 1662. Ludlow, while keeping a keen eye on events in England, was to remain in Switzerland for the rest of his life; he compiled his memoirs most probably between the years 1663 and 1673. However, they remained unpublished until 1698, six years after his death. Because of the time lapse involved his writings cannot be accepted as wholly reliable; sometimes the details of incidents are inaccurate and the chronology is confused. Notwithstanding these shortcomings, however, and in the absence of anything better, Ludlow's memoirs remain a valuable account of the proceedings of the war in County Clare for the autumn and winter of 1651.

During these transactions, the deputy of Ireland [Henry Ireton] labouring with all diligence to carry on the public service, ordered the army to rendezvous at Cashil; from whence he marched by the way of Nenagh to that part of the river Shannon which lies over against Killalo, where the Earl of Castle-haven lay with about two thousand horse and foot, disposed along the side of the river, and defended by breast-works cast up for their security, resolving to endeavour to obstruct our passage into Connaught. The deputy, as if he had intended to divert the course of the river, set the soldiers and pioneers at work to take the ground lower on our side, that the water venting it self into the passage, the river might become fordable; which so alarmed the enemy, that they drew out most of their men to oppose us. Whilst they were thus amused, the deputy taking me with him, and a guard of horse, marched privately by the side of the Shannon, in order to find a convenient place to pass that river. The ways were almost impassable by reason of the bogs, though Col. Reeves and others who commanded in those parts had repaired them with hurdles as well as they could. Being advanced about half way from Killalo to Castle-Conel, we found a place that answered our desires, where a bridge had formerly been, with an old castle still standing at the foot of it on the other side of the river. We took only a short view of the place, lest we should give occasion to the enemy to suspect our design. The way hither from our camp was so full of bogs, that neither horse nor man could pass without great danger, so that we were necessitated to mend them, by laying hurdles and great pieces of timber across in order to bear our carriages: which we did under pretence of making a passable way between our camp and Castle-Conel, a garrison of ours, where provisions were laid up for the army. It was about ten days before all things necessary to this design could be prepared, and then Col. Reeves was commanded to bring three boats which he had to a place appointed for that purpose, by one a clock in the morning. At the beginning of the night three regiments of foot, and one of horse, with four pieces of cannon, marched silently towards the place where the boats were ordered to lie, and arrived there an hour before day. They found but two boats waiting for them, yet they served to carry over three files of musketters and six troopers, who having unsaddled their horses, caused them to swim by the boat, and were safely landed on the other side. Two sentinels of the enemy were in the castle, of whom one was killed by our men, and the other made his escape. Our boats had transported about sixty foot and twenty horse before any enemy appeared; but then some of their horse coming up skirmished with ours, wherein one Mr How, a hopeful daring young gentleman, who had accompanied me into Ireland, distinguished himself. About a thousand of the enemies foot advancing, our horse was commanded to retire, which they did, not without some reluctancy; but the hasty march of their foot was retarded by our guns which we had planted on a hill on our side of the river, from whence we fired so thick upon them, that they were forced to retreat under the shelter of a rising ground; where after they had been a while, and considered what to do, finding ours coming over apace to them, instead of attacking us, they began to think it high time to provide against our falling upon them; and having sent to all their guards along the river to draw off, they retreated farther through the woods into their own quarters. . . .

In the mean time the enemy was endeavouring to draw their forces together to relieve the place [Limerick], well knowing of what importance it was to their affairs. To that end the Lord Muskerry had brought together about five thousand horse and foot in the counties of Cork and Kerry, and David Rock between two or three thousand more in the county of Clare. The Lord Broghil and Major Wallis were sent to oppose the Lord Muskerry, whilst I with another detachment was ordered to look after the other. The Lord Broghil soon met with the Lord Muskerry, and after some dispute entirely defeated him, killing many of the Irish, and taking others prisoners, with little loss on our side. I passed the river at Inchecroghnan [Inchicronan], of which the enemy having advice, drew off their forces from Caricgoholt, a garrison of ours, which they were besieging, whereby Capt. Lucas, who was governor of the place, wanting provisions, took that opportunity to quit it; and being joined by Capt. Taff's dragoons, came safe to us. Whilst I was endeavouring to find out the enemy, advice was brought to me, that they, to the number of three thousand horse and foot, were marching with all diligence to possess themselves of the pass at Inchecrohgnan, thereby designing to obstruct our return to the army before Limerick: which being confirmed by a letter we intercepted, I drew out two hundred and fifty horse with sixty dragoons, and sent them before, with orders to take possession of the pass, marching after them with the rest of my party. When I was almost come to the pass, I was informed by those sent before, that they had found a small number of the enemies horse there, who immediately retreated upon the advance of our men, some of whom were in pursuit of them. Presently after advice was brought, that the enemy made good a pass leading to some woods and bogs which they used for a retreat; whereupon I went to take a view of their posture, that if it were necessary I might order a greater force to succour our men. Being come up to the place where the dispute was, I found that Connor O'Brian, deputed by the Lord Inchequin to command in the county of Clare, had been shot from his horse, and carried away by his party. The enemy retreated to a pass, and fired thick upon us; but we advancing within pistol-shot of them, they quitted their ground, and betook themselves to their woods and bogs. Divers of them were killed in the pursuit; yet the ground was so advantageous to them, and their heels so good, that though we pursued them with all possible diligence, and sent out parties several ways, yet we could not take above two or three of them prisoners. Having dispersed this party, and relieved the garrison of Caricgoholt, I returned to the army before Limerick, where I found a considerable progress made in our works on the other side of the town, and a reinforcement from England of between three and four thousand foot, whose arrival was very seasonable and welcome to us, having lost many men by hard service, change of food, and alteration of the climate. The deputy [Henry Ireton] fearing that the plague, which raged fiercely in Limerick, might reach our army; and to the end that care might be taken of our sick and wounded men, caused a hospital to be prepared, and furnished with all things necessary; and whilst the works were finishing against the town, he went to visit the garrison of Killalo, and to order a bridge to be made over the river at that place, for the better communication of the counties of Tipperary and Clare. . . .

Though the news of these successes much discouraged our enemies in Ireland, yet those in Limerick were not without some hopes, that either the plague, or scarcity of provisions, together with the badness of the weather, might constrain us to raise the siege; and therefore refused to accept such conditions as we were willing to grant. The line which we had made about the town, and the forts being in a condition of defence, the deputy resolved to look after the enemy in the county of Clare, and if possible to get some provisions from thence for the relief of the army. He took me with him, knowing I had been in those parts before, and between three and four thousand horse and foot. At our approach to the places where the enemies usually were, we divided our body, the deputy being at the head of one, and I at the head of the other party; hoping by this means so to encompass the enemy, that they should not escape us: but though we sometimes came within sight of them, and used our utmost endeavours to engage them, yet by reason of the advantages they made of the woods, rocks, hills, and bogs, for their retreat, we could do them little hurt, save by seizing their horses and cattle. In the absence of this party from the army, the enemy with two thousand foot made a sally out of Limerick so unexpectedly upon our men, that they had almost surprised our guard of horse; but ours immediately mounting, and being not accustomed to be beaten, charged them, and notwithstanding the inequality of the forces, they being much superior to us in number, put them to a stand, till a party of horse and foot came to their relief, and forced the enemies to retreat under the walls of the town, from whence their men fired so thick upon ours, that their own men had time to get into the town.

When this account was brought from Sir Hardress Waller to the deputy, he was upon his return to the army before Limerick, having left me with about two thousand horse and foot, as well to ease our quarters about the town, not knowing how long we might lie before it, as to endeavour to persuade the garrison of Clare-Castle, a strong place, and situated upon the river, to surrender. To that end being arrived in the army, he sent one Lieutenant Colonel White, who had served the enemy, and now had a commission to raise forces for the king of Spain, with an order to me, to permit him to go the said garrison, that he might inform them of the impossibility of their receiving any relief, and of the necessities to which Limerick was already reduced, and thereby prevail with them to make speedy provision for themselves, and to list under him: but his design proving ineffectual, I found myself obliged to return to the camp before Limerick, where we made provision for a winter-siege. . . .

Whilst the deputy was settling affairs at Limerick, he ordered me with a party to march into the county of Clare to reduce some places in those parts. Accordingly I marched with about two thousand foot and fifteen hundred horse to Inchecroghnan, fifteen miles from Limerick; but it being late before we began our march, and night overtaking us before we could reach that place, as we were passing the bridge, one of my horses that carried my waters and medicines fell into the river, which proved a great loss to me, as things fell out afterwards. The next day I came before Clare-Castle, and summoned it, whereupon they sent out commissioners to treat, though the place was of very great strength; and after three or four hours debate, we came to an agreement, by which the castle was to be delivered to me the next morning, the enemy leaving hostages with us for the performance of their part. That night I lay in my tent upon a hill, where the weather being very tempestuous, and the season far advanced, I took a very dangerous cold. The next morning the enemy marched out of the castle, and received passes from me to return home, according to the articles. After which having appointed Col. Foulk and a garrison to defend it, I marched towards Carickgoholt. That night my cold increased, and the next morning I found myself so much discomposed, that Adjutant General Allen, who was then with us, earnestly pressed me to go aboard one of the vessels that attended our party with ammunition, artillery and provisions, and to appoint a person to command them in my absence. But being unwilling to quit the charge committed to my care, I clothed myself as warm as I could, putting on a fur coat over my buff, and an oiled one over that; by which means I prevented the farther increase of my distemper, and so ordered our quarters that night, that I lay in my own bed set up in an Irish cabin, where about break of day I fell into so violent a sweat, that I was obliged to keep with me two troops of horse for my guard, after I had given orders for the rest of the men to march. In this condition I continued about two hours, and though my sweating had not ceased, I mounted in order to overtake my party, who had a bitter day to march in, the wind and the hail beating so violently in our faces, that the horses being not able to endure it, often turned about. Yet in this extremity of weather the poor foot were necessitated to wade through a branch of the sea, near a quarter of a mile over, up to the waist in water. At night we arrived within view of Carickgoholt, my distemper being but little abated, and my body in a continual sweat. The next day I summoned the garrison to surrender the castle: in answer to which they sent out commissioners to treat, who at first insisted upon very high terms; but finding us resolved not to grant their propositions, they complied with ours, and the next day surrendered the place. Liberty was given by the articles to such as desired it, to go and join the Lord Muskerry's party in the county of Kerry: the rest to return home, with promise of protection as long as they behaved themselves peaceably, excepting only such who should appear to have been guilty of murder in the first year of the war, or afterwards. Having placed a garrison in Carickgoholt, I returned towards Limerick, and being on my march thither, I was met by an officer of the guard, with orders from the deputy for my return; who thinking it impossible to reduce this garrison by force in such a season, was unwilling that the soldiers should remain longer in the field, exposed to such cruel and sharp weather. The messenger also acquainted me, that the deputy was coming towards us, which he did, as well to view the country, in order to the more equal distribution of winter-quarters and garrisons, as to let us see that he would not command any service, but such as he was willing to take a share of himself. Upon this advice I hastened with a party to meet him, giving orders for the rest to follow as fast as they could conveniently. At our meeting I gave him an account of what I had done, with which he was very well satisfied. After two days march, without anything remarkable but bad quarters, we entered into the barony of Burren, of which it is said, that it is a country where there is not water enough to drown a man, wood enough to hang one, nor earth enough to bury him; which last is so scarce, that the inhabitants steal it from one another, and yet their cattle are very fat; for the grass growing in turfs of earth, of two or three foot square, that lie between the rocks, which are of limestone, is very sweet and nourishing. Being in these parts we went to Lemmene, a house of that Connor O'Bryan whom we had killed near Inchecroghnan; and finding it indifferent strong, being built with stone, and having a good wall about it, we put a garrison into it, and furnished it with all things necessary. The next day the deputy with a party of horse went to view some other places where he designed to appoint garrisons, in order to prevent the sending of provisions into Galway, to which this country lies contiguous. I was very desirous to attend him according to my duty, but he having observed my distemper to continue upon me, would not permit it; and when I pressed it more earnestly, he positively commanded me to stay. That day there fell abundance of rain and snow, which was accompanied with a very high wind, whereby the deputy took a very great cold that discovered itself immediately upon his return; but we could not persuade him to go to bed, till he had determined a cause that was before him and the court martial, touching an officer of the army, who was accused of some violence done to the Irish; and as in all cases he carried himself with the utmost impartiality, so he did in this, dismissing the officer, though otherwise a useful man, from his command for the same. The next day we marched towards Clare-Castle, and found the way so rocky, that we rode near three miles together upon one of them, whereby most of our horses cast their shoes; so that though every troop came provided with horse-shoes, which were delivered to them out of the stores, yet before that day's march was over, a horse-shoe was sold for five shillings.

The next morning the Lady Honoria Obryan, daughter to the late earl of Thomond, being accused of protecting the goods and cattle of the enemy, under pretence that they belonged to her, and thereby abusing the favour of the deputy's safeguard, which he had granted to her, came to him; and being charged by him with it, and told, that he expected a more ingenious carriage from her; she burst out into tears, and assured him, if he would forgive her, that she would never do the like again, desiring me, after the deputy was withdrawn, to intercede with him for the continuance of his favour to her: which when I acquainted him with, he said, 'As much a cynic as I am, the tears of this woman moved me'; and thereupon gave order that his protection should be continued to her. From hence I would have attended him to Limerick; but so much more care did he take of me than of himself, that he would not suffer it; desiring me to go that day, being Saturday, and quarter at Bonratto, a house of the earl of Thomond's, in order to recover my health, and to come to him on Monday morning at Limerick. Accordingly I came, and found the deputy grown worse, having been let blood, and sweating exceedingly, with a burning fever at the same time. Yet for all this he ceased not to apply himself to the public business, settling garrisons and distributing winter-quarters, which was all that remained to be done of the military service for that year. . . I was unwilling to leave him till I saw the event of his distemper; but he supposing my family was by this time come to Dublin, would not permit me to stay, and I finding I could in no way be serviceable to him, submitted to his desires. I found the commissioners of parliament at Dublin, and acquainted them with the state of affairs in those parts from whence I came, and with the resolutions taken by the deputy at Limerick; but soon after my arrival, the sad news of his death was brought to us, which was universally lamented by all good men, more especially because the public was thereby deprived of a most faithful, able and useful servant.

Extracts taken from *Memoirs of Edmund Ludlow Esq.* (Vivay, Switzerland 1698), i, pp 346-83.

Fr Anthony MacBrody,
Description of Thomond, 1669

In 1669 the Franciscan Anthony MacBrody, a friar of the Irish college in Prague, published a large work called *Propugnaculum Catholicae Veritatis*, in which he defended the Irish nation against the calumnies of English writers. He was incensed at the claims of writers such as Camden, Stanihurst and Carew, who claimed that the Irish had been unlearned and were made civil through their intercourse with the English. MacBrody was a descendant of the illustrious Mac Bruaideadha, praise poets and hereditary historians to the O'Briens of Thomond. As a young man he joined the Franciscan order, completing his novitiate in Quin. He travelled to Rome in 1643, where he studied under Luke Wadding. He later transferred to the province of Bohemia and taught at the college of St Mary of the Snows, Prague. While much of his account of Clare is based on his own experiences, he obviously had access to William Camden's *Britannia* and Sir James Ware's works on Ireland. MacBrody viewed his native county through the uncritical eye of an exile and was clearly given to exaggeration as he tried to impress his readers on the continent.

Thomond (formerly a most noble principality, the home of the Dalcassian clan), is also known as County Clare, a name derived from the castle of Clare, one of the residences of the O'Brien family, prince of Clare (now called the earl of Thomond). Those who follow Camden in saying that that castle was built and named by Richard, the earl of Clare, who once lived there, are completely wrong. The castle, together with Clare Abbey was built by the most devout prince Donald O'Brien before the English made their way into Ireland about 1158. Donald was the first of his family to personally pay homage to Henry II. It was his son Donat O'Brien known as Caribrac, prince (or king) of Limerick, who was held in the highest esteem by King John on account of the many loyal services rendered to the crown of England. That place, then, is not called Clare after the earl of Clare; it comes, rather, from the name of a bridge which once spanned the river Fergus; the word clare means a board in gaelic. And so from that wooden bridge which was once the only crossing over the Fergus, the place came to be called Clare.

British writers have not been adverse to describing my native Thomond (which has three baronies, respectively soft, mountainous and stony), but they err magnificently. So I shall try to defend it briefly against false histories such as [Geraldus] Cambrensis, Camden and others of their ilk, by describing it in a way which never strays even one step from the truth.

Thomond, a fairly important part of Laithmogia (old name for southern half of Ireland), is situated in the northern corner of Munster, beyond the Shannon (Ireland's principal river). It is bound on the east and south by the curving flow of the Shannon river. On the west it is bound by the open sea, and to the north by County Galway in Connacht. It is so circumscribed, in fact, that access to it by land is possible only from the south through Limerick (the finest city in Munster) or from the north through the border with Connacht.

It has beautiful skies and healthy air; its land is fertile in many places, and it abounds in wild birds (especially pheasants, partridges, falcons, hawks, eagles, quails, ducks, geese, wild cocks and hens, woodcocks, blackbirds, thrushes, cranes, swans, and many other species of birds) in great profusion. It also has a great variety of woods and forests, as well as many mountains, sunny hills, fields and plains. It is rich in rivers (the principal ones being the Shannon and the Fergus) and lakes (the most important being Lough Derg which extends long and wide along the noble Shannon and forms the division between Ormond, Thomond and Clanricard near Athlone; so large that it is at least fifty miles around it), and these abound in almost every kind of fish, especially salmon, eels, trout, etc. It is so blessed in all of these things that it could not be better. So great too is the abundance of wheat, barley, and oats gathered into the barns in Thomond that it would be right to call it the seat of cereals. Hence the fact that it often charitably helps out neighbouring provinces. It is also rich in metals, especially silver, and so abounds in ironore that from the ironworks at Tomgraney alone great quantities of iron are exported to England every year. The great multitude of flocks of sheep further enhances the splendour of this blessed fatherland. Day and night, they wander along the hills and fields and shady groves, without fear of thieves or wolves (though the kingdom is not entirely devoid of the latter). Like almost every county in Ireland, this province also abounds in the finest horses; I have sometimes seen as many as sixty well-groomed horses in the stables of the head of the O'Brien family, the earl of Thomond, at Bunratty. You will also find almost every kind of domestic and wild animal there, except camels, mules, donkeys, elephants, etc. I know of no better place in the world for hunting; wolves, deer, foxes and hares are hunted and captured.

Not least of this province's ornaments is the great quantity of fine multi-coloured marble. There are also many towns, castles, churches and monasteries. The chief towns are: Ennis, Clonroad, Killaloe (episcopal see), Kilfenora (episcopal see), Killinnaboy, Coroffin, Quin, Drekud [Six-mile-bridge?], Scariff, Clondegad, Kilrush, and Tobar Rian Douin (the well of the king of the world).

Saints and Holy Wells

Beside these, and several other gifts of nature, Thomond is also blessed with supernatural gifts, such as several wells formerly made holy by saints. People who drink of the water from these wells with devotion are cured of various ills, as the daily experience of several centuries testifies. One of these wells is called Tobar Rian Douin, from which the town takes its name, not far from the house of my father Miler Brouder in Ballyogan. He died in 1668, the year I wrote these things; he was then in the 81st year of his age and the 58th of his marriage with my mother Margaret Moloney. There are also wells dedicated to Saints Senan, Donatus, Caimin and Cronan, and two to St Brigid. St Michael's well was first found 36 years ago, and since God worked many miracles through it (as everyone in Ireland knows, even the heretic English), I shall say a few words about how it was found, lest the memory of it perish.

A lady of ancient lineage, Lady Marian O'Gorman, lost her husband Sir Thomas O'Gorman, Lord of Tullycrine in the barony of Clondegad in Thomond. She was about fifty-two years old at the time; I knew her well as she was a close relative. She suffered so much from sciatica and a stone in the kidney that she could not sleep day or night with the pain. She tried several doctors, but in vain; the human skills of the doctors could do nothing to relieve the pain. The devout Lady Marian left aside vain hope in human medicine, and drawing on her Catholic faith, she sought divine help through the intercession of St Michael, the most glorious prince of archangels. Michael, commander of that angelic army, hastened to the aid of the suppliant lady. The pain lessened. The following night he appeared to Marian in a dream and spoke these words to her: 'Tomorrow, you will go to the shrine dedicated to my name'. (In Irish it is called Cill Mhichil, which means the shrine dedicated to St Michael, where there is a chapel dedicated to his name). 'When you have heard mass, you will go the cemetery and where you see a clump of reeds you will dig the ground. When you have done that, a copious flow of health-giving water will flow forth. As soon as you drink of this water, and wash your hands and feet in it, you will be completely cured.'

Good Catholic that she was, Marian paid no heed to the angel's advice the first time, for she knew that dreams were not to be trusted unless they were clearly from God. The prince of angels appeared to her a second time in her sleep, and warned her to give top priority to what he had previously ordered her to do. Still, on her confessor's advice, she wanted further proof of whether this inspiration was coming from God or not. So, in spite of increasing pain, she declined to carry out the order. But at the same time she continued to pray to St Michael for help. The Archangel appeared a third time; if she did not heed the divine warning this third time, he said, she would suffer irreparable damage.

Next morning, Marian called her confessor and her son Thomas O'Gorman, and told them of what she had seen and heard in her third dream. With the consent of both men, she had herself driven immediately to the designated place, about an Irish mile from her home. There, she first went to confession and received holy communion. Then, in the presence of many people, she ordered the earth to be dug up. The parish priest, Mr Dermot O'Queely, took up the spade in the name of God, and he had no sooner sunk it in the ground than a spring of the clearest water gushed forth. All the Catholics sank to their knees at the sight of this miracle, and gave thanks to God for this unexpected grace. Marian wept for joy and, calling on further help from her heavenly protector and the assistance of her servants, she approached the full well. She tasted the water, washed her hands and feet, and she was instantly restored to full health as if she had never been ill. That same week, so greatly did the devotion of the people to the glorious prince of angels and to the recently blessed water increase, two people who had been blind from birth had their sight restored. Three cripples also walked; one of whom could only crawl about on his hands and knees for the previous fifteen years.

The fame of the miracles worked at the new well increased daily, and a huge crowd began to gather there from all over Thomond and the whole of Munster. Eventually they came from all the provinces of Ireland, especially on the feast of St Michael and on the anniversary of the apparition; there were times when as many as 6,000 received holy communion there on one day.

Miracles at the Well

As God continued to favour the place with miracles, the faith and devotion of the people grew towards this sacred place. In the first year alone, the parish priest listed out 300 miracles to the late bishop of Killaloe, the most reverend John O'Molony, a cousin of mine. All of these were people who has tasted the water from St Michael's well with devotion and were restored to their former health by the power of God. The following years too, up to my departure from the country in 1643, an equal number of miracles were authenticated by a notary public appointed for this purpose.

The only miracle I witnessed with my own eyes happened on the feast of St Michael in 1642. A poor man called Donatulus (little Donat, or Donnachin) was so crippled from birth that his heels were attached to his buttocks. For many years he used to be carried about Clanricard and Thomond from house to house on a horse, or sometimes propelled himself in a little hand driven cart, in search of food. With the assistance of some devout people he was present at St Michael's shrine, along with thousands of others from all over Ireland, on the day and year I mentioned. About 11 o'clock in the morning, just after the sermon, Donat (I forget his surname) was brought to the well by some devout person, in spite of the milling crowd, and washed in its waters. No sooner had he done so that Donat suddenly stood up before all those people, rejoicing and praising God as if he had never been crippled. He did the customary rounds of the church and cemetery on his bare feet in the most lively fashion.

I was already a Franciscan at that time, and I was able to see for myself the marks of his heels and calves on his buttocks; I even touched them out of curiosity. Nor must some heretic say that several such ailments can be cured by the natural powers of water. No, it was not customary for the sick to bathe there as they do at the Caroline Spa and elsewhere here in Bohemia and at the various healthgiving waters around Europe where doctors send people. Here, people first armed themselves with firm faith in God, and hope in the invocation of the Blessed Archangel Michael, and then drank a little of the water and wet their faces with it rather than washed themselves properly. The power by which they were healed came from elsewhere, not from the natural properties of that water. But let's get back to the subject.

The Diocese

In olden times there were three episcopal sees in Thomond, namely: Killaloe, Scattery Island and Kilfenora. But in the reign of King Murrough II, Scattery was joined to the cathedral of Limerick. The episcopal seat of Killaloe was on the west bank of the Shannon, which was occupied in the sixth century by the abbot St Molua; hence the name Killaloe (or Kill-Maloe) by which it is known in popular parlance. After Molua's death, he was succeeded by his disciple St Flannan, son of King Theodoric, who was consecrated in Rome by Pope John IV. He is credited with being Killaloe's first bishop. King Theodric continued to be one of this see's greatest benefactors; he endowed it with a great quantity of land. Theodoric was succeeded in these generous steps by their highnesses Prince Morrough, king of Ireland (who died on the 6th Ides of March 1124 and was buried at his own request in this church), and Donald O'Brien, prince of Limerick, who, according to Ware, has been greatly praised by historians for his generosity to this and many other churches.

About the end of the 12th century the ancient cathedral church of Roscrea, founded by St Cronan, bishop and abbot, was joined to the see of Killaloe. As a result of this union, the diocese of Killaloe became quite rich and extensive: it was about 60 miles long and, not counting the various small chapels and shrines, it had 126 parish churches. It would be tedious, however, to treat of all of these individually. We will come to Scattery Island when dealing with Limerick, to which, as we have said, it was united.

The diocese of Fenabore, commonly known as Kilfenora, is situated in the barony of Corcomroe, and was founded by St Fachtna, of whom more presently. As far as I know, this see is the smallest in the whole of Ireland; it has no more than fifteen parishes. Nevertheless, the bishop can support himself comfortably.

Princes and Monasteries

There are many holy places in this principality famous as places of pilgrimage, and are still frequented as such despite the tyrannical madness of the heretics. The most famous for their miracles are Iniscaltra, once the see of St Caimin, and Iniscaha, the see of St Senan. There were also 80 churches, parish or other, in Thomond before Henry VIII's time, as well as eight monasteries, namely: Clare Abbey, Scattery, The Island of the Canons (known in the vernacular as Illan na gCanonach), The Island of St Cronan (commonly known as Inishcronan), St John the Baptist's (commonly known as Kiloen), St Mary of the Fertile Rock (known as Corcumruo), Kilshanny, Inish (known as Inishcluanruada), and the monastery of Quin.

The noble monastery of the Canon's Regular of St Augustine by the river Fergus, called Clare Abbey, was founded by Donald O'Brien, prince (or king, as some would say) of Limerick and Thomond, before the coming of the English.

Scattery, also belonging to the Canons, was restored by Terence O'Brien, king of Ireland.

The monastery of the Island of the Canons, belonging to the Canons of St Augustine, was founded by the above mentioned Donald O'Brien, prince of Limerick, as was that of Inishcronan.

The monastery of St John the Baptist was founded by Prince Donald O'Brien for the nuns of St Augustine.

That of St Mary of the Fertile Rock [Sanctae Mariae de Petra Fertili], and its cell at Kilsanna, was founded by the same prince for the Cistercian monks.

The monastery and church at Ennis, on the banks of the river Fergus, was founded about 1280 [*recte* 1240], for the Friars minor of St Francis, by Donat Cairbreac O'Brien, that most devout and powerful of princes, who, according to Bruodin's Chronicles and Miler junior Mac Bruodin, founded up to 80 monasteries, parish churches and chapels throughout many parts of Ireland.

The noble monastery of Quin was built of pure marble for the said Franciscan Friars about 1433. It was built by the illustrious Baron Maconus MacNamara, head of his dynasty, who built himself a beautiful mausoleum in the choir of the church.

In the choir of the Franciscan church in Ennis (now unfortunately used as a parish church by the heretics), the founder had a marble mausoleum built for himself and his descendants; it is known as the burial place of the O'Brien barons of Inchiquin. And since he did not want to be separated from his Bruodins even in death, he had a beautiful marble tomb built for them next to his own, where to this day most of the Bruodins are buried; the Bruodins of Maynoe are buried on St Caimin's Island, i.e. Inishcaltra, as they live too far away [from Ennis].

In the same choir you will find the lineal descendants of Brian O'Brien and the illustrious McMahon family.

They have a beautiful altar tomb, adorned with several marble statues and columns. Further down the same church several noble families, especially the Clanchys, Nealons, Deas, Gilroys, Hehirs, Considines, etc., have fine marble altar tombs. The Earl of Thomond's tomb is in the ornate chapel to St Francis within the church. . .

We shall now name the oldest noble families who ruled the nine baronies of Thomond up to the time of Cromwell's tyranny. Some were 'Most Illustrious', others just 'Illustrious', while finally there were those who were just 'Noble'. They were: O'Brien (from this royal family come the Earls of Thomond, Earls of Inchiquin, Barons of Ibrickan, Viscounts of Clare, to mention but a few of their glories), MacNamara or O'Mara, McMahon or Matthews, O'Connor, Fitzpatrick, Loghlin, O'Dea, Grady, Clanchy, Nealon, Sunigan, Delahoyd, Nerinhy, Bruodin, Hogan, Elmers, Britt, Davoren, Conry, Chruttin, Torenton, Cormican, Bourke, Fanning, Arthur, Blake, Graji, Hehir, Gorman, Gilriagh, Molony, Cahane, Caii [Kay?], Morisy, Considine, Flanigan, Gripha, Carmody. I do not wish to detract from any family by the order in which I have named them, and there may be other noble families which I do not remember just now.

Let that be enough about Thomond.

Taken from Antonio Bruodino, *Propugnaculum Catholicae Veritatis* (Prague 1669), pp 958-71; and Chris O'Mahoney and Brian Ó Dálaigh, 'A Seventeenth Century Description of County Clare' in *Dal gCais* 9 (1988), pp 27-38.

Thomas Dineley, Journal of County Clare, 1681

Thomas Dingley or Dineley was the son and heir of Thomas Dingley, controller of the customs of Southampton. Educated by the dramatist James Shirley in London, he registered as a student at Gray's Inn in 1670 but apparently did not complete his legal studies. Travelling through Holland in 1674, he left an illustrated manuscript of his travels there. The following year he completed a similar tour of France. In 1680 he visited Ireland; unfortunately the circumstances surrounding his Irish visit are unknown. He obviously had a connection with either the earl of Thomond, then resident in England, or with a tenant of the Thomond estate. He travelled from Dublin to Carlow, the principal Thomond manor outside of Clare, and from there to Limerick and Bunratty. He appears to have stayed in the vicinity of Bunratty, making occasional forays into Tipperary and Limerick, and travelling as far west as Ennis and Kilrush in County Clare. The most valuable part of his account are the many line drawings with which he illustrates his tour. Ancient abbeys, church monuments and castles occupied by English settlers attracted his attention. Clearly the newly arrived settlers were not yet sufficiently secure in their holdings to reside in the mansion houses which were to become such a prominent feature of the landscape in the eighteenth century. Dineley's drawings, though valuable, are not always accurate and need to be treated with caution. The last leg of his Irish tour was from Bunratty to Youghal, where he took ship and sailed for England. In 1684 he completed a tour of Wales. In later years he resided at Dilwyn in Herefordshire, where he compiled a *History from Marble*, a collection of epitaphs, church notes and sketches of domestic and public buildings. He died in May of 1695 at Louvain in Flanders. The original manuscript of his Irish tour is preserved in the National Library of Ireland.

Gentlemens' seats, castles, and places near this town [Limerick], are these following, viz., within a quarter of [a] mile. That castle belonging to Henry Ivers, Esq., well situated and capable of very considerable improvement, a draft whereof I took on the other side [of] this leaf. It is five miles and three quarters distant from Limerick. The gentleman, owner hereof, came over (a young man, clerk to one Mr Fowles, a barrister), since the king's restoration, and had in this time by his industry, acquired one thousand pounds a year. The first and chiefest of his rise was occasioned by being concerned in the revenue as clerk to the king's commissioners for settling the quit rents, and afterwards became their deputy receiver, is now in commission one of his Majesty's justices of the peace, not worth less than sixteen hundred pounds a year.

MOUNT IVER'S CASTLE

A mile distant from Six mile Bridge, on the other side [of] the river from hence, is an estate lately purchased from Mr Tiege O'Brien, by a very worthy gentleman, Mr Hugh Percivall, who bears for coat armour this: sable, a horse passant argent, spanceled on both legs of the nearer side gules, by the name of Percivall. Yet the vulgar and most usual way of spanceling, not only of horses, but black cattle, viz., cows, etc., in this country, is by joining their fore legs together by gads or widths twisted. And by this the horse cannot move or gain ever so little ground but by a galloping step, jump, or stretch. Now, a horse by his nature is rather won to this by tractable usage than forced, for such is the horses brisk and sprightly nature, and of all other noble spirited animals, that to bring them to conformity must be rather by gentle handling than severity. . . .

Three miles from Six-mile Bridge, 9 from Limerick, and 7 from Ennis, near the road between Limerick and Galloway, which city stands 27 miles off, is Ballicar castle, belonging to John Colpoys, Esq., whose prospect I have sketched off on the other side; this is part of the estate of the Right Honorable Henry, Earl of Thomond, in the barony of Bunratty, in the parish of Tomenlagh.

The South-East Prospect of Ballicar Castle.

In bogs here, as in most parts of Ireland, in digging for turf, are found large fir trees, and particularly in the Bishopric of Cloyne, in the county of Corke, and province of Munster; in the bogs are found such quantities of fir timber trees that they make benches, tables, wainscot, and floor rooms therewith; they use it also so much for fuel that the town smells of turpentine.

Ballicarr Lough abounds in eels and trout, especially of a stupendous largeness for such as trout, of 30 and 24 inches in length, which very commonly have been taken from here.

It is discoursed also, and by very credible persons, that at Muyree castle, in this county of Clare, towards Galloway side, was taken a prodigious pike with two ducks in its gorge or belly, one whereof was so fresh, that taken out and roasted proved a very good dish. And that upon the rising of the water of a lough, and overflowing some meadows, 3 pikes were shot at once grazing. That at such times they do eat grass, is very certain, and observed by several. The larger the pike the coarser the food, the smaller being the best, contrary to the nature of eels, which improve their goodness by their bulk and age...

Five miles from Six-mile bridge, 11 from Limerick, 8 from Ennis; and 3 miles from Rathlahine castle, is Ballyclogh castle, held for 3 lives by Tho. Cullen, Esq., justice of the peace, of Sir Henry Ingoldsby. This castle is adorned with some modern building according to the sketch on the other side [of] this leaf.

Besides this are 3 castles more in this kingdom, which go by the name of Ballyclogh, viz. two in the county of Limerick, one belonging to Lieut. Col. Eaton, another to Quartermaster Whitroe, and a third to Mr Pordam, in the county of Cork.

Ballyclogh, belonging to Captain Thomas Cullen.

Rathlahine castle, an ancient castle built by John Mac Namarra, Esq., it is founded upon and among rocks. It belonged since to Sir William King, governor of Limerick, and is now in the hands of Giles Vanderlure, Esq., who has built unto it the fairest stable of the county.

Rathlahine Castle.

Twelve miles from Rallahine, near Killaloo, worthy the sight of the curious, is an island called Ennish Caltra: this is two small miles about, in the Shannon river, in which are seen the remains of seven churches called the 7 churches of Asia. Here, once a year, the superstitious Irish go to do penance, and are enjoined to walk round barefooted 7 times, and they who fear hurting their feet, hire others to do it; here is a great concourse of both sexes. This island, by some, is called *Insula Sanctorum*, a name which has been applicable to all Ireland.

Ballingard and the Islands belonging to the Earl of Thomond.

Islands, parcel of lands belonging to the Right Honorable Henry earl of Thomond, touched off from Paradise hill.

Ennish Macony, is at present the interest of the officers of the 1649 security. This island is in the county of Thomond, and barony of [Clonderala].

Cony Island took its name from the great number of rabbits and coneys there; in it is seen the ruins of an ancient chapel, but without monument or inscription.

Coverhane castle was the seat and abode of Henry, the first [*recte* fifth] Earl of Thomond, during the life of his father, the great Donnagh O'Brien, earl of Thomond.

Deer Island, in the county of Clare and barony of Clonderala and parish of Kilchrist, heretofore called Innish Moor. Deer Island's lodge is built out of the ruins of a church or chapel. Among memorable accidents here written upon the door of the bedchamber of the right honorable Henry earl of Thomond are these, with these dates:

'MDCLVI. This hare was then cropped and turned into Deer Island; and in MDCLXXIII, the said earl killed her; and Anno MDCLXXII, a buck was killed there weighing 16 stone and two pounds.'

Inish Chirkey, an island 257 acres profitable, parish of Kildicert in Clonderala barony, county of Clare.

Cannon Island, in the county of Thomond, alias Clare and barony of [Clonderala] in it are seen the ruins of an ancient abbey of regular cannons of the rule of St Austin, whence it took its name of Cannon Island, which in Irish is Illean ne Cannanagh.

This [Bunratty Castle] is the principal seat of the most noble family of the O'Briens, earls of Thomond adjoining to a very fair park with deer.

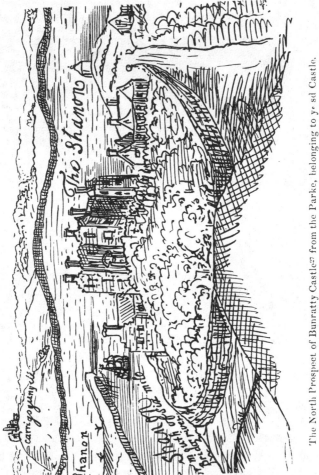

The North Prospect of Bunratty Castle[27] from the Parke, belonging to yᵉ sᵈ Castle.

This whole county being a peninsula, and kind of a park all over, environed with the Shannon river and the sea, except a narrow neck in the county of Galloway, abounding with stags and fallow deer.

[In the] barony of Ibricham, and in the barony of Corcumro in this county of Clare, both which baronies belong to the Right Honorable

Henry, Earl of Thomond, it is said that no mouse or rat will live by any means 24 hours; and it is likewise given out that a clod or piece of the earth of either of those baronies is a sufficient antidote and preservative placed in any other house or castle in this kingdom against these vermin.

Over against Bunratty castle on the other side of the Shannon is a fair castle called Carrig O'Gunnel, situated upon a hill belonging to his Royal Highness, rented by the present primate and chancellor of all Ireland, near which, in a marle pit, was lately taken up the skeleton of a monstrous man, whose thigh bone was seven foot long, and all other parts proportionable, whose skull could contain two bushels, which is half a Bristol barrel of grain.

The Blazing Star (as it appeared to me and others in the county of Thomond or Clare), taken at the castle of Rallahine, belonging to Giles Vanderlure, Esq., one of his Majesty's justices of the peace for that county in Ireland.

At its first appearance here at Rallahine Castle, being on Friday night, December 10th, [16]80, it showed itself with a prodigious long, pale, taper ray of a leaden saturnine colour, without any sign of a star to be discerned at its point. And that it continued to January the 13th following, is all the observation I could make, and communicate to my friends in England, as being unacquainted with astrology. . . .

Ross Roe, in the county of Thomond, barony of Tullagh, and parish of Kilmurry, part of the estate of the Honorable the Lord Viscount Clare, now in the possession of Mr John Fennell, is a fair seat situated among good lands and orchards, with a very pleasant and profitable large pool or lough on the one side thereof abounding with large trout. Here are also great plenty of wild fowl.

Rofs Roe Caftle.

About a mile and half from here, by water, between the castles of Rallahin and Rathfoelane; this lough of Ross Roe runs under ground for half an English mile, being opposed by hills and rocks, at last breaks out so far off that the possessor, John Colpoys, Esq., a very worthy English gentleman says, (as the Spaniards do of the river

Ama), that he feeds sheep and herds upon a green-bridge. Camden takes notice of one much more remarkable than this of the river Mole, in Surrey, undermining for several miles together. . . .

This stream of Ross Roe Lough at its rising again from Mr Colpoys his green-bridge turns a mill belonging to John Cooper, Esq.

Quin or Quyn town distant from Ross Roe castle four English miles: here it was that March 29, 1601, Captain Flower from Limerick lodged and fought the Connaught and Ulster rebels, who were drawn to a head to invade Munster with the assistance of Teg, son and heir to Sir Tirloghe O'Brien. The Lord Thomond's company here hurt and slew many, among which of note were Walter Burk, son to the blind abbot, and Tegg aforenamed.

Quin town is twelve miles from Limerick, six from Six-mile-bridge, 4 from Rallahine castle in the road to Galloway. It has nothing worth the note of a traveller but the ruins of an abbey, which I sketched off on the other leaf.

The Ruins of QUIN-ABBY lately harbouring some Friers of the order of S^t. Francis.

There are two fairs a year, which in times past were famous for quarrelling of two families of numerous offspring hereabouts, viz., the Molounys and Macnamarras, in which 8 persons, Ulster men, were killed and buried in one hole. It is storied also that at the drinking of a small barrel of sack, that the Ulster men being absent often, and thought to go out to leak between every other glass: it seems they went out to drink Usque bath, *Aqua vitæ* so called, they said to warm their stomachs which they thought would be overcooled with the sack, so accustomed they are to extraordinary hot liquors more than any people I ever heard of. The fairs of Quin are of black cattle, as cows, oxen, etc., which are so called here.

The abbey was anciently of the order of St Francis; here are seen the ancient vaults and burial places of the Mac Namarras and the Molounys, and hither they are brought if they die in the kingdom to be interred with their ancestors.

On the south side on the floor of the abbatial church of Quin-barony is seen this monument.

On the right hand of the altar at the east end of the abbey church of Quin is seen this monument of black marble of the Molounys. Family very ancient.

Opposite to the last monument are seen the remains of that belonging to the ancient family of the Macnamarras. . . .

This castle [Clare castle] and the lands belonging thereto are part of the estate of Henry, earl of Thomond, governor of this county, whose deputy governor, George Stammers, Esq., now High Sheriff 1681, holds it of the said earl. It was founded by Lionel Duke of Clarence, surnamed Antwerpe, the chief city of Flanders, and the marquisate of the Holy Empire, where he was born,

The Prospect of yᵉ Castle of Clare towards the Town of Clare, in the sayd County, and from the Road leading to Ennish Town.

third son of Edward III, earl of Ulster and lord of Connaught, the first who came over under the title of Lord Lieutenant of the Kingdom of Ireland in the year 1361, and in the reign of his Royal Father Edward the third; he died in the year 1361, and lies buried by his first wife Elizabeth, daughter and heir of William de Burgh, Earl of Ulster, in the chancel of the priory church of Augustines in Clare in the county of Suffolk.

Clare Castle, its Prospect from the Road between it and the Town of Six mile Bridge.

The Lord Ireton and Sir Charles Coot, in the year 1651, besieged and took this castle of Clare, and the most considerable pass in the country, whence they then sent a summons to the city of Galloway.

CLONROND CASTLE.

ENNIS. Its South East Prospect.

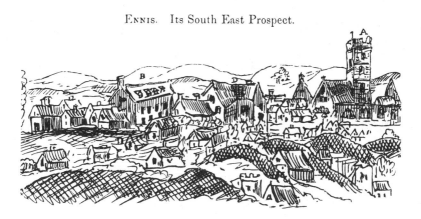

A. The Abby Church.   D. The Hall of the Azyses.   B. Lenthalls the Chief Inn.

The abbey of Clare, which lies between the castle of that name and the town of Ennis, is also thought to have been founded by the said Duke of Clarence, for the love he bore and in memory to a priory of that name in Suffolk where his first wife lies buried, after whose death he was married again unto Violenta the sister of John Gáleas Duke of Myllane whereto he journeyed. . . .

Ruins of the Abbey of Clare.

Clare. { S. Castle.
{ G. Abbey.

Loopshead is a promontory belonging to the Honorable the Lord Viscount Clare not far off the mouth of the Shannon, [here is] a stone whereon if anyone turns round upon the heel, and thinks on any other of either sex for a husband or wife, are said never to fail of their thought; on this several have written and engraved their names, but none ever ventured to make the turn, the stone being so dangerous an eminence over the water that it is thought impossible.

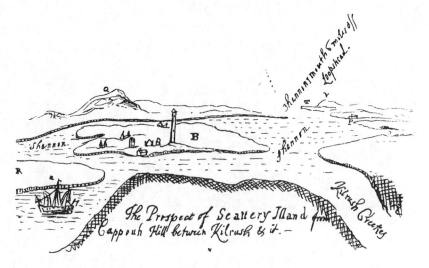

Q. Knockannore, in the County of Kerry. P. Carrigoholt, belonging to my Lord of Clare
O. Queren, a neat box belonging to Mr. Abraham Vanhogarden, who built it. R. Ennis
Bigg, or Hog-Island. A. Customehouse boat. T. Kilcardane poynt. V. Knock Ray-hill.

Kilrush is a town in the county of Clare, belonging to the right honourable Henry, Earl of Thomond, at this time, 1680, in the tenure of Major Granniere; opposite, with a league and half of river between, to the castle of Carigofoile in the county of Kerry, hither 28 July 1601, from Limerick marched the president of Mounster Carew against the rebels of Kerry with 1050 foot of Queen Elizabeth's soldiers and 75 horse, he being forced to take his way through the county of Clare, the mountain of Sleuglogher, by reason of the rain, being unpassable for carriages; the honour of this despatch is worthily attributed to the then earl of Thomond, who provided boats.

Barony of Burren, in the county of Clare, famous for physical herbs the best in Ireland, and equal to the best of England. Here are eringo roots in great quantity. Oysters of middle size, salt, green finned, far exceeding our Colchester, as owned by several judges of both; this barony affords not a piece of timber sufficient to hang a man, water in any one place to drown a man, or earth enough in any part to bury him. This consists of one entire rock with here and there a little surface of earth, which raises earlier beef and mutton, though they allow no hay, than any land in this kingdom, and much sweeter by reason of the sweet herbs intermixed and distributed every where. Earth or mould is so precious here, that it is reported process has been several times made for one neighbours removing earth in baskets from one another's land. Here horses 4 abreast draw the plough by the tails, which was the custom all over Ireland, until a statute forbade it.

Yet they are tolerated this custom here because they cannot manage their land otherwise, their plough gears, tackle, and traces being (as they are all over the rest of the kingdom) of gads or widths of twigs twisted, which here would break to pieces by the plough share so often jubbing against the rock, which, the gears being fastened by wattles or wisps to the horses' tails, the horses being sensible stop until the plowman lifts it over. Here people live to an extraordinary age, as observed by a gentleman of this country, who has an estate upon the place, that a man and his wife made above 204 years. The rock is a sort of limestone. And their garrens, horses so called, are seldom or never shod. It is not so seriously, as jestingly, reported that a traveller passing over this barony his horses leg chanced to stick in an hole between two rocks and to leave one of the shoes, which he alighting and searching for it, drew up out of the same place above 30 shoes; this is modestly thought the least number, for some undertake to say 30 dozen. Here is but one narrow road, no going out of it, and in this barony the partitions of land are made by broad stones like slate turned up edgewise. The common people here use brogues made of raw hides or untanned leather.

Ballykitt was anciently a castle, but reduced to what it is by Henry Hickman, Esq. Here is yearly kept a fair for black cattle on the feast day of St John Baptist, called Ballykitt fair. This is part of the estate of

BALLYKITT.

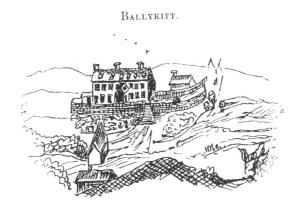

the Right Honorable Henry, earl of Thomond within a mile of Kilrush town. Note, that Irish cattle at 4 years old here are held marketable if fat, wherefore not so fit for long voyages as the English 8 year old stall-fed beefs. . . .

From Knockannaneene [Birdhill] to Obrien's Bridge town is a mile and half.

Two miles from hence is the Bishoprick and ancient city of Killaloo. This bridge parts the county of Tipperary and Clare.

Within a mile and three quarters of O'brien's Bridge is seen the ruins of a very ancient building called Castle Connell built by King John.

A fair view of it is seen on the left hand returning for Limerick from O'Brien's town, from whence to Parteene is 5 miles: this is a small town adjoining to the famous salmon weir belonging to the city of Limerick.

T. The House of the Earle of Inchiquin.

O'BRIEN'S BRIDGE.

Upon Parteen bridge is read this inscription beginning a fair causeway over a bog leading to Limerick

HUNC PONTEM AC VIAM STRATAM FIERI FECIT
PETRUS CREAGH
FILIVS ANDREÆ
MAJOR CIVITATIS LIMERICENSIS. SUMPTIBUS
EJUSDEM CIVITATIS
ANNO DOMINI MDCXXXV.

On the right hand of this bridge is a great decoy for ducks, belonging to James Fitz Gerald of the middle temple, Esq.

Taken from 'Extracts of the Journal of Thomas Dineley, Esquire, giving some account of his visit to Ireland in the Reign of Charles II' in *Journal of the Royal Society of Antiquaries*, 6 (1867), pp 73-91, 177-201.

William Molyneux, Survey of County Clare, 1682

About the year 1676, Moses Pitt, a London bookseller, became interested in publishing a general atlas of the world. Pitt wanted the atlas to contain detailed topographical descriptions of the places mapped. He enlisted the help of William Molyneux, the well known Dublin philosopher and scientist, to gather the information relating to Ireland. In the summer of 1682 Molyneux had a flyer printed with sixteen queries relating to the descriptions of Irish counties; this he despatched to all parts of the country. In response to his queries he received some twenty replies describing counties in various parts of Ireland. However, after four of the projected eleven volumes of the atlas were printed, Pitt was arrested for debt and the scheme collapsed. The accounts of the Irish counties were never used and are still preserved in the library of Trinity College Dublin. Two descriptions of Clare were in fact collected, one by Robert Downing, who appears to have had no Clare connections and who probably worked directly for Molyneux as descriptions of Sligo and Mayo are also attributed to him. The second account was from Hugh Brigdall, an attorney of the town of Ennis. Brigdall was the only individual to reply to Molyneux's queries from County Clare. The fact that he received the flyer is a good indication that a postal service was in operation between Dublin and Ennis in 1682. Little is known about Hugh Brigdall; he clearly had travelled extensively around Clare, having a good knowledge of the Burren and the county's rivers. The Fergus was one of the main channels of communication and much of the produce of the county was transported by river to Limerick. The Brigdall family was associated with Ennis at least from 1613 when one Hugh Brigdall (father or grandfather to the above) was appointed a first free burgess of the town. In 1684 Hugh Brigdall was living at Rosslevan on the outskirts of Ennis. As an attorney he would have earned a lucrative living from the many assizes and courts of quarter sessions held in the town. Merchants and attorneys with surplus cash engaged in extensive land speculation and one would expect Brigdall to have had land in various parts of the county. He was clearly affected by the disturbances associated with the Williamite War, because he was included in a list of Protestants seeking protection of his Majesty's forces in May 1691. In 1705, presumably in old age, he was superseded in the post of county treasurer. Although often quoted, the descriptions of County Clare collected for the Molyneux Survey have never been published. They appear here courtesy of Trinity College Dublin. Spelling and punctuation have been normalised and names of people and places appear as in the original manuscript.

Munster Province: County of Clare by R[obert] Downing

The county of Clare formerly called Tomond alias Tomow or north Munster alias Tomen i Bryen, to which formerly belonged the isles of

Aran now with Connaught, this county was divided into nine principal baronies that is to say:

1. The barony of Tullaghnenaspuil or Tulla formerly east Clancollane or McNemarra Reogh's country.

2. The barony of Dingenyvigane now called the barony of Bunratty formerly West Clancollane or McNemarra Finn's country.

3. The barony of the Islands formerly called the barony of Cluonrawde, O'Bryen['s] demesne originally belonging to the palace or manor of Cluonrawde.

4. The barony of Clonderala formerly called east Corcowaskynn, McMahon's country.

5. The barony of Moyarta formerly called West Corcowaskin another chief family of the McMahon's country.

6. The barony of Ibrekan O'Bryen's demesne to Moygh castle.

7. The barony of Corcumroe formerly called the barony of Dough i Connor or O'Connor of Dough's country.

8. The barony of Gragans now called the barony of Burren or O'Loughlin's country.

9. The barony of Insiquin formerly Tullida barony or O'Dea's country.

And first the barony of Tulla alias Tullaghenaspuil or east Clancollane. In this barony were several religious houses as first of all the cathedral of Saint Faghnanus in Killalo which stands upon the brink of the river of Shannon which bounds the county of Clare and the county of Tipperary. Here is within one mile thereof the place of the ancient palace and habitation of the O'Bryen's, when they were as well kings of Munster as also monarchs of Ireland, called *Tachcincora*; no great remarks there only some heaps of stones fallen. It was built just where the river of Shannon grows small being down for several leagues or miles to that place a spreading lough like the arm of the sea. The word *Tachcincora* signifying the house at the head of a wave. I do not find that the house or palace was ever inhabited since Monertarchus O'Bryen king of Ireland died here about the year [blank]. Here was a house in the barony of Colidei, some say called Moynoe or Moynore where to some lands belonged as may appear by the composition of Thomond or Clare 1585. Here was another religious house alias Tullanaspull aforesaid. It is said of the same order of the Colidei. This was founded by Convarn McNemara R[eogh], then lord of both Clancullanes and granted to his son Tadhg or Teigh McNemara, a priest of that order or rule, about 1367. I find that this house was not found in the crown as a religious house but by the statue of mortmain forfeited as granted without the king's licence in mortmain as may appear by the inquisition in king James' reign in the chief remembrancer's office.

Here was likewise another sort of a religious house at Tomgreny in the barony belonging to the family of the Gradys, one of which family Donogh or Dennis O'Grady going into England to accompany Morrough or Mauritius the last O'Bryen and first Earl of Thomond now knighted by Henry the eighth. Here is likewise in the barony an ancient manor house of the said great family of the O'Bryen's called O'Bryens Bridge now and since the said first earl's time in the hands of his heirs being the family of Insiquin. This barony in many places is coarse land especially towards the county of Gallway by the mountain called Slenoagteen and so it is likewise about O'Bryen's Bridge, but very good limestone lands in all or most part else of this barony.

The barony of Bunratty formerly the barony of Dingenivigeene alias west Clancollane belonging to the McNemara called white McNemara being the eldest house. In this barony stands the Franciscan friary of Quinn alias Quinchy in a market town upon a small fine river and in a very fertile country. The friary was built by Maconus McNemara anno 1433 saith Sir J[ames] Ware. There is a fair and large castle and houses called Bunratty formerly belonging to the family, but for one hundred and fifty years past, the chief mansion house of the earls of Thomond. It lies on the river of Shannon where the river of Knee enters it. Here are very fertile marshes all about the said Bunratty. Here are near the city of Limerick in the barony lying on the river of Shannon three several ancient castles called the Cratallaghs formerly belonging to the McNemaras. Here are likewise about Quinchy aforesaid several castles belonging to the said Mac Nemara, which are very considerable castles as Cnoppocke, Dingen Iviggen aforesaid Danganbrack. Here is likewise in this county a considerable market town called Six Mile Bridge where are oil mills. Here are a great number of castles of lesser note in this barony. The barony is generally mighty fertile land but in some places stony.

Next barony to this Bunratty barony lies the barony of the Islands called formerly the barony of Clounrawde or Cluonrawne. In this Cluonrawde was an ancient hall and castle on the river of Forgus which is related to have [been] the ancient dwelling house of the noble family of the O'Bryen's aforesaid; since the ruin of the other house called *Tachincorra*, where there was one of the fairest greens in this kingdom at this Cluonrawde. Within half an English mile thereof on the same river stands the town of Innis, now the shire town and only corporation of the county, having a [blank] magistrate thereof [blank], which is a very good town being planted for the most part with the inhabitants or burghers of Limerick who came thither when Limerick was taken by the late usurped powers. In this town stands a fair Franciscan friary built by Donagh Carbrach O'Bryen about the year of our Lord 1240. It stands on the said river of Forgus. Here several fair tombs and monuments in this friary or abbey, the chief whereof belongeth to the said family of O'Bryen.

Within two English miles of this town stands an ancient monastery or abbey called commonly the abbey of Clare, but where it stood was called Kilmony. This abbey is called likewise *Monasterium de Forgio*, dedicated to Saints Peter and Paul; it was built by Donaldus O'Bryen, king of Limerick. Upon the west side of the said river of Forgus is the order of Saint Augustin's cannons regular and endowed with great livings. Next place of note to the monastery within two miles thereof is the town of Clare of which the county is named standing in the river of Forgus aforesaid where there was an ancient strong castle and halls much gone to ruin in the late times. Out of this town is also the lord viscounts Clare dignified, which honour was granted by his now Majesty King Charles the second to Sir Donald O'Bryen, Knight, third son of Corneilius or Concubhar O'Bryen, third earl of Thomond. Here are considerable fairs held in this town. Here is a very considerable stone bridge over the said Forgus in this town. It is related that the castle was built by the lord Thomas de Clare of the race of the earls of Heriford and by Sir Richard de Clare his son who are both buried in the Franciscan friary of Limerick. This Richard de Clare was killed at a place called Droumkevan in the barony by O'Bryen in the year 1318. The land about this town of Clare is generally very rocky being limestone land. Here is in the barony, though in the river of Shannon, an ancient abbey monastery or priory of the cannons regular of Saint Augustine's order, built by Donold O'Bryen, king of Limerick, about the year of our Lord 1200.

Note that all the barony did anciently belong to the said family as the demesne of Cluonrawde aforesaid or to their household servants as in Clanchy, O'Bryen['s] brehon, judges or deempster; Hehir his steward of his household and others of lesser employments. Here are several castles of lesser note in this barony. Here is likewise in this barony a house of nuns of the order of Saint Augustin, built by the said Donald O'Bryen, king of Limerick; this nunnery had likewise great livings. This barony is generally very good land but in some places rocky.

This barony of Clanderala formerly east Corcabaskin or McMahons country, next to the barony of the Islands westward, lying in the great river of Shannon in the barony of Cluonderala, belonging chiefly in 1641 to one Sir Teige McMahon of Cluonderala aforesaid of the race of Murtough or Monertagh O'Bryen, last king of Ireland of that family.

Cluonderala house: here was a very ancient castle and a house of great hospitality in as much as when the late rebellion begun, that the said Sir Teige McMahon did give provision and clothes to all the distressed English and Protestants that came near him. And likewise gave succour with fresh meat to the Lord Forbes, his shipping then riding in the river of Shannon; though by his death before any settlement and his son being a child and having no guardians that would make his application, lost his own estate and got no recompense for it and he is reduced to great indigence.

Here was another great castle and hall in this barony belonging to the said McMahon called Dangen McMahon in the east part of the barony where there is very good lands about it, but a great part of this barony is coarse and mountainous. Note in this barony are the largest and fairest structures of parish churches in Ireland built by one of that family of the McMahons called Terlaughndampull by reason he built the said churches. Here was no abbey or other religious house in this barony.

Next barony to this Cluonderala barony is the barony of Moyfarta formerly west Corkabaskinn. (Moyfarta signifying a place of miracles). In this barony stands a town called Killrush on the north shore of the island of Scattery formerly Iniscatt. Here was in this Kilrush an ancient house of the Colidei having a great termon or sanctuary belonging to it. The superior whereof in later ages before the dissolution was a layman called corb or convert of Saint Shennan to whom belonged great livings both in lands and tithes. Here was the island of Iniscatt aforesaid in the Shannon in which there was formerly a bishop sent and an abbey of cannons regular built by the said Shennan about the later end of the fifth century said Sir James Ware. About this island is good anchorage for shipping. This island is now part of the county of the city of Limerick, though fourteen leagues distant from it and the diocese thereof united or added to the bishopric of Killaloe alias *Loanensis*. Here were great beliefs of miracles done formerly on this island. One whereof is that if a woman goes into a certain church or chapel herein (of which there were several) that she shall never after bear children.

Here is about seven miles westward of this island and of Kilrush aforesaid an ancient castle and hall called Carrigicoult, Englished a rock for shipping, which does belong since the later end of Queen Elizabeth's reign to Sir Donald O'Bryen created lord viscount of Clare as aforesaid but this castle and the most part of this barony for several hundred of years before belonged to a great branch of the said family of the McMahons who lost it by attainder in Queen Elizabeth's [reign]. Here are several creeks in this barony but none of the[m] safe harbours. Here was likewise another considerable house and castle of the said McMahons called Ballyket within two miles of Kilrush aforesaid granted to the first lord viscount Clare as aforesaid.

About three miles distant from Ballyket is a famous well called Saint Michael's well, much frequented from far and near and specially on Michaelmas day. Many cures attributed to be done by it; curing the lame and the blind, but whether it be by any extraordinary miracle or by some minerals through which the waters run I answer not. Here are several other castles in this barony. This barony is generally somewhat coarse land. Here is a considerable river in this barony.

Next barony to the barony of Moyfarta in the north thereof is the barony of Ibrekan, being but a small barony and generally coarse land. Nothing eminent herein only that it gives title to the earl of Thomond's eldest son, being baron thereof and that here is an ancient castle herein called Moy Ibrickane being in former time a manor house of the earl of Thomond. Note that all this small barony was the demesne of the earls of Thomond since and before their being created earls and given them in Queen Elizabeth's reign free from composition.

Next barony to Ibrickan due north is the barony of Corcumroe formerly the barony of Doughy Connor so called upon the entry of Inagh into the Western or Virgivian sea. This barony did about the beginning of Queen Elizabeth's reign belong to one O'Connor of Corcumroe of the race of Ire *a quo* McGennis, Lord Iveagh etc. Since that time it was enjoyed till 1641 by the heirs of Donald O'Bryan second brother to Donaty or Donougn O'Bryen second earl of Thomond. This river is not above one mile navigable and that but for very small vessels.

In this barony is the cathedral church of Kilfenoragh, in Latin *Seneborensis*, in which stands the ancient cathedral of Saint [blank] and an ancient palace or mansion house of the lord bishop thereof and a small market and fair. Most of the lands about this is good but generally stony. Here is within two miles distant from the bishop's seat an ancient castle and hall called Ballyogoen or Smithstown belonging to Teige O'Brien second son of Mauritius or Morrough first earl of Thomond which came in frank marriage to the right honourable Lord Wingfield, viscount of Powerscourt's great grandfather with Honora eldest of the said Teige O'Bryen.

Here are likewise within less than two English miles of this cathedral two ancient castles and halls, the one whereof called Cahirmenane, belonging till 1641 to the heirs of Morrough O'Bryen, another brother of Donate second earl of Thomond and another castle called Drumleene, belonging also to the heirs of Turlaugh O'Bryen another brother of the said second earl of Thomond. Here is likewise in this barony another considerable castle and hall called Inisdimaine belonging to the earls of Thomond. This barony is indifferent good lands but toward the barony of Burren rocky.

Next to this barony of Corcumroe is the barony of Burren formerly the barony of Gragans lying on the shore from the bay of Galway. This barony is generally very rocky being all limestone where it is said that there is not earth enough to bury a man, water enough to drown a man nor wood enough to hang a man. This barony did till Queen

Elizabeth's reign belong to one O'Loughlin of the race of Ire aforesaid, but since it was for the most part in possession of the heirs of Donald O'Bryen aforesaid second brother of Donald, earl of Thomond. Here are three ancient castle belonging to the said O'Loughlins, in former time one whereof called Gragans, another Glincollumkill and the other dreioton where there is a harbour for indifferent big vessels in the bay before it.

In this barony stands the abbey of Corcumroe alias *de Petra Fertili Monasterium Beata Maria*, built by Donald O'Bryen, king of Limerick about the year 1194 or others say by Donough Corbrach O'Bryen, his son, 1200 for the Cistercian monks. Note that [although] this abbey is called generally the abbey of Corcumroe it lies in this barony. Here is a monument or statue of one of the O'Bryen's in this abbey nicknamed Concubhar Suidne. Out of this barony of Burren is the eldest son of the earl of Insiquines dignified thereof.

Note also that the isles of Arran did anciently belong to this barony till the reign of Queen Elizabeth, it was joined to the county of Galway then. The propriety of the lay lands and chief demesnes whereof did belong to one of the family of the O'Bryen's called McTeig of Arran. It is in the diocese of Kilfenoragh to this day. These islands are rocky like the continent or mainland abroad. In these isles of Arran were churches, bells and chapels in abundance. It lying in Saint Gregory's sound about 14 leagues from Galway. Here was an abbey of cannons regulars built by Saint Endeus about the year 480. These islands were granted by Engusa son of Natsraicus, king of Munster to the said Endeus abbot. Note that this Natsraicus was the first king of Munster that embraced Christianity was baptised by Saint Patrick. Here was likewise a Franciscan friary in these islands but by whom built it is not very certain but it is generally reported to be by the said McTeig who was Lord thereof as aforesaid. Here is a garrison in the said isles of Arran. Note that the right honourable Richard earl of Arran, lord deputy of Ireland, is dignified out of Arran aforesaid.

Next to the barony of Burren, south east thereof, lies the barony of Insiquin, formerly the barony of Tullyadae from one O'Dea who was the chief of this barony in former time. As one of the said family of O'Bryens then under lords called *taen* and tisaugh or barons. The castle or house of Insiquine of which Dermod O'Bryen, eldest son of Morrough, first earl of Thomond (his father being but earl for life), was dignified baron, granted to him by King Edward the sixth and to the heirs male of his body which so continued till his now Majesty King Charles the second, created Murrough late earl of Insiquin for his eminent services both at home and abroad. The late earl being great great grandson of Dermod or Dermitius first baron of Insiquin. Near this castle is a considerable lough through which runs the Fergus aforesaid. In this barony stands the castle and manor house of

Leamoneith belonging to Donogh O'Bryen Esq. heir of Donnough O'Bryen third son of Mauritius or Murrough first earl of Thomond. Here was an ancient castle called Disert O'Dea, now claimed by the see of Killaloe, but should seem to have been the estate of that family by the denomination thereof. Here was also Tulligy Dea from which this barony was formerly named belonging to the said family. Most part of this barony did belong to the Barons of Insiquin since their creation.

Note that this barony and all the rest of this county, except the barony of Corcumroe and Burren in the diocese of Kilfenoragh now annexed to Tuam, are in the diocese of Killaloe. This barony is indifferent good lands but in some places stony and in some places mountainous. Here is likewise in the barony other castles of lesser note and a good market town called Corrifinny. Here was a parish church of great veneration called Killinaby which in the time of the Romish government a great termon or sanctuary, so that no man that came to that church or church yard, be his crime what it would, could not be touched there. Here is little or no more matters of note in this barony. This county is but thin peopled other than towards the river of Shannon which is but indifferently inhabited also.

Clare County by Mr Hugh Brigdall

Questions to which answers are desired for the illustration of that part of the English Atlas relating to Ireland.

1. The nature of the soil of the county, or place, and the chief product thereof.

The county of Clare is of a different soil on the outsides thereof for the most part, swelling with lofty mountains interlaced with bog and woods. The more inward part is of a better soil, but pestered in most places with crags and loughs. In a special manner the barony of Burren mounts aloft with high soaring mountains of massive rocks in a wonderful sort, laid one upon another, seeming to strangers at a distance as if always covered over with snow, notwithstanding in the deep valleys between them affording very good pasture for all sorts of cattle. Towards the brink of the Shannon the south east bounds of this county lieth a rich vain of land with many thousand acres of marsh defended with banks from the fury of that river; the north part of this county is bounded by that of Galway; the west by the ocean and the rest by the river of Shannon. It is in length from Loopshead in the southwest to Lough Derrigett in the north east about 50 miles but of a very unequal breadth, in some places five, in others ten and at the broadest from Limerick to the ocean is nearly thirty miles. Its ancient name is Thomond signifying in Irish north Munster. So called from the situation being the north part of that province. Its present name is the county of Clare derived from Thomas de Clare, the first English planter thereof.

2. What plants, animals, fruits, metals or other natural productions there are peculiar to the place, and how ordered?

The more particular products of this county are coleseed in the marshland, a commodity first brought hither by Dutchmen; fir trees in an island of the Shannon; yew and juniper in the barony of Burren and an abundance of swans in the loughs of Insiquin; in brief it is a county better for pasture than for tillage wherein is no want of fish, fowl or venison, red or fallow deer.

3. What springs and rivers or loughs, with the various properties thereof, as whether medicinal, how replenished with fish, whether navigable, rapid or slow etc.

Chief rivers peculiar hereunto are the Foragus which rising from a lough of its own name after a crooked course of near twenty miles and spreading into many a pool by the way visits the towns of Enis, Clonrond and Clare at which last its waters tend to be brackish and about six miles lower it joineth its streams to the Shannon with a mouth of a league wide and is navigable by boat as far as the town of Enis. Then there is the Gilsagh that running through Quin mingles its waters with the Foragus. The Kney which passing by Sixmilebridge falls into the Shannon by Bunratty castle. The Eynah runs westward through the bogs of Brentir and pays its tribute to the great ocean at the bottom of Malbay near the castle of Doogh O'Conor but neither this nor the two last before mentioned are navigable above a mile upwards. In this county are several springs reputed medicinal but in the opinion of the people by miraculous operation of the particular saints to which they are dedicated among which that of Saint Michael in the barony of Clandirala is most famous, yearly visited on that saint's day by a multitude of devout pilgrims coming thither from far and near to pay their zealous devotions.

4. What curiosities of art, or nature, or antiquity are or have been found there?

Nothing.

5. What ports for shipping, and their descriptions, and what moon causes high water?

This county hath no port of its own but is served by the city of Limerick standing upon the Shannon; no town of note in this county seated on the banks of that river. Near the mouth thereof is the island of Iniskatry, where is safe anchorage coming up or going down the river for vessels that stay for a wind. From the Shannon mouth northward, the western shore to the bay of Gallway, 40 miles in length, is fenced in with horrible cliffs and precipices, affording certain destruction to all such shipping as by force of weather or mistake of their course, are driven upon it.

6. What great battles have been there fought, or any other memorable action or accident?

Nothing extraordinary.

7. What peculiar customs, manners, or dispositions the inhabitant of each county, or town have among them?

Nothing extraordinary.

8. How each county is inhabited, thickly or thinly?

This county being populous enough before the late fatal rebellion but in years 165[1], 52 and 53 was so afflicted with sword, famine, pestilence and banishment of the natives as scarce left any inhabitants therein, but now with a continued peace of near 30 years, it begins again to be stored with people and containeth about 30,000 souls whereof near 2,000 may be Protestants and English by birth or decent.

9. What places give, or formerly have given title to any noble man, as also what ancient seats of noble families are to be met with?

Henry O'Brien is now Earl of Thomond and the seventh earl of the family, which title was first by King Henry the 8th, anno 1543, conferred upon Morrogh O'Brien for term of life, after whose death Donogh O'Brien, son to Conor, the said Morrogh's elder brother (the law of tanistry being then in force) succeeded his uncle in the earldom and renewing his patent in the time of Edward the sixth obtained that dignity for him and his heirs male for ever. This present earl is the said Donogh's great grandson's son descending from Brien Borvy, sometimes monarch of all Ireland, about the year 1030. Bunratty is his chief seat standing on the Shannon's brink on a fertile soil and pleasant situation. About 8 miles above Enis, on the side of the Foragus is the castle of Insequin, which after the decease of Morrogh, first earl of Thomond, was erected into a barony and the title thereof conferred on Dermot O'Brien, eldest son to the said Morrogh and by his descendants in a direct line enjoyed until our present sovereign for the many virtues and loyal services of Morrogh O'Brien, fifth in descent from the said Dermot, created him Earl of Insequin. His son William (late governor of Tangier) now enjoying that honour. This earl's eldest son is Baron of Burren as the Earl of Thomond's is of Ibrecan. Far in the west on the Shannon's mouth stands Carrighoult, once the possession of Teige Keough McMahon, but he being attained of treason in Queen Elizabeth's days, his estate was by her conferred on Sir Daniel O'Brien, third brother to Donough, fourth Earl of Thomond, which Daniel since his majestie's restoration was created lord viscount of Clare his grandson Daniel O'Brien, being now the third viscount Clare.

10. What towns of note in the county, and especially towns corporate?

The chief town of this county is Enis, seated on the Foragus two miles above Clare amongst flourishing meadows. Corrofin six miles higher on the same river. Sixmilebridge on the Kney three miles from the Shannon, Killaloe, Kilrush and Quin.

11. The names of such towns both antique and modern, English and Irish, and why so called?

Ennis is so called from its situation among waters and meadows, that word signifying so much, as appears by Eniskillin, Iniscorphy, Inis Teog, Inismore and many other places in this kingdom, all islands or places built on some river side.

12. The magistracy of towns corporate, and when incorporated, and by whom built, with their return of parliament men?

This town is the only corporation in the county, whose head magistrate is a provost, assisted by twelve burgesses and was first incorporated by King James in the tenth year of his reign and returns two burgesses to the parliament.

13. Trade of the town, with the number of houses, and inhabitants, and manner of buildings.

It drives a considerable trade in hides, tallow and butter, which are sent thence by boat to Limerick. It consists of about 120 houses whereof about a score are good slated buildings, the rest covered with thatch. The number of inhabitants may be five or six hundred, whereof not above a dozen English families; the rest (for the better sort) are of the birth of Limerick, who settled here upon their turning out of that town when taken by Ireton anno 1651 and now thrive and grow wealthy by the trade aforesaid and by the meetings of assizes and [courts of] quarter sessions constantly held in this town.

14. What public or antique buildings?

Wherein are the courthouse, bridewell and gaol for the county with an old decaying house of the Earl of Thomond.

15. What synods have been held there, what monasteries, cathedral, or other churches are or have been there, and from what saint named?

In the north end of the town by the river side stands a fair abbey of the order of Saint Francis, now serving the town as the parish church. In the chancel whereof is an ancient monument of grey marble, whereon is cut or engraven the story of our Saviour's passion and belongs to the family of the McMahons. This abbey was built by the O'Briens about the year [blank]. In Quin is another abbey of the same order founded by the McNemaras with fair cloisters and outhouses, now all out of repair. Near Clare on the Feragus bank is another abbey founded by Thomas de Clare of the monks of the order of Saint Benedict. Not far [from] it is Killone a monastery of nuns of the same order built by [blank]about the year [blank]. In the river Shannon is another ancient ruined house of cannons regular from whom the island takes its name which was built by [blank] anno [blank].

In the barony of Burren stands the ruined abbey of Corcumroe in a hollow vale encircled about with rocky mountains of the order of Cistercians founded by Donogh Carribreach O'Brien whose father Conor O'Brien, called Conor ne Shudiriny lyeth buried therein with his image of grey marble upon his tomb. In the barony of Corcumroe is a little ruined abbey of Austin friars called Kilshany and in the parish Inyscronane is another abbey of Benedictine monks. In the great lough of Lohderygets is the island of Iniskaltra or Holy Island wherein are the ruins of seven churches, a place of great reputed sanctity unto which on Good Friday and Whitsuntide yearly is a mighty resort of people coming thither to do penance by walking barefoot about the rough and rocky shore of the island. In Killaloe is a bishops see and palace standing on the very edge of the Shannon with a cathedral dedicated to Saint Flannane which was ruined in the last [war] but now beginneth to be repaired.

16. In what bishopric each county or any part thereof is?

Within whose diocese is all this county excepting the barony of Burren and Corcumroe which make a particular diocese by themselves called the bishopric of Kilfenora whose cathedral standing in a poor village of the same name is dedicated to Saint Faghnanus. This bishopric was, since the king's restoration, united to the archbishopric of Tuam in Connaght, though both this of Kilfanora with that of Killaloe be suffragans to the metropolitan of Cashell.

This county contains nine baronies viz. Bunratty, Tulla, Islands, Insiquin, Burren, Corcumroe, Ibreikan, Clanderala and Moifarta in which are 74 parishes, about 1300 ploughlands and 400,000 acres rough and smooth. The chiefest mountains of this county are Slieueculan in the barony if Ibrekan, Slieue Pheylim in that of Burren, Gallows hill in the barony of Bunratty, Slieuerieogh and the large mountain of Slieue Aghty bounding this county from the county of Gallway, at the foot of which last runs into the Shannon the river of Scarriff whose waters drive two iron mills and are replenished with excellent trout, pike and bream.

Taken from Molyneux Survey, Trinity College Dublin, Ms. 883/1.

John Stevens, A Journal of my Travels, 1690

The English Jacobite John Stevens was collector of the excise in Welshpool at the outbreak of the English Revolution in 1668. Leaving his employment in Wales he followed the Catholic King James II into exile in France. There he joined the Jacobite army that was preparing for embarkation to Ireland. Starting on 11 January 1689, the day he set sail from England, Stevens kept a detailed account of his experiences. His journal is remarkable for the light it sheds on the life of the common soldier and the hardships endured by those who supported the Jacobite cause. Landing at Bantry bay on 5 May 1689, he found the people so poor that money could not be changed and troops had to be billeted in cabins no better than pigsties. Arriving in Dublin on 17 May, Stevens was compelled to sell his rings to buy food. He was quartered in Trinity College for the winter of 1689. Conditions were such that the doors, closets and floors of the chambers were used for firewood. Stevens participated in the Battle of the Boyne, July 1690; his regiment which had been 1000 strong was reduced, mainly through desertion, to 400 men. Retreating to Limerick, he was billeted in the village of Carrigogunnel. Here the people were kind and gave them plenty of meat, barley bread and milk. Because of the loss of tents and baggage at the Boyne, some troops about Limerick slept in the open. Stevens suffered all the deprivations with remarkable forbearance. Unlike James II, he did not blame the Irish for the failure of Jacobite arms; rather he praised the endurance of the soldiers, especially at Limerick where they suffered incredible hardships in defending a hopeless position. The surrender of Limerick brought an end to his hopes, but, as he says, he was proud to have been 'a voluntary exile for love of his Prince'. His journal ends 1 July 1691. Stevens was not cut out for the soldier's life and by 1695 he had returned to London where he spent the remainder of his life in writing and translating. Having resided in Spain during his youth, he had an intimate knowledge of Spanish and Portuguese and translated a number of important books into English. Unlike many of his countrymen, Stevens was unburdened by religious or national animosities towards Ireland so that his journal provides an accurate account of Irish conditions as he observed them. The account of his march from Limerick to Athlone, from which this description of Clare is taken, illustrates not just the bleakness of the east Clare countryside but also the primitive state of roads and the absence of urban settlements.

Wednesday, July 23rd, 1690. Athlone having been some days besieged and by Colonel Grace the governor well defended, it was thought fit to send him some relief, the enemy being only on the Leinster side of the river and Connaught side open. Here upon this day one battalion of the guards, the Grand Prior, Slane and Boisseleau's detachments making another battalion, Gormanstown and Bellew a third, Hamilton and Sir Maurice Eustace a fourth, and the French detachments, two other small battalions, marched out of Limerick and lay this night at Killaloe, the men without tents or quarters in the gardens. The officers were quartered in the town, the great ones taking up the best houses which are not many, the inferior were crowded into very poor cabins that only served barely to cover them from the weather. These eight miles from Limerick is part of the county of Clare and is all very bare, there being in this way scarce any corn or meadow, but only a hilly common in some places boggy, everywhere covered with fern and rushes, which is all it produces. The road is hard and pleasant for the most part open and often crossed by small brooks and springs, near a mile at first is a large causeway over a bog, not unlike to the old Roman ways being raised high because of the floods. A little above the midway is the wood whence we [cut] the palisades, it is not large nor produces any large timber. Killaloe is a bishopric, but as to the town the meanest I ever saw dignified with that character, except St David and St Asaph in Wales, having but very few houses that are anything tolerable, the rest and even those in no very great number are thatched cabins or cottages, in fine it has nothing beyond many villages in England, nor is it equal to some, except the church be reckoned which indeed is large, and so all is said of it, having nothing else beautiful or commendable. The bishop's house like the rest has nothing worthy [of] observation. The Shannon runs by the town, and in this place is so rocky it is not navigable, so that all goods must be carried from Limerick till above the town by land, and being embarked there the river is again navigable for many miles. The most remarkable thing here was that the Protestant bishop of the place continued then and long after in his diocese under his Majesty's government.

Thursday, July 24th, 1690. We marched first along the side of the mountain near the Shannon, which about this place makes a very large lough or lake. This way is very close and woody but lasts not long, as soon as out of it the rest is across the barren hills till we came to a small village called Tomgraney, which is five Connaught miles from Killaloe, and the miles here are of an excessive length. We halted a little farther at another village called Scarriff, neither of these places worth the naming but for some iron mills that were there before the war. Close by these two places is a large stone bridge which joins, or rather the river that runs under it parts, the counties of Clare and Galway, the same being also the bounds of the provinces of Munster and Connaught. At Scarriff begins one of the most desert wild barbarous mountains that ever I beheld and runs eight miles outright, there being nothing to be seen upon it but rocks and bogs, no corn, meadow, house or living creature, not so much as a bird. Nothing grows there but a wild sedge, fern, and heath. In wet winters this way is absolutely impassable, in dry summers it is a soft way, but at best in many places very boggy, so that at no time cannon or heavy carriages can pass that way. This day we marched about four miles of the mountain, a violent rain falling most part of the time, which made the way extreme toilsome afoot the long sedge twisting about the feet, and the bog sucking them up, as that which immediately draws in the water being naturally soft and yielding. For our comfort at night we had a bare bog to lie on without tents or huts or so much the shelter of a tree, hedge, or bank. The rain held most part of the night, and scarce any firing to be had the place being furnished but with a few and those small scattered trees, and we tired and without any tools to cut wood. Meat was as scarce as other necessaries, but that we might not be destitute of all, Providence had furnished a small brook which, though foul and ill tasted by reason of the rain and bog, afforded us plenty of drink.

Friday, July 25th, 1690. With the day began our march over the remaining part of this barbarous mountain, just at the end whereof is a wood very thick the trees coarse and misshapen and as the others affords no large timber. It was a great satisfaction to us from the tops of the mountains to discover at a distance ploughed land, pasture and some few scattered cottages. At length having passed what was left of the solitude we came to a small place the English call Woodford and the Irish Graig, where it being St James's Day we halted and heard mass. . . .

Wednesday, July 30th, 1690. Between twelve and one in the morning the general beat, and again ordered that no man upon pain of death should stir from his post in marching. We marched through a very thick wood and extraordinary rough stony way long before the least light appeared, and the road being so uncouth was exceeding troublesome in the dark. We had many falls and that sometimes in the water, some stony brooks crossing the wood and nobody seeing where they set their feet. When day appeared we were out of the wood and in a better way. Soon after day we halted to gather our scattered men and march again with some lighted matches. Now it appeared very many of our men had left us and among them some who had the reputation of being very brave, many of which upon occasions of danger I have found to be the backwardest of all, and that they gained a name only by being mutinous troublesome fellows, always in private broils, yet durst not look upon the common enemy. Having marched seven miles this morning we made a considerable halt to refresh the men at Quin, a small village, where are some considerable remains of an ancient church and abbey, then possessed by the Franciscan friars. Whilst we halted some men of each regiment were sent with officers to look out for provisions in the neighbourhood to bring to the men, who were commanded to pay for what they had. There was no other neighbourhood to seek anything, but those they call the creaghts, which are much like the Tartar hordes, being a number of people some more some less, men, women and children under a chief or head of the name or family, who range about the country with their flocks or herds and all the goods they have in the world, without any settled habitation, building huts wherever they find pasture for their cattle and removing as they find occasion. This is a custom much used in Ireland, especially in time of war as now, when thousands of all sorts fled from the dominion of the usurper and had no other manner of living but this. But the custom I believe is immemorial and was doubtless in use among them before the conquest by the English. They have small cars and garrons or little horses to carry their necessaries and live most upon the milk of their cows. With what they can spare they buy bread and other necessaries, or in these times of confusion make no scruple of taking where they find it. Particularly in gathering cattle they are industrious, for many who came from their habitations in Ulster with only one or two cows by the time they came to the neighbourhood of Limerick were increased some to fifty, some a hundred, and some more head of black cattle. They examine not whose ground they encamp in, and when they march drive all the cattle that comes in their way, and in some places I have heard them complained of as more grievous and burdensome to the country than the army, which seemed to me improbable and almost impossible, but that the country people affirmed the robberies and insolences of the soldiers were much inferior to the extravagant barbarities of those people. In short if they came first they left nothing for the army, and where they came after they carried away whatever the army had left. . . The design was to have marched through this day to Limerick, which was twelve miles from this place, a great march, though the county of Clare miles be not altogether so long as those of Connaught. But being informed there was no danger of the enemy we only marched half-way to Sixmilebridge, which is an indifferent good town and takes its name from its distance from Limerick and a small bridge over a little river that runs through it, and thence into the Shannon, yet we were quartered three or four companies in a house.

Taken from John Stevens, *A Journal of my Travels since the Revolution containing a brief account of all the War in Ireland* (ed.) Rev R. H. Murray (Oxford 1912), pp 151-4, 160-3.

Thomas Moland,
Survey of the Thomond Estate, 1703

The Moland survey was commissioned by Lady Henrietta O'Brien, mother of Henry, eight earl of Thomond. The earl was a junior at the time and the estate was being administered by his mother and her second husband, the earl of Suffolk. The family was resident in England and the purpose of the survey was to facilitate the collection of rent and the issuing of new leases to their Irish tenants. The man chosen to carry out the survey was Thomas Moland, the foremost cartographer of the period. Moland, a resident of Dublin, was employed by the government to survey the forfeited estates of Catholic landowners following the Williamite confiscations. He also received many private commissions: he surveyed the lands of Sir John Perceval, County Cork, the estate of Sir John Courtenay, County Limerick and the lands belonging to the Erasmus Smith foundation. His survey of the Thomond estate was perhaps his biggest assignment for which he received a fee of £376 in 1704. His connection with the earl of Thomond continued: in 1711 he was appointed clerk of the commission established to administer the Thomond estate. In later life Moland resided in Carlow where he became steward and receiver of rents of the Thomond lands in that county.

The survey consists of thirty two folio maps; twenty four of which refer to lands in County Clare and the remaining eight to lands in counties Limerick, Tipperary, Carlow and Dublin. The maps contain, among other things, the earliest known illustrations of the towns of Sixmilebridge, Ennistymon and Kilrush. Opposite each map is a page of reference, giving the content of each tenement and townland and their suitability for agricultural use. A separate 'Book of Reference' gives the size and value of land parcels and includes Moland's observations on each holding. It is these observations from the 'Book of Reference' that are published here. They contain a wealth of local information unavailable in any other source. They show that at the beginning of the eighteenth century the process of urbanisation was just beginning in County Clare, agriculture was in a primitive state and large tracts of countryside were still forested.

Although Moland surveyed the whole of the Thomond estate in County Clare, his observations, unfortunately, end at the parish of Kilfarboy in Ibrickan and do not cover the remaining Thomond lands in the baronies of Ibrickan, Inchiquin or Burren. A full transcript of Moland's observations on the parish of Kilquane (the first parish to be surveyed) is provided below; however, to avoid repetition and publication of unnecessary detail, the remaining observations have been condensed.

A Book of Reference to the Survey of the Estate of the Right Honourable Henry Earl of Thomond in the Kingdom of Ireland.

Barony of Bunratty

Parish of Kilquane

Gortatogher: Arable and pasture 82a. 1r. 0p. at 5s. 6d. per acre. Bog 12a. 0r. 0p. at 1s. 6d. per acre. Content 94a. 1r. 0p. Real value per annum £[ ] 8s. 0d. Distance from Limerick a mile and a half; has on it a farm house and 4 cabins.

Athlonchard: Arable 17a. 3r. 24p. at 6s. 0d. per acre. Low pasture 80a. 2r. 0p. at 5s. 6d. per acre. Content 98a. 1r. 24p. Real value per annum £27 4s. 3d. Distant from Limerick 2 miles, has one farm house, 5 cabins and an eel weir worth about £4 per annum.

Shanakeile: Arable and coarse pasture 87a. 1r. 0p. at 3s. 6d. per acre. Bog 46a. 0r. 0p. at 2s. 0d. per acre. Content 133a. 1r. 0p. Real value per annum £19 17s. 6d. Situate as the former has one farm house and 3 cabins.

Rossmadda alias Blackwater: Arable 114a. 3r. 0p. at 3s. 0d. per acre. Shrubby and coarse pasture 71a. 2r. 0p. at 2s. 0d. per acre. Heath shrubby pasture 272a. 0r. 0p. at 1s. 6d. per acre. Arable 67a. 0r. 0p. at 2s. 6d. per acre. Red bog 79a. 0r. 0p. at 0s. 2d. per acre. Red bog 64a. 0r. 0p. at 0s. 2d. per acre. Red bog 20a. 2r. 0p. at 0s. 2d. per acre. Shrub 8a. 2r. 0p. at 2s. 0d. per acre. Wood 1a. 1r. 0p. at 1s. 0d. per acre. Content 698a. 2r. 0p. Real value per annum £54 14s. 0d. Distant from Limerick 3 miles, has on it two farm houses, 8 cabins, 2 tuck mills and a corn mill which are worth £20 per annum.

Castlebanke: Arable, meadow, pasture and bog 211a. 2r. 0p. at 4s. 6d. per acre. Content 211a. 2r. 0p. Real value per annum £52 15s. 0d. Distant from Limerick a mile and a half; has two farm houses, the ruins of an old castle and 5 or 6 cabins.

Ballykealane: Arable, meadow and pasture 168a. 0r. 0p. at 5s. 6d. per acre. Bog 8a. 1r. 0p. at 1s. 0d. per acre. Content 176a. 1r. 0p. Real value per annum £47 6s. 0d. Distant from Limerick 1 mile has a good slate house, 3 farm houses, 5 cabins and the old church of Kilquane.

Saint Thomas's Island: Arable, meadow and pasture 13a. 0r. 0p. Content 13a. 0r. 0p. Real value per annum £15 0s. 0d. Situate as the former and is part of it, has a good house, tan yard, kill and a store house for the fish caught in the corporation of Limerick's weir which joins it.

Parteene: Arable, meadow and pasture 130a. 2r. 0p. at 8s. 6d. per acre. Content 130a. 2r. 0p. Real value per annum £[ ] 5s. 0d. Situate as the former, has one farm house, 3 ale houses, tan yard, malt house, kill and 9 cabins.

Poulaquen: Arable, meadow and pasture 124a. 0r. 0p. at 6s. 6d. per acre. Content 124a. 0r. 0p. Real value per annum £37 4s. 0d. Distant from Limerick one mile, has a good farm house, an ale house, tan yard and 9 cabins.

Cappanagrissane: Arable, meadow and pasture 106a. 3r. 0p. at 4s. 6d. per acre. Content 106a. 3r. 0p. Real value per annum £23 17s. 0d. Distant from Limerick 1 mile and a half, has on it 5 cabins.

Ballyfineene alias Shanaballyfineene: Arable and pasture 148a. 0r. 0p. at 3s. 0d. per acre. Content 148a. 0r. 0p. Real value per annum £22 4s. 0d. Distant from Limerick one mile has on it 8 cabins.

Parish of Saint Munchions

Knockilisheene: Content 266a. 2r. 0p. Value £67 12s. 0d. Distant from Limerick [blank] has on it a good farm house and 8 cabins.

Ballykenane: Content 347a. 2r. 0p. Value £65 15s. 9d. Distant from Limerick 2 miles has on it about 8 cabins.

Capantimore: Content 260a. 0r. 0p. Value £28 5s. 6d. Situate as the former has on it only 3 cabins.

Coonagh, the earl of Thomond's part, in the north liberty of the city of Limerick: Content 200a. 3r. 24p. Value £91 5s. 0d. Distant from Limerick 2 miles bounded on the west and south by the river Shannon; it is two distinct parcels, besides Mr Dury's house and garden which is separate from both; it has on it a farmhouse and several cabins.

Parish of Killelly

Cratloekeile: Content 264a. 0r. 0p. Value £44 8s. 9d. Distant from Limerick 4 miles has a good farmhouse and out houses, 2 or 3 cabins an old ruined castle and a timber wood worth £500.

Parish of Drumline

Tullyvarga: Content 142a. 0r. 0p. Value £56 12s. 0d. Distant from Limerick 9 miles is all very good corcas land, bounded on the south by the river Shannon.

Tullyvarga bog. Earl of Thomond's and Colonel Ingolsby's properties intermixed. Content 26a. 0r. 16p. Value £9 8s. 0d. Situate as the former and joins to it are parcels of land of the earl of Thomond's intermixed with lands of Sir William Ingoldsby's in five parcels as they appear in the map, on two of which are cabins.

Ballycasey: Content 211a. 1r. 16p. Value £40 12s. 0d. Distant from Limerick 8 miles and 2 from Six mile bridge has on it one farm house and 13 or 14 cabins.

Ballycuneene: Content 186a. 0r. 0p. Value £41 17s. 0d. Situate one mile from Six mile bridge and 8 from Limerick has on it 2 cabins.

Drumline: Content 515a. 3r. 0p. Value £121 11s. 0d. Situate as the former has an old decayed castle and an old church and 2 cabins.

Parish of Bunratty

Clunmunny farm; 8 ploughlands: Content 847a. 2r. 36p. Value £281 4s. 0d. Distant from Limerick 8 miles, has two farm houses and about 30 cabins scattered on the land, bounded on the south by the river Shannon on which is a salmon weir worth £10 per annum.

Bunratty, Key Island, Reet Island, overflown land without the corcas banks: Content 472a. 3r. 0p. Value £170 12s. 10d. Distant from Limerick 8 miles, formerly the mansion seat of the Earls of Thomond, had a noble castle very high and strong with outhouses a joining, the ruins of which only now remain; it was placed too near the water and the model for strength more than pleasure; the land is very good and Key Island is a considerable pleasure and advantage to it.

Parish of Kilfentinane

Knocknabreeky: Content 695a. 0r. 0p. Value £149 0s. 0d. Distant from Limerick 8 miles has on it one farm house and about 30 cabins scattered on the land and the old ruined parish church of Kilfentinane; this is 5 ploughlands viz. Gortfune, Ballymote, Kilfentinane, Tirenowen and Caroogare.

Moyhill, the leeward island, Island Grogan, Island Skeagh, overflown land without the corcas banks: Content 230a. 3r. 8p. Value £83 9s. 0d. Tithes: £30 0s. 0d. Distant from Limerick 6 miles, is part of Knocknabreeky farm and has only an old ruined house and a barn. This is all corcas land and very good but chargeable maintaining the sea banks.

Parish of Finagh

Deer Parke: Content 674a. 0r. 0p. Value £134 16s. 0d. Distant from Limerick 7 miles, containing part of the lands of Ardkeile, Rossmanagher, Curraghvata (?) and Cappagh.

Rossmanagher: Content 459a. 2r. 0p. Value £173 17s. 0d. Situate as the former, has on it a castle in good repair, orchard stables, barn and other outhouses in good order and about 8 cabins.

Ardkeile: Content 147a. 0r. 16p. Value £20 0s. 0d. Distant from Limerick 7 and a half miles, has on it 6 cabins.

Finagh and Seircy Quarter: Content 341a. 0r. 0p. Value £68 4s. 0d. Situate as Ardkeile, has an old decayed church and about 7 or 8 cabins.

Rath: Content 310a. 0r. 8p. Value £65 15s. 0d. Distant from Limerick 8 miles and two from 6 mile bridge, has no improvements but an orchard.

Parish of Kilnasullagh

Dromoland, Rahin, Kilkorane West, Knockrow, Lisnagown, Ballyconnila and Ballygareene, Ballynacraggy, Rathfolanmore: Total content 1500a. 3r. 28p. Value £380 5s. 6d. Distant from Limerick 12 miles and 5 from Ennis, the arable is good for stock and corn and with the corcas are in good heart, though chargeable to maintain the sea banks and sluices; it has a castle on it in good repair with stable, malt house, barn etc. and a kitchen garden with some fruit trees. Ballynacraggy and Rathfolane are colder and a shallower soil than the former and have no improvements but an orchard on the latter and some cabins where cottiers live. There is a hop yard the value or profit of which I cannot tell.

Parish of Tomfinlagh

Ballycarr and Lismultoone, Killullabegg, Granahane, bog in common to Killullabegg, Lismultoone, Lisleagh and Killullamore: Total content 549a. 3r. 8p. Value £89 2s. 0d. Ballycarr and Lismultoone is good land for black cattle or sheep and the arable will bring good corn when manured with lime or sand both of which it's well furnished with; has on it an old orchard, a good castle and 3 houses. Killullabeg is of the same quality and joins to the former. Granahane is a shallow soil and much out of heart, has an old stone house and two mills set at £6 per annum with 2 or 3 cabins.

Boherone alias Newmarkette: Content 57a. 1r. 32p. Value £15 14s. 6d. Distant from Limerick 9 miles and 3 from 6 mile bridge, has 4 good tenantable houses, 6 or 7 cabins and 2 mills set at £10 per annum.

Parish of Inchycronane

Doonmulvihill, Ballycasheenmore and Knockmeal: Content 762a. 1r. 12p. Value £100 0s. 0d. This farm joins on the county of Galway; distant from Galway 18 miles, is good land for corn when limed, of which stone they have plenty and turf to burn it. There is on it a good farm house and orchard and an old castle.

Bonahow alias Monahow: Content 83a. 1r. 8p. Value £18 13s. 6d. Situate as the former has a good thatched house and a corn and tuck mill.

Ballyvaneene: Content 435a. 0r. 32p. Value £47 18s. 0d. Situate as the former but is a colder soil and hath no improvements but 3 or 4 cabins.

Island [of] Inchycronane: Content 42a. 1r. 0p. Value £9 9s. 0d. Distant from Ennis 5 miles and 13 from Galway surrounded by the lough of Inchycronane, only at a narrow isthmus which is the entrance into it; has one thatched house out of repair and 6 or 8 acres of the island now overflown.

Carrowhill: Content 235a. 3r. 16p. Value £17 7s. 6d. Situate as the former, has a dairy house in good repair and good convenience of fire and water.

Shanclone: Content 23a. 3r. 16p. Value £4 15s. 0d. Situate as the former.

Ballynagranagh: Content 135a. 2r. 0p. Value £20 11s. 0d.

Gortlurkane: Content 48a. 3r. 16p.   Value £7 3s. 0d. Situate as the former has no improvements but 3 or 4 cabins.

Kiltowlagh: Content 24a. 0r. 0p. Value £6 12s. 0d. Situate as the former, has 2 eel weirs set for £3 per annum and no other improvements.

Kilvoydane south: Content 136a. 0r. 0p. Value £28 2s. 0d. In the parish of Inchycronane, distant from Ennis 3 miles.

In Muckirish 3 cartrons and one third of a cartron viz. Castle Cartron, Ulane Cartron, Knockaghrim Cartron, one third Kile Cartron: Total content 70a. 3r. 24p. Value £15 13s. 9d. Distant from Ennis 3 miles, is good land for any kind of stock or corn.

Cahirshaghnesy: Content 144a. 3r. 32p. Value £21 5s. 0d. Situate as the former has no improvements but a few cabins.

Curragh Mohane: Content 38a. 0r. 32p. Value £5 7s. 0d. Situate as the former has no improvements.

Cranacher: Content 172a. 2r. 32p. Value £24 7s. 9d. Distant from Ennis 3 miles has no improvements.

Parish of Clooney

Racloane part of Mahery east: Content 87a. 3r. 16p. Value £14 3s. 0d. Distant from Limerick 13 miles and 5 from Ennis, has on it three cabins.

Craganashanagh: Content 124a. 0r. 24p. Value £21 10s. 3d. Distant from Limerick [blank] miles, is a good wholesome sheep walk, but has no improvements.

Knockaphreaghane: Content 223a. 1r. 16p.   Value £23 11s. 0d. Distant from Limerick 12 Miles and two from Tullagh, has no improvements.

Fiagh: Content 132a. 2r. 32p.   Value £23 10s. 0d. Situate as the former, has on it a good thatched farm house with stable and barn all in good repair and a corn mill set for 30 shillings per annum.

Classagh: Content 42a. 3r. 32p. Value £7 17s. 2d. Situate as the former has on it only 3 cabins.

Cahirloghane: Content 126a. 2r. 32p. Value £20 5s. 0d. Distant from Limerick 11 miles and 2 from Tullagh has on it 5 cabins.

Ballymaconagh: Content 297a. 3r. 13p. Situate as Cranaher has on it one farm house and outhouse; in the shrub are several oak plants which if preserved would in time be good timber.

Ballyfinshan: Content 191a. 0r. 32p. Situate as the former has no improvements but 5 or 6 cabins.

Carhookile: Content 298a. 0r. 0p. Distant from Ennis 3 miles and has on it about 5 cabins.

Knockaclara: Content 72a. 1r. 24p. Situate as the former and has on it 3 or 4 cabins.

Ballyogan: Content 26a. 2r. 0p. Of the same nature situation and quality with the former.

Parish of Kilraftis

Ballygaffa East alias Coolbane: Situate as the former. Total content [of the six former denominations] 959a. 0r. 37p. Value £98 12s. 0d.

Cullinagh part of Balinlinemore: Content 50a. 1r. 8p. Value £10 1s. 0d. Is about a mile distant from the rest of the farm and has 3 or 4 cabins.

Doorlas part of Mohallow East: Content 19a. 0r. 0p. Value £[ ] 15s. 0d. Situate 3 miles from Ennis.

Clonkerry: Content 103a. 0r. 16p. Value £17 5s. 3d. Situate as the former.

Drumgranaghbegg: Content 54a. 0r. 0p. Value £10 0s. 3d. Distant from Ennis 1 and a half miles, has on it some oak plants in thriving condition.

Carrouroe Quarter not surveyed.

Kilnahow: Content 50a. 1r. 0p. Value £10 9s. 0d. Distant from Ennis 6 miles and 12 from Limerick has a good thatched [house] near the bridge and two new mills set at £8 per annum.

Knockmoyhell alias Knockmegh etc. and Carownalogha: Content 22a. 2r. 32p. Value £5 1s. 3d. Situate as the former has no improvements.

Kilfeilim: Content 62a. 2r. 16p. Value £8 16s. 0d. Situate as the former.

Parish of Doory

Ballaghboy alias Doory: Content 38a. 2r. 0p. Value £5 15s. 6d. Distant from Ennis 2 miles, is a coarse stony farm and has 2 or 3 cabins.

Gortglass: Content 4a. 2r. 0p. Value £1 0s. 3d. Situate as the former.

Knockaskibole: Content 33a. 2r. 8p. Value £5 4s. 4d. Situate as the former has only two cabins.

Drumdulaghtna: Content 34a. 2r. 24p. Value £6 16s. 0d. Situate as the former no improvements.

Nohavall: Content 66a. 2r. 16p. Value £8 6s. 9d. Situate as the former has 3 cabins.

Poulmore a cartron of madara's: Content 23a. 0r. 0p. Note this farm was not surveyed but is set down here from Mr Wilson? by the Stafford survey; the rent is £1 8s. 4d. per annum; it is a parcel lying near Cooleshannog but is separate from it.

Parish of Templemaly

Ballymale: Content 203a. 2r. 0p. Value £[ ] 6s. 4d. Is distant from Ennis 1 and a half miles has a thatched house, barn etc.

Knockballymacory: Content 60a. 0r. 7p. Value £[ ] 19s. 6d. Has a good thatched house and barn with 2 or 3 eel weirs worth £3 per annum (and so set).

Knockinderry: Content 122a. 0r. 0p. Value £[ ] 4s. 6d. Distant from Ennis 1 mile has on it a cabin or two.

Dulick: Content 123a. 0r. 0p. Value £[ ] 10s. 0d. Joins Knockinderry has one or two cabins.

Gortleavane and Cappagharde: content 108a. 0r. 22p. Value £[ ] 16s. 0d. Rinegarrane: Content 29a. 2r. 0p. Value £6 0s. 0d. Are half a mile from Ennis of the same nature and quality of the former.

Parish of Quinhy

Killane alias Cullane: Content 122a. 3r. 16p. Value £15 16s. 6d. Cloghrinagh: Content 11a. 1r. 0p. Value £1 13s. 0d.

Killys: Content 5a. 3r. 24p. Value £1 3s. 3d.

Cluonmore: Content 13a. 1r. 8p. Value £2 5s. 6d.

Drumgoornagh: Content 14a. 0r. 24p. Value £2 16s. 0d.

Leacamuricuane: Content 8a. 0r. 0p. Value £0 16s. 0d. Distant from Six mile bridge 3 miles, the arable is good for corn or sheep if the bushes were destroyed; it has a good farm house, barn and kill and an old decayed orchard. These 5 parcels are set together and called Killane farm. Total content 175a. 1r. 32p. Value £24 10s. 3d.

Kilbrickane Begg: Content 71a. 2r. 16p. Value £14 8s. 0d. Distant from Ennis 6 miles has on it a good thatched house and barn.

Cooleshamrogue: Content 68a. 2r. 0p. Value £10 5s. 6d.

Parish of Kilmallery

Island Macknavin a parcel called Annavidoge: Content 78a. 3r. 0p. Value £25 5s. 3d. Distant from Ennis 6 miles has no improvements.

Parish of Kilconry

Finish, an island: Content 101a. 0r. 0p. Value £28 0s. 6d. Distant from Limerick 10 miles, has on it an old ruined castle, a tenantable thatched house and stable.

Inish McNaghten Island: Content 157a. 0r. 0p. Value £47 2s. 0d. Distant from Limerick 12 miles, has on [it] a barn and two small cabins.

Parish of Clonloghan

Drumgeely: Content 117a. 0r. 0p. Value £39 17s. 0d. Distant from Limerick 11 miles, has on it one cabin and barn.

Caherteagbegg: Content 20a. 0r. 0p. Value £6 0s. 0d. Distant from Limerick 11 miles, has on it a thatched house and one small cabin.

Ballyhenisa farm containing these sub denominations viz. In Ballycallagh one third of a quarter called Kilconnery; in Garinamona one cartron called Ballyhenisa; in Rynanagh one cartron and one third called Clanderlagh; in the same two cartrons called Tirenegeragh in several parcels, in all 17 parcels: Rynana, Craigleig and Gortmona, Gortnacoragh, Clanderlagh, Ballyhenisa, Gortinashana, Eribole, Earl of Thomand's bog, One third of Kilconnery, Keilty, Clonecoragh,

Kilkekaghaneapeek (?) Gortneclogh, Gorteen McNemara, Corkasuna Corcas, two thirds of Coolcumist corcas, part of an island in the corcas: [Total] content 164a. 2r. 21. Value £45 6s. 0d. Distant from Limerick ten miles and 4 from 6 mile bridge, all the parcels separate from each other.

Barony of Tullagh

Parish of Kiltenanlea

Donassy Farm

Nedanora: Content 993a. 1r. 0p. Value £130 0s. 0d. Distant from Limerick 4 miles, has on it an old ruined castle, two ordinary farm houses, and an old orchard and about 25 cabins.

Killeene: Content 491a. 0r. 0p. Value £114 6s. 0d. Situate as the former, has on it an old decayed castle and three ordinary cabins.

Island Regan: Content 215a. 2r. 0p. Value £62 12s. 0d. Situate as the former, has on it no improvements but one cabin and an eel weir, worth £4 per annum; bounded on the south by the river Shannon.

Donassy: Content 195a. 2r. 0p. Value £68 5s. 0d. Joins to the former has on it a good stone house, stable, barn and other outhouses with orchard gardens and all in good order, lying on the Shannon side on which is a salmon leap and an eel weir worth about £4 per annum.

Coolesteige: Content 619a. 3r. 0p. Value £151 7s. 6d. Distant from Limerick 5 miles, has on it an old castle, a farm house and 5 or 6 cabins.

Errinagh: Content 533a. 1r. 16p. Value £95 9s. 0d. Situate as the former, has on it a ruined stone house, an orchard hill in some order and 5 or 6 cabins bounded on the east by the river Shannon.

Total content [of Donassy farm] 3048a. 1r. 16p. Value £621 15s. 6d.

The Farm of Annaghbeg

Cloncarrie: Content 153a. 0r. 0p. Value £45 18s. 0d. Distant from Limerick 2 miles is bounded on the south by the river Shannon.

Derryfadda: Content 393a. 2r. 0p. Value £54 9s. 9d. Distant from Limerick 3 miles, has on it about 13 cabins transpersed about the land and the wood is of oak saplings about 12 years growth.

Cappavilly: Content 311a. 1r. 0p. Value £50 15s. 6d. Situate as the former has on it 5 farm houses and 4 cabins and a wood of young oak and ash which if preserved would be of considerable value; £50 value might now be cut of timber stripped of the bark.

Garranes: Content 144a. 1r. 0p. Value £46 16s. 0d. Distant from Limerick 2 miles, on it an old brick house, formerly a very good one, but now out of repair and almost a ruin, an orchard and about six cabins.

Shramucky: Content 219a. 3r. 0p. Value £60 16s. 0d. Distant from Limerick 3 miles, has on it a farm house and about 16 cabins, a wood of young saplings and half an eel weir set at £3 per annum.

Total content [of Annaghbeg farm] 1215a. 3r. 0p. Value £258 15s. 9d.

Parish of Killallow

Ballycarnes: Content 469a. 0r. 0p. Value £39 16s. 0d. Distant from Limerick 3 miles and has on the premises about 4 cabins.

Glaunlan: Content 323a. 0r. 0p. Situate as the former has on it 7 cabins.

Agherinaghmore: Content 163a. 2r. 0p. Distant from Limerick 4 miles and has about six cabins on it.

Agherinaghbegg: Content 579a. 0r. 0p. Situate as the former is a good convenient farm and has on it about 12 cabins.

Knockanerbla: Content 68a. 0r. 0p. Situate as the former a parcel of mountain without any improvements.

Curubane: Content 191a. 2r. 0p. Distant from Limerick 11 miles and 3 from Killallow and has on it 8 cabins.

Currugare and Curhunakilly: Content 308a. 1r. 0p. Situate as the former and has 2 cabins on it.

Total content 499a. 3r. 0p. Total value £67 5s. 0d.

Lackanabranar: Content 287a. 0r. 0p. Value £11 10s. 0d. Situate as the former and has on it 2 cabins.

Mountain common to Carrabane, Carragare and Carhunakilly: Content 953a. 3r. 0p. Value £15 17s. 8d. No improvements.

Ballycuggerane: Content 325a. 1r. 0p. Value £31 9s. 0d. Situate as Carubane and has on it 8 cabins.

Gortmagee and 4 tenements, with fishing weirs at Killallow: Content 430a. 3r. 0p. Distant from Killallow one mile from Limerick 9 and 4 from Tomgraney has 5 cabins on Gortmagee.

Ballykilledea: Content 155a. 2r. 0p. Joins to the former and has on it 3 or 4 cabins.

Gorteahelrow alias Lackamore: Content 153a. 1r. 0p. Situate as the former and has on it no improvements but a few sorry cabins.

Ballygarreene: Arable 47a. 3r. 0p. Situate as the former and has on it about 4 cabins.

Garranboy, Ballinduff, Lacknabane alias Balinacarrig: Content 304a. 0r. 0p. Joining the former and has only one cabin on it.

Total content 660a. 2r. 0p. Total value £96 5s. 0d.

Clonfadda: Content 414a. 1r. 16p. Value []. 7s. 5d. Distant from Lymerick 7 miles and one from Killallow, it is a well improved farm having on it a good stone house slated, one storey high, with stable barn and other out houses; an orchard by the side of the Shannon and several enclosed parks which render it a commodious farm.

Parish of Kilfinaghta

Castle Cappagh: Content 227a. 2r. 16p. Distance from Limerick six miles has on it an old castle, two cabins and [illegible] firing in the bog belonging to the premises.

Cappagh Lodge alias Cappagh north: Content 150a. 1r. 24p. Value £46 11s. 0d. Situate as the former, has on it a good stone house built by the Lord Thomond where he used to reside when he came in these parts; a good stable, barn, brew house, store house, kill etc. and a pleasure garden with 2 orchards and an avenue to the house, very handsome which makes it a pleasant and convenient seat.

Lower Cappagh alias Oyl Mills: Content 139a. 2r. 0p. Value £45 6s. 6d. Situate as the former, has on it a dwelling house thatched, an orchard, 2 corn mills and a tuck mill and about 4 cabins.

Sixmilebridge Cappagh: Arable meadow and pasture including all the tenements of the Sixmilebridge which are that side of the river: Content 160a. 0r. 24p. Value £64 0s. 0d. The town £112 0s. 0d. Total value £176 0s. 0d. On this land stands the town of Sixmilebridge on the south side of the river, consisting of about 20 good tenements and about 32 cabins; the tenements I compute to be worth about £5 per annum, taken one with another, valuing the cabins but at £1 per annum a piece, but the place improves everyday.

Ballysheene: Content 409a. 3r. 8p. Value £80 6s. 0d. Distant from Lymerick 6 miles, has on it a good slated house and out houses.

Moygalloe: Content. 145a. 0r. 0p. Situate as the former, on it a good slated house and out houses, an orchard and 2 or three cabins.

Beallycullin, Gortnepishy meadow: Content 507a. 0r. 0p. Value £39 7s. 0d. Distant from Lymerick 5 miles and one from Sixmilebridge; it is a mountain farm and has on it an old castle and 2 or 3 cabins.

Corlea part of Moygalloe: Content 326a. 0r. 0p. Value £10 17s. 4d. Distant from Limerick 4 miles is a coarse mountain farm but good bedding and shelter for black cattle in winter; it goes with Moygalloe farm.

Ballymulcashell part: Content 102a. 3r. 0p. Value £[ ] 7s. 6d. Distant from Lymerick 8 miles and 2 from Sixmilebridge, consists of two parcels, about a quarter of a mile distant from each other; there is a castle half of which only is said to stand on my Lord Thomand's land and convenient out houses.

Parish of Feakle

Knocknehaneene: Content 347a. 3r. 10p. Value £10 9s. 0d. Distant from Limerick 19 miles, from Gallway 17, from Ennis 13; there has been a fine wood on the premises but almost destroyed, few of the young oaks remaining or anything of value, but some birch and ash trees and bald pikes fit only for the iron works; on it 2 or 3 cabins.

Fahyalurane: Content 2337a. 0r. 3p. Value £67 5s. 0d. Situate as the former, has on it the ruins of an old chapel and there is in the wood some oak saplings which if care be taken of them will come to be good timber; there are likewise some decayed oaks fit to be sold to the iron works and is every day stolen away. There are likewise cinders of old iron works of which the people make money by digging them up and selling them to the iron works near the premises.

Gortigen alias Gortedune: Content 596a. 1r. 8p. Value £17 2s. 6d. Gortigen has no improvements but 3 or 4 cabins.

Knocknegehy alias Killanenagh: Content 433a. 0r. 0p. Value £18 6s. 7d. Distant from Lymerick 18 miles, from Gallway 18 and from Ennis 13 miles. There is on the premises a young wood which if preserved will be of value.

Knockanenagh alias Killaneny: Content 124a. 3r. 3p. Value £5 0s. 6d. Situate as the former has on it no improvements but 3 or 4 cabins.

Carrowkeile: Mountain in controversy. Content 1684a. 0r. 0p. Value £28 14s. 0d. Distant from Lymerick 20 miles, from Gallway 22 and 16 miles from Ennis, has on it no improvements but 3 cabins.

Parish of Tullagh

Lissafin Farm viz. Ballyblood, Darragh, Cottenmore, Cottenbegg, Liscolane, Lissafin and Forhy: Distant from Limerick 12 miles and six from Ennis; the land is very good being a limestone soil and has on it an old castle in good repair and 18 or 19 cabins.

Munmore alias Moeghmore: Content 191a. 0r. 29p. Value £26 4s. 10d. Situate as the former on it an indifferent good stone house thatched something out of repair; no other improvements of any value.

Clonteene: Content 88a. 2r. 22p. Value £17 14s. 3d. Situate as the former has on it only one cabin.

Lackarowbegg part of Liscolane: Content 71a. 1r. 17p. Value £8 12s. 0d. Distant from Lissofin one mile no improvements but 4 or 5 sorry cabins.

Fomerly: Content 189a. 3r. 0p. Value £37 15s. 0d. Distant from Lymerick 11 miles and 2 from Tullagh, has on it a castle out of repair and the walls of an old house joining to it, an orchard and 6 cabins.

Parish of Killnoe

Cloonmoher: Content 93a. 3r. 5p. Value £6 10s. 10d. Distant from Lymerick 11 miles and the same from Ennis, has on it no improvements.

Culreabegg: Content 272a. 3r. 36p. Value £16 1s. 6d. Situate as the former, has on it an old castle out of repair and 2 or 3 cabins.

Total content 366a. 3r. 3p. Total value £22 12s. 4d.

Parish of Tuogonila

Island Coskery: Content 159a. 0r. 0p. Value £29 12s. 0d. Distant from Lymerick 12 miles and 4 from Killallow, has on it a very fine oak timber wood of well grown trees of which I compute there might be now sold the value of £1000 at the least.

Parish of Killurane

Tiravaneene farm

Tiravaneene: Content 334a. 0r. 12p. Part of Island Oughtarush alias Lackarow and Gortnapishy: Content 80a. 1r. 0p. Craig Oughtarush: Content 86a. 2r. 0p. Tiravaneene farm is distant from Lymerick 9 miles and 7 from Killallow, there is on the premises one farm house and seven cabins.

Total content [of Tirvaneene farm] 500a. 3r. 12p. Total value £47 4s. 2d.

Barony of Islands

Parish of Killone

Kilmeranemore: Arable and pasture, Coarse heathy pasture, Bog. Content 192a. 3r. 16p. Value £25 17s. 6d.

Knockenira: Content 158a. 1r. 24p. Value £[ ] 7s. 0d. Distant from Ennis 5 miles, has on it [a] good thatched house well sheltered with trees; the soil cold and shallow but good for a dairy.   Killerk   east: Content 137a. 3r. 0p. Value £27 11s. 0d. Situate as the former the soil cold but yields good corn when manured with lime; it has on it 4 or 5 cabins.

Killerk west: Content 168a. 3r. 16p.   Value £23 4s. 0d.   Of same quality and situation has on it 1 cabin.

Darraghs: Content 273a. 2r. 0p.   Value £[ ] 15s. 9d.   Situate as the former is good land for rearing black cattle or for corn when manured with lime; has on it two good thatched farm houses.

Cloonane: Content 113a. 0r. 8p.   Value £22 12s. 0d.   Distant from Ennis 5 miles, a limestone soil and has on it four cabins.

Ballyhay: Content 173a. 0r. 0p.   Value £32 0s. 0d.   Situate as the former, has on it six cabins and a mill now set at six pounds per annum.

Ballyvullagin: Content 142a. 0r. 0p.   Value £27 13s. 0d.   About 5 miles from Ennis, the arable is good for corn and the lowland good pasture; on it a cabin.

Lisvealbridy alias Lismoylbreedy: Arable and pasture, Heathy and boggy mountain. Content 245a. 2r. 16p. value £29 7s. 0d.

Barnagihy and Carhoonganana: Content 242a. 2r. 24p.   Value £72 11s. 6d. Lisvealbredy and Barnegihy are 4 miles distant from Ennis, the soil shallow and cold but indifferent good for black cattle; on the land of Barnegihy is a good thatched house and three or four cabins.

Tiriculane alias Tyrmclane: Content 249a. 1r. 20p.   Value £27 11s. 6d. Tiricullane is distant from Ennis 4 miles; this is a very well improved farm, divided into handsome enclosures, thatched barn, stable and orchard; there is a platform of a house laid out before the war with orchard and pleasure garden and in thriving condition.

Parish of Clareabby

Ballyveeregane and Ballyveskill: Content 329a. 0r. 0p. Value £94 7s. 0d. Situate as the former and the land well enclosed and improved.

Buncraggie: Content 345a. 3r. 24p. Value £108 1s. 0d. Buncraggie is distant from Ennis 3 miles, has on it a good stone house with stables, barn, malt house, pigeon house, orchard and garden; and at a distance from the house [on] the road are 2 ale houses or inns with convenient outhouses; it is a well improved farm with good land.

Island Macragh: Content 211a. 0r. 0p. Value £79 2s. 6d. Joins to the former it is an arable hill surrounded with corcas, the banks of which are much exposed and often damaged by the river which here is very broad.

Barnantick and Ballyfada north and south: Content 638a. 2r. 24p. Value £182 16s. 6d. Distant from Ennis 2 miles, the land is good for corn or stock with several stone wall enclosures, has on it a good house, stable, barn and other outhouses and is a fine well improved farm.

Carhoocoyne, Craiganeihulla and Corkykealahir: Content 164a. 2r. 16p. Value £42 0s. 6d. Situate as the former and of the same quality.

Ballybeg alias Kilaroghane: Value £25 6s. 0d. Distant from Ennis one mile has on it only 1 or 2 cabins.

Carhoonakilly: Content 100a. 3r. 8p. Value £18 15. 6d. Situate as the former has on it five or six cottages and gardens.

Clare Abbey: Content 138a. 3r. 0p. Value £36 16s 6d. Distant from Ennis one mile, has on it the ruins of an abbey which gives it its name, a good thatched house, an orchard and 2 or 3 cabins.

Knock and Lissane: Content 201a. 1r. 0p. Value £56 18s. 6d. Distant from Ennis 2 miles has no improvements.

Common whereon the town of Clare stands: The value in the tenements: £40 0s. 0d. Content 32a. 0r. 0p. Clare was formerly the county town, now very poor and little, consists of one old stone house out of repair, a stone walled thatched house of wherein Mr Stammers now lives, an ale house or two and about 17 other small tenements and gardens, worth about 30 shillings apiece one with another per annum; and 2 fairs are held here yearly the best in the county in peaceable times, worth £10 or £12 each fair per annum.

Shehannagh and Derry: Content 181a. 3r. 8p. Value £40 1s. 0d. Distant from Ennis 2 miles on it 5 or 6 cabins.

Knock and Knocknagananagh: Content 130a. 1r. 0p. Value £42 5s. 0d. Joins to the former has no improvements.

Killow: Content 342a. 0r. 8p. Value £36 1s. 0d. Killow is situate as the former, there is on the premises about 5 or 6 cabins.

Carhoogarr: Content 103a. 0r. 0p. Value £27 1s. 0d. Joins the former has on it no improvements but 3 or 4 cabins.

Carhoonelly: Content 162a. 0r. 0p. Value £48 12s. 0d. Situate as and joining to the former, has on a good house and barn.

Common: Content 28a. 2r. 8p. Value £5 14s. 0d. A public common.

Ballyvanavan: Content 190a. 3r. 8p. Value £37 6s. 0d. Distant from Ennis 2 miles, has on it only two small tenements.

Cloughaneboy Farm

Cloughaneboy and half ploughland of Ballyvanavan: Distant from Ennis 3 miles, has on it 2 or 3 cabins.

Ballyveehane: Content 175a. 1r. 24p. Value £56 17s. 6d.

Manusmore: Content 164a. 2r. 8p. Value £53 6s. 0d. Ballyveehane and Manusmore are distant from Ennis about 3 miles and have on them five or six small tenements.

Island of Vana: Content 18a. 0r. 0p. Value £5 8s. 0d. An island in the Shannon.

Parish of Clondegadd

Drumquin and Lacky and Craigkernan, Inishshaghmurra: Content 322a. 2r. 0p. Value £92 13s. 6d. Distant from Lymerick 20 miles and five from Ennis; limestone land and both the arable and corcas in good hearth but has no improvements.

Cragbrian: Content 330a. 2r. 16p. Value £59 0s. 0d. Situate as the former, the land very good and well improved, on it a castle, stone house, stable, barn and pigeon house; three farm houses a good orchard and gardens, a corn and fulling mill worth 7 or 8 pounds per annum; limestone land and well improved.

Lisheen: Content 570a. 3r. 0p. Value £117 3s. 6d. Joins the former, there is some corcas by the river side; it has on it a good lime and stone walled thatched house and out houses, an orchard and three cabins; it is very good limestone land.

Ballyhorigg and Knockmenagh, Inishelane: Content 329a. 2r. 16p. Value £74 0s. 0d. Distant from Lymerick 22 miles and 6 from Ennis, has on it an old castle, a thatched farm house and out houses, an orchard and two cabins; there is some corcas by the river side but no limestone on the premises.

Ballycloghus: Mr O'Brien's part, arable meadow and pasture 57a. 2r. 16p., 4s. 0d. per acre. Mr Burton's part, arable meadow and pasture 60a. 3r. 0p., 4s. 0d. per acre. Common to both, turf bog 4a. 2r. 0p., 0s. 3d. per acre. Content 122a. 3r. 16p. Value £23 13s. 0d. Situate as the former, has on it no improvements but 2 small cabins.

Clonmore: Content 386a. 3r. 16p. Value £30 0s. 0d. Situate as the former, this land is mountainy and coarse; there is on the premises about 4 cabins.

Cahera east: Content 399a. 0r. 0p. Value £31 9s. 0d. Distant from Lymerick 20 miles and 6 from Ennis, a coarse mountain farm has no improvements but 4 or 5 ordinary cabins.

Cahera west: 805a. 3r. 0p. Value £57 4s. 10d. Situate as the former a large mountain farm, great part heath and bog, has on it about twelve or thirteen cabins.

Lannagh: Content 262a. 3r. 0p. Value £31 4s. 0d. Situate as the former but the land not so bad, has on it an indifferent good lime and stone walled farm house, an ordinary corn mill out of repair and three cabins; the land is much overgrown with shrubs.

Cappanageragh: Content 184a. 1r. 0p. Value £114 11s. 0d. Joins the former and has on it 3 cabins, some oak and ash trees on the land with a shrubby underwood, great part of this land is overrun with heath or bog.

Cloncolmond: Content 429a. 2r. 0p. Value £37 7s. 6d. Distant from Limerick 23 miles and 8 from Ennis, a mountain and on it has four or five cabins.

Gortnegehy: Content 1099a. 1r. 0p. Value £[ ] 3s. 0d. Situate as and joining to Cloncolmond has on it nine or ten cabins, the farm is large and coarse, part shrubby with some old oak trees and a great part heath and bog.

Decomade: Content 1512a. 0r. 0p. Value £58 6s. 8d. Situate as the former a large coarse mountain farm house and nine other cabins, a parcel of coarse old oak timber, stripped of the bark, some birch and alder shrub.

Secasa: Content 1046a. 0r. 0p. Value £63 16s. 0d. Distant from Lymerick 24 miles, has on it nine or ten cabins, some old oak trees stripped of the bark and some birch and alder shrub; the farm is coarse and mountainy.

Furrour: Content 1528a. 0r. 0p. Value £[ ] 5s. 0d. Situate as the former, a large mountain farm, something better than the former, has on it five or six cabins; there are likewise several oak trees stripped as aforesaid with some alder and birch.

Inisdadrum an island alias Coney Island: content 144a. 1r. 0p. Value £46 16s. 0d. Distant from Lymerick 18 miles, has on it an old chapel or church and one cabin.

Parish of Drumcliff

Clonerodebegg: Content 178a. 2r. 0p. Value £75 18s. 0d. On this land stands the town of Ennis, the chief town of the county for largeness and trade where the assizes are kept, having two markets a week and two fairs per annum, its a pleasant and well situated place.

Clonrodemore: Gardens in Clonrode town. Content 392a. 1r. 30p. Value £[ ] 18s. 6d. Distant from Ennis a quarter of a mile, is limestone craggy land with some extraordinary good meadow; the town of Clonrode is prejudiced by its nearness to Ennis, it consists of one good house and castle, a few shops; there are two fairs kept here yearly and the mill is worth £10 per annum.

Liffords: Content 279a. 1r. 0p. Value £78 4s. 6d. Lifford is just joining to the town of Ennis, is limestone craggy land intermixed with copses; there is on the premises about 20 cabins and a tuck mill about £5 per annum.

Mill Park, part of Drumbigill: Content 21a. 2r. 0p. Value £6 9s. 0d. Situate as the former, has on it two corn mills worth about £20 per annum, the miller's house and two other cabins.

Drumbigill: Content 164a. 3r. 0p. Value £[ ]. 1s. 9d. Joining to the lands of Ennis, is all arable land intermixed with shrubby craggy land, all limestone, on it about 20 cabins.

Kilty part of Kilnakalla: Content 30a. 1r. 0p. Value £6 16s. 0d. Situate near Ennis has no improvements.

Killnakalla: Content 75a. 0r. 0p. Value £16 17s. 6d. Distant from Ennis one mile, there is no improvements on the premises nor cabins except a barn.

Cahercallamore: Content 412a. 2r. 3p. Value £[ ] 18s. 0d. Distant from Ennis one mile, is a well improved farm, has on it a stone house, one story high thatched with convenient out houses, one stone walled park for rams and stone horses and about 12 cabins.

Cahercallabegg: Content 138a. 0r. 0p. Value £17 5s. 0d. Situate as the former, has no improvements on it but one cabin.

Barony of Clonderalaw

Parish of Kilfaddan

Muy alias Moyeralla: Content 423a. 3r. 36p. Value £37 17s. 0d. Muy is distant from Ennis twelve miles, from Kilrush 9 and 28 from Limerick; it has on it two stone houses thatched, two or three cabins and a fine grove well preserved which is a great ornament to it.

Der'ynegehy: Content 130a. 1r. 0p. Value £5 17s. 3d. Derrynegehy is about half a mile distant from Muy, there is no improvements on the premises except on cabin.

Drishane: Content 208 a. 1r. 20p. Value £21 14s. 3d. Joins to Muy but has no improvements.

Efernane: Content 208a. 1r. 20p. Value £20 2s. 1d. Distant from Lymerick 30 miles and 15 from Ennis, has on it an indifferent good cabin and an orchard, both our of order, no other improvements of value.

Eroble: Content 486a. 1r. 0p. Value £58 0s. 10d. Distant from Lymerick 31 miles and 16 from Ennis, has on it one indifferent good house and five or six cabins.
Scott's Farm.

Shanacroemore: Content 490a. 3r. 4p. Shanacroemore is thirty miles distant from Lymerick, from Ennis 15 and 24 from Sixmilebridge;

there is on the premises about seven or eight cabins, no other improvements of value.

Shanacroebegg: Content 182a. 3r. 0p. Shanacroebeg is situate as the former and has on it about 5 or 6 cabins.

Cahiracon: Content 322a. 3r. 32p. Situate as the former, has on it a fine young wood, a good orchard, an old ruined castle, a small stone house and barn, a mill seat and about five or six cabins.

Parish of Kildizert
Lisconolan: Content 400a. 1r. 7p. Joins the former and has no improvements except three cabins. Total content [of the four former denominations] 1397a. 3r. 3p. Value £104 15s. 0d.

Gortnagaul: Content 43a. 2r. 8p. Situate near the former has no improvements on it but one cabin.

Drumonduff: Content 65a. 0r. 11p. Situate as the former has on it 3 cabins. Total content 108a. 2r. 19p. Value £16 1s. 0d.

Ardgereene: Content 15a. 0r. 11p. Situate as the former has no improvements.

Kildizert: Content 169a. 3r. 27p. Kildizert is distant from Lymerick 25 miles and 10 from Ennis, has on it the ruins of an old church and several cabins.

Gortinacoragh: Content 14a. 2r. 38p. Gortinacoragh joins the former.

Inishcater Island: Content 110a. 3r. 9. An island in the Shannon has no improvements on it except one cabin. Total content 310a. 2r. 5p. Value £56 12s. 6d.

Inishtubber: Content 51a. 0r. 6p. Value £17 17s. 0d. This island has no improvements on it but one cabin.

Cannon Island: Content 136a. 2r. 8p. Value £34 0s. 0d. There is on this island the ruins of an old abbey and two cabins; all these islands are about 7 leagues from Lymerick by water.

Inishloe Island: Content 83a. 0r. 3p. Value £28 5s. 0d. The island of Inishloe is about 20 miles distant from Lymerick by water it has no improvements but one cabin.

Crourahane alias Ballybegg: Content 303a. 3r. 0p. Value £57 19s. 0d. Crourahane is distant from Lymerick 24 miles and ten from Ennis, it is a well improved farm having a good stone house joining to a castle with garden, orchard and parks about the said house and five or six cabins; this farm is pleasantly situated by the Shannon side.

Lackanakilleen alias Coogy: Content 401a. 1r. 13p. Value £55 15s. 0d. Situate as the former, the corcas land is very good and in good order, it has on it no improvements but five or six cabins.

Inisharke: Content 17a. 1r. 9p. Value £5 2s. 0d. An island in the Shannon without improvements.

Parish of Kilchrist

Ballynegardon: Content 302a. 2r. 8p. Value £30 0s. 0d. Situate as Crourahane on the Shannon side, has on it a good stone house 2 storeys high and slated with convenient out houses; the farm well improved and divided into handsome enclosures.

Roscleave: Content 115a. 3r. 25p. Value £34 15s. 0d. Joining the former has no improvements.

Inismore alias Deer Island: Content 268a. 1r. 0p. Value £104 11s. 6d. Distant from Lymerick by water 18 miles, the soil is very good, now under deer and black cattle, has on it an old stone house out of repair and an ordinary orchard.

Inishdea: Content 220a. 0r. 0p. Value £[ ] 2s. 6d. This island is extraordinary good land, as are all these islands, limestone soil, has on it one cabin.

Knapoge: Content 26a. 3r. 0p. Value £6 14s. 6d. This land has some part of it overrun with copse and part subject to the tide.

Burren: Content 463a. 2r. 0p. Value £25 14s. 6d. Distant from Lymerick 23 miles and 8 from Ennis, a mountain farm, has on it 2 cabins; the wood is some part alder and birch with some ash and oak, most of which are young and small but will be of value if preserved.

Parish of Killimore.

Desart: Content 140a. 2r. 1p. Value £13 14s. 3d. Distant from Lymerick 34 miles from Ennis 18 and one from Kilrush, has no improvements but 3 or 4 cabins.

Ballymacrenan: Content 587a. 2r. 8p. Value £53 17s. 3d. Situate as the former has on it seven or eight cabins.

Carrodoty alias Carrinbeg: Content 454a. 3r. 36p. Value £65 11s. 8d. Situate as the former, has on it a small house lately built with stone and clay walls thatched and an indifferent good orchard.

Carrinlongard: Content 309a. 0r. 0p. Value £39 6s. 3d. Distant from Lymerick 33 miles and 5 from Kilrush, has on it 5 cabins.

Derrylogh alias Torinane: Content 433a. 2r. 17p. Value £27 8s. 0d. This farm is about a mile distant from the former, but has no improvements except a few very ordinary cabins.

Tarmons and part of Carrownisky: Content 1195a. 1r. 32p. Value £99 7s. 0d. Distant from Lymerick 32 miles, from Ennis 16 and three miles from Kilrush, there are scattered on the premises about fifteen or sixteen cabins.

Parish of Kilmurry

Carronisky: Content 448a. 1r. 11p. Value £26 7s. 0d. Distant from Lymerick 32 miles and 3 miles from Kilrush, has on it a large mud walled thatched house and barn and 3 or 4 cabins.

Barony of Corcumroe

Parish of Kilmanahine

Reneene: Content 266a. 0r. 0p.   Value £16 0s. 6d. Distant from Lymerick 30 miles and 13 from Ennis has no improvements except 2 cabins and a salt house.

Tredane alias Carrorotedane: Content 258a. 0r. 0p.   Value £28 15s. 0d. Situate as the former has no improvements.

Carrowgare: Content 258a. 0r. 0p. Value £28 6s. 4d. Situate as the former has on it two small cabins.

Craig alias Craiginmulvihill: Content 153a. 1r. 0p. Value £19 2s. 6d. Distant [from] Ennis 12 miles.

Callonora: Content 174a. 2r. 0p.   Value £21 16s. 3d.   Situate as the former has no improvements except a dairy house and 2 small cabins.

Tullagaran: Content 336a. 0r. 0p.   Value £20 6s. 6d.   Joins the former but has no improvements.

Maghery: Content 287a. 3r. 16p.   Value £27 8s. 0d.   Situate as the former but has on it a very pretty wood and well preserved.

Inistymond Farm viz.

Castle quarter, Lissionagh: Content 129a. 0r. 0p. Cloncoule west: Content 286. 0r. 23p.

Killcornan: Content 96a. 2r. 20p.   The farm of Inishtimond is 30 miles distant from Lymerick, from Ennis 13, and 17 from Kilrush; it is a manor and has on it a good castle and a house joining to it, two storeys high and in good repair, a stable and other convenient out houses with a small garden, a corn mill worth about £5 per annum and seven or eight cabins. Total content 641a. 0r. 3p. Value £51 19s. 0d.

Parish of Kilmacrehy

Liscanor: Content 109a. 1r. 39p.   Liscanor is distant from Lymerick 32 miles and 15 from Ennis, on it an old castle out of repair and three cabins.

Ardnahay: part of Liscanor: Content 23a. 3r. 28p.   Ardnahay is a mile distant from Liscanor and has on it 3 cabins.   Total content 133a. 1r. 27p.   Value £19 18s. 10d.

Barony of Moyarta

Parish of Kilmacduane

Cloonwhite alias Cloneitrogh alias Cloneenagh: Content 497a. 1r. 0p. Cloonwhite is distant from Ennis 12 miles and 6 from Kilrush; a coarse mountain farm, has on it 3 or 4 cabins some old stripped oak trees, as likewise a birch and alder wood, convenient for building tenements or the like on the premises.

Crighe alias Clonotrogh: Content 757a. 0r. 0p. Clonotragh joins the former has on it a good lime and stone walled house, something out of repair and three cabins. Total content 1254a. 1r. 0p. Value £105 13s. 8d.

Carrickfiny: Content 560a. 0r. 0p. Value £49 17s. 1d. Distant from Ennis 14 miles and 6 from Kilrush, has on it an old lime and stone walled house slated and 4 cabins.

Dangonanelly: Content 392a. 3r. 0p. Value £28 10s. 0d. Distant from Ennis 14 miles and 4 from Kilrush; a shallow coarse farm, has on it 3 or 4 cabins.

Parish of Kilferagh

Farryhey: Content 386a. 0r. 0p. Distant from Lymerick 34 miles, from Ennis 18 and six from Kilrush, has on it a stone and clay walled farm house thatched. Joins the sea and is generally coarse and heathy.

Tarmon, half quarter: Content 333a. 2r. 0p. Value £14 0s. 0d. Distant from Kilrush 4 miles, from Ennis 20 and from Lymerick 36 miles, has on it seven or eight cabins.

Racoan a parcel: Content 31a. 3r. 0p. Value £1 17s. 0d. This parcel joins the former and has on it no improvements.

Tarmonque and Lehind alias Lequid: Content 344a. 0r. 0p. Value £37 3s. 0d. Distant from Kilrush 3 miles has on it 7 or 8 cabins.

Kilnegallagh: Content 110a. 0r. 0p. Value £13 9s. 6d. Situate as the former, has on it an old church and three cabins.

Parish of Moyarta
Quiren Farm viz.

Gortaclara: Content 365a. 2r. 0p. Ballyraght: Content 192a. 0r. 0p. Gortaclara and Ballyraght are distant from Kilrush two miles over the water; the land is indifferent good bearing any kind of grain and have on them about 13 or 14 cabins.

Curragh: Content 374a. 1r. 0p. Curragh is distant from Kilrush 3 miles is a well improved farm with quickset enclosures, a good brick house with barn, stable and other outhouses of lime and stone, an orchard and 2 gardens, the walls of 2 old houses and 12 or 13 cabins.

Clooncarn: Content 599a. 2r. 0p. Joins the former on it 9 or 10 cabins and some underwood, very useful to the tenants, but the westerly winds coming from [the] sea hinder the growth of trees in this and all the lands by the seaside to the great discouragement of the improving tenants.

Tulla and Faran Willion: Content 702a. 0r. 0p. Joining to Clooncarn, the land is very coarse and the bog scarce pasturable at any time of the year, has on it five or six cabins. Total content 2233a. 1r. 0p. Value £169 17s. 0d.

Parish of Kilrush

Knockerry east: Content 564a. 3r. 0p. Value £36 6s. 0d. Distant from Lymerick 30 miles, from Ennis 15 and three miles from Kilrush, it is a coarse mountain farm and has on it eight or nine cabins.

Garran: Content 170a. 3r. 0p. Value £14 5s. 0d. Situate as the former has on it an indifferent good farm house and 2 cabins.

Moyne: Content 365a. 3r. 0p. Distant from Kilrush one mile, on it a good lime and stone walled farm house and outhouses and several dry stone wall parks and enclosures, but the land poor and hungry.

Ballynole: Content 275a. 2r. 0p. Joins the former lying on the sea side, has on it five or six cabins.

Inishbeg an island: Content 25a. 0r. 0p. An island near the shore, used for rams or stone horses, formerly a coney warren. Total content 666a. 1r. 0p. Value £78 1s. 6d.

Kilrush Farm

Distant from Lymerick 32 miles by land and 36 miles by water, the town of Kilrush is composed of six clay and stone walled houses, which with their gardens are worth about £4 per annum, one with another; and six cabins, which one with another are worth about 20 shillings each with their respective garden[s]; the parish church stands on the premises, there is a bridge of stone over the river, a very commodious haven for barks or small ships, good conveniency of fishing which may be improved here considerably; the land is good for corn and the situation of this town makes it capable of improvement [and] answerable to the charges laid out on it.

Part of Kilrush ploughland as now held by Patrick Rochfort: Content 124a. 1r. 0p. Value £20 12s. 9d.

Part of Kilrush ploughland as now held by Messrs Vandelure, Brown and Connor: Content 158a. 2r. 0p. Value £26 19s. 6d.

Part of Kilrush ploughland as now held by Richard Mead and Michael Roche: Content 377a. 1r. 0p. Value £45 0s. 0d.

Tenements and gardens part of the ploughland of Kilrush and some meadow on the north side of the river held by several tenants: Tenements, gardens and meadows 11a. 3r. 0p., 10s. 0d. per acre.

Cappagh: Content 122a. 2r. 0p. Value £30 15s. 10d. Mill £6. 0s. 0d. Cappagh joins to the land of Kilrush and has on it a corn and tuck mill worth £8 per annum.

Leadmore: Content 366a. 1r. 0p. Value £55 18s. 9d. Leadmore lies on the west side of the bay of Kilrush, has on it a good farm house and outhouses and 3 or 4 cabins; very conveniently seated for fishing.

Caronocoyle: Content 647a. 3r. 0p. Value £58 0s. 0d. Coronocolly is distant from Kilrush one mile, has on it an ordinary farm house and 3 or 4 cabins.

Monemore: Content 1605a. 3r. 0p. Value £55 0s. 0d. Monemore is distant from Kilrush two miles, from Ennis 16 and 31 from Limerick, has on it about seventeen or eighteen cabins, wherein live only poor cottiers; this farm is for the most part boggy unpasturable most of the year. Kilrush farm as set on the cant to Mr John Vandelure for £900 fine, reserving £183 18s. 9d. out of the same.

Barony of Ibrickane

Parish of Kilfarboy

Muybegg: Arable and pasture, coarse mountain. Content 150a. 3r. 0p. Value £24 5s. 3d. Distant from Limerick 28, from Kilrush 15 and 12 from Ennis, a well improved farm having good enclosures which when saved makes good meadow as also a stone walled thatched house.

Muymore: Arable, mountain, red bog. Content 697a. 3r. 0p. Value £28 16s. 7d. Situate as the former on it a large castle well roofed and in good repair with barn, stables, malthouse and also an orchard and some small parks well fenced with double ditches.

Taken from Petworth House Archives, West Sussex, Ms. 9342.

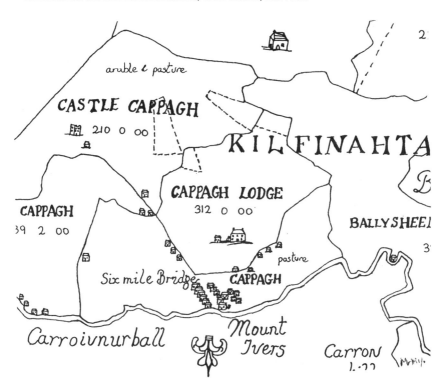

Map of Sixmilebridge, 1703, from Moland's Survey.

Letter of Charles Lucas to Sir Hans Sloane, 1736

Charles Lucas, apothecary, pamphleteer and politician, is best remembered as a tireless campaigner against the corrupt practices of Dublin corporation in the mid eighteenth century. Today a large statue of him stands in the lobby of the city hall, Dublin, in recognition of his contribution to municipal reform. Lucas was born at Ballinagaddy, Ennistymon, County Clare in 1713. His father, a descendant of a Cromwellian army officer, was a wastrel, who left several illegitimate children and died in so much debt that the family lost their ancestral home. In his teens Charles was apprenticed to an apothecary in Dublin where initially he lived in poverty. In 1735 he published a pamphlet on the abuses of the sale of drugs. The following year he wrote a letter to Sir Hans Sloane, President of the Royal Society in London, describing the cave of Kilcorney and commenting on the flora of the Burren. Elected to the city council, he campaigned against corruption and advocated parliamentary independence for Ireland. He translated and printed *The Great Charter of the City of Dublin* in 1749. His writings were held to be treasonable and, threatened with imprisonment, he fled to Europe. Taking advantage of his stay on the continent he graduated in medicine from the university of Leyden in 1752. Returning to Ireland in 1761 he was elected M.P. for Dublin and succeeded in holding his seat until his death ten years later. He founded the *Freeman's Journal* in 1763 and was a frequent contributor to the newspaper. While in exile Lucas took the trouble to study the spa waters at Europe's fashionable resorts - a relevant detail since he is traditionally credited with the discovery of the spa wells at Lisdoonvarna. His letter to Hans Sloane indicates that he was extremely familiar with north Clare and must have spent much of his youth there. In his later years Lucas rekindled his Clare interests; he was made freeman of Ennis in 1766 and voted in the Clare election of 1768. While an edited version of his letter to Sloane appeared in the *Philosophical Transactions of the Royal Society* (1740), the entire text of the original is printed here.

Sir,

The great figure you deservedly make in the learned world and the pains you have taken in publishing a most excellent natural history of a foreign nation, emboldens me to offer to your consideration the following account of a very extraordinary cave in this kingdom, before I have had the honour of being known to you; and hope such a relation will not be disagreeable to you, from a poor country that has the vanity, of boasting of your birth in her.

Before I give a particular description of this cave, it may be proper to give a short sketch of that part of the country in which it is situated, being mostly neglected or deemed unworthy of the notice or observation of any historian hitherto.

The part of Ireland called Burren, is a small barony in the northwest part of the county of Clare, and bounded on the north side by the bay of Galway. It is from one end to the other a continuation of very high, rocky, lime-stone hills, there being little or no plain land throughout the whole. It is that part of which it is reported that Oliver Cromwell said (when he came to storm a few castles in it) that he could neither see water enough to drown a man, wood enough to hang a man or earth enough to bury a man in; notwithstanding it is most fertile and produces immense quantities of juniper and some yew, besides great variety of the capillary herbs, *virga aurea*, verbena and some other common plants. I have found the *teucrium alpinum*, mango flore of Casper Bauhin and a large shrubby cinquefoil answering the description Mr Morison gives in his second volume of *Hyst[oria] Oxon[iensis]* of his *Pentaphilloides Rectum Fruticosum Eboracense*.

The inhabitants are but few and they mostly poor cottagers whose chief stock is a parcel of goats. They are courteous and good natured to strangers, though very wild and unpolished; weak, blind, superstitious zealots of the church of Rome, (like some more polite people in the world) led and enslaved by a set of mean, ignorant and illiterate priests.

The place where this cave lies, is called Kilcorny; it is a pretty low valley in comparison to the hills that surround it; the entrance is into the east end of it (for it lies east and west) about midway, there is the ruins of an old church and a little westward of it, an even plain of about an acre of ground; on the north side of which, under a steep rugged cliff lies the cave.

The mouth of it is level with the plain, about three foot diameter. It has been much larger, but was blocked up with lime and stone, which plainly appears still, but to what purpose is not known. Some conjecture it was an attempt to restrain the great flux of water, but the fabulous natives who tell numberless romantic tales of it say, it is a passage to the antipodes and that a stud of fine horses have been seen coming out of it very often to eat the corn sown in the valley. They further add that many stratagems have been tried to catch some of them, but with the loss of some men's lives they could catch but one stone horse the breed of which being very valuable, they say is kept to this day by O'Loghlen, which with them is a kind of titular king that they pay great respect to. But to return to the cave, when you pass this narrow entrance it grows much wider and loftier. The floor is a pretty even rock from two to four or five yards broad, the sides and top are rugged and unequal from six to twelve, or fourteen, feet high.

About forty yards from the door there is a pretty deep pit seven or eight yards over, but when passed the floor is plain and even as before for about two hundred yards which is the farthest that any one known has ventured into it; for my part I did not pass this pit, but have seen several that did whose veracity I can depend upon; most people that have gone into it went by a thread or clue, others have carried a bundle of straw and dropped it by the way, to guide their return which seems altogether unnecessary there being no windings or chambers throughout of any extent. It is all over, even in the depth of winter, as dry as any place of the kind underground can be, and what seems very prodigious is that it often powers forth such a deluge as covers the adjacent plain, sometimes with above twenty foot depth of water.

The times of its overflowing are uncertain and irregular; sometimes it does not happen above once in a year or two, but most commonly three or four times a year. It is sometimes observed to succeed great rains and storm though it often happens without either.

The neighbouring inhabitants are alarmed at its approach, by a great noise as of many falling waters at a distance, which continues for some hours before and generally all the time of the flood.

The water comes forth with extreme rapidity from the mouth of the cave and likewise from some smaller holes in the low ground attended with a surprising noise. It flows for a day or two and always returns into the same cave and partly into the small holes from whence it was observed to come before, but with a more slow and tardy course. The water is of a putrid quality like stagnated pond water insipid as spring water. It always leaves a filthy muddy scum upon the ground it covered which greatly enriches the soil.

It has been known sometimes (though rarely) to overflow and ebb in six or eight hours time but in a much less quantity.

There is neither river or lake anywhere in that part of the country and it is above six miles from the sea. There are very near it several much lower valleys, in which there is no appearance of water, unless a little rain water collected in a pit in the fissure of a rock or the like.

If there be any queries about further circumstances relating to it any way material to be asked, I shall be always ready to answer them having spent a good deal of time upon the spot examining of it myself, so that I can aver this whole narrative for truth from my own actual observations.

I thought it a pity so remarkable and wonderful a phenomenon of nature should lie hidden from the learned, and though conscious of my own insufficiency and incapacity of writing or stating the case methodically have at last resolved at all adventures to send you a true simple and naked description of it.

I have been very cautious in saying more than any man may see there for I know the ill consequence of making a false report in matters of this kind from an account sent the learned Royal Society (of which you are the worthy president) of squills growing in the county of Kerry, which my curiosity leading me to enquire into, I find there is no such thing and the person who delivered the reputed Irish squills to the ingenious gentleman, who transmitted you the report made him; is one that supplies the markets with medicinal herbs, upon strict and close examination confessed to me, they were a parcel of run'd squills which he sold by that name to prevent their being seized.

If there be anything else in this kingdom which deserves your notice in this way, that you desire being satisfied in, I shall take a great pleasure in being honoured with your commands; I have been bred an apothecary and understand the customs, manners and language of all parts of this country, so that I am so vain as to think myself in some measure qualified, for looking into the natural history of it.

If this rude piece be worth your while I beg you will do me the honour at least of letting me know you received it which will be an obligation on

> Sir
> Yours Most Obedient
> and
> Most Faithful
>   Humble
>   Servant
>   Char: Lucas

Taken from Charles Nelson, 'Charles Lucas' letter (1736) to Sir Hans Sloane about the natural history of the Burren, County Clare', *Journal of the Irish Colleges of Physicians and Surgeons* 21 (April 1992), pp 126-31.

George Whitefield, Stormtossed
on the Clare Coast, 1738

Rev George Whitefield, Methodist Evangelist, was a leader of the religious revival that took place on both sides of the Atlantic in the mid eighteenth century. He was educated at Oxford university where he came in contact with Charles and John Wesley, the founders of Methodism. Whitefield was renowned for his preaching, his captivating voice could be heard over immense distances and it is estimated that he preached up to 18,000 sermons during his lifetime. He made seven voyages to America where he established a special mission to Georgia. Returning from his first voyage in 1738, his ship suffered severe storm damage and after a sea journey of two months eventually made landfall on the coast of west Clare. Being imbued with intense religious fervour, Whitefield attributed his deliverance to divine intervention. He was hospitably received by a Mr McMahon in the Carrigaholt area before passing on through Ballynacally to Limerick. In Limerick he was entertained by the bishop, William Burscough, and preached to a large congregation in St Mary's Cathedral. Like most eighteenth century travellers in Ireland Whitefield was astounded at the depth of poverty of the common people. His journals were originally published 1738-41 to raise money for his missionary activities in America.

Sunday, Nov. 12, [1738]. This morning, the doctor of our ship took up the Common Prayer Book, and observed that he opened upon these words, 'Blessed be the Lord God of Israel, for He hath visited and redeemed His people.' And so, indeed, He has, for about 8 o'clock this morning news was brought that our men saw land, and I went and was a joyful spectator of it myself. The air was clear, and the sun arising in full strength, so that it is the most pleasant day I have seen these many weeks. Now know I that the Lord will not always be chiding, neither keepeth He His anger for ever. For these two or three days last past, I have enjoyed uncommon serenity of soul, and given up my will to God. And now He hath brought us deliverance - from whence I infer, that a calmness of mind, and entire resignation to the divine will, is the best preparative for receiving divine mercies. . . .

Tuesday, Nov. 14, [1738]. Let this day, my soul, be noted in thy book, for God has visited thee with His salvation. On Monday midnight, as I was lying on my bed, my sleep departed from me, and I had no rest in my spirit, because although the weather was so exceeding calm, and we in so great distress, yet no boat was sent to fetch us provisions. Upon this, I spoke to the captain, and he to the mate, who, in the morning went with a boat, and about noon this day returned loaded with provisions and water, and not only so, but told us, he was kindly entreated by the people he met with, especially by a great country gentleman, who came from his seat at midnight, on purpose to relieve him and his companions; furnished them with a fresh boat and other necessaries, most kindly invited me, though unknown, to his house, to stay as long as I please, and has ordered horses to wait ready to take me thither. . . .

A little before our provision came, I had been noting in my diary, that I believed deliverance was at hand; for last night and this morning, I had the most violent conflict within myself that I have had at all. Thus God always prepares me for His mercies. Still greater mercies God confers on His unworthy servant. For after our provisions were brought aboard, the wind still continued fair, and by six at night blew us to a little place on Carrigaholt Island, before which we cast anchor. Praise the Lord, O my soul, and all that is within me praise His holy Name. . . .

Just as we had cast anchor, a violent wind arose, which (had it happened sooner) must have greatly hurt us. Marvellous are Thy works, and that my soul knoweth right well. About seven at night I dressed myself and went on shore, and was received in a strong castle belonging to Mr MacMahon, the gentleman who sent me an invitation. He himself was not at home, having gone some miles to meet me; but his maidservant kindly received us. I asked for water, and she gave me milk, and brought forth butter in a lordly dish, and never did I eat a more comfortable meal. About ten, the gentleman (having missed me at the place appointed) came through the rain, and entertained us most hospitably, and about one we went to bed - I hope with hearts full of a sense of the Divine Love. My song shall henceforward be always of the loving-kindness of the Lord. I will make mention of His Righteousness and Truth, in the assemblies of His saints. Now our water is turned into wine.

Kilrush in Ireland

This morning about 11 o'clock, after being most hospitably entertained by Mr MacMahon, and furnished with three horses, I and my servant and my new convert set out for Dublin and reached Kilrush, a little town, eight Irish miles from Carrigaholt, about two in the afternoon, where we were refreshed and tarried the remainder of the day with Captain Coc, who last night, with his whole crew was like to be shipwrecked; but this morning by the good Providence of God, was brought hither on shore. Surely my shipmates will, of all men be most miserable if they continue impenitent, having such loud and repeated calls from God.

As I rode along, and observed the meanness of the poor people's living in these parts, I said, if my parishioners at Georgia complain to me of hardships, I must tell them how the Irish live; for their habitations are far more despicable, and their living as hard, I believe, as to food; and yet, no doubt, content dwells in many of these low huts.

At my first coming into our inn, we kneeled down and prayed, and again at night sang psalms, and prayed with the captain and several of my shipmates - the first time, I believe, the room was ever put to such a use by a ship's crew and their chaplain.

Forthfargus

Friday, Nov. 17, [1738]. Had a very pleasant ride, over a fine fruitful open country to Fourthfargus [Ballynacally], a village that was reckoned only ten, but at a moderate computation, thirty English miles from Kilrush. But this is not the first piece of Irish I have met with - their innocent blunders often extort smiles from one.

As I stopped to have my horses shoed I went into one of the poor people's cabins, as they call them; but it may as well be called a sty, a barn, or a poultry-coop. It was about twenty feet long, and twelve broad, the walls built with turf and mud. In it was a man threshing corn, two swine feeding, two dogs, several geese; a man, his wife, three children, and a great fire. Georgia huts are a palace to it. Indeed, the people live very poorly in this part, some walk barefoot with their shoes in their hands to save them from wearing out, others out of necessity. I observed many of their feet to be much swollen, and ready to gush out with blood, through extremity of cold.

Whilst I was in the cabin, as they call their little Irish huts, I talked with the woman in the house, and found she was a Roman Catholic; and, indeed, the whole commonalty almost, are of the Romish profession, and seem to be so very ignorant, that they may well be termed the wild Irish. No wonder, when the key of knowledge is taken from them. Woe unto their blind guides. I can think of no likelier means to convert them from their erroneous principles, than to get the Bible translated into their own native language, to have it put in their houses, and charity schools erected for their children, as Mr Jones has done in Wales, which would insensibly weaken the Romish interest; for when once they could be convinced they were imposed upon, they would no longer suffer themselves to be misled. Oh that some man, in whom is the Spirit of the Holy God, would undertake this!

Taken from *George Whitefield's Journals*, (ed.) W. Wale (London 1905), pp 173-6.

Richard Pococke in County Clare, 1752

Richard Pococke was born into a well established Church of England family, several of his ancestors having served as prelates of the established church. He attended Corpus Christi College, Oxford, from where he graduated with a number of degrees between 1725 and 1733. Influential family connections ensured his preferment to a lucrative church benefice in early life. He was little more than twenty when his uncle, the bishop of Waterford, appointed him precentor of Lismore. It was the first of many appointments. He became vicar general of Waterford in 1734, precentor of the diocese in 1744 and twelve years later Bishop of Ossory. The leisure and affluence such positions afforded allowed him to indulge in travel, the passion of his life. No sooner had he completed his doctorate in Oxford in 1733 than he embarked with his cousin on a three year excursion through Europe. Between 1743 and 1745 he published a two volume record of his five year expedition to Egypt and the Middle East. In later years he completed extensive tours of the remote parts of Scotland and England. His travels around Ireland were a feature of his later life. He toured the Giant's Causeway on a return trip from Scotland in 1747. In 1749 he travelled through Galway, Clare and Limerick but unfortunately no record of this tour survives. Three years later he embarked on his most ambitious Irish tour, completing a circuit of the whole island in four months. It is the Clare section of the 1752 tour that is published here. Pococke did not visit Ennis in 1752 because he had previously visited the town in 1749, and so modern readers are denied what would have been a valuable description of the county town. Coming from Galway, Pococke abandoned the turnpike road at Crusheen and proceeded east along a minor road to the village of Quin; following, incidentally, the route proposed for the new Galway to Limerick bypass of Ennis. His description of Quin friary reveals his abiding interest in antiquarian enquiry. Pococke had no agenda to pursue in his writings. Unlike previous writers, he had no interest in military conquest, colonisation or religious conversion. His comments on the whole, therefore, are objective and free of sectarian bias.

27th. [August 1752]. At Tuberein we crossed a stream from the county of Galway in Connaught, to the county of Clare in Munster, we came to Loughed bridge which I conjecture to be the river which in part forms those loughs that are to the west of Crusheen: half a mile further we crossed another stream and in half an hour more came to Crusheen on an eminence where there is a very good inn, at which I dined. 'Till we come to the county of Clare the face of the country is all rocky being a greyish marble as I conjecture; about Galway it is full of cockles and the conchae anomiae, and in almost all parts the petrified coral more or less. But here the face of the country is entirely different, all in little well improved hills, not without wood and something like

Northampton Shire. We went on and immediately crossed a stream and had a fine view of Lough Rinchacrounah, we passed three streams in a mile and come to Brin-Castle, and crossed three more below, I come to a village called Span [ ] Hill, where the road strikes out to Ennis which I had formerly gone in. This place is three miles from Crusheen, we soon came to Molieth [Moyriesk] Mr Macnamarrah's, well improved and a fine situation, and at the end of three more came to Quin, having had a view of Col. Hickman's house and of the plantations of Mr Burton and Sr. Edward Obrien we had passed in our former journey through this country. Here I saw fine lime-stone with much of the coral in it entirely consolidated with the marble. We had also in this ride a view of that pleasant bay beyond those gentlemens' seats, which extends to the north from the Shannon and is full of islands. At Quin is one of the finest and most entire monasteries I have seen in Ireland, it belong'd to Franciscan Minorities, and is called in Ware Quinchy; it is situated on a fine stream, there is an ascent of several steps to the church, and at the entrance one is surprised with the view of the high altar entire, and of an altar on each side of the arch to the chancel; to the south is a chapel with three or four altars in it, and a very gothic figure in relief of some saint probably of St Patrick: on the north side of the chancel is a fine monument of the Macnamarahs' of Ranace. On a stone by the high altar I saw the name of Kennedge in large letters; in the middle between the body and the chancel, is a fine tower built on the two gable ends. The cloister is in the usual form with couplets of pillars, but particular in that it has buttresses round by way of ornament; there are apartments on three sides of it; what I supposed to be the refectory, the dormitory and another grand room to the north of the chancel with vaulted rooms under them all; to the north of this large room is a closet over an arch, which leads to an opening, that seemed to be anciently a private way to go down in time of danger, in order to retire to a very strong round tower, the walls of which are near ten feet thick, though not above seven or eight from the ground; it has been made use of without doubt since the dissolution, as a pidgin house, and the holes remain in it. In the front of the convent is a building which seems to have been a forastieria or apartments for strangers, and to the south west are two other buildings: on the other side of the river is the parish church, with a tower built to the corner of it. Half a mile to the north east is a beautiful turret of a castle. We went on three miles further to a small neat town on a fine rivulet.

On the 28th [August 1752] I went three miles to Six Mile Bridge, where there is a handsome new church, and near it Mr Ivers has a pleasant new built house. The ride from this place to Limerick is very delightful, being well wooded and in sight of the fine river Shanon, and of the beautiful country on the other side of it. The appearance of the country on this side of Galway is very different from what it was farther north for I observed the corn ready for the sickle, and when I passed Gort, I found the harvest in several places far advanced: it is all a hot lime stone which makes the harvest very forward; and I was told that the cattle turn themselves frequently in the night on account of the heat of the ground. In about 2 miles I saw a large old house, near the river called Bunratty, which was the mansion house of the Obrians, the ancient earls of Thomond.

Taken from *Richard Pococke's Irish Tours*, (ed.) John McVeagh (Dublin 1995), pp 95-6.

Rev John Wesley, Visits to County Clare, 1756-73

John Wesley, founder of Methodism, came to preach in Ireland on no fewer than twenty one occasions between 1748 and 1789. Educated at Christ Church, Oxford, he was ordained in 1728. Following a spiritual conversion in 1738, which centred on the realization of salvation by faith in Christ alone, he devoted the remainder of his long life to evangelism. He travelled on horseback and preached constantly in Britain and in Ireland. He journeyed to County Clare on five occasions between 1756 and 1773, usually at two yearly intervals. There were no preaching houses in Clare so meetings were held in the open street or in the chamber of Ennis courthouse. Initially Wesley was received with enthusiasm and many Catholics attended his sermons. Gradually numbers dwindled and on his fourth visit in 1767, he found that 'the preaching had been discontinued and the society was vanished away'. Catholics no longer came to the meetings, perhaps on the orders of their priests, and local Protestants showed little interest in his evangelical zeal. Wesley left declaring that 'at Ennis the god of this world has wholly prevailed'. It was another six years before he returned to County Clare and then he came only as far as Clarecastle to preach to the soldiers stationed in the barracks there. Wesley met with much opposition in Ireland and despite valiant efforts, failed to bridge the sectarian divide. He was, however, an informed observer and his journals are of particular interest for the insights they provide into religious practice and affiliation in the eighteenth century. They are also of value for the light they shed on contemporary modes of travel, weather conditions and life in provincial towns. Following his experience in Clare, Wesley avoided the county in his subsequent Irish tours. He died in 1791 at the age of eighty eight, still travelling and still preaching.

Wednesday 23 June, 1756. I took my leave of Limerick and rode to Six Mile Bridge. There I left Mr Walsh to preach in Irish and went on to Ralahine.

Thursday 24 June, 1756. I went on to Ennis, a town consisting almost wholly of papists, except a few Protestant gentlemen. One of these (the chief person in the town) had invited me to his house, and walked with me to the courthouse, where I preached to a wild unawakened multitude, Protestants and papists, many of whom would have been rude enough, if they durst.

Friday 25 June, 1756. Mr Walsh preached at six [a.m.], first in Irish and then in English. The papist priest had contrived to have his service just at the same hour; and his man came again and again with the bell, but not one in ten of his people would stir. At eight I preached to a far more serious congregation and the word seemed to sink into their hearts. We took horse about ten and rode through the fruitful and pleasant county of Galway.

Thursday 29 June, 1758. I rode to Clare, and at six [a.m.] preached in the street to many poor papists and rich Protestants, almost all the gentry of the country being assembled together. Thence I went on to Ennis, and at ten the next morning had another genteel meeting in the courthouse. In Ennis many suppose there are not less than fifty papists to one Protestant. They would have been very ready to show their good-will; but the sight of Mr Bindon kept them in awe. A report, however, was spread of some terrible things they were to do in the evening; and many were surprised to observe that more than nine in ten of the congregation were papists. But none spoke an unkind or uncivil word, either while I preached or after I had done.

Friday 11 July, 1760. I preached in the new house at Clare to a genteel congregation. What a contrast between these and the poor people at Killeheen? We had still a more genteel congregation the next morning at nine in the courthouse at Ennis, to whom I spoke with all plainness. I did the same on Sunday morning; so, if they hear me no more, I am clear of their blood. I took my leave of them at Clare in the afternoon, and in the evening returned to Limerick.

Thursday 27 May, 1762. We had another Georgian day; but having the wind again full in our face, after riding about fifty English miles we got to Ennis in the afternoon. Many being ready to make a disturbance at the courthouse, I left them to themselves and preached over against Mr Bindon's house in great quietness.
Friday 28 May, 1762. I was informed that two days before, two of Mr Bindon's maids went to bathe (as the women here frequently do) in the river near his house. The water was not above a yard deep, but there was a deep hole at a little distance. As one of them dashed water at the other, she endeavouring to avoid it, slipped into the hole, and the first, striving to help her slipped in too. Nor was either of them seen any more, till their bodies floated upon the water. Yet after some hours, one of them was brought to life. But the other could not be recovered.
Saturday 29 May, 1762. We had a pleasant ride to Limerick. The violent heat, which had continued for eight days was now at an end, the wind turning north.

Thursday 6 June, 1765. Between five and six we reached Ennis, after a warm day, which much exhausted my strength; but it was soon repaired, and the serious well behaved congregation (though many of them were people of fortune) made amends for the turbulent one at Galway. Such is the chequered work of life.
Friday 7 June 1765. I rested at Ennis; and it was well I did; for even in the house the heat was scarce supportable.

[111]

Saturday 8 June 1765. I rode to Limerick and found the preaching house just finished.

Saturday 9 May, 1767. I rode to Ennis, but found the preaching had been discontinued, and the society was vanished away. So having no business there, I left in the morning and preached at Clare about eight and in the evening at Limerick. The continued rain kept me from preaching abroad this week; and I was scandalised by the smallness of congregation in the house. I am afraid that my glorying touch of mark of these societies is at an end. In Munster a land flowing of milk and honey, how widely is the case altered! At Ennis the god of this world has wholly prevailed; at Clare there is but a spark left; and at Limerick itself, I find only the remembrance of the fire which was kindled two years ago.

Wednesday 12 May, 1773. I took my leave of this affectionate people, in the evening preached at Clare. What a contrast between Clare and Limerick, a ruinous little town; no inn that could afford us either meat or drink or comfortable lodging; no society and next to no congregation, till the soldiers came. After preaching I spent an agreeable hour with the commanding officer; and having procured a tolerable lodging in the barracks, slept in peace.

Thursday 13 May 1773. We went on through a most dreary country to Galway.

Taken from *The Works of Rev John Wesley*, 4 vols., Journals 1735-70 (London 1872), ii, pp 379, 452; iii, pp 10, 95, 223, 279, 490.

Fifth Letter of Chief Baron Edward Willes
to the Earl of Warwick, 1761

Edward Willes, an Englishman from Warwickshire, achieved a life-long ambition of becoming a judge, when he was elevated to the office of Chief Baron of the Irish Court of Exchequer in 1757. Willes, a man of high integrity, was determined that the law would be freely and impartially administered. He scrupulously avoided family and party politics and declared that, like Caesar's wife, judges should be above suspicion and reproach. Between 1757 and 1762 he wrote six letters describing Ireland to the earl of Warwick. The letters describe the six circuits Willes travelled as judge of assize. His accounts, though never intended for publication, were recognised from the outset as perceptive portrayals of the country and its people. Clare formed part of the Connacht circuit in 1761. Willes made a five day journey from Dublin to Ennis, the first town of that circuit. He was impressed by the excellent condition of the turnpike road between Limerick and Ennis and gently chided the crowd of Catholic onlookers that gathered to observe him enter the near empty Protestant church in Ennis. The tensions generated by the Williamite land confiscations were still apparent. The earl of Clare, then an exile in France, continued to keep a register of the leases issued on his ancestral homelands in County Clare.

From Limerick to Ennis, where I held the assizes, is about 22 miles and a very rich country, great numbers of gentlemen houses and many orchards. The cider of this country is I think in general equal to the Devonshire cider, and that made from the Cagogee apple is the finest liquor I ever drank. It has the strength of the stire without its very disagreeable roughness. It is a dispute whether this apple was brought into Ireland by the Courtney family, or transplanted from hence by them to England (where it bears the same name) and I believe will not be settled 'till the place of Homer's birth is.

The road from Limerick to Ennis is as fine as a gravel walk. The town of Ennis is a dirty old town; streets very narrow. I believe it is near as big as Stratford upon Avon; nothing worth remarking as I heard of in the town. The church, by the ruins now extant, seems to have been a very large one, but consists at present only of one of the [a]isles of the old church. However, 'tis large enough for the Protestant inhabitants for, except the people of fashion a pretty many of whom live in and near this town, the common people are in general papists. I could not help remarking that though generally when the judges go to church at an assizes, curiosity draws to gather a great concourse of people, and so it did here, in the streets and at the church door, yet there was but three ordinary people in the [a]isle at church, and indeed the whole county of Clare has 20 papists to 1 Protestant.

The earl of Clare, who is in the French service, claims a great part of the county of Clare as his patrimony. Mr Burton, who has a large estate in this county, tells me some few years ago before the war broke out, when he was in Paris, the earl of Clare showed him great civilities and he used to dine with him often, that he knew all the gentlemen and the estates of the county and their private affairs as well as if he had lived among them. [He] told Mr Burton that he had an exact rent roll of all his own estates, that he had a register kept of every part that was sold and to whom and for what. He added that he was in possession of only about £600 a year of his estate, for says he, you sold such a part at such a time, and to Mr such a one. He said the time might come when such a registry might be of use to him, and indeed it was reported last year that he was to command the French forces, which were inten[d]ed for Ireland. Had not Admiral Hawke defeated the French fleet, it is more than probable he would before this time have found the benefit of his registry.

From Limerick to Ennis I met near 70 cars drawing packs of wool from 5 to 700 weight each going to be shipped at Cork for England. The price of it upon enquiry was 14s. 6d. at a medium for a stone (the Irish stone is 16 lb). This is a larger price than I ever knew English wool to be sold for. If our woollen staple manufactory bears so high a price, surely our merchants can't complain, and the farmers must pay their rent well. From Ennis to the city of Galway is a long day's journey - 30 computed Irish miles. We dined at Gort, near which place, at about 2 miles distance, is a very extraordinary river that runs out of a lough. It sinks and rises again in the compass of six miles, and one of the apertures that it sinks into is (as I am told for I had not time to go to see it) a most magnificent natural Gothick arch of limestone. When we left Ennis and got into the county of Galway, the face of the country was quite changed: the roads rocky and rough, scarce a gentleman's house upon the whole road; miserable cabins at 3 or 4 miles distance one from another presented themselves; not a hedge or a tree to be seen, but yet the land was enclosed in very large pastures with stone walls of a very singular construction.

Taken from *The Letters of Lord Baron Edward Willes to the Earl of Warwick*, 1757-1762, (ed.) James Kelly (Kilkenny 1990), pp 78-80.

Observations made in 1766 by Colonel William Roy

William Roy, military surveyor, was noted for his mapping skills and the excellence of his cartographic surveys of Scotland. In 1752 he was employed making military sketches of the southern coast of England against a threatened French invasion. Later he was appointed to make a general survey of the whole island of Britain. Roy came to Ireland in 1766 to report on the state of the country's defences. He toured that part of the country south of a line from Dublin to Galway. He described the countryside from the viewpoint of a military commander and the opportunities the features of the landscape offered for defence and the marshalling of troops. He was impressed by the quality of Irish roads and attributed their good condition to the lack of heavy traffic. He was, however, critical of the defences of forts and walled towns and their lack of ordnance. Roy made a detailed military sketch of the southern half of Ireland which was studied by subsequent map makers, in particular Daniel Beaufort before the publication of his *New Map of Ireland*, 1792. In later years Roy devoted his leisure time to the establishment of an accurate base line for the connecting of the London and Paris observatories and for the triangulation of the southern counties of England. Roy's Irish survey is preserved in the Library of the British Museum with manuscript copies in the Royal Irish Academy and the National Library of Ireland.

The east part of the county of Clare is mountainous and rugged, consisting of that range which begins near Cratelagh to the west of Limerick and extends by Killaloe and Feakle towards Loughrea, they are generally heathy stony and uncultivated.

The middle part [of Clare] is low and at a distance has the appearance of being smooth and level but in travelling over it is found to be everywhere broken with little rising grounds or collines which are almost universally quickset with sharp pointed stones. The intervening plains are generally boggy and interspersed with lakes of fresh water some of them of a considerable extent.

Notwithstanding the apparent ruggedness of this part of the country, yet it feeds great numbers of sheep, and a spot which here and there happens to be less encumbered than the rest with rocks is ploughed and produces good grain or where the inhabitants have with prodigious labour and pains cleared a field from the immense stones, collecting them in heaps, there they plant their potatoes.

Scarcely one tree is to be seen and the ground is only enclosed by gathering the stones and piling them one on another, thereby forming an open wall or fence called sharp dykes similar to those of Galloway in Scotland, that serve to confine their cattle, which the country people allege are afraid to come near least they should fall upon them.

The west part of Clare is mountainous, particularly the district of Burrin and some parts of Ibrickan. The former consists of groups or ranges of high mountains which from their barrenness, being covered only with stones, appear quite white and shine at a distance. The small valleys between these hills do, nevertheless, produce the finest pasturage for sheep. . . .

The Shannon is the largest river in Ireland, it springs from Lough Allin in the county of Leitrim and in its course southwards forms several lakes whereof the principal is that between Lanesborough and Athlone called Lough Roe, and that between Portumna and Killaloe called Lough Derg. The river falls into the western ocean between Kerry head and Cape Lean, 50 or 60 miles below Limerick to which place the tide flows up and whereat spring tides, ships of near 300 tons can come close to the quay, but as there are many rocks and sands in the Shannon, to avoid which, it requires good pilots. The navigation to and from Limerick with contrary winds is always very tedious.

Within the limits of the sketch there are five bridges over the Shannon viz. at Limerick, Briansbridge, Killaloe, Roghra and Athlone.

In summer the river is sometimes fordable between Limerick and Briansbridge, particularly near Newcastle, but between Killaloe and Athlone it is nowhere fordable, excepting immediately below the bridge at the last mentioned town. To the westward of the Shannon in the counties of Galway and Clare there are few rivers of any consequence.

The Fergus is navigable for boats to Ennis. Clare Castle is from its situation a post of considerable strength at the bridge on this river. . . .

There is no country whatever where there are more or in general better roads than in Ireland. The gravel or other material for making them so are found in plenty and, excepting where the bogs intervene, constantly near at hand. They appear to be likewise judiciously enough constructed and substantially made, but what contributes greatly to their lasting is the little repair that is upon them, being entirely free from heavy carriages. Those chiefly made use of in the country being only small cars or sledges drawn by one horse or two at most.

The Irish have been at great pains in this respect as well as in the article of bridges, for there are not only great roads leading from Dublin in all directions to the most distant quarters of the kingdom but likewise from any considerable town there are crossroads leading to the next adjacent places, and in this manner the communication is continued from town to town almost through the whole extent of the kingdom which would otherwise be inaccessible by reason of the bogs and rocks that so frequently intervene.

The mountainous parts of Kerry with some other rugged districts, such as Burrin and Ibrickan in the county of Clare must however be excepted, there being few roads in these parts practicable for carriages. . . .

If the English soldier, who is accustomed in this country, to live so much better than the inhabitants, shall not be supported as usual, but shall be suddenly put upon their miserable diet, I much fear that the same diseases, which carried off the greatest part of King William's army in 1691, will affect our own and occasion an increase of that desertion, which disgraces the army of this country.

Extracts taken from Royal Irish Academy, Ms. G/1/2.

Arthur Young, An Agriculturalist's
Account of Clare, September 1776

Arthur Young, agriculturalist and travel writer, was already famous when he came to Ireland in June of 1776, having established his reputation with *Farmers' Letters to the People of England* (1767) and *Political Arithmetic* (1774). In Ireland he visited twenty nine of the thirty two counties and travelled some 1,500 miles. Being principally concerned with the social and economic consequences attendant on the practice of agriculture, he had little interest in Irish antiquities or topography. Young was a gifted social observer and an insatiable recorder of facts and figures. He gathered his information though, not from farmers or agricultural workers but from the Protestant landlords, who were in possession of nine tenths of Ireland's land surface. Nevertheless he had a natural sympathy for the rural poor and praised their cheerfulness and the liveliness of their music and dance. He was shocked at the rapaciousness of landlords and roundly condemned the humiliation and economic exploitation of their tenantry. Consequently he was much quoted by nationalist writers in the nineteenth century. While Young was an experimenter and innovator in agriculture, as a practising farmer he was a failure. In 1777 he was appointed resident agent on Lord Kingsborough's estate, Mitchelstown, County Cork; his fourth venture into practical agriculture, but he resigned within the year and returned to England.

Young's description of farming in County Clare is not reflective of the county as a whole. He focuses on the fertile meadowlands along the Fergus and Shannon estuaries in the south east of the county. The farming culture and high yields of these areas were untypical of the agriculture of the rest of the county. While in Clare, Young lodged with Sir Lucius O'Brien of Dromoland, the largest and most prosperous landowner in the county. He also communicated with two neighbouring landlords, Mr Fitzgerald of Shepperton, and Mr Singleton of Ballgireen House. Young confirms what Chief Baron Willes had previously recorded in 1761, that this part of Clare had an established reputation for the production of cider. Clare cider was noted for its deep green colour, hence the name by which it was known, Cagogee (*cach an ghé*, goose excrement). Arthur Young's achievement in his *Tour in Ireland 1776-78* has never been equalled, it is a classic of its type. The tour was one of the unacknowledged sources used by Hely Dutton in his *Statistical Survey of the county of Clare* (1808), and even today may still be read with profit by aspiring agriculturalists.

September 5th [1776], to Drummoland, the seat of Sir Lucius O'Brien, in the county of Clare, a gentleman who had been repeatedly assiduous to procure me every sort of information. I should remark, as I have now left Galway, that county, from entering it in the road to Tuam till leaving it to-day, has been, upon the whole, inferior to most of the parts I have travelled in Ireland in point of beauty: there are not mountains of a magnitude to make the view striking. It is perfectly free from woods, and even trees, except about gentlemen's houses, nor has it a variety in its face. I do not, however, speak without exception; I passed some tracts which are cheerful. Drummoland has a pleasing variety of grounds about the house; it stands on a hill gently rising from a lake of 24 acres, in the middle of a noble wood of oak, ash, poplar, etc. three beautiful hills rise above it, over which the plantations spread in a varied manner; and these hills command very fine views of the great rivers Fergus and Shannon at their junction, being each of them a league wide. For the following particulars I am indebted to Sir Lucius O'Brien.

Average rent of the county of Clare, 5s. The bad tracts of land in the county, are the east mountains, part of the Barony of Burrin, and the great peninsula, which forms the north shore of the Shannon. Great tracts are let at nothing at all, but there are 20,000 acres from Paradise hill, along the Fergus and Shannon to Limerick, which let at 20s. an acre. These lands are called the *corcasses*. The soil of them is either a rich black loam, or a deep rich blue clay; and all the higher lands are lime-stone, or lime-stone gravel. The mountains are generally grit-stone. The size of farms is various. Captain Tim. Macnamara farms 7,000 acres, but part in other counties. Mr Singleton, 4,000 acres. A farm of £300 a year is a very small one; £500 a year middling; this is speaking of stock-farms. The tillage of the country is carried on by little farmers, from £20 to £100 a year; but most of it by the poor labourers, who are generally under-tenants, not holding of the landlords. The courses of crops are,

1. Potatoes. 2. Bere. 3. Wheat. 4. Oats. 5. Oats. 6. Oats. 7. Lay it out to grass.

1. Beans. 2. Bere. 3. Barley. 4. Wheat. 5. Oats. 6. Oats. 7. Oats 8. Lay it out, or beans again.

Of wheat they sow 10 to 15 stone an acre; the crop, in the corcass grounds, 8 barrels, in the other lands 5 or 6; 20 stone to the barrel. Potatoes they measure by the barrel of 48 stone: they plant 6 to the acre, and the average produce 50 barrels. They never plant them on the corcass lands, for they will not grow there. Mr Fitzgerald, of Shepperton, has had 100 barrels per acre; the favourite sorts are the apple, the Castania, the Buck, being a species of the Howard. They fat pigs on them; but, what much amazed me, was fattening hogs on grass, which they do very generally, and make them as fat as a bullock, but put them up to beans for three weeks to harden the fat. Of barley they sow 14 stone an acre, and get six barrels, at 32 stone each. Bere, two rowed barley, called *English* here, and four rowed, called *Dutch*, and of these the bere yields best. Mr Singleton has had

40 barrels of bere per acre, each 16 stone on the corcass land. Of oats they sow 21 stone to the acre, and get 12 barrels, on an average 14 stone each; and on the corcass land 16. Of beans they sow 35 stone to the acre, sow them on the green sod soon after Christmas, and plough them in; never hand-hoe or weed them: the average crop 20 barrels, at 20 stone; 30 the greatest; they are used for home consumption in dear years, and for exportation in cheap. The poor people make bread of them, and eat them boiled, and they prefer a bushel of them to a bushel of wheat; but they will not eat them, except in a scarcity. No peas sown, but rape in considerable quantities in mountain grounds, or boggy, both of which are burnt for it. They plough the furrow very shallow, and burn it: they never feed it. The crop of seed 8 barrels, at 16 ft. at from 7s. 6d. to 18s. a barrel, generally from 14s. to 17s. It is pressed into oil at the mills of Six Mile Bridge and Scariff, near Killaloe; but the greatest part is bought up by the merchants of Limerick for exportation for Holland, and last year some part of it had been sent to Great Britain, in consequence of the Act which passed last sessions. The rape cakes are all exported to England for manure: the price of them at 45s. or 42s. per ton. The rape and the bean straw are burnt to ashes for the soap boilers; and Mr Singleton has a kiln contrived on purpose for burning lime with it, collecting the ashes at the same time that the lime is burnt. No clover is sown, except by Sir Lucius O'Brien. Flax is sown in small quantities by the poor people for their own consumption; and some yarn sold, but not much from the whole county. Spinning is by no means general; not half the women spin. Some linens, bandle cloths, and Clare dowlas, for exportation in small quantities, and other sorts, enough for home consumption. Wool is spun for clothing for the people, into worsted yarn for serges, and into yarn for stockings. Great quantities of frieze are sold out of the county.

Much heath waste land, many hundreds of acres every year are brought in by paring and burning for rape, but use no manure for it; after that wheat, and get good crops, and then two, three, or four crops of oats, good ones; then left for grass, and comes tolerable herbage, worth 5s. an acre.

The principal grazing system consists in a union of both rearing and fattening; the rearing farms generally at a considerable distance from the rich lands on the Fergus and Shannon. The most profitable management of grazing, is to buy in year-olds upon this system, but it can only be done by hewing a variety of land, commonly at a distance. It is found much more beneficial than buying in bullocks in autumn, and cows in May, as the Meath graziers do.

The average price of the year-olds, is from £2 2s. to £2 10s. and the price sold at four and a half years-olds, weighing 4½ cwt. 4¾, to 5¼ cwt. is on an average at £8. For cows bought in in May, £3 3s. to £3

12s. and sell at £5 10s. An acre of the corcass land will fatten one of these bullocks, but then it must not be winter-fed at all. Sheep, on an average, shear three to a stone of 16 lb. and sell at 1s. per lb. Mr Macnamara sold this year 55 bags, besides his lambs' wool; the weight is from six hundred to seven and a half, fifty stone, and this year's price 17s. 6d. a stone. Upon the lime-stone sheep-walks of this county, they keep from one and a half to five; on a average, three. The loss on stock-sheep, bullocks, etc. will not amount to more than one per cent on the value. For hiring and stocking a grazing farm, three rents are reckoned to do. Those bullocks that are to be fattened the summer following, they give hay most part of the winter, for four or five months, as much as they will eat, which will be half an acre of good meadow.

There are 4,000 bullocks fattened annually in the county of Clare; bought in at £6 and sold out at £10 and 3,000 cows, bought in at £3 and sold fat at £5, also 6,000 fat wethers, sold out of the county annually at 20s. each.

This country is famous for cider-orchards, the cakagee especially, which is incomparably fine. An acre of trees yields from four to ten hogsheads per annum, average six, and, what is very uncommon in the cider counties of England, yield a crop every year. I never beheld trees so loaden with apples as in Sir Lucius O'Brien's orchard; it amazed me that they did not break under the immense load which bowed down the branches. He expected a hogshead a tree from several.

Land sells at twenty years' purchase. Rents fell in the rearing lands 5s. or 6s. in the pound, but rich lands fell very little. Tithes are compounded by a composition made every year by the piece. Fat bullocks nothing. Sheep, 20s. per hundred. Wheat, 5s. Barley, 3s. Oats, 2s. Potatoes, 10s. Middle men, not common, but much land relet, arising from the long tenures which are given of three lives, etc. The poor live upon potatoes ten months of the year; but, if a mild winter, and a good crop, all the year on them. They keep cows very generally, but not so many as in the list of Sir Lucius's tenants. Labour is usually paid for with land. Working-days of Roman Catholics may be reckoned 250 in a year, which are paid for with as much land as amounts to about six pounds, and the good and bad master is distinguished by this land being reckoned at a high or a low rent. The state of the poor, on comparison with what they were twenty years ago, is that they are much increased in numbers, and better clad than they were, and more regularly fed, in being freed from those scarcities which were felt before the laws for the increase of tillage. Relative to religion, there was a return to the Committee of Religion, in the House of Commons, in 1765, when the return of Clare was as follows, in five divisions:-

No. 1.	896	Protestants	16,831	Catholics
2.	1,089		12,156	
3.	291		2,694	
4.	99		786	
5.	101		4,677	
	2,476		37,144	
			2,476	
		Total	39,620	

16 to 1, and 404 over.

Lucerne, Sir Lucius cultivated for some years, and found while it was attended to, and kept clean, that it was of great use for horses; but his absence and neglect destroyed it. Relative to smuggling wool from Clare, he gave me several strong reasons for believing that there had not been any for some years; that county is well situated for it, and some ships smuggled brandy and tobacco, and could carry it away with great ease, yet not one goes. Sir Lucius was executor to a man who made a fortune by it twenty-five years ago, but he would never smuggle when above 10s. a stone; I had the same account in Galway. The cause of the high price of wool is the admission of woollen yarn in all the ports of England, and the increased demand in the Manchester fabric for that yarn, which demand would have operated in England as in Ireland, had the cheapness of spinning been equal. Another cause, the increase of population, and the people being better clad. Sending a pound of wool to France, smugglers compute to be sixpence, which is fifty per cent on the present prime cost. Thus the French could get wool much cheaper from England, where the prime cost is lower. There is none from Cork, for being a manufacturing town, the people would not allow it. A duty of 4d. per stone of 18 lb. on woollen and worsted yarn exported, marks the quantity which Ireland grows beyond its own consumption. Raw wool, two thousand to 10,000 stone, the rest yarn, which is nearly doubled in value by the manufacture. The quantity of broad-cloth and serges, that is, old and new drapery, imported from England, equals the export of woollen yarn. It is remarkable that upon the corcass lands in this county, there are several tools in use, which are called *Dutch*, a *Dutch* spade, a *Dutch* plough, etc.

Sir Lucius O'Brien introduced me to two of the most considerable graziers in the county, Mr Singleton, and Mr Fitzgerald, and rode through a part of their farms. Mr Singleton's corcass meadows were one continued bed of rushes, till he destroyed them by a method which alone proved effectual, which is digging up the rush, and turning it topsy-turvey into the hole again, this he finds effectually destroys them, and the expense is not so great as might be imagined. This gentleman has more tillage-land than common upon grazing farms; he showed me a *haggard*, well filled with wheat stacks;

Particulars of some of Sir Lucius O'Brien's labourers.

Men.	Souls per cabin	Cows	Horses	Sheep	Potatoes, acres	Corn, acres
No. 1	7	3	1	6	½	3½
2	5	1	2	8	1	4
3	3	2	0	10	1	1
4	6	2	1	9	1¼	3
5	7	2	0	20	¾	3
6	8	3	0	3	½	2½
7	7	1	0	3	1	1½
8	7	3	1	12	1½	1½
9	6	0	1	6	½	1
10	5	1	1	6	¼	1
11	6	1	0	4	¼	1
12	5	0	0	6	½	0
13	5	0	0	0	½	0
14	3	1	0	4	½	½
15	6	1	0	4	½	½
16	3	0	0	6	½	½
17	3	0	0	6	½	1
18	9	3	0	0	0	0
19	3	0	0	0	¼	0
20	5	5	1	12	1½	6
21	8	5	1	10	2	4
22	4	4	0	6	1½	2
23	7	3	1	18	¾	4
24	8	2	0	6	1	2
25	5	4	1	6	1	3
26	5	0	0	5	¼	2
27	6	0	0	0	0	0
28	7	1	0	6	¾	2
29	4	1	0	6	1	1½
30	4	1	1	6	½	2
31	8	3	1	12	1½	3
32	9	5	1	10	1½	4½
33	6	6	1	16	1	3½
34	4	2	0	6	½	2
35	7	2	1	6	1	2
36	7	3	1	11	1¾	2
37	8	3	1	12	1¼	2
38	4	3	1	10	1¼	2
39	10	0	1	20	2	2
40	10	4	2	12	1½	2
41	12	8	5	40	4	3
42	7	5	2	20	3	4
43	8	5	2	12	3	3
	267	109	31	381	45¼	89
Average	6	3	1¼	9½	1	2¼

seventeen acres of that grain yielded him 196 barrels. Mr Fitzgerald is a very attentive farmer, and in several particulars, conducts his business upon principles different from those which are common in Ireland. He has built excellent farming-offices; particularly a barn, exceedingly well contrived; the corn may be thrown at once from the part of the barn where it is stowed on to two threshing floors, the one over another, and from the stacks through a window into the barn. His hay is also thrown in the same manner, down into the cow-house, and his potatoes into a vault. These conveniences, which are a great saving of labour, are gained by the buildings being raised on the side of a steep hill, cut away for the purpose. His cows he keeps in the house all winter, by which means they are better wintered, and he raises a great quantity of manure. The chaff of his corn crops he saves carefully, which is directly contrary to the country; and what is much more, cuts much hay and straw into chaff, with an engine, which he finds to answer perfectly well; the man works it with one hand, and supplies it with the other, being fixed against the wall.

September the 8th [1776], left Drumoland. Sir Lucius rode with me through Clonmelly, to the hill above Bunratty Castle, for a view of the Shannon. Clonmelly is a division of Drumline parish, 900 acres of corcass land in one lot, which is cheap, at 30s. an acre. I went into some of the pastures, which were stocked with very fine bullocks, at the rate of one to every acre. In this neighbourhood, Mr Hickman has a close of 20 acres, which, when in his own hands, fattened him 2 cows per acre, and in winter fed him 100 wethers, to the improvement of 6s. each. The profit by the cows was £4, and by the sheep £1 10s. per acre: in all £5 5s. I had this fact from his own mouth. The richness of these corcasses, which are flat lands on the river side, that have been gained at different times from the salt water, is very great. When in tillage, they sometimes yield extraordinary crops; 50 stat barrels an acre of bere have been known, sixteen of barley, and from 20 to 24 of oats are common crops. . . .

At the foot of this hill is the Castle of Bunratty, a very large edifice, the seat of the O'Briens, princes of Thomond; it stands on the bank of a river, which falls into the Shannon near it. About this castle, and that of Rosmanagher, the land is the best in the county of Clare; it is worth £1 13s. an acre, and fats a bullock per acre in summer, besides winter feed.

Taken from Arthur Young, *A Tour in Ireland; with general observations on the present state of that kingdom; made in the years 1776, 1777, and 1778*; fourth edition, ed. A.W. Hutton 2 vols (London 1892, reprinted Shannon 1970) i, pp 284-92.

John Howard, Public Institutions of County Clare, April 1788

John Howard, self appointed inspector of prisons, was born in Hackney, London into a well off family. At twenty six he married his landlady, a widow of fifty two, under obligation, as she had nursed him through a long illness. Appointed sheriff of Bedfordshire in 1763, he was appalled at the intolerable distress of prisoners. Thus began his career as a prison reformer. Prisoners could be kept in gaol even if found not guilty before a court until certain fees were paid to the gaoler. Howard travelled all over Britain visiting gaols and bridewells, paying particular attention to the ravages caused by prison fever and small-pox. Two bills were eventually introduced into parliament for the abolition of gaoler's fees and the improvement of insanitary conditions in gaols. Howard continued his self imposed task of inspecting gaols, visiting prisons in France, Holland, Flanders and Germany. In 1787 he commenced his fourth inspection of English gaols and his third of Ireland. He had previously visited gaols in Ireland in 1767 and gaols and hospitals in 1775. Howard was a deeply religious man with a powerful will and great endurance. In Clare he visited the charter school at Newmarket where orphaned children received a Protestant education and the county gaol and infirmary in Ennis. He also inspected the Erasmus Smith foundation, built in 1775 for the education of better off students.

Newmarket school. April 4, 1788. Eighteen girls and fourteen boys. The rooms clean and free from disorders. The master does not live in the school house.

Ennis county gaol has been built about seven years. Only one dayroom for both men and women. The criminals have beds and proper bedding. Allowance, a threepenny loaf (weight one pound eleven ounces); a twopenny loaf and a penny worth of milk, as at Limerick and Tralee, would be better. April 4, 1788. Debtors 6. Felons etc. 19.

The county infirmary at Ennis, built about fifteen years ago, has two wards on the first floor, one for each sex. The floors and walls were very dirty. None of the patients had sheets, two excepted, who said they brought in all their bedding; the others lay on a little hay or straw, and had hardly any blankets to cover them. No fuel. (The criminals in the county gaol had blankets and fuel.) The allowance is two pennyworth of bread a day and three halfpenny worth of milk. April 4, 1788. 16 patients.

A poor house adjoins to the infirmary at Ennis, in which were twenty aged persons, who had an allowance of four pence a day for diet but no fuel. The house was not very dirty and they seemed to have an attentive and honest keeper.

At Galway and Ennis I visited the schools of the Erasmus Smith foundation, which are well conducted and provided with able masters. With the worthy master of the former, the Rev Mr Campbell, I had much conversation relative to a more general and liberal mode of education in that country. Mr Campbell testified the readiness of many of the Catholics to send their children to Protestant schools; and he is of the opinion that many would by these means be brought over, were the most promising of them enabled by moderate aid to pursue their further education in the university. It might also be advisable to remove from the charter schools some of the most improved children to these schools, or such provincial ones as might be established.

Taken from *The Works of John Howard Esq., An Account of the principal Lazarettos in Europe*, (London 1791) pp 93-4.

Daniel Augustus Beaufort,
Journey Through County Clare, August 1788

The Beaufort family was of Huguenot origin; one of the many Protestant families who fled to England in the early decades of the eighteenth century to avoid persecution in France. In 1746 Daniel Cornelius de Beaufort accompanied the Viceroy Lord Harrington to Ireland as chaplain. He was subsequently appointed rector of Navan, County Meath, with pastoral responsibility for Dublin's large Huguenot community. His son, Daniel Augustus, was a gifted student with a versatile and enquiring mind; he entered Trinity College Dublin in 1756, gained a scholarship the following year, graduated B.A. in 1759 and M.A. in 1764. Daniel Augustus succeeded his father as rector of Navan in 1765. He travelled on the continent and in Britain and, being interested in most things, became an expert on many subjects. Because he found the diocesan boundaries of Ireland so inaccurate, he determined about 1785 to produce a new map of Ireland on a scale of six miles to an inch. This involved him in a considerable amount of research and travel. He toured the west and north of Ireland in 1787 in search of accurate topographical information, a journey of 1,320 miles. The following year he set forth again travelling the north, west and south of Ireland. It is this second tour which concerns us here, because in August 1788 the Rev Beaufort passed from Galway into County Clare. He was accompanied on the journey by two competent artists - his sons James and William. Regrettably, except for a plan and some rough sketches of Corcomroe Abbey, none of the drawings executed by the Beauforts in Clare appear to survive. Evidently the roads of the county were sufficiently improved by the 1780s to accommodate vehicular traffic, as the Beauforts were able to travel the length of the county in a horse drawn carriage. Beaufort also carried with him some recently published works of reference to which he refers: John Ferrar's *Directory of Limerick* (Limerick 1769), Taylor and Skinner's *Maps of the Roads of Ireland* (Dublin 1778), Mervyn Archdall's *Monasticon Hibernicum* (Dublin 1786) and possibly also William Wilson's *The Post Chaise Companion* (Dublin 1786). Beaufort's Map of Ireland and Memoir of the same were published after much labour in 1792. However, his projected *Grande Topography of Ireland*, for which much of the information was collected in the tours of 1787-8, was never completed. That portion of his 1788 tour relating to County Clare is published here courtesy of Trinity College Dublin. Spelling has been modernised; names of persons and places remain unchanged.

August 2nd [1788]. Left Galway at 7 and passed through Oranmore. Good large cleared fields (interspersed with some rock) for about one mile. Old church as in Taylor and Skinner. See Tyrone house, large and new but very bleak and too high though some low woods about it.

Claranbridge a very small village with an inn - omitted by Taylor and Skinner. Hereabouts there is much fine corn among the rocks.

Passed Kilcolgan, old castle and church but no village, only two or 3 cabins. Just above the bridge the river from Cragwell and Rahassan (about one mile off) rises out of the ground. Here we quit the Gort road and turn to the right and at ½ past ten reach Kinvarra a small village with a ruined church (not marked in any map). Just near it is Dunguerrin Castle, perched on a quay over a small bay. Under this castle we saw (it being low water) 3 or 4 great streams issue from the rocks, much below high water mark on the strand, being the rivers of Gort and which disembogues by a subterranious passage here most curiously. James drew the castle for me.

Kinvarra is at south end of bay. The church 60 by 27 feet in clear, had only a small spike-hole east window and near the altar a small one on the south side - no other. This village is frequented by boatmen. The inn kept by Mr and Mrs Sille, where we had a good breakfast and afterwards she took me for a doctor and consulted me but I declined prescribing. The whole village belongs to Mr Gregory and is distant 14 miles from Galway, 14 from Loughrea, 12 from Corrofin (computed) and 7 from Gort. Tithes set at 7 and 4 and twenty shillings for 100 sheep, none for hay. Of this parish Mr Upton had 2 quarters, bishop one and vicar Mr Ficher 1, and of 8 others united to it and Kilcolgan.

Clare

Three miles farther enter Clare county over Curranroo bridge, built across a small creek now dry and rocky, the tide being out. There [are] a few neat whitewashed cabins here. From Kilcolgan here the whole country is covered with grit, stones and rock, worse if possible than Arabia Petrea and continues the same into Clare.

We soon ascend a long steep mountain between two high summits, quite covered with rock and loose stones, yet among them were many sheep feeding. From hence have a distinct view of Galway across the bay. On the summits of these rocky moores they say that there is good grassy plains.

About 1½ mile from this abbey [Corcumroe] on the steep side of the hill 4 or 5 hundred yards above the sea is the clear and plentiful well of Rose Keilly, shaded by an old thorn. Accessible but by a narrow path on the hill by which cattle go and drink and so pass on in a string never attempting to turn about and return.

From this summit by a gradual descent into a valley with good grass among the rocks and at our right hand on the slope see the ancient abbey of Corcomroe in a field without a way to it. The horses were taken off and turned to grass and we walked onto the ruin which is very mean architecture. There were side aisles to the nave but that on the north is now quite down and the arches on both sides walled up.

The choir was very dark only one small window at south end. The chancel indeed is a small chapel, on each side are screened off by handsome pillars and arches of which William made a drawing. This chancel is walled up by a rude modern wall, with an open door, up to the springing of the arches. Inside are two large square tombs, 2 ornamented ones in the walls and in a deep niche a recumbent figure of a chieftain of the O'Briens called in this country Chraghool na Seuderny which upon Archdale relating that he was a king of Thomond interred in 1267. James designed the figure and also some elegant capitals formed by rows of descending tulips or rather hyacinths or lily of the valley bells. Some pillars have no capitals. The east window is triple but very narrow in the spike-hole stile. No inscription anywhere. The choir is separated from the aisle by a wall 4½ feet thick with a very small door in the middle 3½ feet by 7 and from that wall arises a very low steeple 10 feet long by 6 broad only. N.B. No door in the middle. The detached buildings seem to have been extensive and numerous.

We left this abbey at half past 4 being told that we had only 8 miles of excellent road to go and being disappointed of a reception at Mr Skerrit's to whom we had sent a letter of introduction from Mr R. Marsh, was not at home. We saw his house at a distance behind us as we went on. On the west side of the mountain over Puldhuda bay famous for the best Burrin oysters.

The road descends for 3½ miles, very good but the grass on it points out how little it is frequented. From thence the road becomes hilly and in one place skirts a deep precipice. The whole country is rocky and desolate but yet we saw many castles and one tree.

Passed by Croofield church, a ruin on our right. Near it we met Mr Skerrit returning home, who pressed us very politely to turn back but we persevered and soon after decoyed by a good road on the right we omitted keeping the left hand road and soon got into a lane of the most horrible rocks that [the] chaise was ever dragged over. At last we met a man and one that spoke English too, a rarity here, who told us we were but between high stone walls. We could not turn about, however he told us that by going [on] we should fall into the Kilfenora road. We took his advice, the road mended and passing by the castle of Lemenagh turned into the great road to Corrofin. Lemenagh was the residence of Sir Lucius O'Brien's ancestors and was taken by General Ludlow who slew Conor O'Brien in the action, father of Sir Donough of whom the people talk hereabouts as a great man. Lemenagh they tell us signifies Horseleap, about it the grass is excellent and the land rich though rocky. All the rocks in Clare are limestone, those in Galway whin and grit.

From hence we drove onto Corrofin through a vale of mixed grounds, fine, fertile, rocky, hilly and well watered by the lake of

Inchiquin on the banks of which are the seats of Mr Burton, who is planting all the hills with oak; and the ruined castle of Inchiquin the ancient residence of the earls. Burton lately purchased the estate from Lord Inchiquin.

Round towers. Upon arriving I wrote a letter to Mr E. Burton for information and in the hope of some civilities. In the last I was disappointed but he informed me that Kilfenora was not worth seeing. That Killnaboy was dedicated to Saint Necaron and mentions the round tower there, that at Dysart and one at Drumcliffe with some directions for an Ogam inscription.

By the roadside on the left stands the ruined church of Killnaboy and on the north west side of it the butt of a round tower . It was ½ past 9 when we reached Corrofin, a poor small market town with a neat church, but a wretched carrier's inn; the parlour clay floor still damp. But the good landlady soon made us a fire and got us excellent mutton chops and 2 spatchcocks with good new potatoes. So we supped heartily, lay in our clothes and slept very well after a fasting and fatiguing day's work and having been out during all the great heat.

August 3rd [1788]. Rose very early and walked about this little town, which is wholly the property of Sir Lucius O'Brien. There are about it some trees and some good land. In the room over the market house Lucius O'Brien has for some years encouraged the spinning and weaving of woollen goods. Met here Mr Hickman a very old gentleman, uncle to Sir Lucius and father to Lady Charlemont and Mrs E. O'Brien. He lodges here for the sake of the fishing, the Lough of Inchiquin being famous and that of Tydan still more so for the quantity, excellence and size of their trout. They are commonly taken of 6 and 7 and sometimes even of 12 lbs. weight. He represents this as the cheapest county in Ireland to live in. Fish is so exc[eptionally] plenty from its extensive coasts and numerous lakes (about 70), wild and water fowl in equal abundance, meat and tame fowl good and plenty.

He told us of a remarkable cave south west of Innistymond, called Puhl-a-Thydane where the sea roars in a most tremendous manner.

The country hack horses are called staggeens, 2 and 3 year old heifers bulsheens.

Ennis
At 7 we set out for Ennis through a fertile vale interspersed with rocks but very thinly adorned with trees. It improved however as we advanced and we went through a very fine country before we came to Ennis. The roads were excellent the whole way. On the right of road see Dromore (see Skinner and Taylor) passed by an old church of Ruan they said with a large modern tomb and monument at the east

end. Near Nutfield is an extensive turlough, partly rocky and very much indented, marked by Skinner and Taylor as water erroneously but connected with the river Fergus. Across a small lake had a full view of the ruins of Drumcliffe with its lofty round tower.

Our entrance into Ennis was through a very long straggling mean suburb, from which instead of going over the great bridge, up to which large boats are brought with the tide, we turned to the right along a new excellent road by the side of the river, having on the opposite side several neat looking places and the school house, large well planted and elegant, and on the other side of the river a neat place of the Pattersons, with iron gates on the town side and just at the foot of a very handsome stone bridge and opposite to which stands the west end of the church; altogether forming a very English scene. The church now used was the aisle of the old one so that the east end is a ruin as well as the transepts, two very fine windows of which appears from the bridge and make the scene very picturesque, many trees being interspersed. Had it not been Sunday we should have taken a view of it.

The town is large and very populous, but streets crowed and narrow, many good houses have an air of comfort and opulence. The serge manufacture is carried on with spirit here. The inn, Mrs Loughlin's, is most horribly situated in a narrow lane through which one must walk, is dark, dirty and ill attended. Here for a cloacina they have across the end of a little yard a board with round hole and a tub thrust under it and drawn out when full, but now omitted cleaning, for its appearance and smell were odious in the extreme. After paying very dear for a bad breakfast, dressed and went to church, where Mr Weldon the curate gave us a very sleepy sermon. The church is pretty large but gloomy, owing to a gallery on each side lately erected and not quite finished. This supposes a large congregation but they are not very polite, for they let us stand in the aisle full ten minutes without offering a pew. No sexton and the clerk sent this morning to jail for robbery but he got out again to officiate.

Immediately after church we set out and passed through Clare, a small town at the confluence of the Shannon and Fergus over which there is a good bridge and large vessels at its quay. Here is a castle now converted into a barrack for two companies who march to church to Ennis. Half way between these two towns are the ruins of Clare Abbey. The country here is rich and good and full of gentlemen's seats: Morriesk, Mr McNamara's, which we saw at a distance, a Major Grant's which we passed by are said to be very good and pretty places. But the largest in this country is Dromoland the seat of Sir Lucius O'Brien. Just before we came to it we crossed on a high bridge a little river with deep muddy banks - the Wye in miniature. At the gate of Dromoland, we applied for leave to drive through the grounds which the porter told us every gentleman was welcome to do. So we went on by a pretty lake and then turned short by the offices, not to be seen, and were passed them a good way and making out of the avenue as fast as we could, when a man on horseback overtook us, whom we were striving to avoid and determined to refuse if he came with an invitation. But when we found it was Sir Lucius O'Brien himself, such a hospitable exertion was not to be refused - *ergo* - we turned to the antique mansion and spent a very pleasant day.

Dromoland

A large old house not regular and only part of a vast design, intended to connect with a castle, since pulled down, standing between terraces with gravel walks, grassy smooth slopes and distant objects seen through vistas in front. In the rear commanding a small lake, with fine woods overhanging a fine rising ground full of haycocks beyond it. The house covered with jasmine, a great aloe in a tub at the front and many very beautiful trees make this old fashioned place cheerful as well as magnificent.

In the house are several old family pictures of the O'Briens and some better ones of all the Clarendon family, from whom Sir Lucius is descended by the women. In a long tiled gallery full of maps and stags' horns and other such things is a very curious massy table of some kind of mahogany, with four lions for legs and in the middle Hope on one side and Charity on the other for supporters, all rudely carved. This table was taken out of one of the ships of the armada wrecked on this coast 200 years ago and can be lengthened at both ends, in an uncommon manner, by drawing out two half leaves which are under it and the great upper leaf falling in between them which keeps all level and fast. Here we saw also an ancient sword which was in the hand of his ancestor Conor O'Brien when slain by General Ludlow.

Sir Lucius cultivates hemp and lucerne but R. W. had not time to stay for us to see this farm tomorrow.

Lady O'Brien is a very pleasant and very affable woman, has been very handsome, talks a good deal and was very attentive to me. Offered to write to Mr Pelham the painter and surveyor to meet me at Killarny. She showed us many miniatures of her father's and uncle's and of other paintings. She showed me Pelham's original drawing of the County Clare. In short they were as civil as possible and pressed us to stay another day. They have eleven very fine children. Here are also two of his late brother's Edward, James and Harriett: the boy a most beautiful intriguing face and seemingly very industrious to be informed, the girl handsome but, I think, not quite so pleasing in her manner as Nichola, Miss O'Brien's name. But all these young people extremely well behaved and very attentive and civil to William.

The dinner was plain and plenty. We drank full enough, had coffee and a slight supper and at ½ past eleven retired to rest. This whole day has been intensely hot.

August 4th [1788]. At 7 we took leave of the Baronet, for he was up, and passed through Ardsallas, a very small village where a great fair is held, to Quin where a few scattered houses form a little hamlet.

Quin

The abbey of Quin stands on a bank on the east side of a small river, which we passed yesterday, and makes a grand picturesque object. The west door is square on top and the ascent to it up several steps, 8 or 10, which are not quite destroyed, adds to the dignity of its appearance. The west aisle is 56 [feet] long by 23 wide. The steeple 15 [feet] square raised on four arches 7 feet 9 inches wide, and very lofty, at least 35 feet. In the choir over the stone arch of a tomb, are distinct remains of a large crucifix and other figures in stucco. On the south side there is a chapel called McNamara's, well built of cut stone 39 feet long and 24½ wide, arch that breadth in the south wall of church. In this are 4 windows one at south end, one at west but not central and 2 at east side regular and a niche between them. There were several detached buildings to this abbey but at the east end are two circular projections which look like the stumps of castles, the north one however seems to have been a dove cote, the south is more levelled.

William and James each made a handsome drawing of this abbey, while they were at work we proceeded to Sixmilebridge to breakfast, passing by a good inn on the road called the Coach and Horses. Here having occasion to look into the Monasticon - missed it - as well as Ferrar, so James was obliged to go back to Dromoland for it, after his drawing was finished.

In the way saw some rich grounds but much rock and few trees. The abbey belongs to Mr McNamara. The village to Sir Lucius and the opposite side of the river, where stands the ruined parish church, is Lord Pery's.

Sixmilebridge is a small village with a market house on the east side of the river, belonging to Mr Ivers. The west side, where our inn was, is Sir Lucius O'Brien's - (a church here).

Near this we saw a bleach green and on our road to Limerick, see at some distance, Bunratty Castle, the seat of [the] earls of Thomond, close to both rivers. Pass on our right the church of Cloghan. Overtake a young lady with a broken brace, repair her calnole and go on in. From the high ground over which the road goes, a noble view of Shannon and of Carrick-a-gunnel on the opposite side. Meelick church which we pass on our left about 3 miles from Limerick (see Wilson) seems a handsome one.

Limerick is scarce seen till we come within ½ a mile of it, has but one old tower to St Mary's, no spires to set it off. Thomond bridge, the castle and the Shannon make a grand appearance. The streets are narrow but flagged on the sides, excessively crowded and full of shops.

We stopped opposite the exchange at a Widow Murphy's, but found the accommodation so bad, that we went on to Taylor's new inn in the new town and found that very good.

Taken from Trinity College Dublin, Ms. 4029.

Charles Bowden, A Tour of West Clare, 1791

County Clare tended to be outside the compass of professional travel writers in the eighteenth century. The first writer to include the county in a contemporarily published account was Charles Topham Bowden. Little, unfortunately, is known about him. He resided in London and had visited many of the capitals of Europe. Bowden disembarked at Dublin, August 1790 and, travelling on horseback, completed a circuit of the whole island in two months. Having taken the ferry at Tarbert he crossed the Shannon estuary to Kilrush. He is unusual in that he avoided the main centres of population. Travelling along the west coast of Clare he passed through Kilmurry Ibrickan and Ennistymon and on to Galway. Bowden was a well informed observer, and being aware of Ireland's historical experience, he was sympathetic towards the people and praised their civility and resilience.

At Ballylongford there is a large and convenient ferry on the Shannon, which we crossed over to Kilrush. Near this ferry in the Shannon, is Inniscathy, formerly an episcopal see, founded by St Senan, in the fifth century. I was told this island had its name from Cathy, a sea monster, that ravaged the country for a long time. The monks of Inniscathy abbey, from its foundation to its demolition, are said never to have permitted a woman to enter the island. There is a passage in the life of one of those monks, relative to a lady who having requested to speak to him, he replied, 'What have women to do with monks? We will neither admit you nor any other woman into the island.' She said, 'If you believe Christ may receive my soul, why do you turn away my body.' 'That (he answered) I verily believe, but we never permit any woman to enter this place. So God preserve you. Return to the world, lest you be a scandal to us; for however chaste you may be, you are a woman.'. . .

Mr Vandeleur has a most delightful seat at Kilrush, where I dined in company with two very convivial gentlemen, Mr Hackman and Mr Studdart. Hence I went to Innistymond by Kilmurry. The castle of Innistymond was the residence of the earls of Thomond, the last of whom was attainted, and though the immediate descendant of that nobleman possesses the property, he does not enjoy the title. The roads in this country are extremely bad, and the accommodations they afford are worse.

Taken from Charles Topham Bowden, *A Tour Through Ireland* (London 1791), pp 210-12.

A Frenchman's Tour of East Clare, 1797

Chevalier De Latocnaye, an aristocrat from Brittany, having fled the terrors of the French revolution, came to reside in England. He wrote a book based on a walking tour of Great Britain, another on the French revolution and a third on a walking tour of Ireland, 1796-97. His Irish tour is of value because it describes the country on the eve of the 1798 uprising. De Latocnaye aroused much curiosity walking the roads of Ireland; he dressed in bright breeches and silk stockings and carried all his possessions in a handkerchief tied to the end of an umbrella. His company was in such demand among landowners that he scarcely needed to use a country inn. De Latocnaye walked from Limerick to Castleconnel, to O'Brien's Bridge and Killaloe before passing on through the county of Galway. He records the digging of short bypass canals around obstructions in the Shannon in order to make the river navigable from Limerick to Lough Derg.

The inhabitants of Castle Connell were assessed with a rate to provide means to build a catholic chapel. I do not know what fault had been committed by the priest of the parish, but the catholic bishop of Killaloe interdicted the work, and the church remained half built, and without a roof. Mass, however, was celebrated in a corner covered by a few planks, and the people continued to come as before, but resolutely resolved not to finish the church unless or until the favourite priest should be recalled.

Crossing the mosses which surrounded this village, I came by O'Brien's Bridge to Glanamore to Mr Thomas Arthur, with whom I spent several days. His house is at the end of a fertile, little valley, surrounded by mountains covered with peat. I saw with him bones representing almost an entire skeleton of that monstrous animal which is called in this country 'moss' or 'moose deer,' and the name of which I do not know in French. . . .

I returned to O'Brien's Bridge, and after having taken a plunge into the Shannon in order to put him in a good temper with me, I ascended the river with Mr Waller in a little boat, for which my umbrella served as sail. The river was charming, beautiful, calm, and it seemed to be deep, but soon we came to a waterfall and were obliged to land. They are here digging a little canal of about one hundred paces long, to join the two navigable parts of the river. Returning in the boat we travelled about ten miles and were again obliged to land and even to leave the boat. Here they are making a canal which shall be about a mile long, and which will terminate near the beautiful palace of the bishop of Killaloe. The fall of water here is very considerable, and in a distance of about fifty feet it falls fourteen or fifteen through large, round stones. This is the kind of obstruction in the rivers which forms the lakes. This one makes an immense lake of thirty miles long by twelve or fifteen wide, and although it offers, at different parts, interesting and pleasing views, like the greater part of the lakes of Ireland, it has rather the look of a great inundation, and the islands through it give *vraisemblence* to the appearance. A company offered to drain nearly the whole of this lake, provided that the riverside proprietors would give them half the new-formed land. Difficulties arose, and the matter has not been carried through. This company had calculated that, in lowering the bed of the river at Killaloe by twelve feet, they would drain fourteen thousand acres. The cost of the works would have amounted to over twenty thousand pounds sterling. It would not have been a great deal to pay for seven thousand acres of land, but it is to be presumed that it would not produce very much in the early years, and perhaps one-third of it would be sandy or unfit for cultivation.

The little town of Killaloe is very ugly; the cathedral is large and appears to be fairly well built. The stone bridge which crosses the Shannon here has eighteen arches, but they are very small, and the bridge will have to be rebuilt - a modern one need not have more than nine or ten arches. I paid a visit to the minister of the parish, who has a superb house at a little distance from the town, on a height dominating Lough Derg. From there is to be had a really magnificent view of this vast sheet of water, whose banks are almost everywhere high, and cultivated with care. There is a bay of seven or eight miles, which cannot be seen without climbing to the summit of a fairly high mountain in the neighbourhood. From this height the Shannon can be seen winding through the plain as far as Limerick, with all the little towns which are on its banks, the principal of these being Nenagh.

It is disappointing that there is nowhere to be seen any appearance of industry. There are no manufactures. Beyond the labouring of the soil there is nothing to do, but patience! - a certain time must be allowed to a nation to come out of its stupor of seven hundred years. It is only fourteen years since its genius made effort to fly, and already thought is being taken to find means to surmount the immense difficulties which the navigation of the Shannon presents. A certain measure of success has followed through the use of communicating canals. The Grand Canal is proceeding very slowly, but it will be finished in a few years, when interior communication will be opened across Ireland from Dublin to Limerick, and industry will grow in proportion as the means are provided for the disposal of its product.

The first step in the civilisation of a country is to cut the woods, drain the marshes, lower the beds of rivers, and allow stagnant waters to flow away. The people of this country have succeeded perfectly well in the matter first mentioned, seeing that they have not left wood enough to make a toothpick in many places, but they have hardly yet commenced to think about the remaining works.

Near Killaloe is to be seen one of those round forts which are so numerous in Ireland. This one is called 'O'Brien's Palace.' Tradition reports that Brian Boru, who defeated the Danes at Clontarf, and perished in the battle, lived here. It is well situated for defence at the point where the river leaves the lake. The fort is not as large as several that I have seen, but the parapets seem higher and the fosses deeper. I cannot conceive the sort of palace or, indeed, dwelling of any kind which could be erected inside such an enclosure, unless it were simply an arrangement of plank shelters or tents.

I followed the western course of Lough Derg, and on the way met an honest attorney going gaily to put the surrounding country under contribution. He pointed out to me, at some distance from the shore, a square tower situated on a rock. Some determined contrabandists had there established a distillery, with intention to pay no duties. They barricaded the place, and being provided with firearms, no customs officer dare hazard his life in approaching these friends of the 'creature.' To dislodge them, it was necessary to send troops with cannon, but the distance from the bank being considerable, and there being also a wish not to proceed to extremes, they proceeded to starve out the illicit distillers, who did not surrender until the fifteenth day, and then only after having affected an honourable capitulation.

I paid a visit to Mr H. Brady at Tomgrany, which is a rather pretty village situated at the end of the bay of which I have already spoken. From it can be seen many of the islands in the lake, among others one which is called Holy Island, which has a high round tower, and where formerly were seven churches, the inhabitants still going, with great devotion, to make their pilgrimages round the ruins. The Catholics of the country have taken exclusive possession of the cemetery, and will not permit that the bones of a Protestant should there be deposited. A rich man of the parish threatened to send a labourer out of it. 'All right,' said the other, 'but I have more right in the parish than you, for you can't take me from my six feet of earth in Holy Island, and with all your riches you will never have that.'

Walking through the ruined town of Mount Shannon, I came to Mellick to Mr Thomas Burke. Near his house was formerly an abbey, and its ruins are still regarded with veneration. Near the chapel is a species of cell which is of singular form. There is just room for a person standing in it to turn round - it would seem to have been a confessional. Above a tomb there is a stone, squarely hollowed and full of the *water of heaven*, which water is said to have the virtue of curing corns. How charming it is to travel in Ireland! I hope by the time my promenade is finished that I shall be cured of every ill.

The borders of the lake in this district were some time ago covered with wood, but this has all been cut down, and the whole country is naked and arid. Near Woodfort the landscape begins to improve, and is rather pretty near a village called Abbey, on the confines of the provinces of Munster and Connaught. Formerly there was a considerable abbey here, with a church dedicated to the Virgin. It was a *fête* day on which I saw it, and the place was crowded. This ruin is one of the few of which the inhabitants have had the good sense to make use, so as to avoid the trouble and expense of building a new church. Catholics have lately obtained permission to use two of the lateral chapels, of which the vault remained intact; it is hardly possible to exaggerate the miserable look of these chapels and of the poor folk who frequent them. In the cemetery two or three priests were occupied in confessing the penitents. They sat on stones, and each held a little flag, which was used to separate the penitent from the crowd. The priests, as I am told, receive something for their trouble, according to a fixed tariff; this is said to be their principal source of income. After all, they must live, and it is only through the little charges they exact from the faithful that their kitchen can be kept going. I have, however, seen some, to my great surprise, who are by no means badly off, having between one and two hundred pounds sterling per annum of income, besides a passable house, and, according to custom, dinners without end with their parishioners who are in easy circumstances.

The law allows to every Catholic priest who will turn Protestant the sum of forty pounds sterling per annum, to be paid by the county in which he lives; he has also the promise of the first curacy vacant. The insults which the people heap on the few who profit by these advantages are sufficient to disgust those whose conscience would allow them to place their temporal interests before all other considerations. However, the law is on the side of these, and yet I do not believe that there are a dozen of them in the whole of Ireland.

Taken from *A Frenchman's Walk Through Ireland*, 1796-7, translated from the French of De Latocnaye by John Stevenson (Belfast 1917, reprinted Belfast 1984), pp 128-135.

John Harden, Voyages on the Shannon,
August 1797

Almost at the same time as Chevalier De Latocnaye was compiling his tour of
east Clare, another group of travellers were recording their experiences on
Lough Derg and the Shannon Estuary. John Harden, a Tipperary landowner
of Cromwellian descent, together with the artist and travel writer George
Holmes, and another friend William Sinnet, went on a tour of the south west
of Ireland in August 1797. Both Holmes and Harden have left accounts of
their tour. Holmes' account was published in 1801 as *Sketches of Some of the
Southern Counties of Ireland*, which included watercolours made on tour.
Harden's much more detailed and discerning description, on the other hand,
was not published until 1953. Harden, a gifted amateur artist, also included
line drawings of historical monuments in his account. After 1800 he went to
reside in England where he perfected his artistic skills and became in time an
accomplished artist. And although he was practically unknown in his own
period his works of art, principally domestic interiors, are today highly
regarded. Harden's description of the Shannon is by far the best account
compiled before the introduction of steam boats on the river in 1825.

Thursday, 17 August 1797. After taking leave of our good friends Mr
and Mrs Lawrence we got on Thursday 17th through as charming
country as any possible, variety, improvements and fertility
everywhere abounding; arrived at Killaloe, (7 miles). We were
delighted with the windings of the Shannon which runs here of great
breadth and rapidity but full of shallows under a bridge of 19 arches.
These shallows interrupt the free navigation of the river up to Lough
Derg, but, in order to obviate that, there are canals cut from hence to
Limerick here and there, wherever it is impassable in the river, but I
believe 'tis but ill attended to and neglected. The bridge here divides
the counties Tipperary, Limerick, and Clare, Killaloe lies in the latter.
The Shannon is navigable up to Carrick on Shannon and will be
shortly complete to the cut of the Grand Canal at Portumna so that
there will be inland navigation to Dublin.

We spent very little time in viewing the town which has little or
nothing attractive, save the situation which is fine. The cathedral is a
poor building but very ancient (it has undergone some modern repairs
internally under the direction of Bishop Knox who has also added
some addition to the spire, but the style totally incorrect). As you
enter the great aisle, which is of good extent and remarkable for the
prolongation of sound, supporting the human voice for half a minute
or near it, is the entrance to the tomb of Bryan Bourhoime, who was
buried here. The arch is built up, but the supporting pillars, capping

and springing of the arch are exposed, and though of a soft bad quality of free stone and so very long done, are yet curiously wrought and in preservation worth minutely viewing. There is little else worth seeing.

The present Bishop, Dr Knox, has shown a mind much unlike men of the same function in his day who, instead of avarice and sensuality, has planned and superintends a free school for the education of 50 children (at his own expense), is about establishing a factory here for spinning woollen yarn - and moreover has instituted a dispensary which is attached to the buildings of the church where a physician prescribes and the apothecary daily administers relief. What an example for full fed prelates. 'Go ye and do likewise'.

We were showed a small building in the churchyard on the south side of the church of very uncouth and antique fashion but perfect, roofed with stone cut square, and clad with ivy, said to be built by Bryan Bourhoime as a place for confinement or security for his daughter but I think it sounds most unlikely. If Bryan wanted to seclude his daughter there were many lonely islands in the Shannon to build on instead of a populous town as this evidently has once been. The church is supposed to have been built by Donald, King of Limerick, in 1160. The stone for building is very bad, as may be perceived even in the tombstones which are so bad as not to be able to bear a face, or have any letter cut on them. The town is built on the side of a hill - consequently the street is steep and badly paved. There is little worth seeing in Killaloe, but if the traveller takes boat (as we intended) and visits Lough Derg and Portumna he will be highly gratified, the Shannon here forming itself into an extensive sea in many places from 8 to 10 miles across, with beautiful islands (some with ruins) scattered through it. I regret our disappointment of a boat, but having made enquiry of a boatman he answered 'twas too late in the day to set off then but that he and his comrade would take us up next day to Portumna for 5/5d and their dinner. The delay of a day, and no inn to sleep at changed our minds, and we declined: so mounted our horses and kept moving on towards O'Brien's Bridge having the Shannon winding its varied form all the road on our left: we were now in the County Clare. The day changing we pushed on, till we came to O'Briens Bridge (4½ miles). Here we sheltered and had some refreshment a good house and keeps good carriages. The Shannon rolls by the door a fine breadth under a bridge of 10 or 12 arches. We made no delay here as the day still threatened, but rode over the bridge (now in the County Limerick) and through a choice rode through a bog for 2 miles till we came to Castle Connell, a place much celebrated by the virtue of its medical waters and fashionable resort of company. . . .

Monday, 28 August 1797. Rose and a very fine morning. Saw our cold dinner packed and all ready. Having had our breakfast W. S., G. H., self and Lyons embarked on board a small row boat [from Tarbert] that carried us down to deep water where our smack waited for us. We took our flutes. They had a charming effect as we sailed along the winding shore. We passed the forts and saluted them with some loyal air, as also an armed cutter and gun boat which are here fixed to protect the navigation, since the terror of the French. The forts are distant from the town near two miles and are erected upon an isthmus which at high water is separated from the main land. Two of them are mounted with 8 twenty four pounders and 1 six pounder - the highest fort had but four 24 pounders. There are now here 300 men in the forts and camp adjoining consisting of a captain's company of Royal Irish Artillery and the remnant of the Tyrone regiment. In this part the river is 3 miles in breadth. Nothing can exceed the beauty of the surrounding shore. On the opposite side river Kilrush with a number of gun boats make a pleasing object.

We proceeded on our course to the Island of Scattery where we saw the ruins of seven monasatic buildings. In the time of Queen Elizabeth there were eleven, there was also an Episcopal see founded here long before the coming of St Patrick by St Senanus, who enjoined that no woman should set her foot on it and which custom was observed from that period, 'till long after the reformation. There stands adjoining one of them an old round tower very ancient and excessively rude about 120 feet high and - what is not usual in this kind of building - there is a low doorway on the level of the ground. With stooping you may enter it and view the inside which is from top to bottom without floors, but there seems corresponding marks in the wall as if places to lodge timber for flooring distant from each other from 6 to 7 feet and ranging from top to bottom. It is astonishing how this pile stands, having as we were told been rent by thunder, a large chasm made in one side and split from top to bottom, yet it is perfectly perpendicular and now likely to remain many years. The different buildings are not large (and of a worse style than even those at Glandelogh county Wicklow) removed from each other. Some remains of ornamental work is still visible on the stones about the doors. They are very ancient - the tops of the doors are round (not pointed), which my friend G. H. thinks to be the oldest style of Saracenic (or ancient Gothic architecture). The pointed arch he thinks of later date. Upon one of the walls of an old ruin they have erected a communicating flag staff to convey signals which, after the manner of the telegraph, conveys intelligence from Ray Head - the entrance to the Shannon - so on to Scattery, thence to the forts. They have various marks for ships of war, privateers, merchantmen etc. This island contains about 100 acres (is the estate of the Corporation of Limerick and they receive the rents as also of all other islands in the river Shannon) and is in general very fine soil, produces corn, meadows etc., is stocked with cattle, it abounds with rabbits, wild fowl curlew, snipe etc. There are two wretched huts on it, the inhabitants of which I'm told manufacture the wool themselves from the sheeps' back, dye, spin, and weave it into apparel. After rambling about here two or three hours, we embarked a second time and sailed round the island by south west, and passed the mouth of the Shannon where the great Atlantic rolls its waves between two projecting promontories called Bale Sand Banks, and Ray Head.

'Twas under this last point that when the French were meditating a descent on this kingdom (in 1796) two of their ships of war anchored; they sent boats to land for provisions and fresh water which they paid for very civilly. From hence we continued on 'till we came over to Carrig Island in hopes of seeing the castle of that name but the tide being full in, and its being insulated, prevented us coming close to it. However we were near enough to see it was not particularly interesting, re-embarked and so pursued our way home as well as we could, not omitting to do every justice to our cold prag, finding a new appetite with every walk.

Taken from 'Tour in Ireland by John Harden in 1797' (ed.) Michael Quane in *Journal of the Cork Historical and Archaeological Society* (1953, 1954, 1955).

Joseph Woods, Scientific Tour Through Clare, 1809

Joseph Woods, architect and botanist, was born of Quaker stock at Stoke Newington, London in 1776. His family owned an export business but Joseph showing little aptitude for business, devoted himself to the study of design and plants. In July of 1809 in the company of two others, Lewis Dillwyn and William Leach, he landed at Waterford and proceeded to tour round Munster. By 19 July the party had reached Killarney, where Woods decided to stay for reasons of health, while the other two cut short their visit and returned to England. In August he travelled northwards to Limerick where he rested before embarking on a tour of County Clare. Reaching Ennis by stage coach on 5 September, he proceeded up the west coast of Clare through Miltown Malbay, Ennistymon and Kilfenora. He lodged with Mr Lysaght of Ballykeale while examining the antiquities and flora of the Burren. He passed on through Kinvara to Galway and briefly visited Connemara. On his return journey on 20 September he visited the ruins at Kilmacduagh and journeyed on through Crusheen, Quin and Newmarket to Limerick. His tour ended in mid October when he embarked at Waterford for Wales. Woods subsequently studied botany and architecture on the continent. His observations were published in 1828 under the title *Letters of an Architect from France Italy and Greece*. Woods also took an interest in education and assisted in the management of schools in London. He returned to Ireland in June 1840 and inspected the newly formed national schools in a number of counties, including Limerick, Clare and Galway. His comments were published the following year in a pamphlet entitled *Notes on Some of the Schools for the Labouring Classes in Ireland*. His greatest work, however, was a book on the study of plants to which he devoted much of his life: *The Tourist's Flora*, a catalogue of the flowering plants of Britain, France, Germany, Italy and Switzerland, appeared in 1850. He died in 1864 while engaged in a revision of his great work at the age of eighty seven. In his Irish tour of 1809, while he deplores the absence of woodland and the depletion of the natural environment, he has, unfortunately, little to say about the social or economic condition of the people. He is chiefly concerned with topography, the occurrence of rare plants and the recording of ancient buildings of architectural interest.

On the 5th of September [1809] I again left Limerick to make an excursion westward and set out on the stage for Ennis. The road passed through a pleasant country with fine views over the Shannon and Fergus and the rich lands which border both rivers. We overtook the funeral just on leaving the town of a Mr Fitzgerald, a funeral I lamented much in the course of the day as two or three gentlemen to whom I had letters had left home to attend it. We passed through

Newmarket where we changed horses at an inn most charmingly situated.

Beyond this begin those tracts of naked rock which are said to be so abundant in the county of Clare. About Clare there is a great deal of this. It is all limestone. There are patches of green among the worst parts but in some places these are very diminutive. At Ennis no gentlemen to whom I had letters were at home. I therefore amused myself with a walk to Clare Abbey, a pleasing ruin in itself but exciting the usual regret from its nakedness. I afterwards walked into the church yard at Ennis where there were two funerals and several people besides crying over the graves of their deceased relatives. This is a common practice. A new funeral recalls or is supposed to recall the emotions of grief for those who had been not long buried. The church has been a large building but a very small part of it is now used for divine service the rest is unroofed - the east window is singular and has a very fine effect.

After this walk I called in on Mr Weldon to whom I had a letter and by his assistance procured a man and car to carry my baggage and in the morning set off to cross Mount Callan to Miltown. The road offers extensive views over the vale of Fergus but they are naked with only here and there a patch of woods. Mount Callen and the whole country round it is covered with a peat bog. There is a pretty strong chalybeate spring on the ascent. Before reaching the top at a very great distance to the north appear the summits of two distant mountains the smaller conical the larger with a flat top at a distance that implied great elevation. These lofty eminencies always excite my attention - the rarest plants are found on high mountains or their neighbourhood.

Near the highest part of the road is a druidical altar or as it would be called in Wales a cromlech composed of two thick slabs placed on edge parallel to each other and another laid upon them. I got on the top and had an extensive view in three directions.

The road hence to Miltown is all on a peaty soil but most of it very dry. A great quantity of oak and fir is dug up in these bogs, not turned black as is frequently the case, but preserving at a little distance from the surface the appearance and colour of fresh wood. Some native oak still remains in Ireland but the fir formerly the most abundant seems to be totally extirpated. I was informed that in this neighbourhood the trees uniformly bore marks of fire near the roots - the tradition of the country is that they were burnt in order to destroy the wolves and robbers with which they were infested. The whole shore shows evident traces of having been once covered with a forest extending many miles in all directions though now trees will not bear the violence of the western winds.

On the 7th [September 1809] the morning was wet. Miltown is a long Irish mile from the shore to which after breakfast I walked down. It is bordered by sand hills consisting in great measure of broken shells. In one part they are traversed by some old foundations which [are] very slight, but not easily accounted for in such a situation. There is a great deal of the brownstone which is used in the rougher parts of some new buildings but it does not bear the tool so well as the limestone - which is either brought by sea from the isles of Arran or (as the landing is very bad so that nothing can approach the shore in rough weather) by land from Kilfenora. Mr Morony is here building or rather has built a large hotel with excellent baths and there are many lodging houses scattered about. The look of the lodgings is not very tempting but the hotel is well contrived. I confess however that the best accommodations seem to me but poor inducement to spend the summer in so dreary a situation as Miltown Malbay. Mr Morony has taken a great deal of pains to make trees grow. He plants them under the shelter of the wall but as soon as they reach the top they are cut off by the north west winds - all except the tamrisk which flourishes in spite of them but its branches are very brittle. The winds are exceedingly violent and nothing will grow exposed to them not even currants and gooseberries. Vegetables thrive well - Mr Morony showed me some *sea kale* which he had got from Mutton Island where it grows wild but it is not found in any other place.

Large trees are frequently dug up in the bogs here and the timber as before observed seems very little altered - it is the principal, I believe I might say almost the only, timber to be procured, and is used not only in the cottages but in the hotel above mentioned. Pieces of fir generally squared and not very large are sometimes driven on the shore and now and then a stick of mahogany of considerable value is found. A still better prize is a hogshead of claret - such a one once fell to Mr Morony's lot sound and full. It seems to be determined by custom that these drifts belong to the gentleman whose land they first touch and this sometimes is the source of very warm disputes.

On the 8 [September 1809] I set off by the road nearest the coast to Ennistymond. The solid brownstone gravel covered with bog and some copse wood on the side of one long hill. The road does not come down to the shore till we reach Laght [Lahinch] where the rocks are similar to those at Miltown. This village is at the opening of a little valley and enjoys by that mean a more sheltered situation and a pleasanter country than Miltown but this indeed is saying no great deal in its favour nor can much be said. I could procure no breakfast at this place and therefore walked on to Ennistymond where with some difficulty I obtained what I wanted. Ennistymond is seated among little hills with a pretty little river running over its rocky bed. Nature has been favourable but the usual complaint occurs of want of wood. Major O'Brien has a seat on a rocky knoll half surrounded by the river - the opposite shore just at that point is covered with wood and there is wood and an orchard on the same side as the house. These may appear trifles but a person who travels much in Ireland will learn to consider them of importance. The house is admirably placed but as usual very ugly. About noon I reached Kilfenora situated in a limestone valley imperfectly covered with a bed of rich loam.

Kilfenora is a bishops see now united to that of Killaloe. It certainly does not look like a rich bishoprick as the town consists only of a few miserable cabins.

The cathedral is said to be one of the oldest in Ireland. It has not an atom either of the magnificent or the venerable. The tower (if it can be called so) is very singular. There are some respectable looking farmhouses in the neighbourhood but they are all in ruins and replaced only by poor cottages. I had a letter from Mr Morony to Mr Lysaght, (originally Collesaghta) who was good enough to invite me to spend a few days in his house while I looked about the country.

On Saturday I walked to the Castle of Lemineg an ancient seat of the O'Briens. Like several of the Irish castles it consists of an ancient tower with an addition comparatively recent. The addition is a mere shell - the old tower is still inhabited by some poor families. I had imagined in England that the Irish were much in the habit of sacrificing the younger to aggrandise the eldest son. The county of Clare would offer materials of a very different story. It seems always to have been the practice to divide the estates and the event has almost uniformly offered the same illustration of the effect of the practice. A father may bring up the younger son to some profession or employment and may leave the elder in a state to continue the stile and respectability of the family but if he has several sons and divide his property no one can occupy his father's place in society and no one will be content with a lower. Their possessions are soon dissipated and if one more prudent than the rest do not amass instead of dispersing his wealth the estates soon pass into other hands and other names. There is I believe hardly a family in the county which has not experienced *vicissitudes* of this sort. Sir Donough O'Brien, the builder of the additional part of this castle, collected an immense property which was divided in this way and of which only a few fragments remain to his descendants. The situation of the castle is neither beautiful or romantic - among barren looking limestone hills forming the extremity of that singular tract of country called the barony of Burrin. There are three crosses in the neighbourhood of Kilfenora and a few fragments of one or two more castles: within a short distance are some large cromlechs or druids altars as they are here called but these are said to be larger as well as more numerous in Burrin. The most singular remains of antiquity are what are called Danish forts - these are merely thick circular walls of large stones built without cement and perhaps from 50 to 100 feet in diameter. I saw one in Burrin which I think exceeded the latter dimension. They are very numerous about Kilfenora and in the barony. I do not know when I have been more puzzled than I was with the first of these that I met with. The large circle caught my attention. I went to it - I walked round it - I got on the top and walked round it there - I went down on the inside which was nearly filled up with rubbish and again returned to examine the out[side]. It had no door and its form and arrangement seemed to baffle any attempt to guess at its use. Was it ancient? Was it modern? There were indeed bushes on it but nothing that could determine any considerable antiquity. I have since learned that they are well known and are called Danish forts - why I know not and as for their use and date I am now about as much in a puzzle as ever Ledwich says.

A little below Kilfenora is a large turlough and there are several smaller ones in the neighbourhood. These are among the singularities of this country. They are pieces of flat land generally very fine and rich pastures. After continued rain the water rises through some holes or under some holes or under some rocks on the borders and presently converts them into lakes. After a time the water runs off again generally by the same openings. The subterraneous rivers whose overflowings supply the turloughs are the only streams in the limestone country - there is no continued stream of water and no constantly descending valley in which such a stream could run. Mr Lysaght has cut through a hill and drained one of these turloughs at the expense of about £150 and converted a property of £15 per annum into one of about one hundred. Indeed it is impossible to conceive a finer and richer black mould than that of these turloughs or a closer and more luxuriant herbage. How far this latter might suffer by the draining I cannot tell but I conceive that one advantage is the throwing into one hand what before was common to many - for these turloughs are mostly commons and they are the only commons I met with in Ireland.

On the 10th [September 1809] about half past seven I set out to walk to Doolin the nearest place on the coast. At a small elevation we left the limestone and soon had to cross a bog. The road passes by Lisdoon Varna where there is a good chalybeate spring and considering the accommodations very much frequented. Another spring rises near it which appears by the taste to be aluminous. The peasantry wash their ulcers in it and think they receive great benefit. A number of little shining crystals in the bed of earth in which it is found were pointed out to me as alum but as they were perfectly tasteless I concluded them rather to be gypsum. Both these springs were in a deep ravine whose half naked banks exposed a soil rather earth than rock, of a crumbling shale. Many little streams about have in like manner worked themselves deep and narrow beds. There is something romantic in the larger but they want wood - the smaller are so deep and narrow as to be totally inaccessible. I had the good fortune to meet a Mr Perry at the *Spa* who invited me to breakfast with him - a very acceptable offer as it otherwise seemed doubtful whether I should be able to procure even potatoes and sour milk.

As the shore on the north of Doolin is limestone I was in hopes of being able to observe the junction of the different soils but a space of sand hills intervenes between the ranges of hill and prevented my observation. The cliffs to the south of Doolin are the abrupt termination of a range of schistose or rather perhaps of shaly hills. They are very high, black and perpendicular - the edge of the summit is quite sharp and there can be no doubt that it is the continual action of the sea undermining the base and gaining on the shore which preserves their absolute perpendicularity. They are said to be 1100 feet in height - I think they must be more than half that. I was too late for the tide to search for seaweeds on the rocks - but hunted a long while in vain for the maiden hair on the shore and returned from a long and dreary walk without meeting any botanical recompense.

Here and at other places along the coast of Clare the fishermen use a boat they call the *corragh* or *navióg* and the English Irish a *canoe*. A slight frame of wood gives the shape. The rest is a coarse sort of wicker work covered with a horse skin and secured with woollen yarn. The inhabitants assert that they answer better on these rocky and inhospitable shore than any other make. If by chance they should get a hole some sea weed will stop it up. An Irishman will make shift *anyhow*. Sure it has done for their fathers before them! They have no keel and are so light that a man may easily carry one on his shoulders.

At a little after 12 on the 11th [September 1809] I took leave of my hospitable entertainers and began my walk through the barony of Burrin. Who has not heard of the barony of Burrin where there is not water enough to drown a man wood to hang him or earth to bury him and really this is nearer the truth in a tract of country about 14 miles long and 11 broad (Irish measure) than will readily be conceived by a person who has not seen it or some similar country. It is moreover added to enhance the wonder that the stone walls are transparent - it is the custom of the country to build these walls with stones that shall touch if possible only by the angles and this is said to be done under the notion that the wind passing through the intervals will not blow them down. Every field is encumbered by stones which in many almost cover the surface so that it certainly is not from any want of materials.

I only observed one cromlech in the way and that not very large, but there are several of the circular ramparts some of great size. In one of the largest and most perfect the external walls are about 7 feet thick. A cross wall passes through the centre and one half is again sub-divided. I thought that in all of them a similar arrangement might be traced; in many it is very distinct.

A little before reaching Corcomroe is a small ruin rather picturesquely situated on the banks [of] what was when I saw it a small lake. It must be remembered however that there is neither tree nor bush in the neighbourhood and not very frequent vegetation. The abbey of *Corcomroe* is in the same valley but in a still more desolate part. It appears large and I should like to have visited it, but I was tired, it was growing late and I was uncertain where I could meet with any sort of accommodation.

Even the valley here is rock with scarcely any covering but straggling patches of the *Dryas octopetala* - called here the Burrin rose, and I think it might almost be called the Burrin grass it constitutes so large a proportion of the whole vegetation. A variety of *Saxifraga hypnoides* or rather perhaps a distinct species, is abundant through most of the district. Yet Mr Lysaght assured me that great part of the land of the Burrin lets for £2 per acre - its value depends on affording good winter feed for cattle. I endeavoured in vain to find some sort of lodgings at Corcomroe. I therefore proceeded to Kilvara [Kinvara] where bread is sold and where I got a pretty decent bed. . . .

At 5 o'clock on the morning of the 20th [September 1809] I found not the least preparations for my departure and at half past 7 left Galway in a Gort post chaise which I was lucky enough to meet with. A thick mizzling rain prevented all view and I could only see that I still continued in a low limestone country. After breakfast it cleared up a little and engaging a boy and horse to carry my luggage I set off on foot for Kilmacduagh. By the time I arrived there the weather was worse than ever and it was in a thick rain that I observed the following particulars.

Kilmacduagh is seated at a considerable distance from the Burrin mountains. The most conspicuous object is the round tower. It is nearly perfect but the point of its conical roof has been broken away. The section of this cone appears to have been a equilateral triangle, the base exactly coinciding with the upper diameter of the tower. Immediately below this are five windows two opposite each other and 2 in one semicircle and one in the other. Lower down are four other windows at different elevations placed as one might suppose them to be if the tower to be occupied by a staircase. All these are pointed but are not arched. The door which is very considerably elevated is rounded at [the] top but without an arch. . . .

I slept at Crusheen. At these Irish country inns I have usually found myself very comfortable. The accommodations indeed are sometimes but indifferent but the people are civil and attentive and the best of everything they have is at the traveller's service.

After leaving Crusheen the country alters. Small gravelly hills enclose winding sheltered valleys. The shelter however is from the ground not from the wood, of which there is none, but the appearance of nakedness is very much taken off by many well grown hedges. The abbey at Quin stands without a tree and the first view of it is of a number of pointed gables (no fewer than 12 remaining perfect) round a lofty square tower. The usual fault of an Irish abbey is the number of gables. The roofs have in no one instance been hipped into one another but wherever there is a change of direction each roof is terminated by a gable. As we approach, some of the gables and part of the height of the tower are hid by the nearer walls and the parts then combine exceedingly well and offer from different points of view very pleasing compositions. The walls are very perfect and exhibit the plan of [an] Irish abbey to great advantage with its small and lofty tower, the large chapel opening on the south side of the nave, the vaulted rooms round the cloisters and the chambers above them and the cloisters. Quin abbey has also two detached buildings which are not usual appendages and vestiges remain of a wall with four round towers which appear to have been intended for defence.

From Quin I walked to Newmarket - the situation of the inn is remarkably pleasant. The Shannon is seen at some distance between the stems of some trees and over the tops of others and beyond a range of hills whose varied forms and sweeping lines make a very agreeable boundary to the prospect. Trees, rock and meadow occupy the foreground. A little to the left is a small lake in the midst of a rich pasture and beyond it a ruined house half buried in ivy and sheltered by a grove of fine trees exhibiting great beauty and richness of colouring. The accommodations at the inn are very comfortable. The next morning I got into the stage and returned to Limerick.

I had intended in this excursion to have visited Bunratty castle but the weather and other circumstances prevented me. It looks at a distance like four of the common castles of the country united by walls into a large square. On one side the connecting wall appears to be perforated with a large and lofty arch like that at Listowell.

Taken from 'A Scientific Tour Through Munster: the Travels of Joseph Woods, Architect and Botanist, 1809' in *North Munster Antiquarian Journal* 27 (1985), pp 34-42.

William Reed, Rambles in Clare, 1810

William Reed from Thornbury, Gloucestershire, was a cobbler by trade. Born in 1770, his education was limited to reading, writing and arithmetic. With little interest in shoemaking, he spent a wandering life touring England and Scotland. He was disappointed in love, when the father of his intended bride refused her permission to marry. His lady love, however, dying young, left him an annuity, which made him financially secure. Reed settled in Bristol and indulged his passion for books, music and poetry. He had a number of essays and poems published in *The Ponderer*. In September of 1810 he came to Ireland; landing at Cork, he proceeded through Millstreet and Macroom to Killarney. 'Irish towns' he wrote 'invariably commence with a row of cabins; all of which smoke like so many bacon houses, and would disgrace a village of Hottentots'. Although a member of the Baptist congregation, he had a fascination with Catholic ritual and attended several masses at a nunnery in Killarney. Proceeding northwards, he crossed the Shannon and landed in Kilrush. Reed provides a very valuable account of a Mass and funeral he attended in the chapel at Kilrush. Agricultural matters also interested him. 'The Irish farmer' he declared 'is less to be envied than the common beggar, to make his payments good and keep himself from gaol, he is obliged to work as a slave and half starve himself and his family'. Leaving Clare, Reed travelled to Limerick and eventually embarked at Dublin for England. He visited Guernsey in 1813 and shortly after his return died at Bristol. His Irish tour, a rare and valuable work, was published posthumously in 1815; only fifty copies were printed.

It was my intention to proceed to Ballylongford, for the purpose of getting a conveyance to Limerick in one of the turf-boats, but was persuaded to cross the river to Kilrush, by a young man who overtook me on the road, telling me that I should more readily succeed at the latter place. At Carrick we found a small group of labourers just ready to embark in a crazy fishing skiff; and as it stood about one hundred yards from the shore, we were all huddled into a machine exactly like a baker's dough-tub, exposing ourselves to no inconsiderable danger in this prefatory voyage to gain the vessel. It blew a heavy gale, and the water, which is here three leagues wide, became so extremely agitated as to strike terror into the hearts of the passengers, one of whom cried and prayed, but to which of the saints I have now forgotten, believing his last hour was come. For myself, though among the most courageous on board, I expected in cutting the channel we should be overset. In a better vessel I should have very much enjoyed the scene. It was extremely wild and picturesque. The billows, which were of a light and almost transparent green colour, rose into mountains, and were also variegated with broken patches of thin white foam, that with every motion of the water assumed some new and strange configuration. It bore some resemblance to a Scottish landscape at the close of winter, where hills rise behind hills, as far as the eye can reach, and the last vestiges of snow are melting and vanishing from the sight.

In this excursion we passed under the shores of Scattery, a small but celebrated island. In ancient times it was much resorted to for religious purposes. Saint Seanus, who I believe was the immediate successor of St Patrick, chose this sequestered spot for the asylum of his old age. There are on this island a few farm-houses, and a round tower, rising to the height of one hundred and twenty feet, which is said to have been a species of ecclesiastical architecture peculiar to this country. I have seen many of them in the western parts of Ireland, but they appear to me more like places of military observation than religious temples. Although this place does not, I should think, contain more than one hundred and twenty acres of land, there are still to be seen the ruins of seven churches, which are said to have grown up spontaneously in one night, like mushrooms, not at the sound of a magician's flute, but through the powerful intercession of the saint. The present inhabitants of the country believe these tales of superstition, and there are no tales too absurd for them to believe.

Kilrush is a neat little and greatly improving seaport-town on the shores of the Shannon, in the county of Clare; and resting there the whole of the following day, it being the sabbath, I had an opportunity of witnessing a circumstance or two which, to a stranger, had some novelty in them.

I went to mass, but found the chapel so crowded as not to be able to proceed farther than the door. The court was also full of people; some of whom were brought, on account of their age or infirmities, in little dog-carts and wheel-barrows, counting and conning their bead-strings with all the care and punctuality of a school-boy casting up his pounds, shillings and pence. There was also among this grotesque assembly a blind woman, singing ballads in the Irish language, and who to all appearance had the power of exciting more attention than charity. The holy water was contained in a common washing-tub on the outside of the door. I, though a Protestant, was rather shocked at this apparent vulgarity. Between the hours of mass, and after it is finally over, every trace of the sabbath is completely expunged. The people have then recourse to a variety of games and sports, among which, dancing to the bagpipe is a common amusement. This sudden transition from the solemnities of devotion to the frivolities of an Irish jig, to say nothing of its immorality, appeared to me a very gross violation of good taste and common sense, and more closely resembled the manners of monkeys than of men. The very same mortals who at twelve o'clock most devoutly sprinkle themselves with holy water on the outside, will, before it strikes one, as devoutly bathe their inside with whiskey. Harnessed with external forms and ceremonies, they toil by fits and starts, like a horse in a mill, dreaming that they go onward, when, alas! they are only going round. The priesthood, in the country at least, take no pains to dissolve this fatal enchantment, being either too lazy or too ignorant for its accomplishment. . . .

At Kilrush, I had another opportunity of being a spectator of the extravagances of an Irish funeral. The deceased was a medical man, young and skilful in his profession, and alike distinguished for the elegance of his person and the courtesy of his manners. Only a week previously he was in full health; but he was now fallen to the dust, and the subject of the most poignant and general regret. When the corpse was about to be removed from the house, his wife, children and friends, amidst the howlings of the women who attended, detained it so long, that the undertakers were at last obliged to seize their charge by actual violence. Every thing being now adjusted for departure, the sash was thrown up, and the females of the family, with looks of agony, sent forth such a wild and piercing scream, that if Stoicism had heard it, she must have stood still and wept.

As the funeral procession is generally composed of a large and motley group of persons, it not infrequently happens, on account of some trifling circumstance, that a quarrel ensues on the road, and the passive solemnities of death are converted into a lively field of battle. When the place of interment has been the subject of dispute, the coffin has sometimes been demolished in the scuffle, and the corpse carried away in triumph by the victorious party, to their favourite place of burial. Some difference arose on the present occasion; but for once the mourners had the good manners, whilst on their sorrowful journey, to suppress the ardour of their resentment. This apparent sense of decorum was however of short duration, for when they returned to town in the evening, the flame broke out with the greater violence for having been pent up, and a general engagement took place, with sticks and with stones, in which many of the combatants were felled to the ground, and carried home to their friends dreadfully wounded. The person at whose house I lodged, had his head laid open in several places, and a relative of mine host was said to be dying through loss of blood. I went to see this unhappy man, and found him weltering in his gore and raving with delirium. His temporal artery had been opened by the stroke of a poker. The neighbouring surgeon was sent for to close the wound; but he was found sprawling before the fire on the carpet, in a most helpless state of intoxication. Another of the profession was now applied to, who resided at the other end of the town; but this son of Æsculapius was imitating the example of his fallen brother with all possible haste, in company with an old friar, and could not on any account be prevailed upon to leave his cheerful companion of the battle.

On the following morning I sailed round the Island of the Seven Churches. The Shannon is a river of great beauty and grandeur, and maintains its noble character from the ocean to Limerick. There are a variety of fine islands in its course, richly cultivated; and its shores are every where adorned with villages and elegant villas, situated at the foot of mountains covered with herds and flocks, and sheltered by groves of the richest verdure.

Taken from *Remains of William Reed late of Thornbury; including Rambles in Ireland with other composition in prose*, ed., by Rev John Evans (London 1815), pp 36-42.

Joseph Lancaster,
A Brief Visit to Ennis, 1812

The English educator Joseph Lancaster was one of the developers of the monotorial system of education a system which sought to provide inexpensive mass education, for the poor. While still in his teens, Lancaster had begun teaching children in London. No system of public education existed and as a result large numbers flocked to his schools. To deal with the influx Lancaster developed a system, whereby a monitor or advanced pupil was placed in charge of every ten children. Lancaster's boast was that he could teach a thousand children in a class and apparently often did. He wrote widely on the subject and raised funds to support his work. Eventually 30,000 pupils were enrolled in thirty five schools in Britain. Lancaster came to Ireland for a brief tour in the winter of 1811-12. He lectured in the main urban centres and on the invitation of Sir Edward O'Brien of Dromoland came to Ennis, where he found a receptive audience for his views. A committee was set up, composed both of Catholics and Protestants, for the establishment of a Lancastrian school. The Catholic bishop of Killaloe, James O'Shaughnessy, was a supporter of the project and before long two schools were in operation, one in Ennis and the other at Corofin. Lancaster eventually went bankrupt and in 1818 emigrated to the United States. He established schools in several American cities before again overspending. He died in 1838 at the age of fifty. Lancastrian schools were the first serious attempt to provide a basic education for all children in Clare regardless of religious persuasion.

In passing through Ireland my whole soul within me was often moved for the poor. The children are interesting children; but they need our help for they are poor indeed.

At the special desire of Sir Edward O'Brien, Bart. of Dromoland, (one of these few 'owners of the soil' who can spend an ample fortune in Ireland, promoting agriculture and manufactures, in ameliorating the condition of his tenantry, and giving employment to the poor.) I visited Ennis and lectured to 400 persons in this populous place, receiving from them all the attention and politeness for which the inhabitants of that town are distinguished.

It was at the close of the lecture of Ennis, for the first time, I expressed my love of Ireland. . . The bursts of applause were reiterated and indescribable. Protestants of that place told me afterwards, they never knew such a cementing opportunity in the place during their lives. I had the happiness of seeing a Dean of the

Roman Catholic church, venerated for his years and a man much esteemed, lifting up his hands over me and praying for blessings on my head and on my progress, as if he had never heard of an heretic being in the world. These instances of liberality cheered my mind to arduous labour, lightened the fatigue of my exertions and literally helped to make hard things easy and rough ways smooth.

A school is to be immediately established in Ennis; at a meeting of the gentry of the county held during the assizes under the title of 'Friends to the Lancastrian System'; a sum was raised by subscriptions, amounting to £250; and an annual grant amounting to £36, have been ensured for the support of the institution.

Sir Edward and Lady O'Brien have a Lancastrian school in great perfection at Dromoland, and I have the further pleasure to add, that a late *Ennis Chronicle* acknowledges the receipt of 'a sum of £50 by the Rev Fredrick Blood, from Sir Edward O'Brien, for assisting the establishment of a Lancastrian school in the village of Corrofin'. The long room over the market house, (the property of Sir Edward,) is to be made the theatre of instruction; and the patriotic Baronet has, in addition, given an annuity of £10 to assist the maintenance of a school master.

Taken from Joseph Lancaster, *A Brief Report of a Tour in Ireland in the Winter of 1811-12* (Tooting 1812), pp 11-12.

Rev James Hall, Tour of East Clare, 1812.

James Hall of Walthamstow, Essex, was a native of Clackmannan, Scotland. Educated at the University of St Andrews, he came to Ireland in 1812 for the purpose of exploring the interior and least-known parts of the country. Little, unfortunately, is known about him. He had previous experience of travel writing because in 1807 he published a work entitled *Travels in Scotland by an Unusual Route, with a Trip to the Orkneys and Hebrides*. Hall served as chaplain to the Earl of Caithness which explains his special interest in northern Scotland. In 1812 he made a comprehensive tour of Ireland visiting practically every county in the country. He was preoccupied with economic improvement and comments at length on social customs and living conditions. He observed Ireland at its best, enjoying the boom years of the Napoleonic wars before the economic collapse of 1815. Hall was among the first to discuss the practical advantages of telegraphic communications between Ireland and England. Being a committed unionist he was convinced of the benefits that would accrue to Ireland from the Union with Britain. In keeping with his political viewpoint, he published in 1814 a pamphlet entitled *The Blessings of Liberty and Peace: or the Excellence of the British Constitution*.

When I left Limerick, and was proceeding through the county of Clare, to Killaloe, my next resting-place, I found a countryman sitting by the way-side, counting his rosary. After he had gone round it three times, and said some Pater-Nosters and Ave-Marias, he told me that he had counted it fifteen times every day, for many years; and trusted in God, that nothing would ever happen which would prevent him from performing a duty so important. As the man could not read, and the beads in his rosary, by being of a more than ordinary size, called up to his mind certain of the patriarchs, prophets, and apostles, I advised him to be careful in imitating the piety and virtue of these; if he wished to be happy either here or hereafter. On giving him this advice he said he would think of it, but must consult the priest, who had, as he termed it, his soul in keeping.

At Donoss, between O'Brien's bridge and Limerick, the Rev Mr Massy, the rector, has tithes to the amount of seven hundred pounds a-year; while the salary of the schoolmaster is only two pounds. Some parishes in the interior, as well as the south of Ireland, have neither school nor schoolmaster. Where parishes have a schoolmaster, they have often neither house nor garden. This circumstance, and the little encouragement otherwise given to school-masters, naturally damps their ardour, compels them to betake themselves to other pursuits, and bestow little trouble on the improvement of their scholars. Proceeding up the banks of the Shannon, I arrived at Killaloe which the Hon. Robt. Tottenham, brother to Lord Loftus, is bishop. The cathedral is small, without any organ, and there is generally no person either to instruct the clergy, or the people, except the Rev Mr Allan, who is the bishop's curate, and who keeps a school. It is no uncommon thing in Ireland to see cathedral churches without an organ. In the Archbishop of Cashel's church, it seems, there is none. The bishop here, however, who has a noble palace in the midst of a park, containing above two hundred acres of excellent land, is extremely humane. When a blind man came to him, soon after he was made bishop, to ask something, the bishop gave him a guinea, desiring him to come every month, and he would get the half of that sum. When the bishop heard that a poor man had lost his cow, he sent him seven guineas to buy another; that being the value of the one that died: and, having learned that many of the poor had not a sufficient number of blankets to cover them in cold weather, he sent and bought a hundred to be distributed among them.

The late bishop erected a school of industry for poor children here; and, among other things, paid a school-master to teach the Roman Catholics their own catechism. The present bishop continues the salary.

There belong to the bishopric a dean, archdeacon, vicar-general, chancellor, and many others, who all receive considerable revenues from it; but who are scarcely ever seen here, except when they come to receive the money. One item of the bishop's income is the tenth of the eels caught in the river, at Killaloe.

Dr Parker, rector of Castleton, who lives on the banks of the Shannon, has a beautiful house and farm on a long lease, and a right, at the end of it, for any improvements whatever that may be made. The doctor, who gives employment to many, in draining, planting, inclosing, levelling, building, and the like, will (which is said to be his object) be able to give in an account, at the end of the lease, equivalent, if not greater than the whole value of the farm.

While standing, not far from Killaloe, observing a stout young fellow driving out manure in baskets on a horse, and a young woman stooping and spreading it with her hands, Major P--- came up, with his lady and parasol, in a gig; and, with much complaisance, entered into conversation with me. But, when I hinted, among other improvements in each county, the propriety of raising a subscription to buy something with prongs for spreading the manure, and preventing women from the humiliating employment of doing it with their hands, and said I was certain that every feeling person would be glad to give less or more, the Major, who has extensive estates in this corner, sneaked off, without saying a word.

A few miles from Killaloe, on my way to Woodford, I found high words, which ended in blows, between three men with some pigs and cows, on the one side, and two men on the other. The three men were the tithe-proctor and his assistants, who were carrying cows, calves, pigs, and the like, to the pound-park of the parish; and the two other were the sons of tenants in the vicinity, who would not permit the tithe-proctor to carry off the cow of a widow in their neighbourhood, who had got a few shillings in arrear to the parson.

In every parish there is a pound-park, to which they take the cows, pigs, calves, and the like, of those who are in arrear for tithes. In eight days after the cattle have been in pound, if the owner do not come and relieve them, by paying the tithe and other expenses, the cow, or whatever it may be, is sold to the highest bidder; and the balance, if any, after paying what had been due, and all expenses, is given to the person to whom the animal, or thing, belonged. There is generally also a pound-park in the parish for the landholders; and middle-men, or receivers, do the same when there happens to be any arrear of rent. One of the young men, opposing the tithe-proctor, had his head tied up, which had been bruised in defending the widow's cow. The young man argued that the widow, though industrious, was poor; that she had a number of children to support; that she had no money, and only that cow to give them milk; and that the rector, who has many hundred pounds a-year for doing nothing, was more able to want the few shillings than the widow was to pay them. While I was speaking to the tithe-proctor in behalf of the poor widow, the young man went off with the cow; nobody preventing him. . . .

For about twenty miles above Killaloe, the Shannon forms itself into a lake, in some places from two to three miles broad. The ground rising gradually from its banks gives a beautiful variety to the country all around.

At Mount Shannon, where was once a linen-factory, the inhabitants are all Presbyterians. The manufactory was, however, some time ago, given up, and the village is going to ruins; he who set it going, being dead, and the property squandered by his son and heir.

About half way between Mount Shannon and Woodford, to which I next directed my course, there being no public-house near, and the evening approaching; at the recommendation of a priest, with whom I fell in, I put up at a farmer's near the road, who has a numerous family. When the mistress of the house, who was extremely hospitable, showed me where I was to sleep, I found three beds in the room, and, in one of them, two fine young women, her daughters, fast asleep. Having appointed me what she termed her best bed, she went away. The good woman and her husband, however, came soon after, and occupied the one next to that in which I lay. Being good Catholics, and seemingly not bad Christians, before they lay down, each of them muttered some Latin prayers, crossing their forehead, breast, and farther down, several times, both at the beginning and end of each prayer.

In the morning, when I awoke, the good man and his wife were gone, as were also the two young women; but a beautiful girl, another daughter, about seventeen or eighteen, who had been at a wake in the vicinity a part of the night, lay on the bed in which her sisters had been. Having awoke while I was shaving myself, she said, 'Good morning, Sir'; begged to know whether I wished for a little hot water or anything, and sat up in bed a considerable time, repeatedly enquiring if she could be of any use. And such is the innocence and simplicity among the people in this part of the country, that she felt no shame; nor seemed to think there was either impropriety or danger in being in bed in the same room with a man she had never seen, except a few minutes at supper in the evening.

On enquiring what they did at the wakes? she told me, while she lay a-bed, that some go there with their faces blacked, and men in women's clothes; that various amusements are introduced, even where they have no whiskey. At one of these amusements, which they call, *mending the old coat*, she told me that a coat is spread on the floor, and that two persons, a young man and woman, sit down, and pretend to mend it, while the rest are dancing in a ring around them, wheeling sometimes one way, and sometimes another. At length, the young man and woman get up, then kiss, and join in the dance; that another couple sit down and do the same; and so on, till all have mended the old coat.

Though they have no manner of acquaintance, or relationship to the dead person, young people, she told me, sometimes come a dozen miles to a wake. The priest, having given to the dead the extreme-unction, and prayed for the repose of the soul; they think that all will be well with their departed friend, and that grief would be improper. Hunt the slipper, and blind-man's-buff, are also common amusements. On some occasions, where there is plenty of whiskey, the singing and music stop, and the old women set up a howling for the dead in general; at which, if they please, young women may learn to howl.

Extracts taken from Rev James Hall, *Tour through Ireland*, 2 vols., (London 1813), i, pp. 315-24.

John Curwen, Observation on Agriculture, 1813

John Christian Curwen came from a Manx family. On his marriage to an heiress he adopted the surname Curwen. He represented the constituency of Carlise and Cumberland in parliament for close on forty years. A pioneering agriculturist, he was awarded the silver medal of the Irish Farming Society. The occasion of his Irish tour was Curwen's retirement from parliament; he wished to divert his thoughts from England and by observing conditions in Ireland suggest means by which living standards might be improved. He arrived from Scotland in the company of a Manx lawyer in August 1813. Bringing their own carriage and coachman, the party travelled round the country visiting such well known tourist attractions as the Giant's Causeway and the Lakes of Killarney. Curwen was passionately interested in agriculture and much of his tour is taken up with farming methods, crop yields and the reliance on potatoes. Coming from Galway, Curwen intended to visit the ruins at Kilmacduagh, but finding the road could not accommodate his carriage he proceeded on the turnpike to Ennis. His favourable comments on the neatness and opulence of the county town contrasts sharply with the views of travellers twenty years later. In dairying he noted the absence of cheese making and the dominance of butter. Grassland, reflecting the continuing prosperity, commanded rents four times the amount recorded by Arthur Young in 1778. Indeed Curwen's whole work appears to have been inspired by Young's tour and regular comparisons are made between the state of agriculture in 1813 and as it was recorded by Young thirty five years previously.

The country, for some little distance before we arrive at Ennis, is broken into a variety of hills, on which the crops appeared to be very good. The immediate approach to the town is delightful; every cabin has its garden, and these we were gratified in seeing highly cultivated. Such an appearance of comfort we had not before witnessed. The town is celebrated for its onions, the growth of which is much attended to, and they are sent to other parts of Ireland from this neighbourhood. There seems to be also a great profusion of the common fruits. I do not know that I was ever more pleased with the entrance to any town. In itself, Ennis is tolerably neat, and has a thriving appearance; it has a communication by water with the Shannon, at the distance of two miles. The remains of the abbey, in the best style of architecture of any Gothic building we had yet seen, we had an opportunity of observing at [Ennis]. Within two miles of the town is the castle of [Clare]; as a source of influence to government, the appointments about it may have utility to them, but it would be difficult to discover any other.

The recent act against illicit distillation, imposing fines on the parishes where private stills are discovered, has created much discontent. The people cannot be reconciled to sugar whiskey - potcheene is their darling liquor. We offered some whiskey to a fruit woman, which she refused; exclaiming 'The country was in danger of being poisoned by the abominable parliament combustible stuff' - but as soon as she understood it to be real honest potcheene, she received it with great courtesy. On the whole the comparative comfort which prevades all classes here makes Ennis one of the most interesting little places we have yet seen.

The first turnpikes we have met with are between this town and Gort; and I must say, at the same time, that in the three hundred miles we have travelled, this is among the worst specimens of road we have encountered. A serious evil attends the rearing of cabins close to the high roads. The children make them their play-ground, and heap on them numbers of stones in various directions, so as to require great attention in driving, to avoid them. The inconvenience is especially found as the day closes, - it is incumbent on the surveyors of the highways, or the persons charged with the care of them, to have this nuisance removed.

Limerick, Sept. 8, 1813. In the neighbourhood of Ennis there are many great dairy-farms; and though there did not appear to be any impediment to the making of good cheese, the produce from the cows was almost exclusively employed in making butter. No attention at present is paid to the selection of stock, the greater proportion of the milch cows being from the Kerry breed, which are very neat small animals, much resembling the Kylo, though the land on which they depasture is admirable, and equal to sustain the largest species of cattle.

Sir Edward O'Brian's beautiful seat of Dromoland is about four miles from Ennis. The house seems modern; great additions have lately been made to the pleasure grounds, and the plantations are extensive over the domain, which is happily broken into the great inequality of surface. Sir Edward farms on a large scale; last year he grew one hundred and twenty acres of wheat, and his green crops bore a good proportion to those of his grain. One hundred head of oxen are fed annually for market, besides a great number of sheep. A grass farm adjoining his residence is now to be let; the rent demanded is six guineas per acre, which is four times as much rent as Mr A. Young speaks of in the year 1778. I certainly do not know of a soil superior in quality: as a proof of the value in which it is held, a level has been driven in limestone for a considerable way in order to drain a few acres of it, which are liable to be flooded.

Great improvements are making in the road near Dromoland, and a large cut is nearly completed, which will considerably reduce the ascent of the hill. We stopped to take a view of the mode in which the work proceeded, by a number of labourers, under the super-intendance of a manager. It was really farcical to observe half a dozen stout fellows loading a car, each not lifting, at any time, more than five pounds weight in their shovels; two English labourers would have done more in the same time than all six. The poor fellows petitioned very earnestly for tobacco; but they would have been much affronted to have had it supposed they were capable of begging. Their wages were thirteen pence a day.

As there was no other place where our horses could be fed, we breakfasted at Newmarket, though but eight miles from Ennis. The country we had passed through was very rich and beautiful, and the inn at Newmarket neat and orderly.

The new road to Limerick is quiet flat, and but twelve miles; the old one fourteen, and very hilly. We were led by the absence of guide posts into the old road, and while our distressed horses suffered by climbing over Clonnelly hill, we became gratified by a noble prospect of the Shannon, from Limerick to Foyle's Island, at the distance of nearly thirty miles. At the foot of the hill is Bonnelly the seat of the O'Brians, the Princes of Thomond.

Meadow land here is from six to seven pounds an acre: the grass is sold and built into hay by the purchaser, who pikes it on the ground, and there it remains until it is paid for; this arrangement accounts for our seeing so much unstacked. Indeed the general management in matters of husbandry is very wretched. Nothing can be less excusable than the neglected state of the grounds within four miles of Limerick, notwithstanding the excessive price at which they are rented. The potatoes are cultivated in lazy beds of an undue proportional width, which must be highly prejudicial to the crop, while the want of thatching to the ricks of grain must subject the farmers to loss, against which the enormous rents and small produce might be supposed to be a sufficient guarantee.

The hills which extend from Clonnelly to Limerick were covered with coppice wood. We found the peasantry busily employed in threshing out their grain in the open fields: their cabins seemed to be extremely poor and wretched; and, if I am correct in estimating the general poverty of the inhabitants by the appearance of the sex, whose hair was no longer the object of their attention, but hung in disfiguring disorder and neglect, I should conclude the people of these southern districts to suffer more privations than those in the north.

Taken from J. C. Curwen, *Observations on the State of Ireland, Principally Directed to its Agriculture and Rural Population; In a series of Letters Written on a Tour Through that Country*, 2 vols. (London 1818), i, pp 361-7.

John Trotter, A Walk through County Clare, 1817

The aptly named John Bernard Trotter conducted a walking tour of Clare in 1817, just at the time when the economic recession associated with the ending of the French wars began to bite and following the widespread failure of the potato crop in 1816. Trotter, born in County Down in 1775, was a son of a Protestant clergyman; he was educated first at Downpatrick Grammar School and later at Trinity College Dublin where he graduated a B.A. in 1795. He subsequently travelled to London and befriended the Whig statesman and leader of the opposition Charles James Fox. Fox espoused many liberal causes including reform of parliament, repeal of the penal laws and the abolition of slavery. Trotter's increasing interest in politics became apparent when in 1799 he published a pamphlet entitled *An Investigation of the Legality and Validity of a Union*. He was called to the Irish bar in 1802 and in the same year accompanied Fox to Paris following the conclusion of the peace of Amiens. On Fox's appointment as foreign secretary in the wartime 'ministry of all talents', 1806, Trotter became his private secretary. Fox, however, died a few months later and Trotter returned to Ireland. In 1808 he published *A Letter to Lord Southwell on the Catholic Question*. In later life Trotter lived in poverty and his misfortunes appeared to affect the balance of his mind. In 1813 he was arrested for debt and lodged in the debtors prison in Wexford. The previous year he had begun a series of letters on a walking tour of Ireland. On his release from jail he continued with his letter writing and completed walking tours in 1814 and 1817. He died destitute at Cork, September 1818. Trotter's tour of Clare is of interest principally because of his method of travel. Walking allowed him to visit villages, observe conditions and interact with people in a way not possible for the mounted or horse-drawn traveller.

This morning we left the memorable city of Limerick. . . The day proved very fine, and the harvest went on merrily in every field. We saw many fine crops of wheat and oats. Reaping and hay-making employed every busy hand, and the joyous laugh, and jocund Irish song, frequently struck our ears. We did not perceive as much flax as we wished. . . Directed to avoid the six-mile bridge-road, we turned to the left in our progress to Newmarket, and from an eminence beheld, at the end of a great plain, chiefly fine meadow, Bunratty-castle, an ancient seat of the O'Briens. . . Hay-making proceeded on all sides, as we approached the castle, and caused a very cheerful appearance in its vicinity. We were very politely permitted, by Mr Stoddert, who resides in it, to view the interior, which is exceedingly venerable. A great hall, or dining-room, arched with stone, in a very perfect manner, is still quite entire. . . .

At Newmarket we discovered an excellent small inn, beautifully situated at the extremity of the village. We met at it good accommodation of every kind, and a respectable hostess and her daughter, who used every effort to render us comfortable, and to give and procure for us every possible information. As these are attentions pedestrians do not always receive at the head inns in Ireland, they were the more agreeable to us.

Though the unrivalled beauties of the way had so much pleased us, a walk of sixteen or seventeen Irish miles did not fail to be felt, and made the reception we met with from Mrs Serjeant, our worthy landlady, very welcome. . . A refreshing repose, in excellent beds, made us quite alert the succeeding morning. In dressing I perceived, for the first time, and at the stables of our inn, a kind of horse-police, facetiously called, by the Irish - *Peelers*, from the secretary's name who has introduced them, in hope of tranquillizing a country which, alas! my dear L., is already but too much burdened by expensive establishments, and whose agriculture can scarcely bear two years more the rents and imposts it is loaded with! These police are paid by the baronies, or parishes, where they are quartered, in case of turbulence; and the expense, we are told, in some places, amounts to eight or ten shillings the acre. They have been of considerable service, it is said, in several parts of this county, and if the objection as to laying another burthen on the land could be avoided, might for some time be a valuable and unexceptionable aid to the magistrates. I apprehend, such expensive establishments must go a great way to absorb revenue, and can no more restrain a great population than the chains Xerxes ordered to be thrown into the sea could the Hellespont. The expense of one of these flying corps of Peelers is not less than £4,000 in a district annually. . . .

Newmarket on Fergus (which being prettily seated on an inlet of the Shannon, is so called) has suffered dreadfully from the fever. At this town, and in its neighbourhood, it has, until this last week, raged like a plague. 'We knew not,' said our pleasing and intelligent guide, Mrs ---, 'in the morning, of what death we should hear; or, at night, who could be said to lie down in safety. Funerals were frequent, and mourning in every house. But when we were almost in despair, the hand of God arrested this malady, and we are now tolerably free from it.'

The death of Miss Colpoys, a most amiable and benevolent young lady, residing near Newmarket, has been universally lamented. She caught this direful fever by ministering to the wants of the poor, and giving them food with her own hands. . . The Catholic bishop, who is a most worthy and dignified character, near this, has just lost, by the same cruel disease, a beloved nephew, of high respectability, and the father of a young family. When such characters fall, what must be the fate of the wretched inhabitants of the mud-walled cottages we have seen in Clare! And in and near this village! It is from such abodes of poverty that this pestilence emanates - it is in them it lurks - and from their inmates is infection so often personally caught. . . .

After viewing Mr Palmer's house and gardens, we took leave of the respectable family at our inn. . . We very soon reached the beautiful lodge and entrance to Dromoland, the noble seat of Sir Edward O'Brien, a lineal descendant of the royal house of O'Brien. The lodge is one of the best taste and chastest execution we have seen, well-suiting the grandeur of Dromoland. From thence the avenue sweeps through extensive grounds and woods to the house. This venerable mansion stands on a gentle eminence, surrounded by noble trees, and overlooks a large and beautiful lake beneath the windows. . . The ancient appearance of the mansion-house, on which ivy had thrown here and there its leaves of glossy-green, was pleasing to us, as being far superior to that of many modern buildings. Sir Edward O'Brien received us with great politeness. The interior of the house is noble, and many good paintings very much gratified us. . . .

Sir Edward and Lady O'Brien treated us with hospitality peculiarly pleasing to pedestrians, who find the occasional charms of refined conversation and manners the best refreshment on their toilsome and devious way. Sir Edward directed us himself to the best path through his fine demesnes, and we left Dromoland, pleased with every scene, and gratified by every moment we had enjoyed there. Sir Edward O'Brien is a good agriculturist, without too much devoting himself to farming, and by his residence employs many. In the late famine, this family opened wide the stores of private bounty.

We hasten from this princely place on our way to Quin Abbey, a very few miles distant. Our walk led us, by private roads, along the small river of Quin, to this ancient ruin. We were astonished at beholding it. Quin Abbey is one of the most perfect ruins in Ireland, and of wonderful beauty. Its tower, cloisters, and aisles, deserve great attention. There we saw an incredible quantity of bones and skulls, long blanched by time's resistless hand - they were piled in great quantities in the abbey. . . How many busy and thinking beings were these whitened fragments of mortality once! Some devoted to war, some to religion, some to commerce, or agriculture! - all now silent. . . .

When we visit the abbey of Quin you will not be surprised at these thoughts. It is really very grand, and its aisles reminded us of Westminister Abbey. A new church is building near it, however, which will somewhat injure the lonely and grand picturesque of this most venerable scene. The village near the Abbey is wretched; the cabins very poor.

Leaving the abbey of Quin, we proceeded along a wild road, and as the day improved, saw many distant mountains. There is great poverty in Clare, and the miserable attempt to sell unlicensed spirits in their mud-cottages scarcely excites displeasure; in a country where there is no trade, where agriculture is over-whelmed, and the people too numerous, nature struggles to procure some livelihood, and labour and fatigue seeks some humble refreshment. . . .

In the evening we stopped at a village called Spancer Hill. There the houses are poor, but a few neatly thatched ones are respectable. We smiled to exchange the splendid scene of Dromoland, in a few hours, for the very humble reception and fare of Spancer Hill. . . .

Spancer Hill is encompassed by singular round hills, but the country wants wood, and the land is too dear to permit improvement. They commonly give six guineas per acre for their potato-ground. On leaving this village, the evening sun broke out in full splendour, lighted every hill and small lake in this picturesque country, and, penetrating the humble cottage, beamed on the scanty furniture within. The Clare people are civil and friendly, and give every information or direction they could. The high rents afflict them in a considerable manner, and in their conversation we perceived a kind of despair, mingled with the hope that landlords and great farmers must yield the vain pretension of holding them up at war-rates. How happy for Ireland, if all had brought them down promptly, and with a good grace, when the markets fell. . . .

Many landlords have thought it a good expedient to take cattle, or any commodity tenants may have, in lieu of rent they cannot get. This must strip every farm of stock, and ruin the tenant for the ensuing year.

On our way the robin sung his evening lay in the hedge, and the narrow rural road we followed became very pleasing. We passed Moriarty [Moyriesk], a handsome wooded place of Major Macnamara's, and had a distant view of Ennis. As the evening fast closed upon us we reached an irregular but beautiful lake, on a distant bank of which stood a small ruined castle. The rural toils of the day were ending, and the cottagers everywhere bringing home cattle, or plying little household cares at their doors. . . .

As we grew fatigued we saw, with pleasure, the small village of Crusheen, situated in Inchieronan Lake. We were now entering Connaught (according to its last division), and began to perceive one of its peculiarities and great beauties - the picturesque and frequent lakes scattered through it. We had seen several this day. We found an old ruined house converted into a tolerable inn, at Crusheen, and met great civility, an humble supper, and very clean good beds.

Extracts taken from John Bernard Trotter *Walks through Ireland in the years 1812, 1814 and 1817* (London 1819) pp 374-95.

George Calladine, Diary of a Colour-Sergeant, 1828

The diary of George Calladine provides a unique insight into the life of the common soldier in Ireland in the early nineteenth century. Calladine, of Wimeswould, Leicester, was the son of a gardener. His father died when he was young and in his teens he became apprenticed to a framework knitter. Tiring of that he joined the Derbyshire Militia in 1810, where his two brothers had formerly enlisted, and quickly progressed to the 19th Foot, a regiment of the line. His regiment was posted to Ceylon in 1814 and after a six month sea voyage disembarked at Colombo, where they assisted in the suppression of a revolt. Returning to England the regiment was ordered to Ireland in 1821. Calladine, accompanied by his wife and children, was stationed in army barracks mainly in the south of Ireland. The regiment marched regularly from one depôt to another and in this way Calladine got to know the country well. He had the opportunity of travelling to the West Indies in 1826 but preferred to remain in Ireland as a hospital sergeant. While stationed at Nenagh in 1836, Mrs Calladine bore him two fine children, a boy and a girl. However, the rigours of army life ensured that neither infant survived longer than eight months. At Kilmainham Hospital in 1837, Calladine was discharged from the army on a pension of 2s. 1½d. per day after twenty seven years service. He returned to Derby where he found employment as master of a workhouse. Of the thirteen children born to his wife, eleven died in infancy, only two surviving into adulthood. Calladine died in 1876 aged eighty three, his wife having predeceased him by thirty years.

We now began to expect the route, but we did not move until the 29th October [1828], when we marched for Clare Castle, near Ennis, the county town of Clare.

In passing through Cork, which was our first day's stage, we saw a young man belonging to the 70th Regiment, cousin to my wife, named Reading, who had lately enlisted and joined the regiment from England. He appeared a steady young man, and had a wife and child. We passed Buttevant, Mallow, Chareville, Bruff, and Limerick, being our old road over again, which I do not approve of. I would much rather that every march we had should be in a different direction, so that we would have an opportunity of seeing more of the country.

We had now got into a part which had lately been the scenes of the great Dan's electioneering concern, when he was ousted by the Right Honourable V. Fitzgearld and was returned a member of Parliament for the County Clare, though it was against the law at the time for a Catholic to sit in the House.

We arrived at Clare Castle on the 4th November, 1828 and relieved the 15th Depôt, sending detachments out to Kilrush, Scattery Island,

and other small detachments down about a point of land called Loop Head, at the extreme west of the country.

The village of Clare is a poor, miserable dirty place situated on the river Fergus, about one mile from Ennis. The barracks are on the opposite side of the river from Clare, and about the worst barracks and the worst situated of any that I have been stationed at in Ireland.

The barracks, such as they are, are surrounded by an old wall which at one time enclosed a castle of the noted Brien Borhoe, the last King of Munster. At this time there were no remains of the castle left except a round tower at the entrance gate, and which was occupied by the barrack-serjeant, Joseph Modgeley, a curious character, who once belonged to the Blind Half Hundred (50th Regiment).

The castle and property round belongs to the O'Brien family, who, I suppose, are descendants of the great Brien Borhoe.

The hospital was about as good a building as there was in the barracks, and we were very comfortably situated therein, and very happy with my family at Christmas and New Year's holydays, having my two little children, Billy and Ann; but the measles soon made their appearance among the children of the depôt, and it pleased God to deprive us of both our children, Billy dying on the 13th January and Ann on the 15th. We buried them in one grave and on one day, the 16th January, and erected a small tomb over them with the following verse on it, which was the only tribute of love we could pay to them. But it is a great consolation to think they are now two little angels in heaven. Billy was two years and four months old and Ann only eight months.

> Grave of Innocence, surely here
> The sweetest bloom of beauty is,
> Oh ! may I sleep in couch as fair,
> And with a hope as bright as this.

On the 24th December we were inspected by Major-General Sir E. Blakeney, who was pleased to speak in terms of approbation of the state of the depôt.

During our stay at Clare Castle the duty was very severe on the depôt, as the men seldom got above two nights in bed, and perhaps on picquet one of them, and having to find the jail guard for Ennis. As the guard mounted after dinner, it was generally dark before the old guard arrived at the barracks. We were all confined to quarters after retreat beating, so taking all things into consideration it was the worst place the depôt ever lay at.

We lost fourteen or fifteen children during our stay at Clare, having found when too late that the disease had been left in the bedding by the 15th Depôt, and they also had lost a number of children. After the loss of ours my wife took much to fretting, and I was obliged to get her out walking through the country when the days got longer and the

Entrance of Lough Derg
at Killaloe

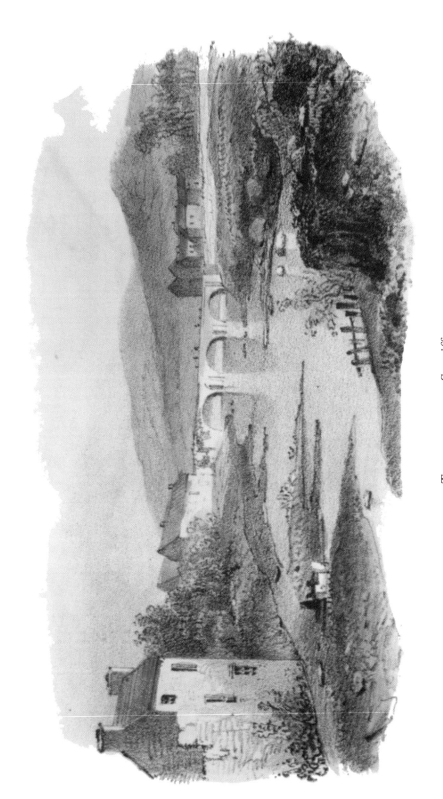

Tomgrany near Scariff.

Killaloe on the Shannon.
With the Cathedral

Scariff Bay

Clare Caftle. Co.y of Clare. 104.M= from Dublin.

Corcomroe Abbey

Court-house at Ballyvaughan

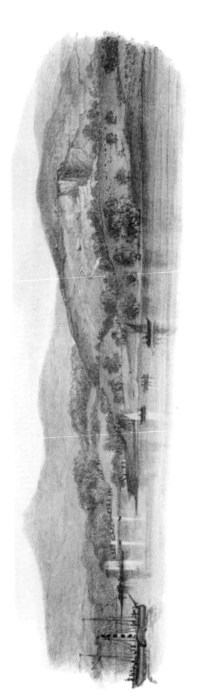

Killaloe Slate Quarry

Clarisford House the Seat of the Lord Bishop of Killaloe

weather fine. During our excursions we visited several gentlemen's seats, at least they should have been such, but they were mostly unoccupied, Buncraig and Barntic being among the number.

The town of Ennis was better than two miles off, and was nothing much of a town. It had been the scene of the election between O'Connell and V. Fitzgearld during the preceding summer, and the summer following was again the place of contest at the general election after the Catholic Emancipation Bill had passed. So I think we were very fortunate in getting away as we did, for the troops assembled at Clare were much crowded and uncomfortable during their stay. We did intend to make up a party and have a trip to Quinn Abbey, about five miles off, but were disappointed, as the route came unexpectedly on the 17th March, and one company marched the next morning for Youghal, in the county Cork, so that our route lay nearly back in the direction we had come.

Taken from *The Diary of Colour-Sergeant George Calladine, 19th Foot, 1793-1837*, (ed.), Major M.L. Ferrar (London 1922), pp 156-8.

William Bilton, The Angler in Country Clare, 1833

William Bilton or Belton, was an Englishman, who came to Ireland in the summer of 1833 to explore the countryside and to indulge in his passion for fishing. His 'rambles' were confined to Munster and Connacht as in the previous year he had made a short tour of Ulster. He admits to being of a 'roving disposition' which had led him to most parts of Europe and every nook of Britain from John O'Groats to Land's End. Ireland had become a point of great public interest in Britain, yet according to Bilton it was very difficult to obtain correct information concerning parts of the country - a difficulty which he hoped his book would help overcome. Ireland needed to know and be known. He had heard much about the Irish character, he longed to study the habits, mode of living and mode of faith of 'one of the most peculiar and most interesting people on the face of the earth'. From his writings it is clear Bilton was a committed Protestant and, unlike others, had few inhibitions concerning Irish religious sensitivities; he broadly declares that 'the greatest obstacle to improvement in Ireland was the Roman Catholic religion'. His habit of fishing led him to explore parts of the country not commonly visited by travellers. In Clare for instance he fished at Broadford and the lakes about Newmarket and Corofin. Although biased in his views, Bilton nonetheless gives a rounded picture of the country as it seemed to the well travelled observer in the 1830s. Bilton's interest in travel and fishing persisted and in 1840 he published another work *Two Summers in Norway*.

Leaving this sweet spot [Castle Connell], I passed through an ugly bog country to O'Brien's Bridge, where I crossed the Shannon; and saw little to interest me, until I approached Killaloe, where I procured very tolerable accommodation at the decent inn, kept by Mr Gilmore.

Killaloe is a very small town, prettily situated at the point where the Shannon issues from Lough Derg. The steamboat from Portumna, an inconsiderable town at the northern end of the lake, arrives here about four o'clock every afternoon, and, of course, contributes much to its prosperity. Close to the town is, also, a long bridge, which is a great thoroughfare into the County Tipperary. Above and below this bridge are numerous eel-weirs, which produce a strong current, where very large trout are said to lie. I carefully fished this part twice or thrice, and could only see small ones move: but then I must add that the weather was in general so bright as to spoil all angling, except very early or very late.

Lough Derg is, however, the great attraction of Killaloe: and each of the three days that I spent there, I was for several hours on its broad and lovely waters. My boatman was named Ellice; whom I can highly recommend for his civility, good conduct, and general intelligence.

Lough Derg extends from Portumna to Killaloe; and is, I believe, nearly thirty miles in length. The scenery at its lower end (which alone I have seen) is extremely beautiful: the expanse of water is very considerable, and of ever-varying proportions. The shores are hilly, sometimes almost mountainous, and are ornamented with several castles and mansions, embowered in very luxuriant woods. . . .

I forgot to mention that my boatman, of whose merits I have before spoken, was a Protestant, the only one of my sporting attendants in Ireland that I remember to have been of that faith. The presence of a Protestant bishop has here encouraged and formed a small colony of highly respectable Protestants in the lower ranks. Whether this interesting community will be allowed to subsist, after the nucleus, round which it has collected, be withdrawn, by the operation of the late act, remains to be proved. I trust it may; but I cannot help entertaining great fears, from the vast desert of popery, by which this little oasis of a purer faith is encompassed. . . .

Illicit distillation seems to be still pursued in this remote nook; and one would think is little attended to by the authorities. We observed, on our voyage, two stills in full work, and so openly situated, that no one who passed could avoid seeing them. The evils, which this illegal practice produces among the peasantry, are so incalculable, that every real friend to the country must wish to see it put down, by as mild, but as effectual, means as possible. The late enactments of the legislature, and the increased vigilance of the excise officers, have greatly checked it within these last few years but I understood it had rather revived again this summer, in consequence of the ruinously low price of corn.

It was close to the very spot where one of these stills was working that a dreadful tragedy occurred, which illustrates some of the collateral evils attending this mischievous traffic. My boatman related to me that a party of men and women, pursued by some excisemen, put off in a small boat, with the worm of the still on board. The officers repeatedly threatened to shoot if they did not instantly put back: but the party disregarding their menaces, one of the excisemen most unjustifiably fired his piece and wounded a woman, who bled to death in the boat. The murderer immediately fled the country, and has not, I believe, been heard of since.

At the end of the bay, we ascended with some difficulty, for about a mile up a sluggish, reedy stream, when we left out cot high and dry, and thence walked another mile to Scarriff, which I found to be a very poor, miserable little village. The *head inn*, also, was unfortunately already engaged by another party: I was, therefore, compelled to take up my quarters at a second-rate *shibeen*. It may be conceived what this must be in such a place. Indeed, I think it was the very worst house I slept at during the whole of my tour.

In using the terms 'head inn,' and 'shibeen,' it may be perhaps necessary for me to guard the reader against misunderstanding the first, and not understanding the latter title at all. In summoning before his mind's eye the 'head inn' of Scarriff, he must not figure to himself the Plough Inn at Cheltenham, or the York House at Bath, or any of the 'head inns' along the North Road. Scarriff's chief hostel consisted, like its worthy second, of a spacious kitchen, with sundry unintelligible cells clustering round it, on the one hand, and of a small parlour, with a still smaller bedroom beyond it, on the other. A 'shibeen' signifies an inferior public-house, where whisky is sold; *mutatis mutandis*, what in the modern attic phrase of England goes by the name of a '*kidney wink.*'

However, if the accommodation was wretched, and the cuisine detestable, these serious deficiencies were much atoned for by the greatest attention and civility, and most excellent whisky, the produce, I fear, of some of the neighbouring stills.

There being nothing to tempt us to prolong our stay, we were off early the next morning on our return to Killaloe. In our way we landed at Holy Island, to examine its antiquities, with which, albeit no antiquary, I was much gratified. Its most interesting object is its round tower, which is of considerable height, and in good preservation, of the usual form and dimensions. . . .

Upon this island I also found, as is so often the case in Ireland, the ruins of *seven* small churches; together with a holy well, whose green margin bore evident marks of having been recently pressed by votive knees. After leisurely examining these curiosities, we resumed our homeward course, and commenced trolling; but hardly moved a single fish until late in the afternoon, when, along the eastern shore, I killed thirteen pike, of from one pound to three pounds in weight, besides losing several others.

The next morning, May 31 [1833], I left Killaloe, loaded with more and warmer blessings from my late daily companions than I had usually been in the habit of receiving. . . .

Affability of manner and liberality of treatment will go far to win poor Pat's heart: and if to these you can occasionally add a good story or good joke, he is yours for ever. . . .

Wishing to vary my route back to Limerick, I took a car from Killaloe to Broadford, a distance of ten miles of a bad mountain road, and not very picturesque. The latter is a very poor village, where I established myself for the day in a moderate country inn. Near it are some celebrated slate quarries; but my chief inducement in visiting it was to inspect two lakes, very celebrated for the enormous pike they contain.

They are situated rather more than a mile from the village, and are connected together by a short deep channel; their entire circuit may be about four miles. The shores are flat, the water dark, with an abundance of rushes and weeds; in fact, it is just the very place for pike, of which there are said to be an abundance of extraordinary size. Wondrous tales are, indeed, told of a monster killed some years ago which weighed ninety-six pounds! And, not long since, a man of the name of Crowe, who constantly fishes the lake, did really kill one forty-five pounds in weight. Crowe and I, however, carefully fished round both the lakes, without succeeding in rousing any of theses Leviathans; I had only two runs of small pike, which both escaped. . .

My success was not such as to induce me to give these lakes any further trial, and I therefore determined, the next morning, to make the best of my way back to Limerick. Such a luxurious invention as a car was not to be had in Broadford; so, hiring a small cart to convey my luggage, I trudged by its side on foot. The distance is about eleven English miles; the road passing for the most part through a barren moorland country, but occasionally affording extensive and fine views over the rich vale of the Shannon. The weather was extremely sultry, and I arrived much heated at Limerick, which made me greatly enjoy a delicious saltwater bath. . . .

On Monday, June 3 [1833], I took the Ennis coach to Newmarket, a rather pretty country village twelve miles from Limerick, where there is a comfortable little inn. The country we passed through was extremely fertile, and occasionally presented pleasing prospects. My object in stopping at Newmarket was again connected with fishing. About two or three miles from the village are two lakes, called Rossroe and Fenloo, which are almost the only ones in the county of Clare that are not infested by pike. These contain nothing but trout, eels, and roach; which last have only lately appeared there, but are increasing so fast as to threaten to starve the trout out of their favourite haunts. The trout of these two lakes are remarkably fine, few being killed less than from one to five pounds in weight; but, occasionally, they are taken as heavy as ten pounds, though seldom with the fly, but by trolling a small roach behind the boat. The flies used are much the same as for Inchiquin Lake, which I shall hereafter have to describe: only they are a full size larger.

Immediately upon my arrival at Newmarket I engaged the services of one Mick Malony, who usually attends strangers, and with him set out for the further lake, Rossroe. We had some difficulty in procuring a boat, but at length succeeded in obtaining a very good one, kept by a plain, honest fellow, named Hicky. They trolled, while I fly-fished; but both without success, although the day seemed favourable for our sport, being cloudy and windy, with occasional showers. I moved three large fish, which would not, however, take the fly. . . .

Finding it mere waste of time to remain here any longer, I took the coach the following morning to Ennis. A couple of miles before reaching it, we passed through the miserable village of Clare, which gives its name to the county. The only remnants of its ancient consequence are an old castle, near the bridge, now used as a barrack; and, a little higher up the river, the venerable ruins of the abbey.

Ennis is the modern capital of the county; and is a rather large town, of the second class, without any apparent commercial activity, or architectural beauty, except the very picturesque remains of an ancient and considerable abbey. The day I arrived, Ennis was in an unusual bustle, occasioned by an election to the surgeonship of the county infirmary; which seemed to excite as much interest as if it had been a contest for the county. This was favourable to me in one respect: for, most of the resident gentry being in the town, I had an opportunity of being introduced to many of them, through the kindness of a well known gentleman of Ennis, whom I had met in Dublin.

I dined the same day, in company with a large and very pleasant party, at his house: when a fishing expedition was most good naturedly arranged for the following morning, to show me Inchiquin the most celebrated lake in this country for trout. It is situated about nine miles from Ennis, near the small village of Corrofin. We drove over in our host's handsome four-in-hand coach: but, as we were a large party, many of whom cared nothing for the fishing, we did not get under way until after twelve o'clock; little, therefore, could be done that day.

The country we passed through, in our way to Corrofin, was particularly ugly. The whole of this part of Clare consists of flat limestone rock, covered in general with little or no herbage, and presenting the most desolate appearance imaginable. Yet not only sheep, but even horses and cattle, contrive to find good browsing among these broken crags. . . .

After travelling this barren and desolate country, it was indeed a great relief for the eye to repose upon the waters of Inchiquin. This is a sweet little lake, about two or three miles in circumference, nestling at the foot of a beautifully wooded range of hills, whose verdure forms the most delicious contrast to the bare limestone rocks, which cover the rest of this tract. On one shore stands an old ruined castle: on the opposite bank is an ancient and spacious mansion belonging to the Burton family, but now converted into a barrack. About a quarter of a mile above the lake, is the very pretty cottage belonging to Mr Fitzgerald, called Adelphi, guarded, as it were, by the picturesque ruins of an old tower that overhangs it.

At the lake's side were several boats and attendants awaiting our arrival. Among the latter was one, whose real name is Darby Fitzpatrick, but who is much better known by his *sobriquet* of 'Sport.' This man's skill and keenness as a fisherman I had afterwards many opportunities of admiring; as well as his intelligence, invariable good humour, and civility. It being late, we lost no time in commencing operations; and had pretty fair sport during the few hours we were able to remain. A gentleman and myself, in our boat, killed eleven trout, the smallest of which was above half a pound, and the largest very nearly two pounds in weight; besides a great number of rises. The other boats were not quite so successful. We dined together on an island, and spent a most agreeable evening. . . .

The trout here are of two kinds, red and white: the latter, in particular, are very strong and active; and, upon being hooked, will often spring a great height out of the water. There are also a few very fine pike, unusually thick, deep, and silvery. One of these, a very handsome fish, ten pounds and a half in weight, was killed during my stay, by a noted and very superior fisherman of Ennis, Mr James O'Gorman: it had almost the shape and colour of a salmon.

The flies generally used here are of the medium size, with red or brown fur bodies, light gold twist, and wings, either of partridge and rail mixed, or else mallard, with a few fibres of the peacock's breast. There is also a very favourite *dropper*, called the rush fly; which has a reddish brown body, with wings of a small rail's feather, *not* stripped of the quill. . . .

I was informed that the largest and most pike were in Lough Tadann, close to Corrofin; and I therefore was one day induced to try it: but, having a very bad and unmanageable boat, I was soon obliged to relinquish the attempt. A day or two before, two pike had been killed there, which weighed, the one twenty seven pounds, and the other nineteen pounds and a half. This lake also contains a few very large trout, and an infinity of roach, any number of which may be killed, either with the fly, or worm. There are also several other lakes round Corrofin, which, I believe, would afford considerable amusement to the keen angler: and very tolerable accommodations may be had at the small inn in the same village. . . .

I soon, indeed, discovered that I was in the centre of [a] disturbed district. Within a mile on one side was the house of Mr Blood, who was so barbarously murdered, chiefly through the means of his own servant: and about the same distance on the other side lived the identical Terry Alts, who has given these midnight legislators the name by which they were usually distinguished. He was a quiet, inoffensive man; and the reason why he has supplied a lawless set of marauders so opposite to himself with their distinctive appellation is, that they used, more out of fun than malice, when executing any of their outrages, to cry out, 'Well done, Terry! well done, Terry Alts!'

These outrages have been put down by a strong extra police force. But there is evidently still a very bad spirit amongst the lower orders, and few parts of Ireland appeared to me in so unsatisfactory a state as this portion of Clare - a blessing for which it is mainly indebted to the excitement produced in order to return Mr O'Connell for this county.

I was surprised and shocked to find that the informer, who was himself concerned in all the outrages, but was the chief means of breaking up the system and hanging several of the ringleaders, is still living in the scene of his exploits. He certainly ought not to be allowed to remain in the country. He several times attempted to join me, but I would not suffer him to do so.

On Wednesday morning I gave the lake a farewell trial; when, *of course*, the trout rose better than ever they had done before. After catching six very fine fish in less than two hours, I bade adieu to my kind and hospitable host, and returned to Ennis. . . .

Leaving Corrofin a few miles to the left, I passed by the miserable village of Crusheen, and through a generally wild, desolate country, in which were only one or two gentlemen's residences and grounds, to relieve a little the monotonous wretchedness of this district. About three miles before reaching Gort, I came to the entrance of Lord Gort's demesne, and obtained permission (neither unsought nor unbought) to drive through the park.

Extracts taken from William Bilton, *The Angler in Ireland*, 2 vols, (London 1834), i, pp. 39-67.

Henry Inglis, Assizes, 1834

Henry David Inglis, journalist and travel writer, was the son of a Scottish lawyer. Trained for a career in business, Inglis tired of commerce and turned instead to his twin passions - writing and travel. At the age of thirty he travelled on the continent and produced his first book *Tales of the Ardennes* in 1825. There followed in quick succession a series of travel books on Scandinavia, Switzerland, Spain and the Tyrol. Perhaps his best book was *The Tyrol with a Glance at Bavaria* which he published in 1833. For two years he edited a newspaper in Jersey and in 1834 published a comprehensive work on the Channel Islands. In the same year he toured Ireland and produced an exhaustive two volume description of the country. With his Irish tour Inglis made his greatest impact; the book received widespread acclaim and reached its fifth edition in 1838. In less than ten years Inglis had established himself as the foremost travel writer of his day but at tremendous personal cost. His prodigious output damaged his health and he died in London in 1835 of disease of the brain, the result of overwork, at the age of forty.

In the summer of 1834 Inglis travelled from Tralee to Tarbert, from where he took the steamer up the estuary to Limerick. He did not delay in Limerick as he wished to be present in Ennis for the opening of the Clare assizes. Inglis provides a wonderful description of the legal proceedings in Ennis courthouse. He uses the cases before the courts to illustrate the 'moral defects', as he sees it, of the Irish character. He mocks the spirit of faction among the people and their propensity for fighting; unable to find a rational explanation as to why members of one faction should wish to murder those of another, he resorts to ridicule. Similarly, cases of pretended rape gave no favourable impression of the female character, and were in many instances rouses to gain husbands. The general untruthfulness of witnesses convinced him of the low state of Irish morals. What perhaps he failed to realise was that such cases reflected more on the human condition than on the morals of a downtrodden people. Ultimately, Inglis was well disposed towards the masses and is a sympathetic interpreter of the scenes he witnessed.

The first part of the road to Ennis, embraces nearly the same views as the voyage up the Shannon; for the road runs parallel to, though at a little distance from the river. From several of the eminencies over which I passed, a great part of the course of the lower Shannon is laid open; and the country on either side of the road was green, fertile, and beautiful. Several of the ruins which are seen from the river, - particularly Bunratty Castle, - I passed close by; and several fine domains, - among others, that belonging to Sir Edward O'Brien, lay in our way.

The little town of Clare, which, from its situation ought to be the county town, in place of Ennis, lies between Limerick and Ennis, and only about two miles from the latter. There is a fine navigation up the estuary of the river Fergus, to the bridge of Clare; so that Clare is the export point of the Ennis market. A very trifling expenditure would extend the water communication to Ennis; and there is no doubt, that, in the event, the prosperity of the town would rapidly increase; for Clare is not only a fine corn country, but an extensive cattle-breeding country. The proposal of a canal, however, has met with every opposition from narrow-mindedness and jobbing. The great Ennis proprietor likes nothing that costs any thing; and the proprietor of Clare is not of course anxious to remove the point of export from Clare to Ennis. Notwithstanding the advantages possessed by Clare, the place looks poverty-stricken.

I reached Ennis just as it fell dark; and found the town in all the bustle that in an Irish county town, precedes the holding of assizes: the inns were all choke full; and for lodgings, the most exorbitant prices were demanded. From three to eight guineas, for a few days, were asked for two rooms; and I was glad to find a place to creep into even on these terms. Although the assize was opened on the following day, no business was entered upon, until the day after; and I therefore employed the interval in those perambulations, scrutinies, and inquiries, which occupy a part of my attention in every town.

I had not yet seen, in Ireland, any town with suburbs so extensive, in comparison with the town itself; or, perhaps, it would be more correct to say, that I had not seen any town with so few good streets, in comparison with the bad; for the rows and streets of cabins form, in fact, the greater part of the town, and cannot properly be called suburbs. There is not, indeed, one good street in Ennis; and there are only two streets which rise above the rank of lanes. Ennis, however, is a populous town, containing 12,000 inhabitants; and is susceptible of considerable improvement in many ways, but especially by the construction of some communication with the river navigation of Clare. The retail trade in Ennis is not extensive, excepting in the necessaries of life. Limerick is so near, and the communication with it so frequent and so easy, that it absorbs a great part of the retail trade of the county of Clare.

I have nowhere yet found land let dearer, or its small occupiers in a poorer condition, than in the neighbourhood of Ennis. I found average good land, but by no means first rate land, situated about a mile from the town, let at 4*l.* and 5*l.* per acre. This is literally squeezing the uttermost farthing out of the soil; and the proprietor of a large portion of the land in this neighbourhood, a Mr Gore, is one of those short-sighted individuals, whose object is, to keep up a nominal rent roll, and to let his land to the highest bidder. This gentleman takes no warning by the frequency of unpaid rents, and possessions relinquished; and finds no difficulty, in the present state of the country, when the demand for improved land is greater than the supply, of letting his land at whatever price he chooses to put upon it. The miserable suburbs of Ennis afford evidence of the same system. I need scarcely add, that there is great want of employment in and about Ennis; and that nothing is done in the way of providing it.

The country about Ennis offers many beautiful scenes. I would particularly name Eden vale and Eden lake, - spots of great loveliness and repose. But the neighbourhood of such charming scenes as these, too often remind one of Castle Rack-rent - a large neglected looking mansion, and a pack of hounds; and congregations of miserable cabins scattered around. Clare is a backward county; little has been done for it; and in no county, has grand-jury jobbing been more unblushingly carried on.

A small Irish county town, during assizes, presents a spectacle that is never seen in England; for even supposing the calendar to be as long, in an English as in an Irish county, - which it never is, - the difference in the character of the cases to be tried, materially affects the aspect of the town and its population. In England, a case of murder or man-slaughter, brings to the county town only the near relations of the party to be tried, - and perhaps, of the party prosecuting; but in Ireland, things are on a different scale. The English murder is a private act, perpetrated by some ruffian for the sake of gain: the Irish homicide has been committed for no reason at all; and not by one cold-blooded ruffian, but by a crowd of demi-barbarians, who meet for the purpose of fighting; and who have no other reason for fighting, than because one half of the number are called O'Sullivan, and the other O'someting else: so that when a manslaughter is to be prosecuted at an Irish assize, the case does not bring up merely the accused and his one or two witnesses, but it brings half the 'boys' in the county who bear the same name as the accused; and as many more, of the same name as the man who was killed, - every one of the former, ready to kiss the book, and swear, that the boy accused of the homicide, never handled a shillelagh, or lifted a stone, or was seen in a 'scrimmage' in his days; and every one of the latter as ready to swear, that the boy that was killed, was the most peaceable boy that ever bore his name, and that he was killed for no reason at all. Besides these homicides cases, which are peculiar to an Irish assize, prosecutions of any kind bring together a greater number of persons than in England, - for be it a robbery, or a rape, or any other crime, of which a man is accused, all his relations come forward to swear an alibi. It may be easily conceived what a motley crowd fills the streets of an Irish county town at the time of an assize. . . .

The most numerous class of cases at most Irish assizes, is that which is facetiously denominated *fair* murders; that is, homicides committed at fairs; and I do not know any means, by which so much insight is to be obtained into the character of the Irish peasantry, and into the condition of the country, and state of things among the lower classes of society, as by listening to these prosecutions for *fair* murders. There were many of these prosecutions at the Ennis assizes; and, although I had already heard much of the factions, into which the peasantry are divided, I had no conception of the extent of this evil, nor of the bitterness with which this spirit of faction is attended. However these factions may have originated, there is now no distinction among their adherents, excepting that which arises from the possession of a different name. The O'Sullivans are as distinct a people from the O'Neils, as the Dutch from the Belgians. The factions have chiefs, who possess authority. Regular agreements are made to have a battle; the time agreed upon is generally when a fair takes place; and, at these fights, there is regular marshalling, and 'wheeling;' and, as for its being a crime to break a 'boy's' head, such an idea never enters the brain of any one. The spirit of faction is brought into court by almost every witness in these prosecutions. I saw a witness, a woman, brought in support of the prosecution for a homicide committed on some cousin, - who on being desired to identify the prisoners, and the court-keeper's long rod being put into her hand, that she might point them out, struck each of them a smart blow on the head. As for finding out the truth, by the mere evidence of the witnesses, it is generally impossible. Almost all worth knowing, is elicited on the cross-examination: and it is always, by the appearance and manner of the witness, more than by his words, that the truth is to be gathered. All the witnesses, examined for the prosecution, were, by their own account, mere lookers on at the battle; nor stick, nor stone had they. *Their* party had no mind to fight that day; but, in making this assertion, they always take care to let it be known, that, if they had had a mind to fight, they could have handled their shillelaghs to some purpose. On the other hand, all the witnesses for the prisoner aver just the same of themselves; so that it is more by what witnesses won't tell, than by what they do tell, that truth is discovered. Half the witnesses called on both sides, have broken heads; and it is not unfrequently by a comparison of the injuries received on both sides, and by the evidence of the doctor, that one is helped to the truth. . . .

The most numerous class of cases (with one exception), and the most important class, as throwing the greatest light on the character and state of the people, were those homicides of which I have spoken. The exception in point of number of cases, is rape: of these cases, I think nearly forty were entered for trial: but only a very few of that number were heard; and all of them terminated in acquittal. In nine cases out of ten, the crime is sworn to, merely for the purpose of getting a husband; and the plan generally succeeds. The parties are married before the cause is called for trial; and I have myself seen an earnest negotiation carried on under the piazzas of the court-house, a little while before a case was called. There was the 'boy' indicted for a capital crime, but out on bail, as he generally is; and the girl, about to swear away a man's life; and the attorneys, and a large circle of relations, all trying to bring about a marriage, before Pat should be called upon to appear, and answer to the indictment that he, 'not having the fear of God before his eyes, and being instigated by the devil,' did so and so. In the case to which I was a listener, Pat and the fair one could not agree: the trial went on; and Pat was acquitted. . . .

I saw tried, one of those singular cases of abduction, which very frequently occur in Ireland; and which also throw considerable light on the state of society among the lower ranks. Sham cases of abduction are frequent. The 'boy' and the girl are agreed; but the girl's relations being dissentient, owing to her being an heiress, and entitled to a better match, it is made up between the young people, that the girl shall be carried away by apparent force. The youth makes known the case to his friends, and collects a number of associates: they come during the night to the house of the girl, force open the door, seize upon the maid, who, though 'nothing loth,' screams and makes all the opposition in her power, place her on horseback, and, after escorting her a sufficient distance, deliver her over to the 'boy,' on whose account the abduction was got up. The charge of abduction which I saw tried at Ennis, was a real abduction however, and a very shameless one, attended with circumstances of great cruelty; and originating, as indeed they always do, in love of money. These abductions are most detrimental to the peace of the country; because a feud is instantly generated, between the relatives of the girl, and those of the aggressor; and many subsequent fights invariably result from these outrages. . . .

I noticed, that great importance is attached to kissing the book; and sometimes, this ceremony is required, for greater security, to be performed two or three times. Without kissing the book, a witness looks upon his oath as very imperfectly taken; and it is necessary that in the act of kissing, the witness be narrowly watched, lest he kiss his own thumb with which he holds the book in place of the book itself. . .

I was much struck at Ennis, as I had been at Tralee, with the acuteness and talent of the Irish attorneys. Their cross-examinations of witnesses were admirable; certainly not surpassed by the very best cross-examinations I ever heard from the mouth of an English barrister.

Extracts taken from Henry D. Inglis, *A Journey Throughout Ireland During the Spring, Summer and Autumn of 1834*, (London 1836), pp 156-67.

Jonathan Binns,
Miseries and Beauties of Clare, 1835

Binns from Lancashire, England took a special interest in agricultural affairs. The opening up of the British grain market to external competition prompted him in 1839 to publish a pamphlet *Cornlaws Superseded by Improved Agriculture*. Previously, in 1833, Binns had been one of the assistant agricultural commissioners appointed by government to inquire into the condition of the poor in Ireland. The Poor Law commissioners visited seventeen counties, including Clare, and collected evidence in one parish of each barony of these counties. Their report, published in 1835, was the most comprehensive inquiry into Irish poverty in the pre-Famine period. Binns appears to have combined his work for the commission with his travel writing. In his introduction he states that his office as assistant commissioner 'afforded advantages and opportunities for the acquisition of information respecting the general condition of the people'. His chief motive in writing was to promote, on the part of the inhabitants of England, a better understanding of the 'real situation and dispositions of the Irish people, and to promote a more practical sympathy for their suffering'. Binns' two volumed work on Ireland was his only travelogue. In England agricultural matters continued to preoccupy him and in 1851 he published a book on his native shire called *Notes on the Agriculture of Lancashire with Suggestions for its Improvement*. Binns journeyed in Clare on at least two occasions; starting at Kilrush in 1835 he toured the towns and villages of west Clare and the following year passed through Lough Derg and Killaloe on his way to Limerick. Binns was among the first to comment on the incipient tourist industry; a well informed observer, he was primarily concerned with agricultural practice, social conditions and economic development.

The lighthouses of Kilkredane and Rehy Head, elevated upon lofty cliffs, are seen on the Clare side of the river. Here part of the French fleet anchored. At Money Point, on the Clare side of the river, some excellent flag-quarries are extensively worked by the Dublin Steam Company, which owes its prosperity in a great measure to the spirited exertions of Mr Williams of Liverpool. Flags are sent from hence to London and other places. Proceeding on our way, we sailed close by the island of Innis Scattery, which contains the ruins of seven churches, and a conspicuous round tower, useful as a land-mark. From the hotel of Kilrush, there is an excellent view of the tower, the diameter of which is the same throughout, and the height 120 feet. It retains its conical top, and has a rent, supposed to be caused by lightning, extending the whole length. The island of Innis Scattery contains 98 acres; a hundred years ago it contained 100 acres, but two have been washed away during the interval. The rental is £100 per annum. . . .

Kilrush belongs to Crofton Moore Vandeleur, Esq., of Kilrush House, who is lord of the manor. His property extends about twelve miles along the Shannon side, east of Kilrush, and, westward on the road to Kilkee, about five miles; and his income is said to be about £15,500 per annum. He is a young man, and is an excellent landlord, giving encouragement by granting longer leases, and ground for building on, and is ready to join any company that may be established for the benefit of the country. Within the last five years, the town and neighbourhood have undergone an astonishing improvement, mainly attributable to the establishment of the steam navigation. The trade of the place is rapidly increasing; several stores are building; branches of the National and Agricultural Banks have been established; a patent *slip* has been constructed; and the Steam Company are about to extend the pier 200 feet. These are unequivocal signs of increased prosperity. Nor are advantages resulting from these changes confined to the town. The agricultural interest is benefited to a very considerable extent, by the opening of the trade of Kilrush: the farmers, for instance, who formerly were obliged to take 2d. or 3d. a stone less than the Limerick prices, now sell their grain within a farthing of those prices. . . .

It was highly gratifying to witness the animation that prevailed in Kilrush, - the neatness of the little shops, the flagged pathway, and the absence of accumulated dirt, so prominent and offensive a peculiarity of most small towns in Ireland. The people about Kilrush (whose population is 5000) are handsome, and appear considerably more intelligent than in many other places. The whole town, indeed, presented abundant proofs of the advantages that result from a spirited and enlightened policy. . .

Kilkee, a well-frequented bathing-place, is nine miles distant from Kilrush; the charge made by the public company for going there is only 1s.; whilst those having private cars charge five. The company, besides what it has done in the *direct* sphere of its operations, has also assisted in making and improving the roads in the neighbourhood.

In going to Kilkee, some bogs are crossed, which contain an extraordinary quantity of wood - the stumps of large trees remaining above ground, as numerous and as close together, and most of them in the same position as in the days when they were portions of an extensive forest. They nearly all belong to the pine species, and the wood is so thoroughly impregnated with turpentine, that the shreds burn most brilliantly, and are substituted for candles. They are occasionally twisted into ropes. This wood makes an excessively hot fire, and kindles in a much shorter time than any other combustible in use; the roots are chiefly applied to this purpose - the stem, which is too valuable, being used for building. . . Turf, to the value of £10,000 annually is said to be sent to Limerick from the neighbouring bogs. . . .

Kilkee is the property of Lord Cunningham, an absentee: his income in Clare is said to be about £7,000 a year; the property is still in lease for lives. Very many of the people here live to the age of eighty and ninety.

The curraghs, or canoes, of the fishermen on this coast, are of the same description as those used by the ancient Britons and Irish, except that they are covered (probably for the sake of economy) with tarred canvass instead of hides; such being the alterations that have taken place in the relative value of these two articles. The curraghs consist of wands of willow or hazel, and are so light that a man can easily carry his canoe on his back. I saw several of them laid up for the winter at the cabins of the owners. The cost price, when ready for sea, is from twenty to thirty shillings. They are sharp in front, and, behind, square but narrow; they have neither keel nor rudder, being guided very dextrously with paddles. When damaged, they are easily repaired with a piece of canvass, stuck on with pitch. The fishery of Kilkee is unfortunately declining, the fish having nearly deserted the shores; and the poverty of the fishermen deters them from trying new banks, for fear of losing their tackle. . . .

The farms in this neighbourhood are from six to twenty acres in size; the rent being from twenty to thirty shillings per acre. For the bog, when part of the turf has been got off, and about ten feet in depth remains, the rent is from fifteen to twenty shillings per acre. For conacre, from fourteen to eighteen shillings per rood is paid; but this is for stubble land, not very good, and the farmer manures it. The rent paid by the farmer for the same land, is £1 per acre. Many of the farmers are now sowing clover, and I was told that in two or three years there will be scarcely a farmer who will not sow a little. No turnips, rape, or other green food, is cultivated. . . .

During the time of potato digging, the labourers receive 6d. per day and diet, after which there is very little to be done till spring, when they may be employed till July. Early in spring they get 6d.; about May, 8d.; and then 6d. per day again. On an average, they are employed about two-thirds of their time. Some of their wives and children go to beg where they are not known, but generally the people are so industriously disposed, and pay such attention to their little potato-gardens, that not many resort to this degrading practice. . . .

Kilkee presents no variation from the rest of places, in respect of early marriages. Girls marry at sixteen, boys from seventeen to twenty. The poorer classes marry under a conviction that their condition cannot be worse, and may possibly be more comfortable. The farmers' daughters necessarily associate with the servants; and the father, afraid of their marrying below their class, is more easily induced than he might be under other circumstances, to allow them to marry, when a tolerable offer is made, although very young.

I would advise all who intent travelling in this part of Ireland in the winter, to go well provided with tea, coffee, and any liquor they may consider necessary. The eggs obtained here are not always the best; tea and coffee are both very poor; good ham or bacon is difficult to find, though in a country overrun with pigs; the fowls are more skin and bone than flesh; mutton may by chance be got pretty good; but the beef is scarcely fit to eat. I lodged at the house of a Mrs Shannon, who treated me with the utmost kindness and civility; and had I taken up my abode there at a time when visitors generally come, I doubt not many of the deficiencies I complain of, would have been supplied.

From Kilkee to Miltown Malbay, a distance of only sixteen miles, I travelled in a very jolting car (for which I paid 8s.) drawn by a horse which was either unable or unwilling to travel at an ordinary rate. Three men in succession undertook to drive him, and so far succeeded as to make him perform the journey in five hours - being at the astonishing rate of three miles an hour. At length we reached the immense inn at Miltown Malbay, which did not contain a traveller besides myself. It presented a comfortless appearance, and in many respects resembled the generality of Irish inns in the winter season: it was, however, comparatively free from the prevailing characteristic of dirt. The rooms were without fires, and the only newspaper they could bring me to read was one of the month of August, the time, I suppose, when visitors began to be scarce. This spacious hotel is a partnership concern, having been built about thirty years ago by four gentlemen, and, including ninety beds, cold and warm baths, and stabling for eighty horses, cost about £7,000. It is built upon a rock, immediately beneath which are the waters of a delightfully sheltered bay, resembling a lake, and occasionally, when the wind blows strong, the spray from the waves dashes against the windows of the house. The water being strong and pure, is well adapted to the purposes of sea-bathing; the sands, moreover, are firm and smooth. The present occupier of the inn pays a rent of £150 per annum; he has five acres of land, and two of bog. Nearly the whole of Miltown Malbay belongs to Mr Marawley [*recte* Moroney] . . . .

The principal proprietors in the neighbourhood, are Mr Marawley, before mentioned, whose income was stated to be about £2,000 per annum, Mr O'Brien, £1,000 per annum, and Sir William Fitzgerald, from five to £6,000. This gentleman resides in France, and has also a seat near Newmarket; he comes over to Ireland occasionally, and is reported to be a good landlord.

The population of Miltown is rapidly increasing. The wages of the labourers are generally 6d., and sometimes 8d. and 10d. per day, with diet. They are occasionally much distressed, being employed only half of their time; their wives are accordingly compelled to turn out and beg, but notwithstanding this, the most complete tranquillity prevails. Land near Miltown lets at from £2 to £3 10s. per acre; bog land, from £2 to £2 10s. Sea-weed and sea-sand are much used for manure, and the latter is held in such high estimation as to be carted from the shore at Miltown to near Ennis, a distance of eighteen miles. But little encouragement, I am sorry to say, appears to be given to agricultural improvements. The morning after my arrival here was exceedingly brilliant, and I anticipated with pleasure a visit to the cliffs of Moher. . . .

A new road from Lahinch to Liscanor was interrupted by a gulf, that had, in consequence of some dispute with the contractor, been cut across it, ands we had accordingly to scramble down a deep decent, covered with large stones, rounded by being rolled by the action of the sea, which is here very powerful. On crossing the beach and the Innistimon River, it was with great exertion we narrowly escaped being swamped in a quick-sand. Between this place and the celebrated cliffs, we passed Birchfield, the residence of Mr O'Brien, whose hospitality to strangers is distinguished; but I had not time to obtrude myself upon his kindness. He is a good landlord; indeed, the great number of white-washed and comfortable-looking cottages that are scattered over his estate, sufficiently indicate the care and attention of the owner, and have been the frequent objects of warm and just admiration. To each cottage is allotted a small portion of land, on which turnips and other green crops are grown. Mr O'Brien, according to the expression of my informant, 'gives the poor a power of employment.' For the purpose of benefiting the poor, as well as for the accommodation of visitors, he built a tower or castle on the cliffs of Moher, to which stables are attached, and all the necessary requisites for the process of cooking supplied. He encourages his tenants in the cultivation of the land, allowing them a car to bring lime from Doolan; and in scarce times he supplies the poor with wool and potatoes, and judiciously takes the price out in work. Mr O'Brien's steward said that as a good deal of work was generally going on, an active man need not be out of employment except on wet days. Two gentlemen of the name of Macnamara occupy a portion of their time in teaching the people to grow turnips and mangel wurzel, and pay them for erecting their own cabins, on condition that they shall whitewash them every year, and keep them clean inside. They also give employment to the women and children.

The low land lets for from thirty to forty shillings; the mountainous part, from thirteen to twenty. The cess is 1s. 5d. per acre. In this barony (Corcomroe) the proportion of Catholics to Protestants is said to be one hundred to one.

From Liscanor the road winds up the hill to the Hag's Heada rock, so called from the striking resemblance of a part of it to the head of an old woman. Here stands an old tower, formerly used as a telegraph, and afterwards as a coastguard station. This cliff was stated by the late Alexander Nimmo, in his report to Government, to be more than 600 feet above the ocean. The celebrated cliffs of Moher extend for three miles to the northward of the Hag's Head - the most remarkable of which is computed to be 900 feet perpendicular. The fearful and sublime effect produced by gazing from the edge of these perpendicular and rugged rocks (the highest in Europe, or perhaps in the world), baffles description. The waves of the sea that rolled below, actually appeared like the diminutive curl upon a pond, when slightly agitated by the wind; and something on the shore, that looked from this dizzy height like rods that a man might grasp and wield in his hand, I was told were large balks of timber. A little southward of the Hag's Head, is a narrow rocky chasm, 500 feet deep, which runs up into the land; within this chasm flows a dark stream. To lie down on these airy heights, and project the head beyond the edge of the precipice, is an act, simple though it may seem, that requires no little resolution. The watery depth below is an awful gulf to gaze into. Fortunately, my visit to these extraordinary cliffs was attended with a transparent atmosphere, and a great extent of rocky coast was visible - its bold headlands jutting into the sea as far as the eye could reach. . . .

Leaving with reluctance the stupendous heights of Moher, which I had been most anxious to see, I returned to Lahinch. The inn is situated at the head of Ballyela Bay, and is much frequented in the summer months by bathers, the sands being remarkably fine. The majority of the company, I was informed, consists of Catholic priests. I was shown into an immense room, a fire of wet turf being carried along with me; and the keen frosty air having produced as keen an appetite, I called for dinner, and was told that a fowl would presently be served up. The promise was literally fulfilled most certainly, for, by and by, *a goose,* as white as when it was uncooked, was brought to table. The 'fowl' was baked.

Leaving Lahinch by the mail-car at seven in the morning, we passed for many miles through a poor, cold, and barren country, destitute of all objects of interest, except now and then the ruins of an ancient castle. Limestone, composed of masses of oyster shells, prevails, as Ennis, the county town of Clare, is approached; and in the immediate neighbourhood of that town the soil improves considerably. At the inn here I happened to breakfast at the same table with Thomas Steele, one of Mr O'Connell's friends, and an able writer on the liberal side. 'Nothing,' said he, in reference to tithe, 'nothing will now satisfy the Irish people but its total extinction, stem, root, and branch.' Poor-laws he considered indispensable.

Mr Steele introduced me to the news-room, where I became acquainted with a gentlemen, a magistrate, who, in the true spirit of Irish civility, kindly accompanied me to inspect the jail, the mendicity institution, the old abbey, and some other objects of interest in the town. Mr Baggot, I found, was an advocate of the silent system, which was about to be adopted in this prison. The arrangements in this jail, with one exception, were very good. That one exception refers to the non-classification of the boys - a point of the greatest importance. This defect will be remedied, I doubt not, when more room is obtained, for the adult prisoners are already classed, according to the character and quality of the crimes of which they are either suspected or convicted. The mendicity institution was also well managed; four hundred persons are fed by it. . .

Ennis is a much cleaner and neater town than I had lately been accustomed to see, and has a population of about 12,000. On the river Fergus, close to the town, are several fine corn-mills.

To Limerick, twenty-two miles. I travelled by the coach, and thence to Dublin, 125 miles, by the mail.

Extracts taken from Jonathan Binns, *The Miseries and Beauties of Ireland*, 2 vols (London 1837), ii, pp 376-408.

Lady Chatterton, Rambles, 1838.

Lady Georgina Chatterton was born Henrietta Georgina Marcia Lascelles, the only child of the Rev Lascelles Iremonger, prebendary of Winchester. In 1824 at the age of eighteen she became the wife of Sir William Chatterton of Castle Mahon, County Cork. After his death in 1855, she married secondly Mr Heneage Dering, formerly of the Coldstream Guards. Her second husband was received into the Catholic church in 1865 and was followed ten years later by Lady Chatterton herself. Heneage Dering ascribed his conversion to 'the conscientious struggles and continual act of Catholic self development' of his wife which marked the whole tenor of her life. A prolific writer of wide interests, Lady Chatterton has over thirty publications to her credit, including such works as *The Pyrenees with Excursions into Spain* (1843), *Jean Paul Friedrich Richter, Selected and Translated* (1851) and *The Heiress and her Lovers*, (1863). Although secondly married, she continued to publish under the name Lady Chatterton. No one can read her work without being struck by her high moral tone and her earnest desire to do good. She bubbles with enthusiasm as she discovers the hidden delights of Kilkee and West Clare. Writing, however, for the growing tourism market, she avoids the scenes of squalor and destitution and her style, while well-meaning, tends to be superficial and non-judgemental.

On Friday last we went to Cratloe woods, to pass a day with its young and interesting owner, Mr Augustus O'Brien. It is opposite to Vermont on the other side of the Shannon; but we drove round by Limerick, and crossed the fine new bridge which has been lately built there. I was curious to see a place which has such attractions for its youthful proprietor, as to induce him to forego all the pleasures which have been inviting him to London during the season. Of neighbours, at least rich ones, he has few; but he is surrounded by the interesting, intelligent, grateful Irish peasantry. . .

The cottage we visited was one of a better class; a well-dressed woman was ironing her husband's linen, and her old mother-in-law was sitting in a comfortable chair near the fire. She showed us to her inner room, where two pretty twin children were asleep in a nice cradle. Besides a china press and wardrobe, this room contained a bookstand filled with religious books. But it was the old grandmother's countenance which riveted my attention more than all these refined wonders of an Irish cabin. She was deaf, and could not hear the musical voice of the young squire, but her eyes were fixed on him with a look of intense gratitude and delight. . .

On Saturday we proceeded to Dromoland. It is a splendid abode, now nearly finished, and offers that phenomenon in Ireland, or indeed in any country, a magnificent place erected without ruining the possessor. Sir Lucas O'Brien lives there in a style of hospitable splendour, which does credit to his good taste and kind heart: the rich are welcome, and the poor taken care of. In both these agreeable employments he has an able assistant in his interesting wife. The comfortable cottages which on all sides may be seen without the walls of the park, bear testimony to the goodness and liberality of their landlord. The castle contains some good pictures, and many interesting portraits of this ancient family. In the entrance hall is one of their great ancestor, the celebrated king Brian Boroihme. The upper gallery is full of these interesting memorials of bygone days; and the present possessor of Dromoland has placed them in richly carved frames, which accord admirably with the florid and beautiful architecture of the building. There are two by Sir Peter Lely, of Lord Clarendon, and his daughter, the Duchess of York. . . .

On Monday we came here, making a detour to visit the ruins of Quin Abbey. It stands in a green plain near the clear river. The cloisters resemble those of Askeaton, and are in as good preservation; indeed the whole building, except the roof, is entire. Most of the chimney-pieces remain; and a peasant woman, who came up to speak to me as I was examining an old monument, said that her grandmother remembered when it was all perfect. I looked on these cloisters with great interest, as the place where the monk who composed those beautiful lines to Lady O'Brien, was wont to meditate and pray.

While we were in the abbey, the funeral procession a young girl entered the ruined building, and, as is always the case in Ireland, several groups dispersed themselves in various directions, each to weep over the grave of their own friends. . .

And a beautiful and strange scene it was to see this crowd - the men in their sober attire, and the women in the brilliant coloured dresses they wear in this part of the country, scattered over the green sward before the venerable ruins of the old abbey. Not one bonnet was there: all the women wore either their own dark hair dressed in the simple Grecian fashion, or the head covered with a sort of white linen veil, or bright coloured handkerchief, or the hood of the red or blue cloak, which forms an invariable part of their costume.

At a cottage, in the village of Quin, we were amused at seeing the following sign over the door.

'Here lives a man who don't refuse
To make or mend both boots and shoes;
His leather's good, his work is quick,
His profits small - so can't give tick.'. . .

After visiting the lead mines of Mr Singleton, where a great deal of work is going on, we continued our journey, passing through Ennis. At Ennistimon, a primitive little place in a mountain valley, we stopped to bait the horses, and took advantage of the delay to enjoy a pleasant walk to a gentleman's place on the opposite side of the river. We went first under the bridge, which is thrown over a broad expanse of flat rock, now quite dry, except a narrow stream at one end; but in winter a torrent descends from the mountains, and rushes over the flat rock with such precipitancy, that we were told, persons could walk under the fall, 'as they do at Niagra,' said our guide, without being wet. Under the first ledge is another not so broad, and so on are successive ledges of rocks to the plain below.

On the steep bank above, a country-house is situated; it is well-wooded, and with a little care might be made a lovely residence. . .

On this spot there stood formerly a castle of the O'Briens, and the rooms still contain many pictures of that ancient family. When I viewed these expressive representations of noble minds, still living on the old canvas, I rejoiced to think that the same generous spirit survives in their descendants, as I had so lately witnessed both at Cratloe and Dromoland. There is also in this venerable house at Ennistimon, a portrait of the celebrated old Countess of Desmond, who is said to have lived to the age of 162. . . .

Miltown; Thursday. We ventured to-day, as far as the Phoul-a-kirché; and were tempted by the report of some boys, to try a visit to the puffing-hole, represented by them as a mile off; but which turned out to be nearly three. . . The sight of the foaming surge was very grand; but the state of the tide was such as not to admit of the puffing-hole exhibiting itself: we determined, therefore, to wait, and took shelter from the high wind under the lee of an old wall - the last remains of an ancient castle. I found a fisherman there, who was waiting until the tide had sufficiently fallen, to enable him to gather the sea-weed which has been detached from the rocks during the late storms; a poor girl, content with some of an inferior description, was hard at work collecting it on the beach.

It is gratifying to know how sea-weed is now valued, when compared with its neglect until a comparatively late period. Formerly, the production of kelp was the only object for which it was collected - the introduction of barilla fortunately destroyed this trade, and sea-weed is now much more profitably made use of as manure.

My friend, the fisherman, told me that they often venture in their canoes ten miles to sea; their fish is bought up by dealers for the Limerick market, and they sometimes get £2 for a boat of fish, turbot fetching from 2s. 6d to 5s. In winter, they catch hake and haddock. The condition of the peasantry here, seems anything but miserable. Potatoes sell so low as 1d. a stone, (14lbs); milk from a penny to three-halfpence a quart; turf is abundant; and fishing sometimes affords a very profitable employment - but it is a dangerous occupation on this coast. The canoes are very frail. They consist of a slight frame-work, over which canvas is lightly stretched, and then saturated with tar, so as to become water-proof: their great lightness and buoyancy enable them to live in a very heavy sea, if properly and steadily managed; and therefore they are perhaps better adapted to this coast, than stronger boats would be. Accidents, however, frequently occur. Only two nights ago, a man and a boy lost their lives; they imprudently crossed a sea, which struck the boat, and broke it in pieces. . . .

Kilkee, Friday. After having travelled so much over the dusty and beaten track infested by the usual summer tourists abroad, I find infinite pleasure in exploring the grass-grown and interesting nooks of deserted Ireland - in arriving at inns where they do not know by rote the whole list of one's wants; where the landlady's face expresses a refreshing mixture of surprise, awe, and pleasure, in which cannot be detected that cold, confident, sum-total-of-a-bill sort of look, which is visible on the blazé countenances of foreign innkeepers.

Then how delightful the feeling that you have put a few rare shillings into the tattered pocket of a post-boy who has returned the touching answer to a reproof you gave him for having his harness in such bad order, 'Plaze yer honor, we haven't turned a wheel this six months, no wonder the harness should break; faix 'tis broke we are ourselves for want o' work.' Then I delight in the blundering eagerness of the chamber-maid, whose kindness proceeds from her good nature, and not from the hope of reward. Good humour and good nature seem to me the great characteristics of Irish women of all ranks; I never saw a people whom it is more difficult to put out of temper. . . .

Monday evening. We decided on a visit to Loop-head, which is said to be about eighteen or twenty miles from Kilkee, and is the point which with Kerry-head forms the mouth of the Shannon. The most striking circumstance of our drive, was the density of the population; the country in every direction being covered with cottages. But when we consider the usual abundance and cheapness of the Irish "staff of life," potatoes, the occasional assistance which fishing affords, and the abundance of fuel, it is not to be wondered at, that as a residence this coast should prove so attractive. All goes well, so long as the harvest is favourable; but the consequences of a failure of the potato-crop are frightful. There is no intermediate step between plenty and starvation.

The road is excellent, being part of the coast-road, constructed some years ago, during a season of scarcity, and still kept in order by the Board of Works. After having passed the village of Cross, we left the Ross-road to the right, and got to a miserable, but singular-looking place on the Shannon, near its mouth, called Kilbaha; there we left our car, and proceeded on foot over a most rugged road, towards the light-house, the distance about four miles. ...

The Head itself is a rock, separated by a perpendicular cleft, forty or fifty feet wide, from the main land. It is the abode of sea fowl, who by their screams expressed their disapprobation of our approach. . . For some time after we left the light-house, we had a delightful walk on smooth turf, along the cliffs, whose ledges were covered with sea-fowl; in some places, drawn up lines, in the most exact order. We saw the place where, three or four years ago, about two acres of the cliff had fallen in, with so tremendous a crash as to shake the light-house, through half a mile distant.

We passed a curious wild bay, where people were collecting sea-weed for kelp, a trade now almost abandoned on this coast; and about three miles from the light-house came to the celebrated natural bridges, the chief objects of our expedition, and which, without the other attractions of this interesting coast, would have amply repaid us. These bridges connect the sides of a long narrow chasm, from thirty to forty feet wide, originally in all probability a cave, the roof of which fell in, leaving, in a wild and beautiful freak of nature, these bridges standing. . . . .

In a quiet little bay, near Ross, is one of the spas which are of frequent occurrence on this coast, and which have performed wonderful cures on invalids.

After getting over a rugged road, now under repair, and having paid contribution to the workmen, who good humouredly intercepted us by drawing a line across the road, to make us 'pay our footing,' a common custom in the South of Ireland, we joined our car at the place appointed, having walked a distance of about nine miles.

Our return was by Carrigaholt, which has the appearance of a thriving village. It is situated in a pretty bay of the Shannon, into which a small river discharges itself. A tongue of land forms one side of this bay; at its extremity is the ruin of a fine old castle, which belonged to the celebrated Lord Clare, who as at one time the proprietor of all this country. . . . .

Carrigaholt holds constant intercourse with Limerick, in the transport of turf and corn. An excellent road leads to Kilkee, along which we dashed right merrily, beating hollow two cars which had the impertinence to contend with us. One of them, to our driver's great delight, was put hors de combat by the loss of a wheel. We reached Kilkee exactly at seven, after a most gratifying excursion. . . . .

Thursday; Vermont. Yesterday we left Kilkee, and returned here. On our road to Kilrush, the first stage from Kilkee, we passed through Moyska [Moyasta], which is the head-quarters of turf, and great indeed must be its traffic in this article to obtain a name, in a country whose bogs are the great features and sources of wealth and commerce. The cottages in that neighbourhood, as I remarked all along the western coast of this county, are excellent. In some parts of Ireland, chimneys are held in contempt, as unnecessary assistants to the doors and windows: here, however, they are in such estimation that one or two false ones are frequently added by way of ornament.

The construction of the cottages is very good; the real bonâ-fide chimney is never at the gable-ends; it always occupies the centre of the house, the flue being in the partition wall between the rooms - by which means the house is more generally and thoroughly warmed. A cottage of tolerable size, such as would probably belong to a 'sthrong farmer,' has generally two sinecure chimneys at the gable ends. The houses are well roofed, and the thatch protected from the effects of the storm by a neat net-work of rope, which whilst performing the most useful office, is very ornamental also. . . .

Kilrush is a thriving place: as it rained, and we could see nothing of it, we were delighted when the pair of horses were ready to convey us to the fair Fanny O'Day's 'half-way house,' between Kilrush and Ennis. There is a police station near it; W--- fell into conversation, while changing horses, with the sergeant of the party. He said the country was perfectly quiet, and the roads may be travelled at all hours in perfect safety; and yet he told W--- of two events which show the singular disregard of the lower orders of the Irish for human life. A woman had that day been committed for having given a piper, apparently without provocation, a blow of a stone on the head, of which he died; and lately, at a neighbouring village, two men quarrelled as to which of them was the better dancer - when one of them went out quietly and brought in a stone with which he killed the other on the spot!

Near Ennis the scenery is rocky and picturesque; the great horse fair of Spancel Hill, which is in the neighbourhood, took place on the day we passed, and gave great life and animation to Ennis. Here we parted with our good-humoured post-boy, who had driven us from Kilkee; for though we exchanged horses, our postillion remained constant to us. For the thirty-six English miles we gave him seven shillings, which delighted him - he said, 'he had never before got so much for a job.' After leaving Ennis we passed near the ruins of Clare Abbey, which are very beautiful.

Killaloe, Monday morning. I am sitting at an open window in Clarisford House, which looks on a lovely view of mountains, valleys, and the fine woods which surround this place. . . We were told that Killaloe is chiefly indebted for improvements to Bishop Arbuthnot. He restored the cathedral, which he found nearly a ruin. The long bridge, over the impetuous Shannon, was impassable when he came to the see, seven of the centre arches having been carried away; owing to the Bishop's exertions, they were replaced by the five large arches which now exist, making the bridge one of fifteen arches. He also rebuilt the Episcopal palace, which is now a most comfortable house; and adorned the grounds and gardens.

In the evening we had a delightful walk through the grounds, and along the banks of the canal, which runs near the Shannon. We then went to evening service, where the effect of the music in the dimly-lighted church, was very solemn and impressive. . . .

Tuesday evening. Yesterday, before nine o'clock, we were at the quay of Killaloe, after having breakfasted at Clarisford with Mrs S ---, who, with her usual kindness and good nature, was up to see us off. The morning was fine, and lake smooth, when we embarked in the steamer for Portumna. . .

The steamer was obliged to anchor near Portumna for want of water, and wait for the arrival of the Dublin packet. We took advantage of the delay, and landed to see the remains of Portumna Castle, the property of Lord Clanricarde. It was unfortunately burnt down about eight years ago; in a few hours nothing but the bare walls were left. The house seems to have been of James the First's time; the ruins are extensive. Soon after we rejoined the steamer, a smaller one arrived - we exchanged cargoes in part, receiving a great many more than we gave, and then returned. A strong wind and heavy sea were now against us, so that cloaks and indianrubbers were very comfortable, as was also a bad luncheon, though off the scanty remains of a bad ham. We stopped for a moment to land a lucky passenger at William's-town, so called for futurity, the 'town' now consisting of a single house. This house is an inn, intended to be the great thoroughfare on a road between Ennis and Dublin, thus avoiding the detour by Limerick.

A high wind ruffles the temper as well as the sea; and ours was not smoothed by another stop to take a great additional lighter in tow, laden with sixty tons of slate. The slate quarries are, I think, near Derry, and are said to produce better slates, in point of quality, than the Welsh quarries, but inferior in colour. We arrived at Killaloe in about three hours and a half, and were delighted to get on shore. Not far from the landing-place there is a hotel, which commands a beautiful view of the lake. We heard it is excellent, and much frequented by persons who come to admire the surrounding scenery, and to enjoy the fishing on Lough Derg - but the hospitality of our friends at Clarisford prevented our seeing more than the outside.

Extracts taken from Lady Georgina Chatterton, *Rambles in the South of Ireland During the Year 1838*, 2 vols (London 1839), II, pp 170-227.

William Thackeray, Clare Sketch Book, 1842.

William Makepeace Thackeray, the celebrated author of such masterpieces as *The Luck of Barry Lyndon* (1844), *The Book of Snobs* (1846) and *Vanity Fair* (1848), was perhaps, after Charles Dickens, the best known of the English novelists of the Victorian era. A master of irony and satire, he explored in his fiction the moral and social pretensions of the age. Thackeray, born in India of English parents, had a number of Irish connections: he was married to Isabella Creagh Shaw of Doneraile, County Cork, whom he met in Paris in 1836; and a relative, Elias Thackeray, was a long serving vicar of Dundalk. He originally contracted to write a tour book of Ireland for publication in 1840. However, due to his wife's deteriorating mental health, he was compelled to abandon his original plan and it was not until 1842, under heavy financial pressure, that he began his Irish tour. Although Thackeray undoubtedly needed the money the publication of the tour would bring, the book is nonetheless cleverly written and gives a straightforward account of Ireland as it appeared to the intelligent traveller before the Great Famine. Sharp contrasts are made between the wealth of the landed classes and the grinding poverty he observed on all sides. His fulminations against government, absentee landlords and clerical indifference reveal how deeply he was touched by the condition of the people. His narrative is occasionally enlivened by fictional interludes: at Bunratty he recreates the scenes of centuries past by peopling the empty chambers with characters such as 'the gallant Lord Hugo', 'the fierce Sir Ranulph' and 'the blind harper of the race of De Clare'. In Ennis he purchased in 'a decent little library' six volumes of fiction which inspired him, while weather-bound in Galway, to devote a chapter of his book to the adventures of one Captain James Freeny. For his Irish tour Thackeray used as a guide book *A Journey Through Ireland in 1834* by Henry Inglis and possibly also *Fraser's Guide Through Ireland* (Dublin 1838). The many subsequent editions of Thackeray's *Irish Sketch Book* are eloquent testimony to the enduring success of the work.

The way to these wonderful sights [Cratloe Forest and Bunratty Castle] lies through the undulating grounds which border the Shannon, and though the view is by no means a fine one, I know few that are pleasanter than the sight of these rich, golden, peaceful plains, with the full harvest waving on them and just ready for the sickle. The hay harvest was likewise just being concluded, and the air loaded with the rich odour of the hay. Above the trees, to your left, you saw the mast of a ship, perhaps moving along, and every now and then caught a glimpse of the Shannon and the low grounds and plantations of the opposite county of Limerick. Not an unpleasant addition to the landscape too, was a sight which I do not remember to have witnessed often in this country, that of several small and decent farm-houses with their stacks and sheds and stables, giving an air of neatness and plenty that the poor cabin with its potato-patch does not present. Is it on account of the small farms that the land seems richer and better cultivated here, than in most other parts of the country? Some of the houses in the midst of the warm summer landscape had a strange appearance, for it is often the fashion to white-wash the roofs of the houses, leaving the slates of the walls of their natural colour; hence, and in the evening especially, contrasting with the purple sky, the house-tops often looked as if they were covered with snow. . . .

After travelling through a couple of lines of wall with plantations on either side, I at length became impatient as to the forest [of Cratloe], and, much to my disappointment, was told this was it. For the fact is, that though the forest has always been there, the trees have not, the proprietors cutting them regularly when grown to no great height; and the monarchs of the woods which I saw round about, would scarcely have afforded timber for a bed-post. Nor did any robbers make their appearance in this wilderness: with which disappointment, however, I was more willing to put up than with the former one. . . .

A policeman shows you over [Bunratty Castle], halls, chapels, galleries, gibbets, and all. The huge old tower was, until late years, inhabited by the family of the proprietor, who built himself a house in the midst of it: but he has since built another in the part opposite, and half-a-dozen 'peelers,' with a commodity of wives and children, now inhabit Bunratty. On the gate where we entered were numerous placards, offering rewards for the apprehension of various country offenders; and a turnpike, a bridge, and a quay, have sprung up from the place which Red Redmond (or anybody else) burned.

On our road to Galway the next day, we were carried once more by the old tower, and for a considerable distance along the fertile banks of the Fergus lake, and a river which pours itself into the Shannon. The first town we come to is Castle Clare, which lies conveniently on the river, with a castle, a good bridge, and many quays and warehouses, near which a small ship or two were lying. The place was once the chief town of the county, but is wretched and ruinous now, being made up for the most part of miserable thatched cots, round which you see the usual dusky population. The drive hence to Ennis lies through a country which is by no means so pleasant as the rich one we have passed through, being succeeded 'by that craggy, bleak, pastoral district which occupies so large a portion of the limestone district of Clare.' Ennis, likewise, stands upon the Fergus, a busy, little, narrow-streeted, foreign-looking town, approached by half-a-mile of thatched cots, in which I am not ashamed to confess, that I saw some as pretty faces as over any half-mile of country I ever travelled in my life.

A great light of the Catholic church, who was of late a candlestick in our own communion, was on the coach with us, reading devoutly out of a breviary, on many occasions, along the road. A crowd of black coats and heads, with that indescribable look which belongs to the Catholic clergy, were evidently on the look-out for the coach; and as it stopped, one of them came up to me with a low bow, and asked if I was the Honourable and Reverend Mr S ---? How I wish I had answered him I was! It would have been a grand scene. The respect paid to this gentleman's descent is quite absurd - the papers bandy his title about with pleased emphasis - the Galway paper calls him the *very* Reverend. . . .

At Ennis, as well as everywhere else in Ireland, there were of course the regular number of swaggering-looking buckeens, and shabby-genteel idlers, to watch the arrival of the mail-coach. A poor old idiot, with his grey hair tied up in bows, and with a ribbon behind, thrust out a very fair soft hand with taper fingers, and told me, nodding his head very wistfully, that he had no father nor mother: upon which score he got a penny. Nor did the other beggars round the carriage who got none, seem to grudge the poor fellow's good fortune. I think when one poor wretch has a piece of luck, the others seem glad here: and they promise to pray for you just the same if you give as if you refuse.

The town was swarming with people; the little dark streets, which twist about in all directions, being full of cheap merchandise and its vendors. Whether there are many buyers I can't say. This is written opposite the Market-place in Galway, and I have watched a stall a hundred times in the course of the last three hours, and seen no money taken: but at every place I come to, I can't help wondering at the numbers; its seems market-day everywhere - apples, pigs, and potatoes being sold all over the kingdom. There seems to be some good shops in those narrow streets; among others, a decent little library, where I bought, for eighteenpence, six volumes of works strictly Irish, that will serve for a half-hour's gossip on the next rainy day.

The road hence to Gort carried us at first by some dismal, lonely-looking, reedy lakes, through a melancholy country; an open village standing here and there, with a big chapel in the midst of it, almost always unfinished in some point or other. Crossing at a bridge near a place called Tubbor, the coachman told us we were in the famous county of Galway.

Extracts taken from William Makepeace Thackeray, *The Irish Sketch Book 1842* (London 1843, reprinted Belfast 1985), pp 150-56.

Johann Kohl, A Tour of Pre-Famine Clare, 1842

The German travel writer Johann Georg Kohl came to Ireland in September of 1842 'without', as he said himself, 'any object in view other than to become acquainted with the country, and to see everything that was interesting and remarkable in it'. A native of Bremen, Kohl had studied at the universities of Gottingen, Heidelberg and Munich, before settling in Dresden in 1838. From there he visited many European countries - including Russia, Hungary, Holland, Denmark, France, Dalmatia and England. He published most of his travel books between 1843 and 1851. He travelled to America in 1854, where he spent four years and prepared a series of maps for his government. In later life he became the city librarian of Bremen and died there in 1878. Kohl was an experienced observer with excellent judgement and his widespread travels allowed him to compare Irish conditions with the general European experience; his book on Ireland therefore is free of the prejudices that retard many writers and provides a most valuable insight into Irish living conditions on the eve of the Great Famine.

Landing in Dublin, he found the houses and buildings there much the same as those of English cities. Proceeding on to Athlone, he arrived at Shannon Harbour, where the Grand Canal intersected with the river Shannon. Steamboats brought canal passengers down river to Limerick. Above Killaloe rocks and rapids compelled travellers to transfer to horse-drawn canal boats, which brought them around the obstacles in the river. The passengers of quality sat on seats in the stern, while in front, sprawled on long benches, the poorer and dirtier sort were assembled. Presently they re-entered the river and in the evening landed at the quay of Limerick. Kohl proceeded to Ennis and Edenvale but, having heard that Father Mattew, the apostle of temperance, was to speak at Kilrush, he set out for west Clare.

Kohl, unlike most visitors, did not travel by steamer down the Shannon, but took instead the mail car from Ennis to Kilrush. He complained that the road, the principal one for the western part of the county, passed through the bleakest and most barren countryside imaginable. Not a single village or hut fit for human habitation was to be seen. What he apparently did not realise was that the road had recently been built and that it would be some years before substantial dwellings would appear along its frontage. The road, in fact, followed the most direct route from Ennis to Kilrush and deliberately avoided existing villages such as Kilmihill and Cooraclare. The stop at the 'mean inn' where the horses were changed was Fanny O'Dea's, the traditional halfway house between Ennis and Kilrush.

Kohl provides a superb description of Father Mathew and the scene in the temperance hall at Kilrush. Although Father Mathew kept aloof from politics, Kohl could sense that the temperance movement, which was then influencing millions of people, had political overtones and duly notes the cabinet-makers' banner with the motto 'Sobriety, Domestic Comfort and National Independence'! Before crossing the estuary to County Kerry, Kohl visited Scattery Island where he declared round towers to be the most interesting of

Irish antiquities. Kohl's book is written with typical German thoroughness; it is an outstanding example of the travel writer's craft and provides the best description by far of County Clare in the nineteenth century.

In company with an Irishman, who joined me in the hire of a car, I started on the following day, a fine Sunday morning, to pay a visit to a friend of mine, a landholder in the neighbourhood of Ennis, the capital of the county of Clare. The road lay at first along the Shannon, and then over a plain, said to be of the most fertile soil in Ireland. The appearance of the country was beautiful, and wherever the ground was slightly elevated, a fine view was obtained of the surrounding landscape, including the beautiful Shannon and its numerous islands. By the side of the river, and partly surrounded by it, lay the rock Carrigogunal, celebrated for its fairies, who take delight in surprising a mortal upon the rock, and making him partake of their hospitality. . .

I was grieved as I passed on the Sunday through several towns to see so many poor fellows loitering about, and on the look out for work. They were most of them in their Sunday attire, but with their spades in their hands, and stood grouped about the churches and market-places waiting to be hired to dig potatoes. I was shocked at the sight of such sad and serious multitudes, and all unemployed.

Clare is a poor and ruinous place, that reminded me of the Polish and Lithuanian cities. Though it bears the name of the county, it is not the chief town, that honour being enjoyed by Ennis, a much more orderly and prosperous-looking place, and celebrated in the history of Ireland, on account of the extraordinary excitement that accompanied the election of O'Connell for the county of Clare, in 1828 - an election that immediately preceded, and in a great measure contributed to bring about, Catholic Emancipation. . . .

Edenvale is one of the prettiest country-seats in the county of Clare, and I had every reason to congratulate myself on having accepted an invitation to spend a few days with the owner, an influential Protestant landholder. The Britons, including the Irish, certainly understand better than any other people the art of selecting an appropriate site for a country-seat, and then converting it into a kind of paradise. . . .

On my arrival, I found my worthy host busy with his trees and flowers, and we immediately undertook a little tour round the lovely glen on the margin of which his house is situated. One of the most remarkable spectacles that presented itself during my visit, was a complete eclipse of the sun, caused by an immense flight of rooks. Never in my life had I seen so many birds collected together. It was as if all the feathered tenants of the hundred thousand ruined castles, abbeys, and towers of Ireland had assembled to hold a monster meeting. The silent glen was at once filled by their loud and discordant cries, and their droppings poured down like a shower of hail; and yet the inhabitants of Edenvale assured me the spectacle was no uncommon one, the rooks having long made the glen one of their favourite haunts. It was at least an hour before the wild concert was at an end, and the air clear of the ungainly vocalists, and when the swarm had passed, I felt as if a thunder storm had rolled away. . . .

In England, where servants are kept at a proper distance, it is seldom that they venture on the familiar impertinence of which I saw frequent instances in Ireland. My worthy friend's coachman, a well-fed, merry-looking fellow, accompanied us through the stables and farm buildings, and pointed out every remarkable object to my attention, with a constant flow of eloquence, while his master followed modestly behind us.

'This stable you see, sir,' proceeded the coachman, '*we* finished last year. And a deal of trouble it cost us, for we had to begin by blowing away the whole of the rock there. But we shall have a beautiful prospect for our pains when the trees yonder have been cut down. And look down there, your honour, all them is his dominions (pointing to his master), and in two months he'll have finished the new building he has begun.' Now no English servant would have made equally free with his master, and yet the Irish servants are taken from a far more dependant class than the English peasants.

At Edenvale I heard of another old woman to whom popular belief ascribed supernatural powers. Her name was Consideen, and I met with her in a neighbouring cabin, into which I entered in the course of one of my excursions. Leaning on a stick the old octogenarian prophetess sat by the turf fire of her friend. She told me she had often seen death, leaning on two crutches, and standing at the end of the meadow, when any of her family was about to die. Old as she was, she said, she knew she should not die yet awhile, for death would be sure to come and give her warning when her time drew near. . . .

During that same walk I visited the stately mansions of some of my host's neighbours. These houses looked to me much more suited for spectral visitation than the fairy meadow I had just left. Scarcely a soul dwelt in them, and the rooms were silent like so many graves. The owners were absentees, who spent their Irish revenues in England or on the continent. These spectral palaces, I am sorry to say, are almost as abundant in Ireland, as fairy grounds and ruined castles. The rich Protestant landowners feel themselves uncomfortable on many accounts among the Catholic tenants. The wildness of the country is not easily remedied, the barbarism of the people leads them often to murderous acts of vengeance against their landlords; greater attractions are unquestionably to be found in English society; the peasantry are often divided into hostile factions, and perhaps many a Protestant may not be insensible to the injustice of which the wealthier class are guilty towards their poorer countrymen. All these causes, combining to keep so many wealthy Irish proprietors out of their country, may have given rise to the universally lamented evil of absenteeism. There are families, also, that have estates in England as well as in Ireland, and who naturally prefer residing in the former country. Those gentlemen, however, all are the most deserving of our esteem, who remain at home, where it is hardly possible that they should not in some measure ameliorate the lot of their poor tenants. There are, after all, many of these voluntary martyrs, and my hospitable host of Edenvale being one of them, I returned from my walk with feelings of increased esteem for him, nor was it without some regret that I took leave of him on the following morning.

The country westward of Ennis and Edenvale is the dark side of the county of Clare, - the wildest, poorest, and most barren part of it. I had, nevertheless, two inducements for visiting these wild regions. Firstly, I had heard that the celebrated Father Mathew was on his way to Kilrush, the most easterly town on the Shannon; and secondly, in the vicinity of this town lies the island of Scattery, on which stands one of the finest of the Irish 'Round Towers,' and, again, the ruins of 'Seven Churches.'

From Edenvale to Kilrush the distance is about sixteen English miles, and along the whole way, though this was the main road for the eastern [*recte* western] part of the county, I passed not a single village, nor a single hut fit for a human habitation. The landscape was everywhere naked and treeless; the colour of the soil was the most melancholy that can be imagined, - black or a dirty brown, - for one great bog seemed to cover all things, even the rocks. If it made me sad, however, how much sadder must such a country make a poor *glebæ adscriptus*, the vassal of a hard landlord, the father of a group of starving ragged children! . . .

A wooden house, with moss to stop up its crevices, would be a palace in the wild regions of Ireland. Paddy's cabin is built of earth; one shovelful over the other, with a few stones mingled here and there, till the wall is high enough. But perhaps you will say, the roof is thatched or covered with bark? Ay, indeed! A few sods of grass cut from a neighbouring bog are his only thatch. Well, but a window or two at least, if it be only a pane of glass fixed in the wall? or the bladder of some animal, or a piece of talc, as may often be seen in a Walachian hut? What idle luxury were this! There are thousands of cabins in which not a trace of a window is to be seen; nothing but a little square hole in front, which doubles the duty of door, window, and chimney; light, smoke, pigs, and children, all must pass in and out of the same aperture! . . .

The Indians in America live wretchedly enough at times, but they have no knowledge of a better condition, and, as they are hunters, they have every now and then a productive chase, and are able to make a number of feast-days in the year. Many Irishmen have but one day on which they eat flesh, namely, - on Christmas day. Every other day they feed on potatoes and nothing but potatoes. Now this is inhuman; for the appetite and stomach of man claim variety in food, and nowhere else do we find human beings gnawing, from year's end to year's end, at the same root, berry, or weed. There are animals who do so, but human beings, nowhere except in Ireland.

There are nations of slaves, but they have by long custom been made unconscious of the yoke of slavery. This is not the case with the Irish, who have a strong feeling of liberty within them, and are fully sensible of the weight of the yoke they have to bear. They are intelligent enough to know the injustice done them by the distorted laws of their country; and while they are themselves enduring the extreme of poverty, they have frequently before them, in the manner of life of their English landlords, a spectacle of the most refined luxury that human ingenuity ever invented. . . .

At times we stopped at a mean inn to change horses. The walls were generally tapestried with proclamations offering rewards for the apprehension of criminals. Fifty pounds were promised for the apprehension of those who had murdered farmer so-and-so; thirty pounds for information that would lead to the conviction of those who had burned a mill, and ill-treated the inmates to such a degree, that two of them had since died; and many others of the same kind. I had not time to read all these placards, instructive as they were respecting the condition of the country. . . .

We carried with us the letter bags intended for the several villages and country seats lying away from the road. At every stage we saw one of these living scarecrows waiting to take charge of the bags intended for the adjoining localities. These *postmen* tried to arrange their rags in a way to protect the correspondence of the country from the effects of the weather. As I looked on these ragged starved beings, I could not help thinking of the comfortable looking fellows to whom, in Prussia and Saxony, is entrusted the not unimportant duty of forwarding the public correspondence from village to village.

Not one in a hundred of those who look like beggars really beg, still the professional mendicants are numerous enough in all conscience. Most of them are decorated with Father Mathew's temperance medal, often as a matter of speculation, inasmuch as many are disposed to give more liberally to those who, having pledged themselves to abstain from intoxicating liquors, are thought less likely to make a bad use of any gift that may be bestowed upon them. Many people in Ireland now make a point of never giving any alms to a beggar who cannot show his temperance medal. . . .

Kilrush is a small seaport town, and, like all seaport towns in Ireland, has fewer ruins and a greater appearance of freshness and comfort than any of the places in the interior. I put up under the roof of an old sailor who had fought, in his time, under Nelson, and now directed the only tolerable hostelry in the place. My first walk was to the ground where Father Mathew was to be received. The temperance societies have their places of meeting in every town in Ireland, and these are called 'temperance halls.' The temperance hall of Kilrush lay in a by-street, a small courtyard was in front of it, and a few steps led up to the house door. The hall itself, if I am not mistaken, was used in the daytime as a national school, and in the evening the men of temperance held their meetings there. A shilling was demanded of every-one who entered, for which he was entitled, in the evening, to partake of the soirée that was to be given. A resident of the town, and one of the most distinguished among the temperance men, whose acquaintance I had already made, showed me the decorated hall, which was still empty. Round about the walls hung the banners of the several corporate bodies of the town, surmounted by mottoes all calculated to please the popular taste of the time. That of the cabinet-makers, for instance, was, 'Sobriety! Domestic Comfort! and National Independence!' This inscription struck me immediately. 'What,' I asked myself, 'has national independence to do with temperance, which is a purely moral question?' I believe, however, that, in point of fact, the two causes are more nearly united than is generally supposed. It appeared to me as if all these temperance men were engaged in a conspiracy against English ascendancy. . . .

Garlands and festoons were wound about the hall. A large horse-shoe table stood in the centre of the room, and boards resting on empty casks and blocks of wood were arranged as seats. At the head of the table were two arm-chairs, one for Father Mathew, and one for the principal Catholic priest of the place, who was to act as chairman. Behind these chairs a gigantic cornucopia was represented, with a multitude of shamrocks falling out; another allusion to Irish nationality. On side tables stood a countless host of teapots and teacups, and huge piles of bread-and-butter, for on all solemn occasions tea is the nectar of the temperance men, and bread-and-butter their chief food. . . .

Suddenly the cry rose, 'He comes! he comes!' and I heard at the other end of the street one of those detestable musical displays with which the temperance men generally open their processions and solemnities. . . .

The great, the famed apostle of temperance, the most prominent man in Ireland, with the exception of O'Connell, entered the room. He advanced slowly through the crowd, for every one wished to shake hands with him, and he had enough to do with his friends to the right and the left. At last he arrived at his place opposite mine, and sat down in his garlanded chair. I was formally introduced to the reverend chairman, who, in his turn, presented me to Father Mathew, with whom I exchanged a few friendly words of welcome. He is decidedly a man of a *distinguished* appearance, and I was not long in comprehending the influence which it was in his power to exercise over the people. The multitude require a handsome and imposing person in the individual who is to lead them, and Father Mathew is unquestionably handsome. He is not tall, he is about the same height and figure as Napoleon, and is, throughout, well built and well proportioned. He has nothing of the meagre, haggard, Franciscan monk about him; but, on the contrary, without being exactly corpulent, his person is well rounded, and in excellent condition. His countenance is fresh and beaming with health. His movements and address are simple and unaffected, and altogether he has something about him that wins for him the good will of those he addresses. His features are regular, and full of a noble expression of mildness and indomitable firmness. His eyes are large, and he is apt to keep his glance fixed for a long time on the same object. His forehead is straight, high, and commanding, and his nose - a part of the face which in some expresses such intense vulgarity, and in others so much nobleness and delicacy - is particularly handsome, though somewhat too aquiline. His mouth is small and well proportioned, and his chin round, projecting, firm, and large, like Napoleon's. . . .

A number of young women, and some lovely and wicked-looking ones among them, crowded round the 'apostle.' Some were sitting by his side, some at his feet, and some in each other's laps, merely for the sake of being nearer to the holy man, and now and then touching him.

Some beautiful old Irish melodies were sung, for Ireland, though its early history has had little interest for the rest of the world, has received from remote ages some melodies of exquisite beauty. Nor was there any lack of toasts, nor did these fail to call forth speeches of more than moderate length. The toast proposed with the most edifying speech, but by no means received with the greatest enthusiasm, was 'The Irish clergy.'. . .

Towards midnight, after a countless succession of speeches, answers, toasts, and countertoasts, Father Mathew retired. The tables and teapots were immediately put aside, and a ball commenced, which must have been kept up till a late hour, for the morning was far advanced when I heard the temperance band returning home, and still playing their favourite melodies as they passed along the street. . . .

At nine o' clock on the following morning, Father Mathew was again in the field, that is to say, in the church, where he read mass, after which he administered the pledge to a few hundred persons who presented themselves for that purpose. The medal which he bestows on these occasions, and of which mention has so often been made, is a round piece of pewter, of about the size of a five-franc piece. The words of the pledge are inscribed upon it, consisting of a solemn promise to abstain from all intoxicating liquors, and to persuade others as much as possible to do the same. Some wear their medals constantly as a kind of amulet, others place them round the necks of their little children, who are often made to pledge themselves to abstain from a vice, the nature of which they are scarcely able to comprehend. . . .

On leaving Kilrush I entrusted my person and my portmanteau to a small boat which I had engaged to carry me over to Scattery Island, and thence to the coast of Kerry. . . We effected a landing on Scattery Island, called in ancient times Inniscattery, and at present occupied by a few tenants of a Mr M'Kean, who graze their cattle there. 'It is a very old ancient place,' said one of the boatmen, as he was carrying me through the water on his shoulders, for we had come to a landing-place where the tide had left one foot of water over a large extent of coast. This pleonasm of 'old ancient' might be applied to many parts of Ireland, where old and older ruins are constantly found in close contiguity. In general, where there are seven churches, in Ireland, some ancient saint is named as having lived and died there, and as having belonged to the first preachers of Christianity in the country. At Scattery it is Saint Senanus, whose grave is still shown amid one of the ruins, and whose fame has been extended far beyond his native isle by one of Moore's melodies. These ancient ruins, however, have many graves of a more modern date; for bodies are still brought over from the mainland to be interred at Scattery. On the occasion of such a funeral, one boat serves generally as a hearse, and the mourners follow in other boats. I saw many tombstones only a few years old, with new inscriptions, from which the gilding had scarcely begun to fade, and their effect upon the solitary and remote island had a peculiar and by no means unpleasing effect. Among them were the tombs of several captains of ships, and it would have been difficult to suggest a more appropriate place of internment for such men than this little island cemetery at the mouth of a great river, with the wide ocean rolling in front. Indeed, there is no other country in Europe where there are such interesting cemeteries, or such picturesque tombs, as in Ireland, partly on account of the abundance of ivy with which they are hung, and partly on account of the practice that still prevails of burying the dead among ruins. Of some of the seven churches on Scattery isle, scarcely a trace remained; but three of them were in tolerable preservation. Their walls, covered with ivy, remained, and into the wall of one of them, that nearest the round tower, a stone strangely sculptured into the form of a human face, had been introduced. Strange to say, it has completely the stiff, masklike features and projecting ears of the Egyptian statues, whence I conclude it must have belonged originally to some other building. On the opposite wall is a stone with evident traces of an ancient inscription.

The round tower stands a little to the side. Although not perfect, it belongs to the most picturesque in Ireland, for it has been struck by lightning, and has received a split on one side from top to bottom. On the south side it is covered completely with mosses and creeping plants; on the north and west side it is bare, the heavy winds, as the sailors told me, making all vegetation impossible there. Lightning and vegetation are the worst enemies the round towers have to contend with, and it is strange that such active foes should not have been able to overturn the whole of them in a space of 2000 years.

All the land upon the little island, except the cemetery, is pasturage. A small battery has been erected here to protect the mouth of the Shannon, the entrance to which river is defended by no less than six batteries and forts, while at the mouth of the Thames there is not one.

On leaving Inniscattery, to repair to the kingdom of Kerry, we had work enough before us, for the tide was against us, besides which we had to contend with such a variety of currents, that the boatmen required all their skill and experience to carry their slight skiff in safety to the little port of Tarbert, whither we were bound.

Extracts taken from J. G. Kohl, *Travels in Ireland*, translated from the German, (London 1844), pp 42-67.

John Manners, Notes on a Clare Tour, 1846

John Manners, a life long politician, was the second son of the fifth Duke of Rutland. Educated at Eton and Trinity College Cambridge, he graduated an M.A. in 1839. He composed poetry and in 1841 published a book entitled *England's Trust and Other Poems*, which is chiefly remembered for the couplet:

> Let wealth and commerce, laws and learning die,
> But leave us still our old nobility,

- lines which, at the time, exposed him to much public ridicule. Entering parliament in 1841 as member for Newark, he espoused many liberal causes. He was a strong advocate of social reform and for raising the conditions of the lower classes both materially and intellectually. He sought to establish public holidays by act of parliament and campaigned for a ten hour maximum working day for labourers which eventually became law in 1847. Being sympathetic towards the Catholic church, he advocated generous treatment of the Roman Catholic clergy in Ireland and supported the financial grant to Maynooth college in 1845. On the death of his brother in 1888 he succeeded as seventh duke of Rutland. His book on Ireland is principally of value because he toured the country as the Great Famine raged in 1846. What is particularly significant about his journey in west Clare is that, despite observing the appalling social conditions, not once does he mention famine or starvation; as an aristocrat Manners was perhaps too removed from the struggle for survival to appreciate the plight of the common people. The tour was first published in 1849 'to amuse and to provide useful suggestions to those who may wish to visit the Emerald Isle'. A second edition appeared in 1881 to show how much progress had been made in the interim.

24 August [1846]. I witnessed to-day some curious and some painful illustrations of everyday Irish life, at Sixmile Petty Sessions, in a wild part of Clare. On entering the little town, every other house in which is a ruin, we met a Mr ---, whom --- introduced to me as one of the most spirited agricultural improvers of the west; we went into court, and the case which occupied most time and attention was one in which Mr --- played a conspicuous part, as will be seen from the following sketch of the attorney's speech for the plaintiff in Maloney v. O'Gorman.

For twenty years Maloney had rented of Mr --- a small farm and piece of bog convenient at £18 per annum. In 1843 the lease expired; Mr --- refused to renew it, and asked £5 a year in addition for the tenancy at will. Maloney agreed, and took the land at that rent: but Mr ---, anxious to improve his estate, said, unless you will subsoil your farm, you must pay 5s. an acre more. To this fresh demand Maloney demurred, and then followed a series of persecutions on the part of

Mr ---, the last of which was the case before us. In 1844 Maloney tendered his rent, minus the £2 5s. for not subsoiling; Mr --- refused to receive it, and served Maloney with a latitat; the cause was tried, and Mr --- cast with costs. Coming out of court, the defeated gentleman saw Maloney and his wife standing outside, and, as their house was some way off, knew they could not reach it speedily, he jumped on a car, and broke into the ungarrisoned place, turning the furniture into the road, and breaking the finger of Maloney's father-in-law, an infirm old man, with the tongs. The work of demolition was nearly complete before the Maloneys came up. On Mrs Maloney attempting to enter, Mr --- presented a pistol at her; but in spite of all this a truce was concluded, the furniture replaced, Mr --- forgiven, and things resumed a tranquil appearance. But twelve days after this attack, Maloney hears Mr --- has issued a summons against them for an assault. The trial came on, but the crown prosecutor, after opening the case, refused to proceed with it, and Mr --- was again defeated. This took place last spring; he then gave Maloney notice to quit next November, thus acknowledging the poor man's right to the land until that period. But in spite of this he affected a right to let the piece of bog to the present defendant for 14s. and had induced him to 'foot' the peats which Maloney had cut; for doing which the action was brought. Imagine this tale, which I have purposely related in as bald a manner as possible, told with all the vindictive eloquence of an Irish attorney, passionately pleading the cause of the poor oppressed against the rich oppressor! Well, O'Gorman said but little in defence. Mr --- had assured him the bog was not let to Maloney, and had urged him to foot the turves; he believed him, paid his rent, and committed the act charged against him. The plaintiff's attorney asked for only nominal damages, to prove once more his client's right, and 1s. fine was imposed on the luckless O'Gorman. What a light does this little history, thus imperfectly told, throw on Irish misery and Irish disaffection! Here you have a gentleman, whose health a few days ago was proposed at the great Irish Agricultural Meeting in Limerick, as the type of agricultural progress, demanding that which no landlord has a right in law or equity to demand of a tenant; persecuting that tenant from court to court for resisting that unjust demand; when defeated in law, having recourse to violence, and with his own arm assaulting an infirm and helpless old man; receiving a double rent for the same bog, and, lastly, urging a man whose money he had wrongfully received to the perpetration of an illegal act, for which that man is punished! . . .

In [another] case, a priest, with a handsome riding whip in his hand, appeared as a witness. One brother charged another with trespass, for pasturing his cows on his, the complainant's, land. The defendant had offered to refer the matter to the arbitration of the third brother, the priest; the complainant rejected the proposal, and the priest came into court to say what he knew of the matter: in the very first sentence, however, he styled brother No. 1, an 'idle lazy fellow,' which drew from that insulted gentleman a storm of the most vituperative vindication. 'Me idle! and it's you who say it: you who, etc., etc.' The constables cried silence, the magistrates, like Lauderdale in 'Old Mortality,' entreated the excited orator 'to keep his breath to cool his ain porridge;' the priest held up his hand, and turned up his eyes in vain: there was the end of his mediation, and fraternal authority. When the storm had somewhat abated, the magistrates recommended the parties to settle it amicably, and the Roman Catholic Bishop and a neighbouring farmer were agreed to as referees.

There were half a dozen other causes, each with some peculiarity, grave or gay, stamped upon it; and I left the court-house of Six-mile Bridge, duly impressed with the conviction that an Englishman can know nothing of Irish nature and Irish habits. . . .

Sunday 30 August [1846]. Young and old, rich and poor, in the west of Ireland have an unbounded faith in the restorative effects of sea bathing; and during the summer months a little bathing place on the iron bound coast of Clare, called Kilkee, receives more visitors than twenty towns of larger dimensions could possibly accommodate. 'He's set a lodge at Kilkee' or 'They're gone to the salt water', is the usual reply to an inquiry after a Limerick family at this time of year. The lower you descend in the scale of society, the more does the faith in the sea approach superstition; and the privations a poor family will endure, the weary miles they will walk, in order to give some sick member the benefit of a month at the seaside, is extraordinary. The sea for all conceivable complaints is a sovereign remedy. Anxious to see this western Brighton, I got on board with considerable difficulty, a Limerick steamer, crowded as never was a steamer crowded before, which carried us rapidly down the noble ever-widening Shannon. The scenery along its banks still continued uninteresting, almost ugly, but the river before we reached Kilrush is well nigh a lake. Kilrush is the port of Kilkee, has a large market place, some granaries, and other faint signs of trade and business. A drunken driver and jaded horse, after sundry mishaps, took us to Kilkee by sunset, through the most wretched dreary country, I have yet seen. Vegetation hereabouts appears not to be stunted only, but to have ceased altogether, as if tired by the long years of constant endeavour and recurring failures.

Tuesday 1 September [1846]. Kilkee itself is the quaintest collection of little whitewashed cottages, some distinguished by the name of 'lodges', that ever aspire to the dignity of a bathing place; and considering it is on the Atlantic I must pronounce the bathing to be bad. The lodges are built round a sandy creek, and here *coram populo*, plies the one bathing-machine, which the decent liberality of Lady

Chatterton presented to this Clare Herne Bay; and if you don't choose to wade a quarter of a mile among a hundred fellow bathers over the said sands, you must do as I did, look out for some cranny among the rocks and trust to the mercifulness of the Atlantic waves. . . As we had only one day to spend at Kilkee, how we should spend it became an anxious question with my two companions, who knew all the charms of this weird coast. . . .

A walk of five or six miles brought us to the Natural Bridges of Ross, which are three in number, and are thrown over narrow creeks of the sea; under them the tide rushes with great violence, and in winter, the neighbouring farmer told us, often dashes over his sheep walk, and endangers the life of his luckless flock. . . In the various little inlets of this terrible coast, where no boat can hope to live, we saw some fifty canoes drawn up, bottom uppermost, looking like stranded whales; these belong to a class of venturous seamen, who catch mackerel at night, and idle or cultivate a wretched acre of land during the day. They sell their mackerel at three-halfpence a piece to the Kilkee tradesmen, but it is only on calm evenings that even they dare risk their frail canoes on that terrible sea. About two hundred men are employed on this dangerous occupation. The farmer on whose grounds these bridges are, asked us into his house and gave us some milk. Several of the fishermen lounged in, and we offered them the remains of our bottle of sherry; all, however, save our wild looking host, were teetotallers, and declined: he gulped down the wine with great relish. I wish I could have sketched his one great room, that like the cobbler's in that touching poem, 'served him for kitchen, and parlour and all'; it rose with an open timber roof, the whole height of the house, and was warmed by an enormous fireplace and chimney. A long-haired daughter was busy at the spinning wheel in one corner, and altogether there was an air of comfort about this marine grange that I have not seen in more favoured localities. Here we found our car, and our kind friend insisted on showing the way onto the high road; and perhaps it was well he did so, for the track lay through several ruined cottages; and as it is impossible to draw a line between the ruinous huts that are, and those that are not inhabited in this country, we might have scrupled to invade, horse and car, the desolate privacy of these sad penates [dwellings]. Guided, however, by him, we threaded our way through kitchen, pig-sty and dung-heap, and so reached the Kilkee road.

Extracts taken from Lord John Manners M.P., *Notes of an Irish Tour in 1846* (Edinburgh 1881), pp 15-20, 54-61.

Quaker Reports on Famine Conditions in Clare, 1847

During the bitter winter of 1846-7, the starving people would have fared much worse than they did, had it not been for the work of the voluntary societies. Foremost amongst these were the Society of Friends or the Quakers, who raised funds for the establishment of soup kitchens, which for many months were the only means of subsistence for large sections of the population. Setting up the Central Relief Committee in London and Dublin in November 1846, the Quakers were careful to collect accurate information on the state of affairs in the west of Ireland. To this end agents were dispatched to report on the prevailing conditions; it was these reports that helped to enlighten, not just British public opinion, but the government itself, about the true nature of the situation on Ireland. The Quakers showed extraordinary commitment and generosity as they helped people in need without religious distinction. A typical example of their generosity is the thirty seven barrels of Indian meal, eight barrels of rye, three of flour, two of peas, one of pork and bales of clothing that were distributed among the poor of Ruan parish in September 1847. In June 1849 the Quakers discontinued their relief work stating bluntly in a letter to John Russel, the British prime minister, that the problem of relief had become too great for any voluntary group and that only the government could raise the funds and carry out the measures to save people's lives. They added that the kernel of the problem was the need to reform the land system, which was a matter for legislation not philanthropy.

Transactions of The Central Relief Committee of the Society of Friends during the Famine in Ireland, in 1846 and 1847.

To the Auxiliary Relief Committee of Friends at Limerick.

In accordance with the wish of the committee, we proceeded on the 15th inst. to Kilrush. On our way from that place to Cooraclare, we observed stacks of corn and hay on several farms, and behind several humble dwellings; this we were unprepared for, being under the impression that all or nearly all the corn had been consumed. The land also presented a less neglected appearance that we anticipated, from all that we had heard of its being left untilled. However, after leaving Cooraclare a mile or two behind us, towards the confines of Kilmacduane parish, the wild bleak hills of Kilmihil broke on our view; and as we proceeded, the cabins and farms assumed a more wretched appearance, and we soon had visible evidence that the description given us of the state of this parish had not been overcoloured.

We soon reached the house of the Roman Catholic priest. He entered earnestly into the subject of our mission; gave us information on every point we sought; and displayed much good sense, good feeling, and candour in his communications.

This parish contains over eighteen thousand acres, and numbers about six thousand inhabitants. All the landed proprietors are non-resident; there are no resident gentry; the priest is the only person to whom the poor can turn for assistance; and from all the accounts we have had, both before our visit to him and since, he appears to be unremitting in his exertions.

After leaving Cooraclare, we proceeded to Kilmurry Ibrickan. This parish contains about twelve thousand inhabitants, and presents a frightful picture of misery and want, more especially along the coast. To this quarter, many houseless wanderers, ejected tenants, and unfortunates of all kinds, and from all quarters, have for some years past been attracted by the free trade in sea-weed manure, there being no check given to squatters; and these are so thickly clustered in some places, that on one townland here of forty-six acres, there are two hundred and ten human beings! There are in this quarter five hundred families (containing over three thousand individuals) located near the shore, none of whom have any land attached to the hovels in which they try to exist. The potato having failed, and with it the trade in sea-weed, not only are they totally deprived of food, but also of the means of procuring it, and as they are unrecognized by any landlord, they are nor considered as tenants of the soil; and thence there is no one bound to them by ties of interest, or upon whom they can urge a legitimate claim for support.

After leaving Kilmurry, we entered the parish of Kilfarboy, and reached Miltown at six, p.m.

On our way to Miltown, and on our return next day by Kilkee, we entered several of the poorer cabins along the road, and in every instance administered some small relief, while we made enquiries as to their modes of life and means of subsistence. The scenes which we witnessed, and the stories which we heard in these abodes of human misery, will not be easily effaced from our memory. All were poor in the extreme - some deplorably so; but it was the same sad tale we heard from all; their potatoes had failed, and their scanty stock of oats being all consumed, they are now solely dependant on the wages received from the road works. The applicants for employment are so numerous, that in most instances only one man in a family, and in some cases one, and a boy, woman, or girl, can obtain it. All work alike on the roads! The pay of a man is tenpence, a woman eightpence, and a boy sixpence per day; and when you consider that there may be broken days from sickness or severe weather - that the price of the lowest description of food is enormously high - and that families here average about seven individuals, you will not be surprised when we state, that they can scarcely support life under their many privations. Indeed, their week's wages, when exchanged for food, is not more than sufficient for three or four day's consumption. They endeavour, however, to stretch it over the week; but it is no uncommon thing with many families to be without any food for twenty-four or thirty-six hours before the succeeding pay - day comes round, with the exception of the man or boy who is at work. And to prevent his strength (upon which all their living depends) from failing, the scanty subsistence of the others is still further reduced, to provide him with sufficient to sustain him. So pressing are the calls of hunger, that when the week's supply of meal is brought home, (perhaps a distance of six miles) it is in many cases eaten before it is fully cooked; some bake it on a griddle; but among the very poorest, and where the family is large, in order to make it go far, it is boiled into gruel. Is it then to be wondered at that dysentery, the general result of insufficient and imperfectly cooked food, should be, as it is, so prevalent amongst them?

James Harvey.

Thomas Grubb.

Limerick, 22nd February, 1847.

Distress in Ireland; Narrative of R. Barclay Fox's visit to some parts of the west of Ireland, 1847

Galway 27 March 1847

At Ennis the chief town of Clare, I observed the streets crowded with gaunt and rugged idlers, male and female, - a consequence of several hundred men having been discharged from the public works within the last two or three days. Whilst there I breakfasted at the house of a benevolent and intelligent man, a landlord and county magistrate, whose wife and daughters are actively engaged in providing employment for the women. I gave them £10 in promotion of their object. My host informed me that he offered to give work to many labourers in drainage, but the owners of the adjoining estates would not co-operate by doing anything to carry off the water. He has offered his tenants seed if they will cultivate their land, but they do not avail themselves of it: he has given one of his tenants six year's rent to enable him to emigrate. The peasantry of Clare has as bad a character for lawlessness as those of Tipperary. Very many horses have been shot while conveying corn to Ennis markets, under the impression that the sale of grain, even in the country, lessens the supply. The aggressors are not brought to justice, - the sufferer simply 'presents' for a new horse at the sessions. The poorhouse at Ennis is well conducted, clean and orderly though containing 240 beyond its full compliment: the deaths are about ten per week, but the fever cases are transferred to the hospital.

At Gort the street was crowded with forlorn beings waiting for relief or employment; some thousands, I was told, have been turned off the public works within the last two days. A crowd of clamorous women laid siege to the coach, many of them evidently suffering from hunger; they said that no soup was given in the place, but sold at a penny per quart (meaning, no doubt, to those not furnished with tickets); their husbands, they said, were without employment, and they had nothing left 'but the mercy of God and the charity of Christians'. It is almost impossible that the new regulations for providing so vast an amount of relief can be organised in time to supply the destitution, which must follow the stoppage of the public works, and a great increase of mortality, will, I fear, be the result. Between Ennis and Galway I observed large tracts of land left utterly neglected. In fact, cultivation is the exception, desolation the rule. The streets of this town teem with miserable beggars, but the ear gets accustomed to the cry for food, and the hand of charity is paralysed by the mass of want to be relieved.

Taken from:
(i) *Transactions of the Central Relief Committee*, 1846
(ii) R. Barclay Fox, *Distress in Ireland: Narrative of R. Barclay Fox's visit to Some Parts of the West of Ireland*, Society of Friends (London 1847), pp 2-3.

Spencer Hall, Life and Death in County Clare, 1849

Spencer Timothy Hall, bookseller, author and homeopath, was one of several English writers to visit the county following the catastrophe of the Great Famine and the numerous reports appearing in English newspapers on conditions in County Clare. Hall was a compassionate man of humble origins; his farther, a Quaker, was a cobbler by trade. Growing up in Nottingham-shire, Hall received little education. He was apprenticed to a printer in 1829 and on the completion of his apprenticeship established himself as a printer and bookseller at Sutton in Ashfield. Appointed postmaster there he printed a monthly publication called the *Sherwood Magazine*. He developed an abiding interest in alternative medicine and spoke and wrote widely on phrenology, the study of the human brain where function was thought to be determined by the shape and size of the skull. This led him to experiment with hypnosis. He allegedly wrought many cures, his most famous patient being Harriet Martineau (a lady who also wrote extensively on post-Famine conditions in County Clare), whom he cured of a hopeless illness in 1844. The results of his labours were published in *Mesmeric Experiences* (1845). Following his visit to Ireland in 1849 he published *Life and Death in Ireland*, a factual account of the famine scenes he witnessed in the west of Ireland, often considered his best book. In later years he became interested in homeopathy. He practised as a homeopath doctor and published *Homeopathy a Testimony* in 1852. Although Hall held a Ph.D. from Tubigen University, Germany, he was not a legally qualified medical doctor and made little from his practice. His later life was spent in poverty; he died in Blackpool, 1885.

It was a very fine morning on which we started upon this excursion, and very busy too for many miles was the road, on account of a great fair at Ennis. Without dwelling on scenes already mentioned, or staying to describe the dejected-looking little town of Newmarket, or the elegant castle of Dromoland, the seat of Sir Lucius O'Brien, with its well-wooded grounds and gleaming lakelet, I may say in general terms that the trip, as far out as Clare, opened up to observation an average variety of Irish extremes. The road, like every turnpike I had travelled on in the country, was excellent; - and, surrounded by undulating green landscapes, lit here and there with refreshing water-glimpses, might be seen buildings of every degree, from the old castle and modern castelet, down to the temporary dwellings of out-driven tenantry in the bye-lanes - the latter (as I examined them on a more leisurely occasion) partaking somewhat in their style of the united orders of the Indian wigwam and the Hottentot kraal.

The town of Clare, with its water-facilities and twenty other great natural advantages, has for some reason been sacrificed to its close neighbour, Ennis, which has altogether superseded it as the capital of the county. It is, in fact, little more at present than a mere village, though not without one or two commercial features. In its castle or barrack, at the time we passed, were quartered some Highland soldiers, who were just being called out by the bagpipes to parade. But what I thought seemed much more in keeping with the country around were the grey ruins of its fine old abbey, in the fields on the right side of our road, as we went on to Ennis.

The latter town was on this day, of course, a scene of bustle if not of gaiety; and although we had very little time, I managed to get a glance at the fair. Irish fairs, like every thing else Irish, have so often been caricatured, and turned into subjects of fun, as possibly to make a homelier description the more agreeable. At this there was a considerable supply of stock, consisting of horses, mules, asses, cows, goats, pigs, and poultry, - which might have been had almost at any price, but there were scarcely any buyers. I have been at many fairs in various parts of England and Scotland; not because of having business at them, but owing to the idea that there one may learn very much in a short time of the character of the district in which they are held; but I never saw one so melancholy as this. And yet somehow the people all looked as if they had been or could be sprightly. The few bargains I observed were made with much clamour, in the Irish language, and in the presence of two witnesses, who confirmed them by uniting their hands over or with those of the buyer and seller - thus forming a cross.

The features, manners, and costume of the majority of the country people, some of whom had come from the wilds of Galway, added to the language they spoke, and (to an Englishman) curious stock of goats, mules, and asses in which they dealt, made me almost start to think that, instead of being in some far-off, primitive land, I was in reality within a twenty-four hours' ride of home and among citizens of the same nation! . . .

Passing by a shattered tower, and turning from the road at the little town of Ballinacally, we struck by an old ruined church, and were soon afterwards met by a number of people, amongst the foremost of whom were the two deputies from the suspended works we were going to see. The works in question were mines of culm, a sort of bastard coal, having a sulphurous smell and casting no flame, but very useful in lime-burning, and for other similar purposes. The manager and the workmen were most anxious to resume operations; and for their interest as well as his own the chieftain stated he was desirous that they should. It is therefore needless to say that his visit was a very acceptable one - since many of them had no other employment to depend upon, and nothing to eat without it. To me the manager and his neighbours seemed on as kindly terms as if they were all one family, and he their father.

Leaving the mines, we visited some drainage works yet higher up the country - the people, old and young, of both sexes, still thronging after and hailing us with blessings and all kinds of pleasantries. At one point where they all gathered round the car, I got into conversation with those who were foremost.

Well boys (said I) of what religion are you here?

'Catholic - all true Catholic, to be sure!'

What! is there not a single Protestant on the estate?

'Not one, then, your honour!'

But does no Protestant minister ever come among you and try to teach you?

'Not at all, then! and what is the need for him to come, when there are no Protestants to come to?'

But what is the distance to your nearest school?

'Between two and three miles.'

And (addressing myself to the best informed of them) do you mean to tell me seriously that no Protestant clergyman ever comes amongst you for any purpose whatever?

'Never!' responded several voices at once. . . .

During the earlier hours of the afternoon, we had met several parties of the armed police, escorting prisoners down to Ennis; but one we passed on returning was more remarkable than the others. Of the races who have in ancient times settled in the country, is one supposed to be of Spanish origin, not yet entirely fused with the rest; and the prisoners in this instance were of that race, with dark hair, and equally dark yet enkindled eyes. One of them was a powerful-looking man, with a large bloody gash upon his brow. A woman well constituted to match him - it might be his wife or sister - and two other persons, were all with him where he lay, bound on a car; the police, with their mounted firelocks, walking before, on each side, and behind. The features of the whole party displayed a working of the darkest passions of the soul. But all I could learn of their case was no more than that it arose, like so many besides, out of some process of eviction or distraint, which they had determined to oppose and risk the consequences.

On our nearing Ennis again, it was a moving sight - that of the crowds of people returning to the country from the fair, many of them taking back their unsold stock, others sad from having been compelled to part with it at most ruinous prices. Whether it were owing to principle or poverty, or both, I know not; but there was much less drunkenness than I had expected to see on such an occasion; and in the evening all was as quiet and orderly in the town as at any fair of equal consequence I had ever known in England.

At the inn where we stayed, there happened to be a frank and intelligent young Irishman - a civil engineer - whom I had seen before at the chateau; and after dinner, as there was still nearly an hour of daylight, we took advantage of it to glance together at one or two points of local interest. Almost opposite was a neat Anglican church, preserved or recovered from the ruins of an old monastery, another part of the interior of which had been turned into a burial ground. These we made an engagement with the sexton - an obliging man - to explore. Considering how extensive and beautiful were some of the architectural remains, I was surprised at the state in which, on one side of the church, they had been allowed to sink. But worse than all - to say, too, that it was in the best quarter of the town - was the dirty and slovenly state of the burial ground itself. My first impression on entering that part of the ruins was, that the place might have been purposely desecrated from religious animosity towards the sect from whom it had passed. But on seeing how the graves of so many of the Protestant towns-people were half-hidden in loose stones and dirt and nettles, it seemed to be in reality little else than a mark of sheer public neglect. . . .

The morrow rose 'with breath all incense and with cheek all bloom,' and at an early hour we were again on our car, accompanied by the young engineer, whose conversation became very interesting to me. . .

Our course this time was north, or north-westward, into a country blending the wild and rugged with the pastoral and beautiful. . . .

In this neighbourhood was a fine natural well, giving the name of 'Fountain' to a residence and farm, and pouring forth a volume half as large as that of Holywell, in Flintshire, - the water abounding with large trout from its very source, and winding away through the green meadows to a lough that was gleaming within the horizon, and making the scene altogether as pleasant and refreshing as the morning that shone down upon it.

Leaving this, we came about noon to another genteel farm-house, on a sort of natural terrace, overlooking a great extent of country. Immediately below was spread out to the south a large tract of half-drained caucass, or meadow, bounded on one side by a branch of the Fergus, and on the other by a prettily winding minor tributary; and here were grazing a herd of good-looking cattle. From the back extended some undulating land, consisting chiefly of arable fields, the crops on which seemed in moderate progress; and beyond these again was a scene altogether novel to me. Here was stretched out, as it seemed for miles, one great unbroken superstratum of grey stone - to the eye of fancy like a lake that had been just ruffled by the wind, then suddenly petrified and left to perpetual sterility. On bringing us to the verge of this *Hibernia Petrea*, where the ruin of an old tower threw its shadow over the head of a lough that flowed away in another direction, the farmer, (who was also a poor-law guardian,) solicited some reduction in his rent, to prevent, as he said, the necessity of his emigrating, and illustrated the destitution which prevailed around him, by informing us that some of the famishing people had come into his field, and taken away the potato seed for food after it had been set!

On hearing the statements of farmers so respectable as this, as to their inability to make their capital and industry answer at the rate they were paying, how mad, thought I, must have been the extortion which, in many places I had seen with natural advantages by no means superior, had set down small holders with large families at proportionably three, four, and even five times the rental these were complaining of, and then depending merely on the potato, the pig, and one small cow, or goat, perhaps, for the means of payment!

We now passed (on the border of the lough or lake) the family residence of the O'Loghlins, and found great numbers of the peasantry cleaned up, in their best attire, and scattered along the road towards Ennis. The reason was this. At the sitting of the board of guardians the day before, Mr O'Loghlin, brother to the late Master of the Rolls of that name, had been suddenly seized with cholera, and was now dead there; and these were the tenantry going to meet the corpse and then to *wake* it, according to the custom of the country.

Of Ennis town, from the hurry we were in, I was enabled to see little more that would be novel to the reader. In truth, one or two of its streets and public buildings reminded me forcibly of some of our large old English market towns, blended of course with much that was especially Irish. But the awful number of poor, half clad, begging creatures, who surrounded and almost overwhelmed us at every step, rendered it impossible for us to make a single uninterrupted observation. The sudden death, too, of Mr O'Loghlin, had caused a species of consternation in the place, which, added to other occasions of gloom, made us anything but anxious to stay; and in the evening we found ourselves once more at the chateau.

Extracts taken from Spencer T. Hall, *Life and Death in Ireland in 1849* (Manchester 1850), pp 58-71.

Thomas Carlyle, Reminiscences of East Clare, 1849

The Scottish essayist and social critic Thomas Carlyle was perhaps the most famous visitor to the county in 1849. Carlyle was among the first of the social philosophers. His influence on the shape of Victorian thought, through such works as *Sartor Resartus* 1833 and *Past and Present* 1843, was pervasive. His writings were a seminal influence on the Young Ireland movement. By 1848 Carlyle was lapsing into despair over what he perceived to be the corruption and greed of English society. In May of 1849 he wrote in his diary 'Am thinking of a tour in Ireland, unhappily have no call or desire that way, but am driven as by the points of bayonets at my back. Ireland really is my problem'. Clearly the accounts of famine in Ireland had touched him deeply. On his return from Ireland in November 1849, he again noted in his diary 'Went to Ireland, wandered about there all through July, have half forcibly recalled my remembrances and thrown them down on paper since my return. Ugly spectacle, sad health, sad humour, a thing unjoyable to look back on'. Carlyle stayed at Castleconnel with Sir Richard Bourke, a former governor of New South Wales. Bourke brought him on a tour of Lough Derg, where Carlyle observed the Shannon navigation works and the slate quarries above Killaloe. The tour included a visit to the former residence of John Fitzgibbon, first earl of Clare and Lord Chancellor of Ireland at the time of the Union. Carlyle's notes on his Irish journey are rough and fragmentary, he attributed little importance to them and clearly did not intend them for publication. After his death in 1881, the manuscript was edited and published by J. A. Froude, under the title *Reminiscences of my Irish Journey in 1849.*

To O'Brien's bridge (by the low road - woody with occasional glimpses of the river); village white, lower end of it pretty in the sunshine, upper part of it squalid, deserted mostly: relief-work road - half breadth cut away, and so left; duckwood ditches, drowned bog, inexpressively ugly for most part, some cleared improved spots, abruptly alternating with the drowned squalor, which produces only bad brown stacks of peat. Sir Richard in mild good humour trots gently along. Two drunk blockheads stagger into a cross roads to be alone; are seen kissing one another as we pass - just heaven, what a kiss with the drowned bog and gaping full ditches on each hand! Long meagre village, hungry single street, Castle Connell. . . .

Scariff; straggling muddy avenues of wood begin to appear; woman in workhouse yard, fever-patient we suppose; had come flat, seemingly without pillow, on the bottom of a stone-cart; was lying now under blue cloaks and tatters, her long black hair streaming out beyond her - motionless, outcast, till they found some place for her in this hospital. Grimmest of sights, with the long tattery cloud of black hair. Procession next of workhouse young girls; healthy, clean in whole coarse clothes; the *only* well-guided group of children visible to us in these parts, - which indeed is a general fact. Scariff itself, dim, extinct-looking, hungry village (I should guess 1,000 inhabitants) on the top and steep sides of a rocky height. Houses seemed deserted, nothing doing, considerable idle groups on the upper part (hill top) of the street, which after its maximum of elevation spreads out into an irregular wide triangular space, - *two* main roads going out from it, I suppose, towards Gort and towards Portumna. - Little *ferrety* shopkeeper, in whole clothes, seemingly chief man of the place, knows Bourke by often passing this way; 'Well, Mr (O'Flanahan, say, tho' that was not it), do you think we can get a car to Gort?' - 'Not a car here, sir, to be had for love or money; people all gone to adjourned assizes at Tulla, nayther horse nor car left in the place!' Here was a precious outlook: Bourke however did not seem to lay it much to heart. 'Well Mr O'Flanahan, then you must try to do someting for us!' 'I will!', cried the little stumpy ferret of a man; and instantly despatched one from the group, to go somewhither and work miracles on our behalf. Miracle-worker returns with notice that a horse and car can (by miracle) be achieved, but horse will require some rest first. Well, well; we go to walk; *see* a car standing; our own old driver comes to tell us that *he* has discovered an excellent horse and car *waiting* for hire just next door to Mr O'Flanahan's. And so it proved; and so, in five minutes, was the new arrangement made; O'Flanahan acquiescing without any blush or other appearance of emotion. Merely a human ferret, clutching at game, hadn't caught it. Purchased a thimbleful of bad whisky to mix in water in a very smoky room from him; 'odd copper, yours.' 'Why sir?' and sent ardently for 'change,' - got none, however, nor spoke more of getting. Poor O'Flan, he had got his house new floored; was prospering, I suppose, by workhouse grocery-and-meal trade, by secret pawnbroking, - by *eating* the slain. Our new car whisked us out of Scariff, where the only human souls I notice at any industry whatever, were two, in a hungry-looking silent back-corner languidly engaged in sawing a butt of extremely hard Scotch fir.

Road hilly but smooth, country bare but not boggy; deepish narrow stream indenting meadows to our left just after starting, - (mountain stream has made ruinous inundation since), - solitary cottages, in dry nooks of the hills: girl *dripping* at the door of one, a potful of boiled reeking greens, has picked one out as we pass, and is zealously eating it; bad food, great appetite, extremity of hunger, likely, not unknown here! Brisk evening becomes cloudier; top of the country, - wide waste of dim hill country, far and wide, to the left: 'Mountains of Clare.'

Extracts taken from Thomas Carlyle, *Reminiscences of my Irish Journey in 1849*, (ed.) J. A. Froude (London 1882), pp 178-83.

George Poulett Scrope, Visit to West Clare, 1849

George Scrope, geologist and politician, was the son of John Poulett Thomson, head of a company of Russia Merchants. Educated at Harrow and Cambridge, he graduated a B.A. in 1821. A keen geologist from youth, he witnessed the eruption of Vesuvius in 1817, which inspired in him a lifelong interest in volcanic studies. He assumed the surname Scrope on his marriage to the heiress Emma Phibbs Scrope in 1821. Elected M.P. in 1833, he represented the borough of Stroud until his retirement in 1868. He was a strong advocate of free trade and of social reform, especially of the poor laws. All his causes were promoted by his pen only as he never spoke in parliament. He was a silent member and was given the nickname 'Pamphlet Scrope'. It is estimated that he published some seventy pamphlets during his political career. The harrowing accounts of famine in Ireland brought him to County Clare in 1849. Scrope was convinced that, with responsible landlords and improved agricultural methods, the land of Ireland could be made to yield sufficient food for the starving people. He had a good understanding of Irish social realities and his proposed reforms were based on sound economic argument. On his retirement from politics Scrope returned to geological research. He published thirty four major papers on the subject and in 1867 was awarded a medal of merit by the Geological Society. In later years, despite a demanding work schedule, he showed no sign of mental decline and died in 1876 at the age of seventy nine.

While steaming down the noble estuary of the Shannon from Limerick to Kilrush, I admired, of course, as all must do, the splendid example of river scenery, the rich land sloping on either hand to the river, the handsome mansions, picturesque old towers and abbeys and thick tufted woods. But it was impossible, at the same time, not to remember the intense sufferings that had been endured for years, and were, even at the moment, borne by the population on both banks - in Limerick county scarcely less than in Clare - the extent to which destitution, disease and death were still at their foul work amidst those smiling and happy looking scenes. And this while the land is, by general admission and avowal, not made to produce one third of what it is capable of producing, nor affords employment to one half the amount of labour which is required to develop its natural fertility. I saw much doing, however, on the estates of Lord Clare, and one or two others. Their hills were scored with drainage works, executed under the Land Improvement Act. But I was assured, upon authority fully to be depended on, that every acre of the extensive tracts stretching around for miles wanted, and would repay the cost of, similar improvements to the full, as much as the comparatively small surface on which they are as yet in operation. Is it not then a sin and a shame that able-bodied men should be starving on all sides for want of work - some literally starving, as alas! I soon saw them too certainly before my eyes - others maintained by the thousand in idleness - uselessly at all events - at the cost of the industrious community, upon local rates, rates in aid, or the national taxation? . . . These were the reflections with which upon my mind I descended the lovely waters of the Shannon, on my way to Kilrush. . . .

I was assured, on the united authority of the admirable poor law officers who are devoting themselves to the perilous task of endeavouring to relieve the unparalleled destitution of this district, that in the Kilrush union alone, within the last two years, 20,000 human beings at least have been turned out of their homes, and their houses for the most part levelled; the population of the whole union being in 1841 but 82,000. What I saw confirmed me in the belief of this otherwise almost incredible fact. Wherever I went - and I drove in many directions over the union, in the company with Captain Kennedy, the indefatigable and humane inspector, whose fearlessness in exposing the horrors of these evictions is beyond all praise - I passed continually the traces of the 'levellers'. Sometimes eight or ten broken gables of stone-built houses were seen to rear their blackened and skeleton frames against the sky, betokening what had once been a comfortable hamlet - now a pile of ruins. Sometimes a few mere heaps of dirt, almost choked by the weeds which grew around, announced the wreck of a mud hovel. Some were single some in twos and threes. At times a whole street in a village had been destroyed. I seemed to be tracking the course of an invading army.

It is needless to particularise the properties on which these sights were visible. This seemed to be the general character of the district. If any exception appeared, I learned that there also the preliminary notice of ejectment had been served, and the fate of the inhabitants was only momentarily postponed. I drove through more than one village in which the sheriff and his posse, and the landlords' bailiffs with their crow-bars, were expected that day or the morrow, and the inhabitants - in the unresisting apathy of despair - were awaiting the execution of the sentence, which would deprive them of home and shelter for ever. On one property alone 600 souls were thus hourly expecting this doom!

And where were those on whom that sentence had already been executed - the 20,000 evicted, destitute poor of the last two years? Where indeed! My informants assured me that, to the best of their knowledge, the greater number of these are dead! And they further expressed their belief, that in spite of all their efforts, notwithstanding the relief afforded through them to some 30,000 recipients at present - a number of which would be largely increased before long, if the present system be continued and no check placed upon the exterminators - one half at least of the remaining population must likewise perish in the ensuing winter and spring. . . .

The general ruin and devastation visible on the face of the country would almost make exaggeration impossible. In each day's drive I passed the sight of many hundred habitations unroofed or levelled with the ground. In some of these ruins a faint smoke, rising from one corner showed the remnant of a family formerly dwelling there, still crouched under a few sticks and sods propped against the broken wall. But of course even this frail shelter would be soon denied them. These wretched beings. And others who yet occupy their houses, but expected soon to be forced out, were the recipients of outdoor relief. And never shall I forget the crowd of miserable objects that clustered around the depots where the weekly meal was being issued. Remember that no clothing, or means of providing it is permitted by the law to be given to outdoor paupers; and yet many may have been on the relief list for years past. No wonder that they are but half covered by rags, which seem dropping off in fragments as they move. What can become of these poor creatures in winter? but the hollow cheeks and emaciated limbs in many, especially the children, too clearly reply. . . .

Orders have been received from the commissioners, just previous to my visit, for the thinning of the relief list; and many hundreds had been struck off belonging to particular classes of the able-bodied, great efforts were being made to fit up a new auxiliary workhouse for their reception. There appeared to be a great indisposition to enter the workhouse, under the impression it was death to do so. This is caused to a great degree by the numerous deaths that have occurred in the house which, however, are not owing to want of nourishment there, but to the fact the poor wretches, postponing their entrance there to the last, carry the seeds of mortality in their constitutions with them. They go in only to die. Others, who have come out, some of whom I questioned, spread the report that the food is insufficient there. But from what I saw myself, both in the central and auxiliary houses, and from the evident humanity of the vice guardians, and their anxiety for the safety of the poor, I am confident this is a false impression, though I believe not a wilful one. . . .

The general surface of the country is an undulating plane, scarcely anywhere rising to elevations of more than a hundred feet above the sea. The soil is deep and friable, easily worked with the spade or plough, of a very good quality, especially suited to green crops, and capable of bearing excellent crops of oats or barley, of which I saw good samples wherever anything worthy of the name of cultivation had been pursued. In some still rarer instances I observed cabbages, parsnip, turnip and mangle growing luxuriantly, and showing the soil and climate to be admirably suited to them. Although the Atlantic breezes seem to be fatal to all vegetation that rises high above the surface (not a tree or bush being visible through the length and breath of the union), there are, from the mild temperature and moisture favourable to the growth of root crops and artificial grasses, and by no means injurious to cereals. Sea-weed and a very fertilising calcareous sea sand are likewise at hand along the coast - where the population most abounds - for application of manure, beyond what might be made of the land. . . .

There is a considerable surface of unreclaimed bog, composed of black peat, and evidently capable of producing very fair crops of turnips, cabbages, oats and potatoes. Of the latter I saw samples dug out which positively whitened the black soil through their abundance and size. And this upon pure peat, ten feet deep, without other drainage than the furrows between the lazy beds. The crop was equally good where the peat had been cut away for fuel, and on the adjoining surface of the uncut bog. I was told by farmers and others that the potatoes grown upon the black peat had scarcely ever failed; which agrees with what I have before stated as to the potato crops of the Lancashire mosses; and excites astonishment that so little of the surface of these bogs have been planted during the last two or three years, in which a sound crop of potatoes would have made the fortune of its possessor. . . .

Moreover, as I have already said, the clearance system must be checked, either by direct prohibition, or, at least, by making those who pursue it responsible for the pauperism they thereby create. . . .

An example may serve to show the expediency of this last proposal. Close behind the small town of Kilrush is an extensive estate, than which in no part of the Union is there a tract of land more wretchedly treated and desolated by mismanagement. I could see nowhere upon it a drain opened - a field well tilled. Everywhere ruined hovels, and a wilderness of weeds. On this estate alone no fewer than 154 houses have been lately levelled; and as many families, comprising nearly a thousand souls driven from their homes and holdings! Nor has this proprietor, like some others, the excuse of insolvency to plead. He is said to be wealthy. Further than this, when it was proposed to send a 'practical instructor' in husbandry down to this wretchedly cultivated district and only £25 was asked for this purpose from the whole body of landowners, not one farthing would this gentleman contribute.

Adjoining to this estate is one belonging to another proprietor, who finding his too crowded for their comfortable maintenance, provided the means of emigration for about 200 of them, and is now employing and assisting the remainder, among whom the vacated farms were divided, to improve and better cultivate their occupations.

Now, as the law stands at present, the latter estate will have to pay an overwhelming poor-rate to support the evicted and pauperised tenantry of the first. Is this just? Is it encouraging to that line of conduct in landowners which alone can save the country and the people?

By the several alterations of the law I have recommended, proprietors would be aided to exert themselves, to employ the people, and to improve their estates; and protected, while fulfilling this duty, from the consequences of their neighbour's neglect, which would fall, as they ought, upon themselves alone.

Extracts taken from G. Poulett Scrope Esq., M.P., *Some Notes of a Tour in England, Scotland and Ireland, made with a View to the Enquiry whether our Labouring Population be really Redundant* (London 1849), pp 28-43.

Rev S. Godolphin Osborne,
Destitution in County Clare, 1849

Sydney Godolphin Osborne, clergyman and philanthropist, came to Ireland in the early summer of 1849 with the purpose of inquiring into the famine conditions in the west of Ireland. Osborne was rector of Durweston in Dorset and a champion of many causes. He was chiefly known for his 'lay sermons' delivered in the columns of *The Times* newspaper. Through his outspoken views he provoked much controversy. In matters of free trade, education, sanitation and women's rights, he was much in advance of his time. In 1855 he visited the Crimea and inspected unofficially the hospitals under the care of Florence Nightingale, a task for which he was publicly thanked in parliament. His knowledge of the agricultural labourer was unrivalled and his forecast of the social and political emancipation of farm labourers was remarkable for its accuracy. Osborne took a special interest in Ireland. In the introduction to his Irish tour he is concerned to establish his impartiality; he points out that he was not a representative of *The Times* newspaper or in any way connected with the government. He had travelled to Ireland wholly at his own expense and reserved to himself 'the liberty to make his opinions known'. Setting out from Limerick, he travelled by boat to Kilrush and by road to Ennis. He continued on to Ballinasloe and Galway visiting the workhouses of Connemara and west Mayo. Osborne inspected eleven union houses in all and was well informed on the condition of the people both in and out of the workhouses. The famine was still raging in 1849 and he estimated that in some areas as much as a third of the population was receiving either indoor or outdoor relief.

From Limerick I went by steamer down the Shannon to Kilrush; the day was stormy, but not sufficiently so to hide the beauty of this noble river; I fear, from all appearance, that it is but little traversed now by trading vessels.

When I reached the union house at Kilrush, I had evidence at its very doors, of the awful amount of destitution for which it is the last refuge. It was 'the admission day'; within the gates, and on the open ground in front of the doors, were collected in crowds, representatives of every species of extreme suffering. Here was ample evidence of the fact, that the workhouse test is in Ireland, a real test of destitution; for one's first impression was, why had not many of these hundreds applied for food and shelter and clothing, before famine, nakedness, and exposure had so defaced and degraded their humanity?

The debility of age, made worse by long borne misery; the debility of disease, aggravated by long neglect; hunger-worn countenances, telling the tale which at once explained the efficient cause which had left the frame just a frame, and that all. Infants at the breast of mothers, with the skin and visage of advanced, careworn childhood; children, whose sores and dirt and squalid famished looks, told of the loss of all the elasticity of their age, of their premature acquisition of that stolid care-blunted nature, which years of common suffering can give. Lazari, to whom the hated workhouse had come to be as the palace of a Dives, in which they hoped to hide their sores and satisfy their hunger, here waited in crowds longing at the gates: the whole picture was one of utter, almost hopeless misery.

The process of admission or rejection was conducted by one of the vice-chairmen of the board, assisted by two other guardians; the relieving officers calling out the names of the applicants, they were in turn ushered in by the porter and some assisting paupers, some of whom, I observed, had sticks in their hands. The cases were disposed of with such celerity, that I presume the relieving officers has taken no common pains to ascertain the different features of each applicant's case. I was shown over the parent house and auxiliaries by the clerk to the union and the medical officer; the numbers in the houses were 4,802. One of the first departments we entered was the infirmary. I do not think my travelling companion will ever forget this his first introduction to the stern reality of famine. There were very many, of all ages, under medical treatment, whose cases were literally those of simple starvation; many, evidently past hope; some whose end was very near. . . .

The whole of the hospital arrangements at the Kilrush Union do the utmost credit to the medical officer and the authorities of the establishment; the wards were it is true sadly crowded, still every possible ingenuity had been exercised, to secure ventilation. The arrangements in detail for the distribution of medicine; for all the various aids the sick require, were most satisfactory. To show what care will do to prevent disease, I narrowly examined, I believe, more than 1,000 children, I did not find one case of ophthalmia; there were only 10 cases in the whole establishment.

There are some twenty acres of ground under cultivation, by the paupers, apparently with good success, but the labourers were sad objects. The mortality in this union is very great, though I hope decreasing; at the end of the month of May last, the number in the house was 3,765, the deaths during the month 197. In June, the number of inmates 4,366, deaths 144.

I cannot dismiss my notice of the Kilrush Union houses, without stating my belief, that it is mainly owing to indefatigable exertions of the inspector, Captain Kennedy, aided by Dr O'Donnell, that so large a number of paupers, coming into the houses in the condition they do, are preserved in the cleanliness and order in which I found them. I have no reason to suppose but that the board of guardians are most efficient, still I could see in the attention to minor details of management, that a very great deal must be owing to vigilant inspection and supervision, by the resident inspector and medical officer. . . .

In a days journey we went by Clonderlaw, Kildysart, Kilchrist, Clondegad to Ennis. The public have heard a good deal of the evictions, *i.e* the house levelling, in the union of Kilrush; the reports made by Captain Kennedy and others, have been often declared to be exaggerations. I had now ocular demonstration, that no report can exaggerate the amount of wholesale house levelling which has taken place in this union.

The rateable tenements in the Kilrush Union
in the years   1846,   1847,   1848,   1849,   1850
were as follows   9050,   8981,   8546,   7952,   7299.

The decrease of tenements at the commencement of the ensuing year, will I think show, that the system of compulsory ejectment is still in full vigour. One place was pointed out to me, where out of 64 houses 54 had been levelled within this last month, there are now 10 caretakers left in possession of the remaining houses. It would only tire the reader to no purpose, were I to particularise the different properties, on which this system has been carried on; the practice seemed almost universal; on both sides of the road, and as far every way as I could command with a telescope, there was evidence of this forcible removal of the population.

Just as the eye and heart of every Englishmen is shocked with the first view he has of his fellow creatures, at death's door, for want of food; beholding in them the mere 'wrecks' of life; so are the eye and heart painfully offended, when mile after mile, 'wrecks' of homes stand forth on every side. I know not how a country looks, after the passage of an enemy through it, bent on desolating its people's homes; but I am quite certain, the work of destruction could not be done more effectually, though perhaps it would be done less methodically, by such an army, than it is done in the western counties of Ireland, by the proprietors of the land. Roofless gables meet your eye on every side; one ceases to wonder that the union houses are so full, when there is this evidence of the fact that no other home is left to so many thousands.

The law now provides, that before forcible possession is taken of the houses of the peasantry, notice should be given to the relieving officer of the district, in order that he may be prepared to offer 'the ejected,' orders for the workhouse. I had, however, one case put before me on good authority, which occurred in 1849, in which 70 houses were down, under the orders of the agent of the property, at once; the relieving officer had never got the notice, through it was said some mistake; the people had for some days to crowd on the neighbouring chapel floor, and by the sides of the ditches; for the neighbours had had orders not to take them in: it is fair to state the whole of this mass of tenantry had been created by a middleman, whose lease was now out.

I was shown one estate on which, in 1847, there had been 482 families, now there are two. A priest to whom I was recommended, and on whom I called on my way from Kilrush to Ennis, told me, in the two parishes in which his cure lay, viz. Clondegad and Kilchrist, the population of the last census being 9,456; in June last he himself took a census, and that he only found 6,360 remaining; a very large number had emigrated, very many died, and the workhouses had received also their full proportion. This gentleman told me, that the present state of distress seriously affected the moral character of the people; many had no clothes in which they could come with decency to the 'stations' to meet their priest; many of a family would often be found in their cabins naked, the clothes being given to those who had to go to the depôt for relief. I had also an interview with one of the coroners of a district in the Kilrush Union; he admitted to me he had had a great many inquests within these last eighteen months on persons 'starved to death.' The accounts he gave of some of the scenes he had witnessed were most painful. . . .

It may be as well, perhaps, here, to give a description of the actual carrying out of the process of 'forcible eviction.' The legal forms necessary to obtain the sheriff's authority to take possession, having been gone through, and the proper notices served on the parties concerned; a notice is also served on the relieving officer, informing him on what day the people will be ejected. At the appointed hour, we will suppose ourselves to be on the spot; there are, say some six dwellings in a group, nearly adjoining each other, and all situated close to a public road side. Some of these dwellings may be larger than others, but in outward form and actual structure, they are all much alike, simply, two stone gables, built of the stone of the country, a thatched roof connecting them, and descending to some five or six feet from the ground. A gig or outside car arrives with the sheriff's deputy; the agent for the property is in attendance on horseback, with some ten or twelve rough looking peasants, one or two of whom have iron crowbars, and other necessaries for their business of destruction. A certain form is quickly gone through by the law's officer, the effect of which is to put the agent of the property in possession, in other words, giving him full power to turn out the people and pull down the dwellings, if it is his pleasure to do so. In very many districts, a small body of armed police attend, in case of any forcible resistance. The relieving officer calls out the names from the list sent to him, and as he may think proper, offers to the parties now to be ejected orders for admission to the union house. These orders are very generally refused, or if accepted, are not acted on.

The word is now given by the agent, to his 'destructives.' If the people will not come out of the dwellings, they are dragged out; with them, the bed, kettle, old wheel, tub, and one or two stools, with perhaps an old chest; few cabins have anything to add to this list of furniture at the time the tenants are ejected; the living and stock being alike out in the road; now begins a loud and long sustained chorus of intermingled prayers, blessings, reproaches, revilings, weeping, etc., generally ending in low monotonous imprecations on the heads of those, who thus are crowning the ruin of the ejected.

The women will 'kene,' beat their breasts, throw themselves on the ground, embrace the knees of the agent's horse, hang on to the steps of the sheriff's car; they will do and say all an excited Irish woman can say and do, to either obtain mercy, or invoke vengeance; and truly poor creatures, they are gifted with powers of eloquence, aided by a power of action and gesticulation, which, as it may be employed, to bless or curse, is in either way most impressive.

Agents and sheriff's officers, however, from the nature of their avocation, have become case hardened against these attacks upon the softer feelings of our nature; the groans and prayers of the ejected, like the dust of the falling thatch of their roofs, are unavoidable evils, the regular result of the routine of 'house tumbling.' 'Don't be all day boys,' is command enough; a man jumps up on the roof, and soon uncovers a part of the beam, which goes the point of one gable to the other; he fastens a rope round it, it may require, perhaps, a little action from a saw, to weaken it; the rope is passed through the door of the house; it is manned at once by some others of the band; an iron bar is now placed under the wall plate, at one of the angles; a pull at the rope, breaking the back of the roof, and the lifting of the bar, hoisting it from its bearing on the wall, down it goes in a cloud of dust, sometimes falling wholly within the walls, sometimes a part will remain resting one end on the ground, the other against the gable.

So clever are a good practised band of destructives, that thirty houses in the morning, would not be at all beyond their powers. Our group of six houses are in about two hours and a half, rendered ruins, there was a little delay from Honor --- going into a fit as they removed her; the tenants are now houseless. They have been told that they may have the thatch and blackened wood of the fallen roofs; but they are significantly warned, not to linger about the spot too long. The relieving officer will now try and persuade them to be wise and go at once to the workhouse. . . .

As there is a certain expense attendant on the sheriff's presence, the people now, seeing that their houses must fall, for a small gratuity, will pull them down themselves. I took a statement from a clergyman, of one case, in which, an old woman, actually worked her own house down, *with her own hands,* on the belief, she was to have 5s. for doing so, she had not however then got it.

One of these lately 'tumbled out' colonies, though a very wretched spectacle, is sometimes a very picturesque one; the women in the red petticoat of the country, the said garment ever in tatters, with the dark bodice only just sufficiently patched to make a bare covering to the bosom; their long dark parted hair; bare legs and feet; the attitudes of the old, crouching under the bank or wall; of the less aged, in active work, drawing the smoke-blackened wood from beneath the thatch; the baby, half out of the queer-looking, half-box half-boat, called a cradle; the younger children, half naked, romping about the ruins, or climbing about the furniture on the roadside; the gables, their heads pointing upwards, as though they would tell the tale to the powers above; the different positions of the fallen roofs, some showing the blackened rafters where the thatch had separated from them in the fall; others, the work not quite finished, still hanging, hesitating as it were, in their fall: a painter could find no little beauty in a scene, which to one, who looks not at the picture, but at its cost, is only a very ugly page in the history of the exercise of man's power, over those who are themselves powerless.

On our journey we had ample opportunity of seeing to what shifts the peasantry will resort before they will face the Union House, after they have been evicted, and seen their homes 'tumbled.' Their usual practice is with the thatch and some of the roof sticks, to build up a dwelling called a 'scalpeen,' the most common form of this species of dwelling is what I suppose an Englishman would call, 'the lean to'. . .

It is a rare thing to find any males at these scenes of desolation; in the majority of cases, I fear, they desert their families, go to seek work at a distance, perhaps in England; very often they start for America as soon as they find they are to be ejected. A very large proportion of the families in the workhouses are deserted families. In travelling in the west of Ireland, it is a curious fact, that you scarce ever meet an able-bodied labourer on the road; the only males you see, are the old and infirm, and the very few small farmers who have yet survived the storm.

At Kildysart, we found a crowd of wretched objects, waiting for the coming of the meal for out relief; my companion, who had an amiable propensity for buying up bakers' shops, to distribute the bread, thereby getting again and again into some trouble, proceeded at once to indulge this charitable feeling, the consequence was, that the shop was very soon in a state of siege; the assaulting party, being, I should think, little less in number than 100, as starved, ill-clad, and desperate-looking as is possible to conceive; by the aid of one of the police, the door of the shop was closed, so as to shut some in, many out; such, however, was the pressure, that it was thought advisable that my friend should surrender his position, and make a retreat by a back-door, then over a wall, and thus escape to the inn. . . .

This is to be a wholly separate union from Kilrush. At present, it is a tributary to it, contributing its full share of pauperage; a few miles further on, after passing many most wretched objects, the least miserable of whom would have caused a crowd in any street in London; we overtook two children, boys, I should suppose, from 10 to 12 years of age; one himself very far from strong, was supporting the staggering steps of the other, evidently sinking in the last stage of famine. I know not how far he had to go before he found a shelter on earth, I feel a comfort in my assurance that his hours were numbered there.

Passing a group of modern house ruins, I thought I saw smoke curling up from a corner, between two roofless gables; we left the car and made our way between the walls; there were a few pieces of turf smouldering on the ground, a board fixed into the walls, immediately over this mockery of a fire, to I suppose conceal all evidence of its existence from any passer by; by it as we came into view, was a woman in mere rags; her child, a girl of about 12, quite naked, and another little thing partially so. She at once hung some rags upon the girl to make her as decent as herself. Her story was the old one - 'her house had been tumbled, she lived as we saw her in the day, at night she was covertly sheltered in a neighbouring cabin.' A little further on, we came to one of the 'lean to's' I have described above, when we looked into it, we found a woman, perhaps some thirty years of age, the place was a mere sty, a lad of four feet could hardly have stood in the highest part of it; the roof descended abruptly to the ground; here this poor creature had dwelt for weeks, with her three children; how she lived was evident; her stock of food was at her feet; *a large bundle of corn-weed and nettles;* she was positively naked to the waist, but with the instinctive modest quickness of her race, as she talked to us, by crossing her arms and hitching up some of the rags which hung about her, she extemporised a bodice.

We were glad enough to arrive at Ennis, for our journey from Kilrush had been one continuous scene of devastation and destitution. As to the crops, it is true we saw here and there a good deal of potato coming up well; there were places too, but few and far between, where the land seemed tolerably well cropped with cereals; but the great proportion of the land, if cropped at all, had as much foul weed as corn growing on it; a great deal was utterly waste, but with evidence on the surface, that it had once been otherwise. . . .

Having a long journey before me the next day, I determined to pay a visit to the Ennis Union workhouse, early in the morning; I left my bedroom at the hotel, soon after five o'clock. . . .

Having reached the gates of the union house before 6 o'clock, I employed a quarter of an hour, in looking at the new court house, now nearly completed, which is a short distance from it. It was another of the many instances I have seen, of the strange love for building at any cost, to the public cost, common to the Irish. It is really a very fine building, the front elevation, as handsome, classical, and substantial, as if it had been built by a people who could well afford it. It must have cost many thousands of pounds; it made me think the statement, in a official document I had with me, must be a libel - viz. - 'That the net liabilities of the Ennis Union at the end of the March quarter, 1850, *over the balance in Bank*, were £21,627,' if this is not a liable, it can scarcely be one, to say that such unnecessary expense, for such a building, under such circumstances, is very foolish, if not very wrong.

Having obtained the assistance of the clerk of the union, to whose kindness I must acknowledge myself much indebted, for it was scarcely reasonable to rouse him so early, I went over every department of the house, and then visited a detached mansion, with large gardens, and some 25 acres of land - an auxiliary inhabited by the boys. There were in the parent house and auxiliaries 3,528 paupers, 6,533 persons on the out-relief list, of whom only 4 were able-bodied. This union is very heavy in debt, and has, I believe, received as much as £7,000 in grants in aid of relief, from government.

The parent house and the auxiliary I visited, were both very clean, and the inmates were in evident good order; they were only just out of bed, and I was much pleased with the celerity with which the dormitories were cleaned, and the beds arranged, so that they should get thoroughly aired, before they were again used. In no house I visited, was there more industrial employment, and employment turned to better account. Every article of clothing is made from the raw material, in the house; except of course, fine linen. They manufacture all the shoes, and even the boys scotch bonnets. The large kitchen garden of the adjoining auxiliary was well stocked, and most cleanly cultivated. I walked over the farm, which was well cropped with root crops, etc. - the labour being superintended by an agricultural instructor; the paupers were generally well enough clothed; the women looked healthy; the boys, equal to the average of workhouse boys, some however bore the familiar 'want' stamp in their countenances. The infirmary was clean - and I was much pleased to see the tenderness, with which two nurses were dressing one of the most distressing cases I ever saw; a child of some 6 or 7 years of age, whose eye from disease had swelled to a size, that had I not seen it, I could not have believed possible; I was thankful to feel it had not long to live.

For a union under great financial difficulty, the Ennis does great credit, to all who take the executive part in its economy; it is satisfactory to see those who must be kept, not kept in idleness; I am satisfied that the health, happiness, and morality of the paupers, are alike advanced, by steady industrial occupation. The average cost of each pauper is at present 10¾d. per week - the bread is half rye, half barley for the adult classes.

From Ennis to Gort the country offers nothing worthy of particular observation, there are the same traces of the hand of the home destroyer as in other places; the peasantry, what few are met on the road, though perhaps not so distressed in appearance as those I have already described, are still in very evident great distress. There was some fair cropping of the ground, but a great deal of it lies comparatively waste.

Extracts taken from Sydney Godolphin Osborne *Gleanings in the West of Ireland* (London 1850) pp 14-39.

James Caird,
Potential of Farming in County Clare, 1849

James Caird, author and agriculturist, had a distinguished public career. A native of Stranraer, Scotland, he was educated at the university of Edinburgh but left without taking a degree. He learned about practical farming in England and subsequently managed farms in Scotland. An ardent free trader he published the treatise *High Farming As The Best Substitute for Protection*. This brought him to the attention of prime minister Robert Peel, who commissioned him to do an agricultural survey of the south and west of Ireland in the autumn of 1849. The report, published in 1850, was favourable to the future potential of Irish agriculture and led to the investment of large sums of English capital in Irish land. Appointed to inquire into the distressed state of farming in England, Caird published *English Agriculture 1850-51*, the most comprehensive review of English farming since the eighteenth century; this earned him an international reputation . Entering parliament in 1857, he was chiefly concerned with agricultural issues. He advocated the importation of cotton from India during the American Civil War 1861-66 and revisiting Ireland in 1869 he published a pamphlet entitled *The Irish Land Question*. Appointed president of the Statistical Society in 1880 and privy councillor in 1889, he died aged seventy six in 1892.

Caird toured Clare after the worst ravages of famine in October 1849. No mention, however, is made of starvation or social conditions. He viewed the landscape with the cold eye of a practical farmer, calculating input costs and potential returns on capital. His detached account of the county's agricultural potential reminds one of an estate agent describing the attributes of property about to be sold. Like Arthur Young before him, it is the rich alluvial lands along the Fergus and Shannon estuaries that he singles out for particular praise.

Proceeding southwards from Galway, after passing Oranmore, the land continues for many miles of the same character, dry light land on a limestone rock or gravel. In some places the rock covers the ground to a very injurious extent. Within a few miles of Gort, the country improves, and some very good sheep-pastures and corn-lands are found here. Gort is a clean, well-built town. Soon after leaving it the fields become more bleak, until crossing into the county of Clare, where good grass-lands are passed through. The cultivated land along the road is everywhere badly managed. A tract of uninteresting, stony, limestone country is then traversed; the fields becoming more open again as we approach Ennis, the chief town of the county. This town is of considerable extent, and is prettily situated on the river Fergus, which is navigable to this point, by large boats, from the Shannon. The streets seemed narrow and old-fashioned, but there are many good shops in the town. A fine suite of new county buildings are just being completed, which will contribute much to the ornament of the place, though, if payable from the grand-jury cess, it may be doubted whether it was prudent at present to proceed on such a costly scale.

Proceeding southwards from Ennis, the country improves. The road crosses the Fergus at Clare, to which town the river is navigable by large vessels. Along both banks of this river to its junction with the Shannon, being a distance of eight or ten miles on each side, are fine tracts of rich alluvial land, called 'corcases,' which yielded very high rents before the famine. These rich flats are banked off from the inroads of the tide, being in many places under high-water mark of spring-tides. Where they have been left in their natural state, they are exceedingly fertile, producing heavy crops of hay year after year, or carrying large stocks of sheep and cattle. They have been generally let in farms of considerable extent, and £3 10s. per Irish acre, besides grand-jury cess, etc., was no uncommon rent for a large farm. The custom of the tenants was to sublet certain portions to the farmers of the upper country for meadow, at rents varying from £6 to £8 an acre; and being fettered by no restrictions in their management, other parts were con-acred for potatoes at even greater rents, the tenant afterwards putting in the grain crop, and frequently selling it, with the straw, before cutting. In this way the actual tenant employed almost no labourers; and the resources of the farmers in the upper country failing with the potato failure, they were unable to take meadow, while the labouring class, of course, for the same cause, ceased to con-acre. The tenant, thrown on his own resources, had neither capital nor skill to meet this new order of things, and the distress and abandonment of farms is accordingly as great on some of these naturally rich lands as on the poorest. The land which had been con-acred is reverting to grass; but any farmer who has ever been accustomed to strong alluvial land, may guess to what a foul state it has been reduced by this most negligent and injudicious management. One acre of land so con-acred, and now reverting to grass, is not one-fourth the value, at this moment, of the land alongside of it, on which the rich old sward has remained unbroken. I am not partial to stringent covenants between landlord and tenant as to tillage, but there is not a point on which, in my opinion, landlords should be more strict than in guarding against the spoilation of their property, by the breaking up of these rich alluvial meadow-lands for a few years' temporary gain. No skilful tenant would wish to see it done.

Dromoland Castle, the residence of Sir Lucius O'Brien, lord-lieutenant of the county of Clare, is finely situated in an extensive park, a few miles south of Ennis, and about a mile to the east of the river Fergus. It is a very extensive and imposing mansion in the castellated form, built of dressed limestone in courses, massive and substantial. To the left of the mansion is a lake of considerable extent; and on a lower level, in the rear, are the stables and farm-buildings, commodious and well arranged, and hid from view by the overhanging woods; while, farther up, the extensive gardens are seen in successive terraces, crowned by a very picturesque cottage under the trees at the summit.

On 22d October I accompanied Sir Lucius in a walk over five or six of his farms in the neighbourhood of the castle. Two of these farms have excellent houses and farm-buildings, and are beautifully situated on the rich slopes overlooking the Fergus and the lower Shannon. They each possess a considerable tract of these rich 'corcase' lands, attached to fine dry arable land, gently sloping up from them. All these farms are situated within a short distance of water-carriage on the Shannon, and about twelve miles from the city of Limerick. When left in its natural state, the land immediately rising from these flats is of the richest feeding quality - a deep, black, earthy soil - dry, and admirably adapted for grazing or green crops. One or two excellent farms are to be let here, which are well worth the examination of farmers.

On the opposite side of the Fergus is the farm of Island Magrath, which by many is considered one of the best farms in Ireland. It is extensive - between 300 and 400 Irish acres - and is at present to be let at a moderate rent; it is said, for something under 20s. an English acre. It is the property of the Marquis of Conyngham.

From the river Fergus, along the north bank of the Shannon to Limerick, the country is all of this naturally fertile character. Passing the old ruined castle of Bunratty, which is beautifully situated close to the waters of the Shannon, the road traverses a very rich country. At Cratloe, four miles west of Limerick, the residence of Mr Augustus Stafford, M.P., which I subsequently visited, I learned from a respectable farmer, and a man of intelligence, that the usual mode of management in this country, is to keep all the tillage-land in a constant succession of crops, and the land which is required for stock always in grass. The course followed is to take -

1. Green crop.	2. Green crop.
Wheat.	Oats or barley.
Oats or barley.	Oats;

then begin again, and so repeat the course: 300 stones of wheat to the Irish acre, equal to 70 imperial bushels, and 300 to 400 stones of barley, equal to 80 to 100 bushels, are said to be no uncommon crops. These are equivalents to 43 bushels of wheat, and 56 to 65 bushels of barley, per English acre, and must be regarded, under the present mode of management, as indicating a soil of the highest fertility. Rents are falling rapidly in this quarter: one farm of fine quality, which used let at £2 10s., is now offered at £1 5s. an Irish acre. Another of 300 acres, principally fine old grass, let to a dairy farmer at nine hundred guineas, has lately been reduced to six hundred.

Leaving Dromoland on 23d October, I proceeded eastward to Kiltanon, near Tulla, the residence of Mr Molony, which I reached in time to walk over part of his estate with him in the forenoon. He has judiciously improved some extent of bog-land, on which there was then growing a very luxuriant crop of swedes, white carrot, mangold, and cabbages. The swedes, indeed, were over-luxuriant, many of them having rotted. This may, perhaps, be attributed to over-manuring, causing a too rapid development of the plant in a bog soil, which had not been previously rendered sound by a sufficient admixture of sand or gravel. In the afternoon I accompanied two extensive north-country farmers over a different part of the estate, where were excellent crops of turnips, and large fields of well laid-out and well sheltered pastures. These gentlemen have been farming extensively in this part of the country for some years back. They complained much of bad times, high rents and rates, and the difficulty of getting landlords to reduce rents, in any case where the tenant was solvent. They suffered much also from the thievish and indolent habits of the people, the sums paid by them for watching their crops and sheep stock amounting to a considerable tax on the produce. They also complained of the wasteful management of the elected poor-law guardians, who were often partners in the contracts for supplying the workhouses. They spoke highly, however, of the natural fertility of the soil, and the prospects of tenants of capital coming to the country and locating themselves judiciously. For such, they think, there is at present an excellent opening, as landlords are prepared to submit to lower rents, and definite arrangements could be made with them as to a limitation of poor-rates and grand-jury cess.

The fears entertained by the more intelligent class of farmers as to the injury they are likely to suffer from the progressive increase of rates, are illustrated by the case of a tenant, on whose farm I was to-day, and which is now to be let. This man came to the country thirteen years ago, with not more than £100 of capital. His landlord lent him £300, and with this he contrived to stock and carry on a farm of 300 acres. He was very skilful in the management of sheep-stock, and introduced the best rams from England, with which he improved his own stock, and then sold their produce at high prices in the surrounding country. So well did this succeed, that in a few years he repaid his landlord the borrowed money, besides, at the same time, greatly increasing the numbers and quality of his farm-stock. The frightful increase of rates, with diminished prices of produce, alarmed him: he found the capital which he had accumulated by skill and industry slipping away; he could not get what he considered an adequate abatement of rent from his landlord, though the increase in his rates amounted to nearly a second rent; so, availing himself of the power of surrender, which is fortunately a clause introduced into most Irish leases, he determined to sell all off, and quit the country for New Zealand. After paying all his debt, he has retired with a capital of £1000, and his farm is abandoned to the landlord, who is now anxious to get a solvent tenant at a lower rent than, I am assured, this man would have gladly paid, and remained in the country. But how much does this single example teach! First, that the soil yields a grateful return to industry and skill; second, that these are marred by the impolicy of placing the pressure of the rates exclusively on the tenant, (which is unhappily the law in Ireland,) thereby driving out of the country a prosperous, skilful farmer, whose example was of the utmost benefit in a district where these qualities are so deficient, but who felt himself compelled to remove his capital from the danger in which it stood of being absorbed in the general poverty of the country and third, the short-sighted policy of the landlord, (too common, I lament to say, and mainly to be attributed to a want of that knowledge of the proper business of a landlord, to which I have already had occasion to refer,) in refusing to share the difficulties of the times with his tenant, because he was a solvent man, - and the natural consequence of this in disgusting the tenant, who then abandoned the farm, for which its owner cannot now get a solvent tenant at the greatly reduced rent he is at length willing to accept for it.

In the neighbourhood of Tulla there are some good farms to be let, sound sheep-land, on the estate of Mr Molony of Kiltanon. I passed several of the roads to-day on which improvements had been begun, but never completed, at the time of the famine. Several of these had been left in a state which rendered them actually dangerous to the traveller, and others were quite useless to anybody.

From Tulla to Scariff and Lough Derg, the land is of various quality. Behind Scariff it rises to a considerable elevation, innumerable little patches of cultivation stretching up the mountain side, and encouraging the growth of a population which nothing but potato culture could keep in existence from the produce of such a soil as that on which they were located. The consequence has been a mass of pauperism, now overspreading the better part of the surrounding country, and threatening eventually to absorb the entire produce of the land embraced in this union.

The banks of Lough Derg are generally fertile and picturesque, there being many very eligible estates and farms in the extensive district between Portumna and Killaloe. A steamer plies regularly on the lake. From Tomgraney the road passes over a comparatively elevated district, between which and the Lough lies much improvable land, which is at present in a very neglected state. Descending the hill near Tinerana, the eye rests with pleasure on the neatly laid out and well-cultivated fields, interspersed with the woods, surrounding the mansion-house of that name, and stretching down to the margin of the lake. Winding along its shores, the road affords many beautiful views to the traveller of the fertile lands of Tipperary, rising from the opposite side of the lake, up the green slopes of the Arra mountains, beyond which may be also seen the tops of the Silvermine and Keeper. Near Killaloe stands an old fort, beautifully situated on a green mound commanding the entrance into Lough Derg, which is here gradually narrowed into the bed of the Shannon.

Proceeding southwards from Killaloe, the land on the road-side is generally inferior as far as O'Brien's Bridge, where, crossing the broad and beautiful river, you enter the county of Limerick. Along this fertile valley, the country is now rich and well wooded; the frowning ruins of ancient castles, and the 'shining morning face' of modern mansions, equally bespeaking the good taste of their founders in their choice of a situation. Passing the demesne of Lord Clare, whose umbrageous woods shut out the river altogether, and proceeding a mile or two farther along fields of deep red friable soil, you reach the suburbs of the city of Limerick, where those who are curious in such matters may have an opportunity of inspecting, by dozens, some of the poorest and most wretched cottages in Ireland.

My time was too limited to admit of my visiting the western portion of the county of Clare, where I was informed that at Miltown Malbay very extensive and judicious improvements are going on. The district round Corofin, to the north-west of Ennis, is famed for its rich pastures. The south-west division, embracing the union of Kilrush, noted for its evictions and its poverty, is situated on the coal formation, (not usually favourable for agricultural enterprise;) but the whole of the north bank of the Shannon, from Limerick to Kilrush, is well worth the inspection of persons in quest of land.

Taken from James Caird, *The Plantation Scheme, or the West of Ireland as a Field for Investment* (Edinburgh 1850), pp 60-70.

Harriet Martineau, Letters from Clare, 1852

One of the many newspaper correspondents to visit Clare in the wake of the Great Famine was Harriet Martineau who reported at length on the workhouses in Ballyvaughan, Miltown Malbay and Ennistymon for the *Daily News*. Unlike later writers Martineau promoted a positive view of work-houses and praised their potential for the improvement of the human condition. By 1852 thousands of people were still dependent on public relief but the worst effects of famine had passed. Martineau, the daughter of a Norwich manufacturer of Hugenot origin, suffered from deafness and ill health throughout her life. Her deafness making it impossible for her to pursue the more conventional career of teaching she turned to journalism. One of her first published pieces was an essay 'Female Writers on Practical Divinity' 1821. She went through a long illness and was left penniless by 1829. Settling in London she became acquainted with literary figures there. She published *Illustrations of Political Economy* (1832) and *Poor Law and Paupers Illustrated* (1833). Her works made an immediate impact and she was consulted on social issues by government ministers. She visited America and wrote *Society in America* (1837). Befriended by the poet William Wordsworth she travelled in Europe in 1839. She returned in ill heath and was advised to try mesmerism. Hypnotised by Spencer T. Hall (who also published an account of his experiences in Clare) she rapidly recovered her health. She travelled in Egypt and Palestine and published *Eastern Life* in 1848. Her *Letters from Ireland* are a series of reports communicated to the *Daily News* during her journey to Ireland in the autumn of 1852. They are an account of 'impressions received and thoughts excited' from day to day. Written 'sometimes in a coffee room to the sound of the harp or in the parlour of a crowded country inn to the clatter of knives and forks'. Her letters provide a vivid picture of the conditions in workhouses in the post-Famine period. Among many other works she wrote an autobiography which was published posthumously in 1877.

[21 September, 1852]. From Galway we have travelled by the unusual route of the coast of Clare, where tourists being, as we supposed, out of the question, we hoped to discover how the people lived. From Galway to Ballyvaughan, and thence on to the borders of Mr O'Brien's estates, was the most desolate region perhaps that we have traversed - almost as unpeopled as the wilds of Erris, without the curious charm of its having never been peopled. It was some relief to find that the unroofing of houses is not at all recent. We were grieving over one mass of good-looking houses, when our driver told us that was the memorial of an old landlord quarrel; that a whole village population - thirty or forty families - all decamped in one night, about thirty years ago, in fear of their landlord. Some good-looking houses on heights and promontories were deserted at an older time; but the dozens and the scores of humble dwellings still have the soot hanging about their gables. The traveller on the admirable road which winds with the heights of the coast looks out anxiously to sea for fishing-boats; but there are none, - only the savage canoe or curragh is to be seen by good eyes, tossing near the shores. A woman here and there climbing barefoot over the rocks in search of bait, or of that seaweed which people eat to give a taste to their meal or potatoes, a boy or girl digging potatoes from out of the stones of limestone fields, are nearly all the people that are to be seen at any one place. There seem to be too few to beg. A very large number of men are gone to England for the harvest, or to America; the wives and children are in the workhouses; and the roofs then come off their abodes. While on the part of the coast of Clare which is almost entirely limestone, we hoped and believed that the excessive subdivision of the land was owing to its stony character. We saw vast heaps in the middle of little fields; and we hoped that the innumerable fences were merely a method of getting rid of the stones. But, since we have come down upon a more fertile district, where there no stones in the middle of the fields, we find the enclosures no larger. Rank and ruinous hedges or turf-banks occupy a large surface, and divide fields which are mere plots, like the sluggard's garden. The first revival that we were sensible of was when the whitewashed dwellings of Mr O'Brien's tenants began to glitter before our eyes. 'Corny O'Brien,' as his neighbours call him, is considered a kind landlord; and is not, we were assured, the less beloved in that capacity for being 'an apostate' - as people here call a Protestant whose parents were Catholic. The care and expense that Mr O'Brien has lavished on making the Moher cliffs accessible, safe, and attractive to strangers, have made his name popular along the coast. The great number of men that we saw employed in getting in his crops of hay - such a quantity that we could not conceive how it was all to be eaten - was an explanation, quite satisfactory, of the affectionate tone in which we heard him spoken of. It is true, there is little more doing in his neighbourhood, in the way of permanent employment of industry, than elsewhere, - no fisheries; but there is something done to attract strangers, and to keep the labouring class from starving. . . .

[22 September, 1852]. Before entering an Irish workhouse, the English visitor is aware that the people to be seen within are altogether a different class or race from those whom he has been accustomed to see in workhouses at home. In England, the pauper population, domesticated in those abodes by legal charity, are, for the most part, a degraded order of people. The men and women have either begun life at a disadvantage, or have failed in life through some incapacity, physical or moral; or they are the children of such that we find in workhouses; and we expect therefore to see a deteriorated generation, - sickly or stupid, or in some way ill-conditioned. In Irish workhouses it is not this sort of people that are to be found. Indeed, the one thing heard about them in England is that they are ready to die rather than enter the workhouse. They are the victims of a sudden, sweeping calamity, which bore no relation to vice, folly, laziness, or improvidence. In the first season of famine, the inmates were a pretty fair specimen of the inhabitants at large; and they are now the strongest and best-conditioned of those original inmates. . .

Matters are not so pleasant everywhere, of course; but still they are a vast improvement on what 'S[ydney] G[odolphin] O[sborne]' and others saw awhile ago. For instance, we stopped at Ballyvaughan, on Galway Bay. In the course of our afternoon walk, we were struck by the situation of a farm-house on an eminence, with a green field before it, stretching down to the bay. Entering the field, we saw below us a number of women washing clothes, evidently from the workhouse. This house was an auxiliary to the auxiliary house of Ballyvaughan. The prevalence of ophthalmia in the house caused this field and dwelling to be hired for an infirmary. Forthwith we went to the larger house, an assemblage of whitewashed buildings, arranged as a workhouse, for the relief of the overcrowded establishment at Ennistymon.

This Ballyvaughan house was prepared to contain 900 inmates. On the day of our visit - at harvest-time - at the most prosperous season of the year, and in a neighbourhood where there is an admirable employer of labour, the number was no less than 667. It was inconceivable to us, when we heard this, what the people could have done when there were no houses nearer than Galway and Ennistymon. People who had to come above thirty miles for relief perished for want of it in great numbers - some at home, and some by the roadside. It will not be so again, for there is to be a proper workhouse built at Ballyvaughan, and the question of its precise situation is now under debate. A proprietor in the neighbourhood is draining his lands largely, and with funds borrowed from the Improvement Commissioners, one of whose stipulations is that the labourers' wages shall be paid in cash. If we remember rightly, as many as 200 men are thus employed regularly, and for sufficient pay. How, then, were there 667 in the workhouse in the harvest month? How many were able-bodied men? One official said twenty, but on inquiry it turned out that they were not able-bodied at the moment. Ophthalmia, or other ailment or infirmity, had incapacitated these twenty. Of children there were 300. That was a fact only too easily understood: they were orphaned by the famine. There were many widows and 'deserted women'; the 'desertion' being that their husbands had gone to England for summer work, leaving their families to the union. The expectation was that most of these men would come back, with more or less money. Some would probably go from Liverpool to America, leaving their families where they were till they could send funds to carry them out to the United States. We heard here again of a scandal which we have since encountered more than once. Some of the guardians have turned out young women, all alone, to shift for themselves. In each case the clergyman and the great man of the neighbourhood have rebuked this practice, and put a stop to it: and it is well; for there will be an end of the well-grounded boast of the virtue of the Irish peasant women, if scores of girls are thus set adrift by their so-called guardians. In one case the excuse given was, that there was no particular notice of their being young women, but that they were included among the able-bodied, and ordered off with that class. Twenty were thus got rid of at Ballyvaughan, and thirty at Kilrush, besides many at other places. We heard with much more satisfaction of the efforts made to enable young women to emigrate to Australia. From Kilrush no less than 450 (some of our informants said more) have been sent across the Atlantic, chiefly to Canada.

On the shores of Malbay, in Clare, stands a little sea-bathing place, called Milltown, all glittering with whitewash; and the most glittering part of it is a large house full of thorough lights, which is described in the guide-books of a few years ago as a fine hotel, where sixty beds are made up for visitors. Travellers had better not go there now in expectation of a bed, for this house is at present a workhouse - another auxiliary of Ennistymon - and spoken of with pride for its healthy situation. Yet, on the way to it we saw a painful sight - a cart or truck, loaded very heavily with paupers - chiefly children, with some women, - the whole being guarded by three of the constabulary, carrying arms. These were runaways, we were told, who were being brought from gaol to Milltown Workhouse. We know nothing of the merits of the case, but the spectacle was not a pleasant one. If the dread of ophthalmia causes any to abscond, we do not wonder at it. The story goes, however, that many put themselves in the way of the disease, actually try to catch it, to avoid work and obtain the superior diet ordered for the patients. The Poor Law Commissioners believe this. We saw the patients at Ennistymon - dozens, scores of them - lying on clean comfortable beds, in rooms coloured green, with green window-curtains, their skins wholesome-looking, and the hair of the young people bright and glossy, but all alike suffering under the painful-looking disease, the consequence of over-crowding, and other predisposing disadvantages.

The aspect of the other parts of the Ennistymon house is anything but depressing. The greatest number receiving relief from its doors at the worst time was 20,000. The house being built to hold 500, of course the chief part of this relief was outdoor, of which there is now none. An incident of the time which happened here explains something of the horror with which the people regarded the workhouse. In order to prevent the sale of the meal given in relief it was wetted by order of the guardians. Much of it became as hard as mortar; and most of it turned sour and caused illness in the already enfeebled people. Popular reports of wholesale poisonings have often arisen from a less cause. Now, however, it is found that the meal and other food agree well with the inmates, whose average of health is high, exclusive of the prevalent ophthalmia. The resident officers spoke cheerfully of the change since last year. During the fever season last year there were deaths daily to the amount of from twenty to twenty-five in that crowded house, whereas there are now only about three in a week. The breakfast is porridge with milk; and the dinner, soup made of meal, with various vegetables; and an allowance of bread, which suffices also for supper. The people are hoping now to be allowed potatoes twice a week; and great is the pleasure with which they look forward to this treat. There is no regular agricultural instructor of the boys at Ennistymon, but some are promising weavers, under the teaching of a zealous Yorkshireman. The women spin and knit, and the sewing of the household is done by the girls, who are also taught fine work, by which they may make money hereafter.

Long before we entered any Irish workhouse Mr Osborne's name was uttered to us with blessings, as we find it still wherever we go. There are no two opinions about him, and the blessedness of his visit - as far as we have heard. Gentle and simple, Catholic and Protestant, Tory and Liberal, bid us believe all that he has said - assure us that his information was precisely correct - declare that he is the best of all the good friends of Ireland - and glow while they tell us that what he said was (in the words of a poor Catholic) 'religion, and charity, and truth, all in one.' We had not doubted this before; but this universal testimony strengthened our desire to see the Kilrush house. We there heard, from resident officials, terrible accounts of the famine and fever times, when people were brought in, and died between the outer gate and the door of the house; when they were laid three in a bed (those beds which are comfortable and decent for one, but which still are made to hold two), and the dead and the living were found lying side by side every morning. But enough has been said about that. There have been auxiliary houses opened to a greater extent than are now needed. Three have been lately closed. The house was built to contain 1100, and the sheds 416 more. The number in the house when we were there was 2735, and the deaths during the last twelve months have been 362. There is a farm of twenty-five acres, where the boys are taught to labour. It was Sunday when we were there; and we neither saw the people at work, nor met the master and matron. Colonel Vandeleur and a party of friends were there. After they were gone we went round. We thought the place very clean, and the people, on the whole, healthy-looking; but our impressions of the management, in the hands of subordinate officers (who seemed to us too young), were not very favourable. There was much confusion and inaccuracy in their statements; and the terms they were on with the people, and the manners of the household, did not seem to us so good as we had expected from what we had seen elsewhere. There can be no doubt, however, of the improvement which has been fairly instituted in the Kilrush house, and which is still advancing.

Extracts taken from Harriett Martineau, *Letters from Ireland* (London 1852), pp 150-64.

Alexander More, Diary of a Naturalist, 1854

Alexander Goodman More, botanist and ornithologist, had an unrivalled knowledge of the fauna and flora of Ireland. Born in London, he spent, for reasons of health, the early years of his childhood in Switzerland where his interest in natural history first became apparent. He was educated at Rugby public school and entered Cambridge University in 1850. He took a certificate in geology in Cambridge but ill health prevented him from taking a degree. As a youth he befriended Walter Shawe Taylor and first visited Castle Taylor, their residence at Ardrahan, County Galway, in the summer of 1850. He became fascinated by the flora of the district and published his first paper 'Notes on the Flora of Castle Taylor'. More was a regular visitor to Castle Taylor in the 1850s and was drawn irresistibly to the unique flora of the Burren. He kept a diary of his botanical and ornithological excursions and added several new species to the fauna and flora of north Clare. His observations on the Cliffs of Moher are of interest for the fascinating account of the bird life and the activities of the cliffmen who made a living from catching birds on the cliff face. More came to Ireland again in 1864 for the purpose of compiling an Irish flora and resided in Dublin. In 1867 he was appointed assistant curator to the Natural History Museum in Dublin. For the next quarter of a century there was scarcely a book or pamphlet on Irish natural history to which he did not contribute. Appointed curator of the museum in 1881, he retired in 1887. His best known works are *Cybele Hibernica* and *A List of Irish Birds*.

Monday, July 24th. [1854]. After passing Kilmacduagh the same loose limestone prevails, only becoming still more exclusively rock and less capable of cultivation; in fact, all through what is called 'Rock Forest,' the surface is very similar to the most barren tracts of the Burren, and inhabited by much the same plants. We looked out in vain for *Potentilla fruticosa* [shrubby cinquefoil]; and the only plant not growing near Castle Taylor was *Carduus tenuiflorus*, close to the boundary of the two counties. Several small lakes seen close to the road had generally one end thickly overgrown with reeds and sedges; *Cladium mariscus* we particularly noticed. No birds were seen on the water.

We soon entered the well-wooded demesne of Mr Blood, and drove through trees for about half-an-hour, quite a novelty in this part of the country. Further on more rock, and a good and rather near view of some of the Burren - a very perfect old ruin of a castle - the exterior wall with its corner tower still remaining. At Corofin, a large village, we first find *Senebiera didyma*. . . Starting hence we noticed the great change produced by the strata. Instead of dry, short pasture appeared heavy clay lands, producing in the valleys luxuriant crops of hay, and even along the hill-sides a most deplorable crop of rushes, docks, etc. The country now became undulating, with streams running along the hollows, bogs in some places, and the conspicuous foxglove reminding one somewhat of Connemara. The rank vegetation of coarse weeds was to my eye anything but a pleasant contrast with the neat and bright flowers of the mountain limestone, and certainly offered far less variety to the botanist. The water, too, besides accumulating on a less pervious soil, has not the drainage afforded by 'swallows' and caverns, but works its way in the usual manner towards the sea. The flat slates or flags were very remarkable at Inistymon, where the road crosses the river, which occupies an enormous breadth of bottom and is very shallow, disappearing in the distance in a dark sluggish stream below some trees.

We soon reached Lahinch, and got an excellent view of Hag's Head, and the hill that slopes down from the Cliffs of Moher. Here a most surprising multitude of people had collected as if the whole population had migrated to the seaside, crowding every available wall and seat, as thick as crows, all inhaling the sea-breeze. It is wonderful how anxious the people here are for a trip to the sea; they appear to consider it quite indispensable. A great number of lodges of every sort, all well white-washed, give one the idea of a very important watering-place. Skirting along the bay to the left, we proceeded through bog and under hill-sides till a second collection of white houses proved to be Miltown Malbay, and we took up our quarters at the Atlantic Hotel, very comfortably, but not in view of the sunset.

There is a good bit of strand below the sandhills, but only for a short distance, since the coast is a low cliff with ledges of the slaty limestone rock, running far and irregularly into the sea, abounding in rockpools and inlets, in which wherever the water remains at low water, there the Purple Urchin quite paves the bottom and is a most curious and interesting sight; each one burrowing a lodgment for itself, and then adhering with its numberless suckers so firmly that it is a matter of difficulty to detach them; the suckers frequently break off sooner than let go their hold. . . .

July 26th [1854]. We left the hotel for the Cliffs, passing Lahinch with its sandhills and bay. . . and made our way to the stables, built, as well as a tower for the accommodation of visitors, close under the best part of the cliff. *Viola* still growing in the grass (not sandy). On reaching the edge, we betook ourselves to one of the little safe crows' nests built expressly, and gazed down this awful height some 700 feet. The descent is quite abrupt, and in some places the cliff overhangs the bottom; the horizontal strata so well marked in most parts as to make it look almost like a built wall. There are two detached pieces, one a long narrow ridge, and the other an isolated pyramidal needle; and there is no better way of realising the stupendous height than to look first at one of these, and after calculating the distance, to carry your eye again to the water. At first I think the very magnitude makes the eye deceive itself, and underrate the height.

Scores of gulls were wheeling round in clamorous indignation, while the cliffsmen were following their avocation not far from the tower, and ever and anon a little puffin or guillemot would shoot out and describe a circle, only to return to the cliff - their quick, straightforward progress very different from the gulls. The birds seen were - herring gull (a few), kittiwake (thousands), puffin (a few), guillemot (plenty), razorbill (plenty), chough and jackdaw (a few), kestrel (several), peregrine (one), cormorant (a few). Many eagles are said to breed near Hag's Head, in a place quite inaccessible from the cliffs, retreating as it descends: one is seen rarely at Moher. The rock-dove is said to inhabit the caves.

The cliffsmen form a company of fourteen, with a captain of long experience from his youth up, and still said to be the best climber. They are seated in a loop at the end, and take the young birds in nooses at the extremity of a rod of some 12 feet. A man brings up four score, sometimes more, at a haul. All I saw were young kittiwakes. The birds are boiled down for oil, and the flesh eaten afterwards by the men. They consider forty birds a-piece an average day's work, and these will produce one bottle of oil, worth two shillings. The season lasts about two months, and their earnings average one shilling per day. The oil is said to be good for bruises, etc.; the feathers are also picked for sale. The names the birds go by are worth notice: the puffin is called 'parrot,' razorbill a 'puffin,' guillemot a 'cliffbird.' The puffins are said to resort to the green grassy ledges where they burrow in the turf, while the others lay their eggs on the bare rock.

Sedum rhodiola (rose root) grows on the cliffs, and *Silene maritima* (sea campion), with a dichotomous panicle of three or more flowers. The weather was too thick to see much, but a little further on we saw all three Isles of Aran, the largest furthest off.

After spending some three hours here, we continued our journey, and this prevented my attempting a descent on the rope, to which I had just made up my mind: the danger being only apparent, not real.

Passing through some extent of similar ground to what we had seen before, boggy, hilly, and varied with streams, we presently regained the stony region of the mountain limestone, and the change was most remarkably apparent in the vegetation, the bright and neat plants of the calcareous soil forming a most pleasing contrast with the land of bog and low rich meadow-ground, through which we had passed. *Geranium sanguineum, Dryas, Sesleria, Antennaria* seemed to smile upon us as old friends, and the first especially in many places quite coloured the ground. Near a glen bounded by some masses of rock, we saw a most perfect square castle placed in a commanding position, accessible only on one side, the outworks built in with the rock, so as almost to be incorporated with it, forming thus a place of immense strength. We also noticed, what is very unusual, a round castle.

The road presently brought us quite close to the sea, and we enjoyed the pleasant breeze off the water, curling so blue under a gentle wind; and, winding along beneath the first point, we alighted at a spot of great botanical interest. Some green tufts caught the eye, and these turned out to be samphire; close by, *Statice dodartii*, quite recently added to the Irish flora, and new to me; under foot the pretty *Arenaria verna* spread its lovely little stars in hundreds, and in great tufts large enough to fill my hat; and in the fissures of the rock *Asplenium marinum*, rather stunted; but we gathered it very fine further on, at Black Head. Hence the road kept close under the Burren, rounding Black Head, and giving us quite a grand view of the mountain-side, very stony, to be sure, but in some places patched with green. This was, perhaps, the most enjoyable part of our whole trip, the water often within a few yards, and on the other side the mountain rising quite suddenly. We found *Saxifraga hypnoides*, like a little to hirta, and the *Cystopteris*.

(But, alas, we missed the great prize; for, under our feet, and only across the road where we alighted to gather *asplenium*, a little nearer the water, was probably growing that lovely fern, the maidenhair. Had I seen Newman before this trip, we had not passed without a good search, at least.)

[July] 27th [1854]. Continued our way, seeing many old castles, and with an indistinct view of Connemara in the distance. At a part of the road, half way up one of the Burren hills, we had an excellent prospect, reaching to Galway (and, I believe, Castle Taylor, too). At the road-side, F. spied out *Nepeta cataria* of gigantic dimensions, *Orobanche rubra*, a thyme, and *Festuca rubra*. After visiting the 'Holy Well,' where the water is wonderfully cold, we followed a foot-path, some three miles over the spur of the mountain, to Corcanroe Abbey, a ruin of some interest; we were especially struck with the angular ornaments of the chancel roof, and the capitals of several of the pillars were well carved. They showed the tomb of King ---, reported to have been represented as a true Irishman, with a pipe in his hand!, of which the traces are still pointed out. At Kinvarra we saw *Coronopus didyma* plentifully, also *Carduus tenuiflorus*, and reached Castle Taylor about 6 o'clock in the evening.

Taken from C. B. Moffat (ed.), *Life and Letters of Alexander G. More* (Dublin 1898), pp 49-54.

Henry Coulter,
An Account of Post-Famine Clare, 1861

Henry Coulter, versatile journalist and author, died 10 August 1911. A native of Newry, County Down, he worked for many years on the Dublin newspapers the *Freeman's Journal* and, later, on *Saunder's Newsletter*. For the *Freeman's Journal* he reported on many of the speeches of Daniel O'Connell and the debates of the Young Irelanders in 1847. He gave evidence for the defence at the trial of William Smith O'Brien at Clonmel in 1848. Working for *Saunder's Newsletter*, he was made a special correspondent for the west of Ireland. Over a four month period at the end of 1861 and the beginning of 1862, Coulter visited seven of the most distressed western counties. His purpose was to gather accurate information concerning the harvest and the general condition of the people. He wrote a series of detailed letters to the newspaper describing the distressed state of the country as he observed it. It is these collected letters that were published in book form under the title *The West of Ireland* in 1862. Coulter devotes over sixty pages to County Clare. He observed that while conditions since the Famine had improved there was still much suffering and deprivation. The book resulted in a lawsuit by an angry reader, but Coulter's remarks were vindicated in court. *Saunder's Newsletter*, one of Dublin's oldest newspapers, closed in 1879, but by then Coulter had moved to London where he was employed as a journalist on the *Morning Post* for many years. He died at the age of eighty two. *The West of Ireland* was his only book; it is a work of considerable interest, not least for its many coloured illustrations of urban and rural scenes, which provide a valuable insight into Irish life in the nineteenth century.

The union of Scariff, which includes parts of the baronies of Upper and Lower Tulla in the county of Clare, and the barony of Leitrim in the county of Galway, was one of those that obtained an unenviable notoriety in the famine years. . .

The unparalleled nature of that calamity had the effect of diminishing the population by death and emigration, and, taking the whole of the union, it is not too much to say that the number of its inhabitants has decreased one-third since the year 1845. . .

During the previous four or five years [tenants] were able to pay their rents punctually, and could have saved a little, had they acted with proper economy and prudence; but, relying on a continuance of favourable harvests, very many spent all, and even ran in debt to the shopkeepers, whose claims are now pressing heavily upon them. A shrewd and intelligent old man, who cultivates about ten acres, when speaking to me relative to the condition of his own class, observed:

'They riz above themselves entirely, and that's why they are so pinched now.' I did not at first catch his meaning, and when I asked him to explain what he meant, he replied: 'Nothing would do them but they should buy fine clothes for their wives and daughters, and now they find it hard to pay for them.' I believe this to be literally true, and that it applies to a large class both in Clare and Galway, for I have it on reliable authority that there are instances of young girls, the daughters of small farmers, who some years ago made their appearance at fairs and markets in bare feet and clothed in tattered garments, now flaunting about in handsome gowns, with hoops of the most fashionable amplitude, and turban hats and feathers of the newest style. Ridiculous as such illustrations of female vanity in persons of a rank so humble undoubtedly are, they afford no slight proof of the prosperous condition of the farming classes during the last few years, and are gratifying as indications of an improved taste and better notions on the subject of personal neatness and cleanness than formerly prevailed, for it is better that the women should be overdressed, than slovenly and unclean.

I am glad to be able to state that I have seen very few beggars since I have to come to the West, and that the labouring people are, generally speaking, respectably and comfortably clad. The battered hat and coat of shreds and patches, which used formerly to characterise the poor Irishman, seem to have disappeared. However, as I have said, many of the small farmers have become indebted to the shopkeepers for articles of dress and other things, and now find much difficulty in meeting liabilities, which is proved by the great increase in the number of processes entered and the decrees issued at the quarter sessions throughout the country.

The extortions of the usurers, who are to be found in almost every country town, also press very severely on the unfortunate people whose necessities force them to have recourse to those harpies, for the mass of the people are absolutely ignorant of the commercial value of money, and though they feel the burden, and sometimes sink under it, they do not really know how atrociously they have been 'fleeced'. Fifty, sixth, seventy, eighty, and one hundred per cent, are frequently charged by these money-lenders. Here are two illustrations of the system - a farmer applies for the loan of £5; he receives only £4 15s., and has to repay the sum nominally borrowed at the rate of £1 1s. per month for five months. In other cases a shilling in the pound is deducted in the first instance on lending the money, and interest is charged afterwards at the rate of six pence per pound per month until the loan is repaid. . . .

The little town from which I write, affords a striking illustration of the prosperous state of the country for some years past. The population of Scariff has suffered a great diminution since the famine year; but the town, which in 1846 had only one little shop of the meanest description, now contains several thriving and wealthy shopkeepers, who have set up establishments and made their fortunes within a period of ten or twelve years. One of these enterprising traders possesses a very large concern, a sort of general miscellaneous 'store', containing all kinds and descriptions of goods, not omitting crinoline, hoops, and other articles of fashionable female attire for the farmers' wives and daughters. The proprietor of this shop is worth several thousand pounds, all realised within a few years in a poor-looking little town - a conclusive proof that the farmers of the surrounding districts had plenty of money to spend. Scariff, too, has its local 'banker', who drives a flourishing business, but whose operations would be very much circumscribed if the usury laws were still in existence.

At the same time I should remark that Scariff contains a great many poor persons of the labouring class, who, if they do not obtain employment, will find it hard to live in their cold and miserable habitations during the winter. I have never seen more wretched-looking hovels than those which are clustered together at the outskirts of the town. The rotting thatch, the fermenting manure-heap before the door, the holes in the mud-walls intended for windows without glass, but stuffed with rags or straw, excluding both light and air - these, and other features of a repulsive character, constitute a picture of wretchedness and poverty which it is not pleasant to contemplate. Occasionally a couple of families live in one of these huts, where they fully realise the condition of the Irish labourer as described in the Devon Commission Report, being 'badly fed, badly clothed, and badly housed'. In 1846 a row of such like squalid abodes extended for more than half a mile on either side of the road from Scariff to Mount Shannon; but death, emigration, and the workhouse have taken away their inhabitants, and they have almost entirely disappeared. . . .

I have traversed the parishes of Feakle, Kilnoe, Tomgraney, and others in the barony of Upper Tulla, forming portions of the Scariff union. The same observations are applicable to all these districts, the potatoes and the corn crops having suffered everywhere in nearly equal proportions. The parish of Feakle is probably the poorest in the union. It is an extensive mountainous district, with, for the most part, a cold unproductive soil.

The following may be taken as a tolerably close estimate of the results of the harvest in this locality. The potato crop is almost a total failure; of those raised some are rotting in the pits, whilst the remainder does not form a wholesome and nutritious food. The return was, however, a bad one, one-third being the average loss, and in some places much more. The quality of the grain is most inferior. There was not much wheat grown, and the yield is at most only one-half of a good average crop. The extent of land under barley this year was very limited, and the produce greatly deficient.

As a general rule, the farmers have but few cattle, and those are of an inferior description, and in poor condition. The loss of pigs in the spring and summer by distemper was a serious addition to the other misfortunes of this season, which has been almost unprecedentedly severe. The rents vary from 15s. to 30s. per acre, according to the quality of the soil, and so far as I can judge, the land is not generally let at too low a figure.

A clergyman, who resides in this parish and is intimately acquainted with the condition of the people, gave me the following description of the present state of Feakle. I give his statement as nearly as possible in his own words, because I think it candid and truthful, and applicable to many other parts of the country -

'There are comparatively but few persons of the labouring class in this parish - that is, of people living, so to speak, from hand to mouth, and depending upon their daily hire for their daily food. These persons do not hold any land except a rood or two in which they grow potatoes, and they will be badly off during the coming winter, because there is no employment going on at present, and no one to give employment. There are several comfortable farmers holding from twenty to thirty acres and upwards; they are independent, and will not find their resources seriously impaired by the failure of the crops. The remainder of the population consists of small farmers, holding five or six acres, many of whom have saved a little capital, and will be able to get through the winter and pay the May rent, which becomes payable this November; but it will distress them sorely to pay the November gale next April, and some will not be able to meet it. The want of fuel will be their greatest privation. Speaking generally, they have scarcely any turf saved; but they will gather underwood, bramble, furze, and heath, to supply its place for the winter consumption. Somehow they will contrive to struggle through; and living constantly, as so many of them do, on the verge of poverty, hardships and sufferings which would appal others have but little terrors for them. There are some aged, infirm, and diseased persons, whose relatives cannot support them during the winter, and who must therefore seek relief in the workhouse, and from this cause there will be an increase, but not a large one, of paupers. There are no resident gentry in this parish. The small farmers till their lands themselves, and employ as few labourers as possible, and do not exert themselves much to improve their holdings. They are generally tenants at will, and are afraid to improve because of the insecurity of their tenure. There will be no starvation in this neighbourhood, and if the people could get employment, there would be no severe suffering for want of food'.

[Ennis] is the capital of the County Clare, and is a thriving, active, busy town, containing at present, according to the last census returns, 7,127 inhabitants. . . A handsome courthouse and Roman Catholic church, and a monument to the memory of the late Daniel O'Connell, erected on the site of the old courthouse, and now fast approaching completion, constitute the most remarkable architectural features of Ennis. Two fine edifices are in progress of erection by the National and Provincial Banking Companies of Ireland, and, when finished, will add much to the adornment of the town.

The observation respecting the prosperity of the traders refers to a recent period, and is not properly applicable to the present, for, in truth, business is now remarkably dull here as in other towns in the West of Ireland. The shopkeepers of Ennis must therefore look forward, for some time to come, to greatly diminished receipts, and they will require the liberal aid of the banks to enable them to maintain their position satisfactorily.

There is a large and poor labouring population in the town, amongst whom severe distress prevails during the winter and spring of almost every year; but in the present year their sufferings will commence earlier, and be of greater intensity, than any of which they have had previous experience. These people depend almost entirely on the potato, which they cultivate in small patches of a quarter of an acre; but, as the failure of the crops has been universal in the uplands, and as there is not much bog land in the immediate neighbourhood of Ennis, on which the potato is grown, they find themselves deprived of the means of subsistence, with no prospect before them but the workhouse. If they could obtain employment all would go well; for the low prices of Indian corn and oatmeal would enable a working man who earned a shilling a day to feed his family even better than he could possibly do with an average crop of potatoes. But beyond the small amount of labour required to carry on the buildings to which I have spoken, there is no employment here for the labouring class, who must remain in idleness, seeing their scanty stock of provisions disappear daily until actual starvation compels them to throw themselves and their families on the union for support, from which wretched fate very few of the miserably poor population of Ennis can hope to escape. . . .

An act of parliament has been obtained, authorising the construction of a railway from Ennis to Athenry, but as yet no steps appear to have been taken to carry out the project, though, if the line is to be made at all, it would be desirable, for the sake of the poor labouring population of Ennis, that the works should be commenced as speedily as possible. Although there must be many persons in this town and its locality who are even now short of food, the anticipated distress will not begin to manifest itself until the beginning of the new year. The potatoes that the labouring class have saved, will hardly suffice until Christmas, but many will contrive to make out a precarious and scanty subsistence for a few weeks longer, after which I fear the workhouse roll will tell a sad tale of want and suffering. . . .

I wish to refer briefly to the position of a class of farmers, some of whom are to be found near this town, whilst others are settled in various parts of the county. I speak of a peculiar class, very rare, I think I may say unique, in Ireland, viz., farmers of humble rank, who have attained to the dignity of being owners in fee. It will be remembered, that a few years ago the great Thomond Estates, including land in every part of the county, but chiefly situate in the baronies of Islands, Inchiquin, and Burren, were sold in the Landed Estates Court. The property was disposed of in small lots, by which a larger sum was realised than would otherwise have been obtained, and nearly the whole of which were purchased by farmers, some buying their own holdings, and others the farms of their neighbours. In several instances the purchaser had accumulated sufficient means at once to pay off the purchase money; but in the majority of cases they were able to make up a portion only of the required sum, and were obliged to borrow the remainder on mortgage. They have since been making strenuous efforts to pay off the loans, but the deficient harvests of the last two years have crippled them considerably, and they now occupy a very critical position. Another season like the last would reduce many to the verge of insolvency, and a fourth bad year would ruin them completely, and throw the Thomond property, or a great part of it, again into the market. It is to be hoped, for many reasons, that these people will be able to struggle through, and to hold permanently the lands which they have thus acquired; since the establishment of a class of independent yeoman farmers amongst us would be an important circumstance, calculated to have no small influence on the social condition of the country. It is wonderful how conservative in their ideas some of these farmers have become under the magic influence of a real estate in the land, and how absolute are their notions of a landlord's rights to do what he likes with his own; for in several instances the new proprietor did not scruple to turn out the occupier of the holding he had purchased, in a summary fashion, and under circumstances which would have formed the theme for much indignant denunciation, had the act been committed by one of the old landlords of the country. . . .

The district of which I now speak includes two parishes - Moyarta and Kilbarryowen [Kilballyowen]; the latter of which is about six miles long, extending from Loophead to within a mile of the village of Carrigaholt; and it is here especially that the greatest apprehension of scarcity and want prevails, for it consists chiefly of arable land, and includes within its boundaries very little *fresh* bog, which is tantamount to saying that the people have no potatoes. Moreover, the oats are said to have been a total failure, as the continuous rain and the unusual coldness of the season did not allow the grain to ripen, and in some instances the cattle were turned into the fields to eat the unripe corn, or else it was cut merely for the sake of the straw.

Notwithstanding the decrease of population throughout the county, the two parishes are thickly inhabited, chiefly by small farmers, labourers, and fishermen. The sea abounds with fish: mackerel and herrings are often taken in large quantities near the shore, and cod, haddock, soles, and ling are caught at the greater distance. The people, however, do not possess the means of carrying on the fishery in a proper manner. They fish from 'corraghs' or canoes, consisting of a light framework of wood covered with tarred canvas, and which, from their extreme buoyancy, dance lightly over the waves, and are quite safe, even in rough weather, when dexterously managed by an experienced boatman; but it is obvious that these frail structures are not suitable for deep sea fishing, and that to a great extent the teeming waters must remain unproductive so far as these humble fishermen are concerned. Bream and other coarse fish are obtained along the rocky shore, which, together with the shell-fish gathered by the women and children, contribute greatly to the support of many poor families.

Those who have no land, rent a small patch for the cultivation of potatoes. This is generally called 'mock' by the people of the West, and in other parts of Ireland it is termed 'conacre'. In the district of which I am now speaking the average rent charged for 'conacre' is £4 an acre, but in other places along the coast it rises so high as £6, £8, and even £10 an acre for bog land which the tenant has to manure at great labour and expense. Persons living near the sea can easily obtain seaweed, sand, and shells for manure, and this fact will account for the comparative density of the population along the coast. Farms which border on the sea are much coveted, because of the privilege given to the tenant of collecting seaweed to manure his own land, he gathers as much more as he can, and carries it to Ennis or some other inland place, where he finds a ready sale for all he brings to market, and thus obtains a few pounds, which enable him to pay his rent or to procure food for his family. . . .

It would also be most injurious to the country at large if the drain of emigration, which has partially ceased, should be again renewed, for it is always the flower of our population, the young, the healthy, and the strong, who quit this country to seek their fortunes in other lands, leaving behind them the aged and infirm. Emigration has already caused a great scarcity of good labour in may parts of Ireland, and I fear the bad results of the last two seasons will turn the attention of many to Australia or the British colonies, if landlords do not act with judicious forbearance, and if some assistance be not given to enable the people to struggle through their present difficulties.

This reference to emigration leads me to mention a resource possessed by the poor of this country, which ought not to be overlooked in considering their present position. There is scarcely a family in Clare which has not some member or members in America or Australia, and remittances are constantly being sent by these exiles to their relatives at home. Sometimes the old couple receive five or six pounds from their son, whose horny hand need never lie idle in his bosom in the new world. Sometimes, as in a case which was lately mentioned to me, a young girl earning good wages in America, sends several pounds to her brother, who is willing to work, but can find no employment in his own country. The large sums thus sent home by Irish emigrants have often excited surprise and elicited the warmest admiration, as proofs of the deep-seated feelings of family affection which characterise our people. Latterly the remittances from America have decreased, in consequence of the fratricidal war now raging in that country; but money is still coming from Australia, and were it not for this timely help many families would have no prospect before them save the workhouse. . . .

[Kilrush] is a remarkable instance of the improvement which has taken place in so many country towns throughout Ireland since 1846. During the interval that has elapsed, the shops in Kilrush have doubled in number, and greatly increased in size. For example, in 1846 there was scarcely a shop in the town more than 24 feet in length, and there was not one having a plate-glass window; whereas now there are twelve shops with plateglass windows, some of 30 feet in front, and over 80 feet from front to rear. These shops are well-stocked with goods, varying in value from £1,000 to £7,000, but they are now almost deserted in consequence of the distressed state of the country; and traders whose daily receipts in prosperous years used to average £30, are now not receiving more than £6 or £7 a day. I was assured by a respectable shopkeeper that in the year 1860 he received for debts due to him for goods sold on credit £1,700. This year he has not received half that amount, and the falling off both in purchases and the payment of bills dates from the 1st of September. Up to that time bills were punctually paid by the farmers, but now it is almost impossible to obtain money from them except by legal process, and in numerous instances the traders who endorsed their bills to the banks, have been obliged to meet them, to their serious embarrassment.

There are branches of the National and Provincial Banks here, but there are complaints that they are restricting the accommodation which they were in the habit of giving, and have refused to renew many of the bills of the small farmers, even though a reduction on them was proposed to be made. . .

It would be a serious omission to finish my description of Kilrush without some reference to the largest proprietor and the best landlord in the district: I allude to Colonel Vandeleur, one of the members for Clare, who is one of the most popular men in the county, and will continue to represent it in parliament as long as he desires to enjoy that honour. In every part of the county which I have visited, but especially in the western portions, where his extensive estates are situated, I have heard Colonel Vandeleur praised as one of the kindest and most considerate of landlords. With the exception of a few town fields, which are set at reasonable rents, all his lands are let at Griffith's valuation.   As a natural consequence, his tenantry are comfortably off, and can bear up successfully against a bad season; whilst the rackrented tenants of other proprietors - and there are many such in Clare - must sink under the losses they have sustained. Colonel Vandeleur recognises a *quasi* tenant right on his property, and an instance was mentioned to me in which one of his tenants, holding 44 acres without a lease, sold his good will, or 'tenant-right', for £500.

The cottier population is very small throughout the country extending from Kilrush to Ballyvaghan, except in the little villages along the coast. The decrease in the population of the county since 1851 is something over 46,000, the diminution being confined to the small farmers and the labouring class. The parish of Killard, which is now in a very poor condition, suffered most severely during the famine years.   The poor rates in the years 1848-9 exceeded the valuation of the land; and the destruction of human life by famine and pestilence was enormous. As an illustration of the terrible condition of this country during that period, I may state the fact, communicated to me by the clergyman of this parish, that within the short space of six weeks the clerk of his church assisted in removing out of two houses no less than twenty-six bodies, the victims of cholera and starvation.   Killard, too, was the scene of evictions on a scale of magnitude and under circumstances of cruelty, which called for the interference of parliament, with a view to prevent the recurrence of such misery as followed that extreme exercise of the power of eviction. On Christmas Eve in the year 1847 no less than 86 families, numbering about 430 individuals - aged, infirm, young, and helpless - were turned out of their cabins, without a roof to shelter them until those who survived the inclemency of the weather obtained admission into the overcrowded workhouse of Kilrush.   These wholesale evictions took place on the property of a gentleman who was then a minor, and the circumstance attracted so much attention at the time, that the late Sir Robert Peel introduced and carried the Evicted Tenant's Bill, by which the landlord is obliged, under a heavy penalty, to serve notice on the relieving officer of the electoral division in which his property is situate, before he can evict any of his tenants-at-will.

The union of Ennistymon, which includes parts of the baronies of Burren, Corcomroe, Ibrackan, and Inchiquin, embraces an area of 99,281 statute acres, and contains 31,612 inhabitants. The poor law valuation is £36,594. The greater portion of the land has been converted into grazing farms, and butter is now the staple produce of the district. People here rarely speak of a man having so many acres of land: they indicate his position in life by saying that he 'has grass for so many cows'. The natural result of the substitution of grazing for tillage has been to restrict the amount of employment, the want of which is most severely felt by the labouring class. The population in the interior is rather sparse, but all along the shore there are numerous little villages inhabited by great numbers of small farmers and cottiers, who are attracted to the seaside by the facility with which the abundance of seaweed enables them to manure their land. The small farmer pays his rent by the sale of his pig, eggs, fowl, and butter, and grows as much potatoes as will supply his family, provided the crop yields a good average return. The cottier generally cultivates half or quarter of an acre of 'conacre' or 'mock ground', as they term it in Clare, for which he pays the middleman a very high rent, ranging from £4 an acre at Kilkee, to £6 and £8 at Miltown Malbay and other places along the coast. . . .

It is at the village of Ballyvaghan, which is situate in the barony of Burren, at the north-western extremity of the county, and along the adjacent coast, that the famous Burren oysters, so highly prized by the lovers of that delicate bivalve, are obtained. Almost the whole barony consists of a mass of limestone rock, interspersed here and there with small patches of arable land, but affording, even in those spots that are apparently most barren, pasturage of the best description, which renders the fat sheep and cattle of Burren proverbial amongst Irish agriculturists. . . .

I find that the potatoes in Burren have been better than in any other part of the county, the light, friable limestone soil being peculiarly favourable to their growth and development. The produce, however, is by no means a large one, and the proportion of black potatoes is considerable. The great and pressing want of the people in this district is *fuel*, as there are no bogs in the immediate neighbourhood of Ballyvaghan; and Connemara, from which in former years the people derived their supply, is now suffering from the universal scarcity of turf. The price at Ballyvaghan of this most necessary article, is treble the ordinary rate, and those who can afford to buy it cannot get enough for their purposes. In fact, a 'fuel famine' has already commenced. The people are literally cooking their food with dried fern, heath, brambles, and branches of hazel, of which there is a scanty growth here and there amongst the stone walls which divide field from field. . .

The population of Ballyvaghan may be roughly estimated at 550 persons, of whom about 100 belong to the labouring class, the majority of them being young, strong, and able men. There is a fishing village in the parish of Gleninagh, near Blackhead; and if the weather does not prove unusually stormy, the inhabitants will not be badly off for food; but, like all others in this locality, they are now enduring much privation from the want of fuel. Whatever may be said of the neglect of the people in other places in not saving their turf earlier, no blame can be imputed to the inhabitants of Burren, for they have no bogs to which they can resort and they have always been obliged to depend on Connemara for their supply. . . .

In closing my observations respecting the county of Clare, I am glad to say, that, although the state of things I have been obliged to depict is for the most part dark and gloomy, there is a bright side to the picture. I have already spoken of the signs of progress which are everywhere visible, and no rational man can doubt but that, when the present temporary pressure has passed away, the country will resume that march of improvement in which it has made such rapid strides during the last eight or ten years. Much, very much, will depend in the exertions of the resident gentry, who, by precept and example, can instruct and encourage their tenantry; and this is a matter of duty and of self-interest, to which the great majority of the landed proprietors of Ireland are becoming more keenly alive than were their pleasure-loving, generous, and hospitable, but thoughtless, predecessors. The better cultivation of the land, the improved habits of the people, both in respect to their dress and their dwellings, are cheering facts which cannot escape the observation of any one who compares the Ireland of to-day with the Ireland of thirty or even twenty years ago. To take a single instance. A quarter of a century back, almost every farmer's house in the county of Clare was built of mud, and presented a most squalid appearance. Now, snug farm-houses and neat stone-wall cottages are to be seen in every direction, and other indications are not wanting of the general prosperity and improved social condition of the farming classes in Ireland.

Extracts taken from Henry Coulter, *The West of Ireland: its existing condition and prospects* (Dublin 1862), pp 21-79.

Thomas Lacy,
Sights and Scenes in County Clare, 1859

Thomas Lacy of Wexford, sometimes styled 'the dacent Lacy' was the author of two books *England and Ireland: Home Sketches on Both Sides of the Channel* (1852), and *Sights and Scenes in Our Fatherland* (1863). In the 1840s Lacy was employed as assistant to the solicitor responsible for negotiating rights of way for the extension of the railway from Dublin to Wexford. The railway afforded him the opportunity to tour extensively in Leinster and Munster. In his accounts he 'always looked upon the sunny side of the picture' and avoids scenes of poverty and deprivation. His second book is a useful record of different tours he undertook in Ireland between 1853-61. Lacy's accounts are remarkable for the detail in which residences, public buildings and the interiors of churches are described. He came to Clare on at least two occasions. His first visit followed the extension of the railway line to Ennis in 1859. Taking the mail car from Ennis he toured Ennistymon and the north Clare area. On his second visit in 1860 he recorded in considerable detail the coastline from Kilkee to Loophead. His detailed description of Ennis cathedral is of particular value as it is the only record we now possess of the interior decoration of the church before the initiation of the extensive changes carried out over the last century and a half. In later life Lacy was employed as borough treasurer of Wexford town.

At six o'clock on Monday morning, the 24th of October [1859] I took my seat in one of the carriages of the train which leaves Waterford for Limerick, and being anxious, with as little delay as possible, to enter the county of my destination, I obtained a ticket for Ennis, where the train arrived at half-past eleven o'clock, and having partaken of some refreshment, I started by the midday car for Ennistymon where we arrived about half-past four o'clock in the evening. . .

In the neighbourhood of Ennistymon the tourist will notice, on the summit of a verdant elevation, the fragment of a once important stronghold, called Glan Castle. The small town of Ennistymon, which is situated in a valley, environed by handsome sheltering hills, forms part of the parish of Kilmanaheen, in the barony of Corcomroe, about seventeen miles from Ennis, and 128 from Dublin. From its low position, it is, generally speaking, remarkable for the moisture of its atmosphere, and, as a matter of course, for the dampness of its streets. The Ennistymon river may be said to intersect the town, leaving, however, the most considerable and important portion of it on the eastern side. This river, after flowing beneath a substantial bridge of six arches, falls over a ledge of rocks that extends across its entire bed, which is about 200 feet wide, and in its descent forms a splendid cascade; thence, at the distance of about a quarter of a mile below the town, it forms a junction with the river Derry. The waterfall here mentioned is a very interesting feature, and the river in its immediate vicinity being, upon each of its banks, enriched with fine trees, appears to great advantage, and excites the notice and admiration of the visitor. On a gentle eminence immediately north of the town stands the Protestant church, a handsome cruciform edifice, of some thirty years' standing, in the later English style of architecture, with an octagon tower on its southern side resting on a massive quadrangular basement. From its situation, at the north entrance to the town, this striking house of worship appears to great advantage. Ennistymon House, a fine square building, is situated on a handsome elevation which overlooks the river, at a short distance from the church. This enviable mansion, the residence of Lieutenant-Colonel Francis Macnamara, is surrounded by a richly wooded demesne, which is margined on the west by the gently flowing river, and on the north by a romantic glen. . . .

The Catholic church, a spacious cruciform structure, with a gallery in the end of each transept, is situated on a gentle eminence west of the river, and forms an exceedingly interesting feature in the surrounding and varied scenery; while the very neat cottage that occupies a still more elevated site west of the town and the church, in which the parish priest and his two curates reside, is also a pleasing and an agreeable object.

The ruin of the old Protestant church of the parish stands within the ancient popular burial-ground of the district, which is situated on the summit of a hill at a short distance from the town; and although merely consisting of the side walls and gables of a small plain structure, from its commanding and elevated position, presents a comparatively imposing and interesting appearance. The school of the Christian Brothers is likewise situated on the eastern side of the town, and is calculated to attract the visitor's notice; while the consciousness of the benefit it confers on the rising youth of the neighbourhood calls up feelings of unmingled pleasure in the minds of those who take an interest in the welfare and happiness of the humbler classes of the community. There is a good Sessions House, with an attached bridewell, in the town. The market, which is held on Saturday, is well supplied with the prime necessaries of life; there are seven fairs in the year. It is to me a source of no small regret to be obliged to say that at this time the town presented little or no evidence of advancing prosperity. It was formerly celebrated for the manufacture of woollen stockings, which, although inferior in quality to those of Connemara, were equally strong and lasting. But, except in the rural districts, even this source of employment has become almost extinct. . .

Proceeding on the following morning to view the celebrated Moher Cliffs, which are situated on the western coast of this county, I passed through the nice village of Lahinch, about two miles from Ennistymon. This place, which is much frequented in the summer season, on account of its fine bathing strand, being favourably situated on the inner extremity of the Bay of Liscannor, contains several new and handsome houses, and some neat shops, with a good Roman Catholic church, a school, under the National Board of Education, and an excellent hotel, called the Victoria. A new and strong boundary wall runs along the margin of the strand in the immediate vicinity of the town, within which the broad and ample roadway forms a delightful promenade. At this period of the year, when the seekers after health or pleasure, like summer birds, had flown, the village looked rather dull; but in the bathing season, doubtless, it is a gay and animated place. . . .

About two miles from this place the tourist will arrive at the town of Liscannor, which is situated on a part of the bay of that name, and to which vessels of small size can find access. A new Roman Catholic church, of oblong form and plain character, has lately been erected in this village, which shows a small chancel on its eastern end, and four windows in its northern side. It is entered in the same side by a neat porch, vastly superior in its style and workmanship to the church of which it is adjunct. A handsome belfry rises above the apex of the western gable, while a plain cross stands upon that of the eastern or chancel end of the building. This small town is situated in the parish of Kilmacrehy and barony of Corcomroe. The ruin of the ancient church, which is situated near the village, and in the immediate vicinity of the old churchyard, consists of the gables, side walls, and the finely pointed arch that divided the nave and choir. On a handsome eminence, south of the village, stands the ruin of O'Connors Castle, which was a strong square fortress of large proportions. It is still in a state of comparatively good preservation, and, from its elevated position, appears an interesting object for many miles on the land, and a striking landmark from the sea. Near this remarkable feature is the handsome cottage, the seat of Charles O'Connell, Esq., which stands close to the edge of the beetling cliff that at this point overhangs the sea. This picturesque and romantically situated cottage, although in an exposed and wild locality, is considered a very healthy residence. Sea Mount, the handsome residence of the Right Rev Dr Fallon, the Roman Catholic Bishop of Kilmacduagh, is favourably situated about a quarter of a mile from Liscannor. The house, which is rented by his Lordship from

George O'Brien, Esq., the son and successor of Cornelius O'Brien, Esq., deceased, presents a rich comfortable appearance, and is surrounded with nice plantations. The tourist will next arrive at Birchfield, the seat of George O'Brien, Esq., and cannot fail to notice the very handsome mansion, which is of quadrangular form, with a nice octangular turret rising on each angle, the summit of which stands one story higher than the main edifice, and is decorated with embrasure battlements; while the mansion on each of its four sides is enriched with an ornamental parapet. The celebrated Thomas Steele, Esq., who was a friend of the late proprietor, and an engineer and architect of no mean pretensions, drew the plan of this building. The grand facade, before which is a rich lawn, displays itself to the south, and is entered from a fine granite platform, which is approached by three or four steps. The grounds, which are of considerable extent, are intersected with handsome drives and walks, while those immediately adjoining the house are richly planted. . . .

Having, within a comparatively brief period, viewed some of the most remarkable and important features on this part of the western coast and its neighbourhood, I returned to Ennis, where at Camody's [Carmody's excellent hotel I found comfortable quarters. This establishment is exceedingly well conducted, the prompt attention and civility of the servants being surpassed only by the politeness and urbanity of the clever and sensible proprietor. . . .

A very handsome bridge of a single arch, with cut stone parapets, was built some twenty-five years ago, at an expense of £800, and crosses the river on the site of a former bridge, nearly opposite the abbey grounds. In the vicinity of this bridge is a handsome modern street, lined with fine new brick houses of uniform height and regular proportions, which is called Binden Street. Extensive mills, some of them belonging to Russell and Co., of Limerick, and others to Mr Ballatine of that city, are situated on the banks of the Fergus, in this part of the town. In this section of the town also, but on the opposite side of the river, is situated the fine Court House, which is considered to be good value for £16,000, although, as I was informed, it was built under a contract for the sum of £12,000. The contractor who, previous to his having entered into the engagement, was worth £4,000 or £5,000, became by the fulfilment of it a ruined and broken man. It is a handsome quadrangular building, the grand façade consisting of a centre and two flanking wings. A splendid portico, extending the entire length of the centre, is formed by six fine columns of the Ionic order, supporting a magnificent entablature complete in all its parts, above which rises an elegant pediment. The centre, the fronts and ends of the flanking wings, are of pure granite, and the rear of hammered limestone. The columns rest on an extensive platform, which is approached by nine steps that, like itself, are composed of granite. At the extremity of the spacious area immediately in front of the grand centre, is a large Russian gun, one of the trophies of the Crimean campaign, which, at the solicitation of the chairman of the Town Commissioners, was presented to the town. In the north-western suburbs, at a short distance from the Court House, but on the opposite side of the river, are situated, close to each other, two seminaries or colleges, in one of which, under the direction of Mr Fitzsimon, the president, are educated a large number of young gentlemen, many of whom are intended for the priesthood, and carefully prepared for entering the college of Maynooth. The other establishment is under the immediate superintendence of the Rev Mr King, a Protestant clergyman, and is partly supported by a grant from the trustees of the charity of the benevolent Erasmus Smith. These valuable institutions, which are surrounded with boundary walls, and entered by handsome gates, being enriched with ornamental trees, form remarkably pleasing and agreeable features.

The fine new Catholic church of Ennis, which is also the cathedral of the diocese of Killaloe, is nicely situated at the entrance of the splendid road which leads to the town of Killaloe. It is a lofty and substantial cruciform structure in the English-Gothic style of architecture, the front, quoins, door-jambs, and window-edgings, being of fine granite, and the remainder of the building of a compact greyish stone. It is entered in the western face of the tower, which at present rises no higher than the first story. There is a door in each end of the transept beneath a fine elliptic Gothic arch, over which is a splendid window in the perpendicular style, of three lights, the pointed arch of which is enriched with elaborate decorations; while from the apex of the gable springs an enriched characteristic cross. The windows of the nave, three on each side, are of the same style as those of the transept, and like them, and the arches of the doorways, are decorated with label-mouldings. The interior presents a fine appearance, the nave being divided from the aisles by nice wooden columns of a rich oak colour. The altar, composed of Caen stone, is strikingly beautiful, the sides, on a line with the rich tabernacle, being furnished with elegant statues, those on the Gospel side consisting of the Blessed Virgin, St Mary Magdalene, and St Bridget, the latter bearing a crosier, the symbol of high ecclesiastical dignity. On the opposite side appear St Joseph, St John the Evangelist, and St Patrick. Above the altar-screen is a beautiful painting, being a copy from one of the first masters, the original of which is said to have cost £12,000, and has been placed in one of the London galleries. The most prominent figure in this splendid picture is that of our Blessed Redeemer, who is represented in all the meekness of early youth. That part of the transept on the Gospel side of the church is furnished with a deep gallery, which is so admirably constructed as to enable every person who obtains access to it to have a full view of the priest during the celebration of the mass. In the opposite portion of the transept, in which there is no gallery, handsome confessionals have been placed. In front of each section of the transept are two magnificent arches, extending from a strong and handsome central column to the side walls. In the western end of the nave, a remarkably strong and well-built gallery has been erected for the beautiful and powerful organ, built by the late Mr White, of Dublin, who was a native of Enniscorthy, in the county of Wexford. This ponderous instrument with its appurtenances, as I was informed by the Very Rev. Dean Kenny, the excellent parish priest, weighs no less than 30 tons. On the left-hand side, within the western end of the nave, and beneath the organ gallery, is an uncommonly fine baptismal font, of black marble. The ceiling of this lofty structure is of rich panelled work, constructed on the principle of the ceilings of the Houses of Parliament, by which the voice of the preacher or officiating priest becomes so far concentrated as to be perfectly audible to the whole of the large congregation. . . .

In the vicinity of High Street, which may be considered the centre of the town, a new bridge was at this time being built across the Fergus, which is considered a great improvement. On a fine open space immediately in front of the entrance to this bridge, a lofty pedestal, based on a massive square platform, was then nearly ready for the reception of the statue of the illustrious Daniel O'Connell, which the patriotic and public-spirited people of Ennis resolved to erect to the memory of Ireland's most distinguished and self-sacrificing public man. In Jail Street, on the site of what was formerly the old county prison, has been erected a new town-hall, which presents a handsome exterior, but which, from want of funds, or from some other cause, had not up to this time been entirely finished. . . .

While proceeding from Ennis to Limerick, I stopped at the Quin station, and availed myself of the interval between the passing of the mid-day train and that of the evening, to visit the celebrated ruins of Quin Abbey, which are situated about two miles from that place. This abbey, which is one of the most perfect and complete ruins that I have seen in this country, is situated on a gentle elevation, which slopes down to the eastern bank of the clear river that flows before its western front, which in its southward course, after passing beneath a handsome bridge of three arches, becomes ultimately lost in the Fergus. . . .

Quin is a parish in the barony of Bunratty, about six miles from Ennis. In the village, which is near the ruins of the grand abbey, there is little worthy of the tourist's notice, save the Protestant and Catholic churches. The Protestant church, which is of long standing, but which has recently undergone considerable improvement, is a plain structure with a square tower. It is handsomely situated on the western bank of the Quin river, at a short distance east of the ruin which, as an appendage of the celebrated abbey, was rendered subservient to the purposes of charity and benevolence, affording shelter and hospitality to the poor and the stranger in the old monastic times.

The Catholic church is a handsome and spacious cruciform structure in the Gothic style of architecture, with a nice portico of cut stone. It was erected about twenty years ago, at an expense of £2,000, which was defrayed by general subscription. At the time I paid my visit it was undergoing considerable improvements, chiefly confined to internal decoration and embellishment. The angles of the nave and transepts are strengthened on the outside by fine buttresses, from each of which rises an ornamental pinnacle; while the apex of each transept, as well as that of the nave, is decorated with a highly wrought Gothic cross. The interior is very beautiful, the fine clustered columns that adjoin the altar, and the part that connects the transepts with the nave, being alike remarkably grand and striking; while the altar itself - which is of Caen stone, with columns of the Cork, Galway, and Armagh marbles - and the elegant statuary command the attention and the warmest commendation of the visitor. The doors leading into the nave and transepts are of elliptic character, with label-mouldings. The windows, three in each side of the nave, are high, and of two mullions; while those above the transept doors, and the three in each of their sides, are of a single mullion. . . .

On my return from Quin Abbey to the Ardsollous and Quin station, I availed myself of the time still at my disposal, and proceeded to take a view of Dromoland, the seat of Lord Inchiquin, which is about two miles in an opposite direction from this station. It is a very handsome place, and the mansion, a fine castellated structure, one of the most magnificent specimens of a modern baronial building to be seen in any part of Ireland. . . .

The Quin river, in its devious windings, flows through portions of this fine demesne. Returning from Dromoland, I was just in time for the last train to Limerick, by which I proceeded to that fine city. . . .

[Kilkee], which is so numerously and fashionably attended, especially by the citizens of Limerick, is about to have a railway opened to it from the maritime town of Kilrush, from which by land it is but seven miles distant, although by sea it is some thirty-four miles from it, being situated at Moore Bay, on the western shore; its distance from Limerick is about fifty statute miles, from Ennis twenty-five, and from Dublin 170. In anticipation of the opening of the railway, Major Macdonnell, the owner of the property on which the town stands, is about to build a large and commodious hotel, the plan of which, together with a new terrace and adjoining houses, has been prepared and exhibited at the principal hotels in the town. The handsome site chosen for these buildings is called, after the gallant proprietor, the Macdonnell Terrace. Moore's hotel, which occupies one side of a quadrangular area called Wellington Square, is an excellent house, and shows its front to the bay and to the Marine Parade, which is a continuation of the fine roadway that extends from the bridge that unites this portion of the town to the older part, and leads to what is called the West End. On the verdant lawn before the front bands of music occasionally play, and fireworks are sometimes exhibited. At a short distance in the rear of the hotel is an old and venerated spring called St Senan's Well, long resorted to on account of its miraculous efficacy in the cure of many diseases; it is enclosed by a small building in the style of a mortuary chapel, with a plain cross on the apex of the western gable, which was erected by the kind and liberal proprietor, Major Macdonnell.

At some distance west of Mr Moore's hotel is a new establishment called the Warren Hotel, from its proprietress, Mrs Warren, who for many years kept the well-conducted house known as the Triton-ville Hotel, in the centre of the Crescent. This house was built expressly for her accommodation by the excellent proprietor, and from her high character and superior management, it will doubtless be considered a desideratum by a large number of the respectable visitors to this rising and very interesting town. It is admirably situated on a gentle elevation immediately above the south-western side of the bay, which can be seen to fine advantage from the commodious dining-parlours and sitting-rooms. The Catholic church, a lofty cruciform building of comparatively modern erection, is finely situated on an elevated site in the eastern part of the town. The principal entrance in the western end of the nave is flanked on each side by a semi-octagon tower surmounted by embattled ornaments, above which, within an elliptic Gothic arch, is a handsome window of two mullions, over which rises the pointed gable, surmounted by a characteristic cross. There is also a door in each transept, over which is a window of a single mullion, with two windows of the same size and style in each side of the nave, and one in each side of the transepts. The altars are very neat and appropriately ornamented, the grand or central one being enriched with a beautiful painting of the Descent from the Cross; with one of the Blessed Virgin above her altar on the Epistle side, and one of the Crucifixion above that dedicated to St Joseph on the Gospel side. In the rear of the gallery in the western end of the nave is the organ, a sweet toned and powerful instrument.

Immediately west of the church is a large substantial building of modern erection, two stories in height, in which are commodious schools under the National Board of Education, for boys and girls. The Protestant church is situated near the centre of the Crescent, and is a handsome oblong building with a neat porch at the western end;

a strong graduating buttress rises on each angle of the church, and a pilaster on each angle of the porch. The east window is of admirable proportions, and, like those in the sides, four in each, is in the Perpendicular style. Near the church is the school, under the direction of the Protestant rector, a remarkably nice house in the Elizabethan style of architecture. There is also a dispensary in the town.

Extracts taken from Thomas Lacy, *Sights and Scenes in Our Fatherland* (London 1863), pp 679-701.

William Barry, A Walking Tour of Clare, 1864

William Whittaker Barry, well known English pedestrian, came to Ireland in the Autumn of 1864. His objective was to complete a circuit of the country on foot. He spent nearly ten weeks in Ireland, visited twenty out of the thirty-two counties and walked upwards of 1,500 miles. His book professes to give a strictly original account of Ireland as it appeared to an intelligent, well informed Englishman. He confines himself to those topics within his own observation and experience. Entering Clare by steamer from Galway he traversed the whole of the west coast from Ballyvaughan to Kilrush where he boarded the ferry for Tarbert. Unable to reach Lahinch in a single day's walk, he was compelled to seek lodgings in Liscannor. He provides a very amusing account of the kind of lodgings a tourist might expect to find in a remote Clare seaside village in the 1860s. Barry appears to have been a lawyer by profession and was the author of several legal tracts including *A Treatise on the Practice of Conveyancing* (1865), and *A Treatise on the Statuary Jurisdiction of the Court of Chancery*, (1872). He also penned a walking tour of Normandy in 1868. He died some years later while attempting to cross the Alps on foot.

Saturday, September 16, 1864. I then took a path which leads into a bye-road leading into the main road to Ballyvaughan. Shortly after reaching the main road there is a ruin to the right of an old castle or mansion. About two o'clock I met an old farmer in a cart, quite 'drunk and incapable'. A friend came up on foot who was in the same condition, and assisted him. I asked a boy whether the men had been drinking potheen at Ballyvaughan. He looked at me with a knowing smile, and said there was none in the place, not a drop. 'Ah!' thought I, passing on, 'you take me for a gauger, I see, my boy; no potheen in Ballyvaughan on market-day - a likely thing, very likely!' On the left, before entering Ballyvaghan there are the ruins of apparently an old church. I pass though Ballyvaughan, a clean neat-looking kind of town with an inn. It was fair-day. Pigs, sheep, drapery, fruit, and salt fish, were the principal articles of merchandise. A good deal of Irish was being talked in the fair, and by two farmers on horseback on the road. I met a woman who said neither herself nor her husband could speak the native Irish, and they found themselves therefore at a disadvantage in doing business in the fair. One of her boys had picked up the language, which was of some assistance. . . .

Shortly before reaching [Lisdoonvarna] I entered a small cabin occupied by two old women. Only one bed in a recess, and underneath a place for the chicken. There was a kind of apology for a chimney, but the smoke went out at the door. I sat down for a short time and had some talk with these old women. One of them said she should be quite contented if she could have this hovel entirely to herself. What a reflection on human ambition! This poor woman would be content to have as a home that which a fine gentleman would hardly think good enough to rest in for one hour.

Arrived at Lisdoonvarna I took up my quarters at Redy's Hotel, to which I had been recommended by my kind medical friend at Kinvarra. It was late in the evening. I asked the waiter for some dinner. He replied, 'I fear there is nothing.' I said, 'But you have a table d'hôte, I hear, at four o'clock.' 'Ah! yes; but the things are all consumed by this time,' he rejoined with a smile. However, though the waiter promised nothing, he produced some very good salmon and a joint of meat. . . .

Sunday, September 17, 1864. After breakfast I sailed forth in my slippers to see the spas, and my object being observed by a respectable Irishman, one of the visitors to the place, he very civilly offered to be my guide to them. We saw three springs, one sulphur, another magnesia, and the other iron. I tasted them all, and neither of the waters was particularly nauseous. We then went on to a place below the site of the small Protestant church, and difficult to find, so that my friend's guidance was of real assistance. As he led me on, in a way to prevent getting wet, he said, 'See how careful I am of you.' The sight here is certainly a curious one. There are two springs close adjoining, one iron and the other sulphur. On our return walk I asked my friend what diseases these waters would cure? He replied, 'Lor, sir, every disease under the sun.' My faith in the spas, however, was somewhat shaken when my friend, who had been here drinking the waters for a month, excused himself from showing me the remaining spring, on the ground that the sulphur made him so weak that he felt too tired to walk any more at present. Of course I wished him good-bye, with thanks for what he had already kindly done, but still on leaving him I could not help reflecting, 'Why, this is my morning stroll in slippers, simply, before taking a day's journey, and yet this man, who looks strong and in the prime of life, is tired already. Can these waters, therefore, be very strengthening?' The wells containing the springs are still left in their rude natural state, and only at the sulphur spring, being that apparently the one most usually taken, is there even an attendant with glasses. At the other places there is only a cup or glass for all comers. The remaining spring I did not see is of copper, and only used I believe for external applications. This spa is much frequented, and there has been a good season here this year, I am informed; but if it be wished to attract English visitors it is essential that the springs should have proper surroundings. An Englishman will never believe in the efficacy of a mineral water which is lathed out of a most primitive-looking well. It should be placed under cover of a splendid saloon, and be made to issue from the mouth of a nymph, a lion, or the like. . . .

Lisdoonvarna is prettily situated in a valley, and very secluded. I should be inclined to think that what does people good here is more the calm and quiet they enjoy, combined with freedom from care and pleasant company, than the efficacy of the springs. But what matter the cause, so the result is achieved. If there were no spas there would be no visitors. Certainly if the post could only be shut out, a person by a little aid of the imagination might fancy himself here in a kind of happy valley.

I left the spa at one o'clock. My first destination was to visit the castle of Ballynacken, near Mr O'Brien's residence, about two miles from Lisdoonvarna. . . .

On arriving at Mr O'Brien's grounds, and on ascending the hill, I was amused to find my progress disputed by a snarling little dog, apparently left behind by his companions to do fag duty while they took their constitutional. However, the little brute did me some service by bringing out a girl from the house, with the key of the tower of the castle. This I forthwith ascended, and enjoyed a good prospect from the summit of Galway Bay, the three islands of Arran, and inland of the surrounding country. I then descended, gained the road, and proceeded through the village of Killalough, where there are four hamlets, one called Fisherstreet, principally occupied by fishermen. Hereabouts I had some talk with a man about the Fenians. He had heard of a person being stopped the other day, on his way home at night from Galway Fair, and made to take the oath. He spoke also of a midshipman having written from the fleet to his mother, saying she must not be surprised if a Fenian army succeeded in landing on the Irish coast. . . .

It was now near nightfall. I had been much misinformed as to the distance by my good friends at the spa, and now felt in a rage with them. According to their information I could easily reach Lehinch, where there was a good hotel; but this place proved to be many miles further than they imagined. The country here is wild and desolate-looking, and did not hold out much promise of an inn of any kind. However, I was informed by a countryman that there was a small inn where I could get a bed at Liscannor, on the bay of that name some miles further on, so there was nothing to be done but to make for this place. I walk on several miles, and pass to the right a monument erected to the memory of Cornelius O' Brien, father of the present proprietor, G. O'Brien, whose residence, Birchfield House, is a little further on, being skirted by the road. It is now quite dark, and with difficulty I keep on my way. I arrived at Liscannor between seven and eight o'clock. I enquire for the inn kept by Mr and Mrs Consedine, to which I had been directed. It is a grocer's, and general shop as well, which I enter, and ask the master whether I can have a bed. He replies, 'I must ask the missis.' Presently she enters from outside - a stout pleasant-looking woman - and I repeat the question, and she says I may have one. The servant shows me up into the coffee-room. It is in a slovenly condition, with the remains of a broken glass on the floor, showing that the room had been in request during the day. The broken pieces are picked up by the servant-woman, but presently a girl with naked feet appears, and I warn her of the débris, at which she is much obliged. . . .

There is but scant fare for dinner. I ask the servant to bring me some whisky-punch. She comes with a glass of it ready-made. I fear it is too strong, and that there may be more than a wine-glass of whisky. 'Well,' says the servant,' I can't say but there may be a little more; trust missis for being able to make a glass of punch.' I ask her whether they have any potheen in the house. She says, 'No; you see, as there is a constabulary next door, it wouldn't do for the master to be having any on't about.' The whisky-punch is certainly strong, but well mixed and very good. At length, soon after ten o'clock I enter the bedroom; but, oh! ye powers, what a sight presents itself. The bed curtains and linen are literally swarming with the three classes of the insect world which so often rob the traveller of his rest. I ring the bell, and the chambermaid appears. 'Cast thy bread on the waters, and it shall return after many days;' but here, within an hour or two, the bread is returning. That care of her unprotected feet now evidently is enlisting this girl's sympathies in my behalf. 'Lor, sir! I have only been in the house three weeks, and never knew of this; bless my soul! what a sight!' I asked her to fetch the other servant, which she proceeded to do. Meanwhile, the insect army, alarmed by the light, began to beat a retreat; but when the head servant appeared, a sufficient number still remained to satisfy her I could not sleep in that room to-night. So I said they must make me up a bed on the sofa and chairs. . . .

Monday, September 18, [1864]. I left Liscannor this morning before breakfast, starting at seven o'clock. There was a good deal of mist, so I could see nothing for a time. The road passes over O'Brien's Bridge, near which are the remains of a castle, and then, by the sea across sandy and undulating mounds of grass-land to Lehinch, a small watering-place. I arrived here about eight o'clock, and breakfasted at the Royal Victoria Hotel, a good-sized and comfortable-looking inn. I met an Irish gentleman here, a clerk in Somerset House, out for his holidays, who had been spending part of his time at Lisdoonvarna, the waters of which he highly commended, and the rest of his holiday he was devoting to this place. This gentleman gave me some information, and on leaving he accompanied me to a lodging-house to learn the prices. The young woman who appeared said the rent for a lodge or house during the bathing season, containing two sitting and three or four bedrooms, was from six to eight pounds a month. The frequenters of English watering-places will be able to draw a comparison, and if I mistake not, very much in favour of the economy of seaside visits of Ireland. Lehinch is a pretty watering-place, with beautiful sands.

Having parted from my friend with thanks for his courtesy, but with some inward annoyance at his pencillings on my map, I left Lehinch at ten o'clock. The road winds round the shore, and presents a fine view of the bay and Hag's Head, with Liscannor, Moher, and O'Connor Castles, and the white houses here and there on the opposite coast. . . .

The visiting part of Milltown Malbay is about a mile from the village, and consists of this hotel, and many lodgings and other houses overlooking the sea. The place is finely situated, with good sands.

I was apparently the only coffee-room guest at the Atlantic Hotel. I was civilly shown into a private room as it overlooked the sea, which the coffee-room does not, though there is a broad expanse of green lawn in front of it. I ordered some dinner, and in a short time appeared roast turkey and pudding. Altogether the Atlantic Hotel is one of the best inns I have yet visited in Ireland. I had here the only perfectly clean bed since that at the Railway Hotel, Galway. . . .

After dinner I sauntered about the grounds, watching the carting of potatoes and looking at the sea. There are some seats in a garden fronting the hotel, which forms an agreeable promenade.

On my way to-day I walked some distance with an old peasant man, and we engaged in conversation on the subject of the Fenians. He disapproved of the movement altogether, and thought it would bring about no good. He did not, however, seem to attach much danger to the conspiracy, and appeared to have full confidence in the power of the government to put it down. The old man said slowly and with emphasis that he had a long memory, but never knew a case of persons opposing the law but it was the worse for themselves in the end. . .

Tuesday, September 19, [1864]. I left Milltown Malbay this morning at half-past nine o'clock. The road winds round the bay, and then joins the high-road to Kilkee. From here a good view is obtained of the Milltown Malbay visiting part. The bay hotel and surrounding houses look well. Then on to the village of Quilty, with a row of thatched cottages by the sea, skirting a large field, and called Sea Field. Opposite is Mutton Island, with a castle or tower in the centre, and two islets to the north. Further on there is a good view of the sea with Milltown and the hills of Clare in the background. Near Quilty, to the right, there is a castle, apparently inhabited, and the village or hamlet of Kilmurry. Then the road proceeds for several miles through a flat but well-cultivated country until you come in view of some low but undulating hills, which serve to relieve a little the monotony of the journey. Then on the main road for some distance, when I took a cross-road to the right leading to the high-road to Doonbeg and Kilkee. . .

On a small bridge over a broad stream which the bye-road crosses there is the following estimate of its cost - 'This bridge was built by John Lynch for 128*l.*, June 10, 1838.' Whether this amount be little or much I know not, but certainly such records if generally given would convey some useful information to succeeding generations of the coast of labour at the time. Shortly after I reached the main road I fell in with a young farmer on horseback. He said Kilkee had been very full this season with the quality, but was now emptying, and partly on account of the Limerick races. He expressed surprise at my walking, and said be would offer me a seat on his pony, only it would not suffer any one to get up behind. A sensible animal!

I then pass through Doonbeg, and cross a bridge, over the river of the same name. Doonbeg is a poor little village, with no inn, and a small chapel. There are two square towers here, one in the village, and the other on the bank of the river before passing the bridge. Further on is Killard Church and the village or hamlet of Bealaha. Shortly after passing through this place I meet a young man, with a rod and a bundle of whiting which he had caught this morning, looking quite black with exposure to the sun. I asked him why he had not put some grass round them. He said he did not know; he could not get any. I am afraid this petty incident lets in a little light on the Irish character. This youth here, after toiling all the morning, is evidently too indolent to secure the fish he has caught from being spoilt.

Then on through several villages and well-cultivated land to Kilkee. About a mile from the town I meet three well-dressed young ladies, as sure harbingers of a watering-place as swallows of spring. . . .

The town consists of two or three back streets, but principally of fine rows of houses, extending round nearly the whole extent of the bay, forming as near as may be a semicircle. Towards the north part of the bay there are some good detached houses, and the best houses are in a row on the north or opposite side of the bay. Towards the south the headlands appear, and in the background a gentle range of undulating hills. The bay is magnificent, with a sandy shore, and shut in by the land with a bar, partly extending across the mouth, with the broad Atlantic beyond. Altogether, Kilkee is the most picturesque and pleasing watering-place I have yet seen in Ireland. It is situated in the south-west and is much frequented by the Limerick people, being so convenient of access for them. The way they come is by the steamboat down the Shannon to Kilrush, and from there to here by car. The distance from Milltown Malbay to Kilkee is about twenty miles. . . .

There are three principal hotels here, Moore's, Warren's, and the West End, all close together on the Esplanade. Moore's I believe is the best. It certainly looks so. I ordered some dinner at the West End Hotel - anything that could be forthcoming. First came some fresh herrings - a good beginning; but then the dinner suddenly collapsed. Not a chop, steak, or bit of fresh meat of any kind could be got in the town; there was only some salt meat, which I declined. The waiter, however, with considerable naïveté, promised that I should have a chop in the morning. Fancy the hungry pedestrian having to wait until the next morning for his second course. . . .

Wednesday, September 20, 1864. I started at eleven o'clock in company of three young English gentlemen, who were doing their tour partly on foot, for Kilrush, distant about eight miles. The road passes through a dull-looking country, with a peep of the sea every now and then to the right. . . .

Kilrush is a small pleasant-looking town on the banks of the Shannon, as it reaches the sea. The principal streets are Henry Street and Frances Street. The Market-place Square is also a good part. There are two hotels, the Vandeleur Arms and Williams's. I intended to cross the Shannon in a boat, wishing to proceed on from the opposite bank to Listowel, but after making many enquiries, and being directed from this place to that, the only chance of crossing, except on exorbitant terms, was by means of a hooker, a kind of fishing smack, the owners of which were regaling themselves in the town, and would not start until the turn of the tide in the evening, and until, I also opined, a good deal of whisky-punch had gone down the throats of the boatmen. So finding those near the harbour endeavouring to make a 'plant' of me, as they say in the vulgar tongue, I went on board the steamboat, just starting for Limerick, with the intention of using it as a ferry, and being put out at Tarbet, the first stopping-place, and on the Kerry side of the Shannon.

Extracts taken from William Barry, *A Walking Tour Around Ireland in 1864* (London 1867), pp 188-214.

Bernard Becker, Disturbed Clare, 1880

By 1880 County Clare was again in turmoil as the land war and the demand for the abolition of landlordism entered a dynamic phase. The new out-break of disturbances aroused interest in England and Bernard Becker, a London journalist with the *Daily News,* was sent to report on the distressed conditions in Ireland. Becker claimed to be an 'intelligent foreigner' with no Irish politics or connections so that his comments could be accepted as fair and impartial. In a series of letters to his newspaper he described conditions in the west of Ireland. He confined his inquiries to counties Kerry, Clare, Galway and Mayo. The letters are claimed to be plain, descriptive accounts of 'a strange phase in national life.' In reality Becker was strongly sympathetic towards landlords. He lodged at Edenvale with Richard Stacpoole, one of the largest and most unyielding landlords in the county. He was critical of tenants and largely unsympathetic to their demands. He paints an insulting and degrading pen picture of Michael Considine, secretary of the Ennis Tradesmen Association and the man responsible for the erection of the O'Connell Monument in the town. His account of the reclamation of lands in the Fergus estuary is informative and, interestingly, records one of the earliest uses of electricity in County Clare. When published, *Disturbed Ireland* made a considerable impact: it gave rise to debates on the 'Irish Question' in the House of Commons. In essence the book is a republication in collected form of his letters from Ireland. Nearly forty pages are devoted to describing conditions in Clare, edited extracts from which are printed below. *Disturbed Ireland* was Becker's only book to achieve public notoriety. In 1884 he published the less controversial *Holiday Haunts by Cliffside and Riverside.* He died in London, January 1900.

Ennis, Co. Clare. Nov. 21st. 1880. The condition of affairs at Edenvale is in many respects even more curious than that at Lough Mask House. There is none of the pomp and circumstance of open war. There is not a soldier or a policeman on the premises. All is calm and pastoral. From a lodge so neat and trim that it is a pleasure to look upon it, a well-kept road winds through a well-wooded and beautiful park, in the centre of which, on the brink of a lake, stands a large and handsome country house. All is ship-shape, from the gravel on the path to the knocker on the door, which is promptly opened, without grating of bolt or rattle of chain, by a clean, well-dressed, civil servitor.

Mr Stacpoole, whose appearance and manner are as frank as his welcome is hearty, is by no means reticent as to the matters in debate between him and the tenants holding from him and other members of his family for whom he acts as agent. To the question whether he goes in fear of his life, he replies, 'Not at all; I take care of that,' and out of the pocket of his lounging jacket he takes a revolver of very large bore. It is a curious picture, this drawing-room at Edenvale. On his own hearth-rug, in his own house, with a silky white Maltese lapdog and a beautiful terrier nestling at his feet, stands no English or Scotch interloper, agent, middleman, or 'land-grabber,' but the representative of one of the oldest, most honourable, and, I may add, till recently most honoured families in the county, with his hand on the pistol which is never out of his reach by day or night. There was once no more popular man in Clare. His steeplechasers win glory for Ireland at Liverpool, whether they return a profit to the owner or not. He keeps up, with slight assistance from members of the Hunt, a pack of harriers, and hunts them himself. His cousin, the late Captain Stacpoole, of Ballyalla, was the well-known 'silent member' who for twenty years represented Ennis in parliament. Finally, he is spending at least 3,000*l*. a year in household expenses alone; but he never leaves his revolver; and he is in the right, for not two hours ago a local leader declared to me with pale face and flaming eyes that he would 'gladly go to the gallows for 'um.'

But the local leader does not, or at least has not yet shot at Mr Stacpoole because he 'can't get at 'um'- a phrase which requires some explanation. I had, with an eye becoming practised in such matters, scanned the house and its approaches as I drove up to the door, and had discussed with the friend who introduced me to its master the chances of 'stalking' that gentleman on his own ground. Trees and brushwood grew more closely to the house than a military engineer would have permitted, and I hazarded the opinion that it would be easy to 'do him over,' as it is called. But on talking to Mr Stacpoole I quickly discover that the real reason why he is now alive is that ninety-nine out of a hundred of his enemies are as afraid of him as the Glenveagh folk up in Donegal are of Mr J. G. Adair. Brave and resolute to a fault, he has openly declared his dislike for what is called 'protection.' 'But,' he observes, quietly and simply, 'I always carry my large-bore revolver, and I never walk alone, even across the path to look down at the lake. Whenever I go out, and wherever I go, I have a trustworthy man with me carrying a double-barrelled gun. His orders are distinct. If anybody fires at me he is not to look at me, but let me lie, and kill the man who fired the shot. And I am not sure that if he saw an armed man near me in a suspicious attitude that he wouldn't shoot first. I most certainly will myself. If I catch any of them armed and lurking about near my house, I will kill them, and they know it.'

There was no appearance of emotion in the speaker, whose collection of threatening letters is large and curious. His position was clearly defined. There was no longer any law in Clare. It was everybody for himself, and he would take care of himself in his own way. Mr Stacpoole's situation is certainly extraordinary. He is not an 'exterminator,' but perhaps he is a 'tyrant,' for everybody is considered one who tries to exact obedience from any created being in the west of Ireland. He has incurred the ill-will of the popular party, mainly through his debate with one Welsh, or Walsh, a small farmer.

So far as it is possible to understand the matter, this Welsh and two other persons held a farm of about fifty acres among them as co-tenants, paying each one-third of the rent. Whether Welsh had reclaimed bog and increased his store is not clear, but it is certain that when the lease fell in he had about half of the farm and the other two tenants the other half between them.

Moreover, the land was not 'striped' in blocks, but remained in awkward patches, so that each man was obliged to cross the other's land, and perpetual squabbling occurred. So when the question of a new lease arose, Mr Stacpoole sent a surveyor to divide the holding into three equal shares as justly and conveniently as might be with reference to the tenants' houses. This was done, the land was re-valued at 12s. 6d. per acre, the tenants preferring to hold it without a lease. Thus two were pleased and one displeased by the new arrangement, and the displeased one, Welsh, or Walsh, was finally evicted a short while since, and his house pulled down. Only the other day a mob assembled, rebuilt Welsh's house, and reinstated his wife and family, who occupy it at this moment. Welsh himself is not with them for the reason that Mr Stacpoole has an attachment out against him. However, the family remains, and no process-server would show his face at the rebuilt house for fifty pounds. Mr Stacpoole could, of course, go and turn the people out as trespassers, but does not think it worth while until he joins issue with all the recalcitrant tenants under his control. Some forty of these will neither pay up nor surrender their holdings, and Mr Stacpoole declares that he will get Dublin writs against the whole of them, and that if they do not yield he will evict them all and compel the authorities to support him. There is no concealment about all this, and it is quite certain that if Mr Adair's action in the Derryveagh matter is imitated it will only be by aid of the military. The landlord declares he will 'have his own,' and the tenants talk ominously of the 'short days and long nights' between this and spring. . . .

Ennis, Co. Clare. Nov. 22nd. [1880]. Ennis, on deliberate inspection, proves to be by far the most interesting western town I have yet visited. To paraphrase a familiar saying, its politics and its liquor are as strong as they are abundant. Ennis is famous for its electioneering fights, for its three bridges, for its public square 'forenint' O'Connell's statue, said to have held thirty thousand people on a space which would not contain a fifth of that number, for its numerous banks, for its fine salmon river, the Fergus, for its police barrack, once the mansion of the Crowe family, and for its long since closed Turkish bath, the ruined proprietor whereof is now in the lunatic asylum on the road to Ballyalla. Ennis is also proud of its County Club, of its handsome drapery stores, of its brand-new waterworks, of its hundred and odd whiskey-shops, and of its patriots. Of the latter by far the most eminent is a certain man named in newspaper reports M. G. Considine, Esq., but better known to his fellow-citizens as 'Dirty Mick.' Mr Considine is a fine specimen of the good old crusted Irish patriot. He has pursued patriotism ever since the day of Daniel O'Connell, and it redounds greatly to his honour that he is now as poor as when he started in that profession.

This Milesian Diogenes is in many respects the most remarkable man in County Clare, after, if not before, The O'Gorman Mahon himself. He is also the dirtiest. But the grime on Mr Considine has a romantic origin. It is the fakir's robe of filth. When he was only a budding patriot the great Liberator once kissed him. Mr Considine determined that the cheek sanctified by the embrace of O'Connell should never again be profaned by water, that the kiss should never be washed off. Without speculating as to the degree of cleanliness previously favoured by Mr Considine, it must be conceded that it is very difficult to wash day by day, or week by week, as the case may be, round a certain spot on one cheek which, moreover, would soon get out of harmony with the remainder of the countenance. It is easier, 'wiser, better far,' to bring the whole face into harmony with the sacred sunny side of it.

This has been done; and the result is a picture worthy of Murillo or Zurbaran. From the grimy but handsome well-cut face gleam a pair of bright, marvellously bright blue eyes, and the voice which bids welcome to the stranger is curiously sweet and sonorous. Mr Considine is quite the best speaker here, and his summons will always bring an audience to Ennis. One enthusiast said to me, 'Whin he dies, may the heaven be his bed, and his statue should be beside O'Connell's in Ennis.' Now this model patriot, whom every one must perforce respect for his perfect honesty and disinterestedness, keeps a wretched little shop in a trumpery cabin. His stock-in-trade consists of a few newspapers, his pantry holds but potatoes. Yet he is a great power in Ennis, and the candidate for that borough who neglected him would fare badly. I am not insinuating that any charge of venality can attach to him. Quite the contrary. He is admitted to be a perfectly disinterested citizen by those most opposed to him socially and politically. He is not only one of those who have kept the sacred fire of agitation burning since the days of O'Connell, but he is possessor of relics of '98. He owns and dons upon the occasion the Vinegar Hill uniform, and has '98 flags by him to air on great days. By dint of sheer honesty and truthfulness this poor grimy old man has become actually one of the chiefs of County Clare. . . .

Ennis, Co. Clare. Friday, Nov. 26th. [1880]. It is noteworthy that the only two persons who are doing much reclamation work in the West of Ireland are Manchester men. Mr Mitchell Henry has awakened Connemara, and Mr Drinkwater has performed a similar operation upon County Clare. Nothing in connection with the Kylemore and Fergus reclamation works, which have brought to and distributed a large sum of money in their respective districts, is more remarkable than the apathy of the surrounding proprietors in one case and their hostility in the other. . .

In 1843 The O'Gorman Mahon himself, as a county member, talked about the grand lands to be reclaimed from the Fergus, and the county talked about it; but nothing was done. This is the pleasant way of the West. All take an interest in any possible or impossible enterprise; but when it comes to finding some money and doing something, the scheme is relegated to the limbo of things undone.

The principal riparian [riverside] proprietors were Lords Inchiquin, Leconfield, and Conyngham, mostly absentees. Lord Conyngham was naturally indifferent, for his estate in Clare was to be sold in Dublin on Tuesday, and his interest in the county thus had ceased. Lord Leconfield is also an absentee, without even an address in the county. Perhaps, as the three noblemen mentioned own between them 85,226 acres in County Clare alone, without counting their other possessions, they thought that at any rate there was land enough, such as it is, in the county. Judging by the government valuation the land held by them is not of the best quality, for it is set down at 38,188*l*., and probably is not let at very much more than that sum; but at the most moderate estimate they draw, or rather drew, more than 40,000*l*. a year from County Clare. When they were invited to share in reclaiming the rich mud-banks of the Fergus, and thus add 10,000 acres of virgin soil to the rateable value of the county, they declined with perfect unanimity. They did more than this. When Mr Drinkwater had bought out the concessionees of 1860 and 1873 - who had not struck a single stroke of work - and was endeavouring to get the necessary bills through parliament, he found himself confronted by the seignorial and other vested rights of these great landowners, who appeared determined, not only to do nothing themselves, but to prevent anybody else from doing anything - unless he paid hand-somely for their permission. . . .

Being sceptical about the 'slob,' I went to see it. . . At last we were on the road to Clare Castle, which might, in the high-flown language of the West, be fitly described as the 'seaport' of Ennis. The river Fergus flows through Ennis, but it is broader and deeper at Clare Castle, a village of ordinary Connaught hovels. There is, however, a quay here, a relic of 'relief-work' in famine time, and affording 'convenience' for vessels of considerable size. Below the bridge and alongside the quay lies a large steam-tug, and lower down the stream is moored a similar vessel. A large number of rafts are being laden with stone to be presently towed down to the reclamation works. As we steam down the Fergus towards its junction with the Shannon at 'The Beeves' rock, the stream spreads out to a great width, enclosing several islands, green as emeralds, of which Smith's Island and Islandavanna are, perhaps, the principal.

There is, however, a marked difference between the area of the Fergus at high and low water. What at one time is an inland sea, is at the other a vast lake of mud rich in the constituents of fertility. As we reach this point of the river a mist arises compelling reduced speed, and as we pass by the upper station of the slob works a low range of corrugated iron shedding shines out suddenly through a break in the vapour, and, as the sun again pierces through, a long, low, dark line is seen stretching from the shore into the water like the extremity of some huge saurian [lizard] of the Silurian period reposing on his native slime and ooze. But the lengthy monster lying in a vast curve is not at peace, for on the jagged ridge of his mighty back a puffing, snorting, smoking plague perpetually runs up and down. The apparent plague, however, is really increasing the size of the saurian. Every day hundreds of tons of stone are carried over his back-ridge and tipped into the water at the end of him, while scores of raftloads are flung into the water on the line staked and flagged out by the officials of the Government. Within a few weeks the growth of the saurian will not cease by day or night, until, as in the case of his kindred ophidian [snakes], his two extremities are brought together. For Mr Drinkwater has contracted with the British Electric Lighting Company to supply him with the electric light. The motive power is all ready, and no sooner is the apparatus fixed than County Clare will be astonished by the sight of work going on perpetually till it is completed, and amazement will reach its highest pitch. The people, gentle and simple, already confess themselves astonished at what can and has been done, and those who at first laughed are now seeking how they may best imitate.

As the tail of the saurian may be said to stretch into the water high above Islandavanna, so may his head be said to project from that pretty patch of verdure. Islandavanna is already a peninsula being connected with the mainland by a massive stone causeway, traversed every half-hour by a locomotive, hauling a train of trucks laden with stone, which, passing over the end of the island, runs out into the water to the 'tip end', as it is called.

So the work is carried on, like modern railway tunnelling, from both ends simultaneously, and when head and tail of the saurian meet the first 1,500 acres will be reclaimed. The 'slob' will be easy to drain, and it is tolerably certain that within twelve months the first instalment will be ready for cropping. It is a sight to make a Dutchman's mouth water - a 'polder' of surpassing excellence, but it is viewed in a different light by enthusiastic wild duck shooters, who, like the owner of a grouse moor, look upon drainage and reclamation as the visible work of the devil. I do not think they need be alarmed for some time to come, for, without exaggeration, I have seen so many duck on the Fergus and the lower Shannon that I hesitate to speak of figures and incur the fate of Messer Marco Polo, who, when he spoke of the vast population of China, was nick-named by his incredulous countrymen 'Marco Millione.' But when I say that I have seen scores of flights a quarter of a mile long, that I have seen reaches of water so full of ducks and other water fowl that they looked like floating islands, I only give a faint idea of the quantity I have beheld between Islandavanna and the abortive ocean steam packet port of Foynes.

Islandavanna is one of three stations of the reclamation works, and is occupied by about a third of the four hundred and fifty men now at work. In the summer seven hundred were employed, but the present season is not so favourable for getting stone and pushing on operations.

The electric light, however, will, it is hoped, help matters greatly, and redress the balance of the 'long nights and short days.'. . .

It is hardly possible to convey more than the faintest idea of the rancour evolved by the jealousy of the Clare men against the Limerick men, of the hatred of both against a Galway man, and of the aversion of all three counties for Mayo and Donegal people. The citizens of the petty republics of Greece and Italy never abhorred each other more fervently. Now on large works with sub-contractors, gangers, artisans, and labourers, by piece and by day, it is no easy matter to keep matters going smoothly. It is needless to say that skilled artisans, such as engine-men and the like, are not picked up in County Clare; but no especial spite is felt against them. They are Englishmen, and that is sufficient; but if a gang of Clare men be dismissed and one of Limerick men taken on, there are signs of trouble in the air. Justice must be done to County Clare. Are the children of the soil to want bread while strangers eat it? For a Limerick man to the poor untravelled folk of Clare Castle, of Kilrush, and of Kilbaha is a stranger. . . .

It is no easy matter to found such a centre of industry as the works on the Fergus, but it is to be sincerely hoped that many such attempts will be made despite of discouragement. Experience has shown that the neglected and, in many localities, degraded West is abundantly capable of improvement. Mr Drinkwater determined to take the only way possible in these parts, that is, to feed and lodge his little army of workpeople, to establish a club for them, to give them a reading-room, to get porter for them at wholesale price - in short, to afford them every inducement to prefer the new settlements on the Fergus to the wretched huts and groggeries of Clare Castle and the surrounding villages. He insists, moreover, that every man shall have his half-pound of meat, either beef, mutton, or bacon, every day but Friday...

There are a store-house and a refectory, a cooking department and dormitories, perfectly ventilated and swept and garnished every day. Tea, beer, and other beverages except whiskey can be obtained, and there is an abundant supply of books and newspapers. Every facility and encouragement is given to the priests to visit their people. In short, the colony on the Fergus Reclamation Works is one of the most extraordinary sights in the West of Ireland. As the entire work will hardly be completed under five or six years, the influence of such a community of people doing their work steadily and thoroughly ought to be very valuable....

The poor people here require to be taught many things; notably to obey orders, to mind their own business, to hold their tongues, and to wash themselves; but it is impossible to expect four such virtues as obedience, industry, silence, and cleanliness to be acquired all at once by people who have been neglected for centuries. But there can be no radical defect in them, for they work hard enough in America, and under strict taskmasters too, for a Yankee farmer is like a Yankee skipper, inclined to pay good wages, but to insist on the money being earned...

In no part of Ireland that I have seen are class distinctions more sharply defined. The landholding gentry are with but two or three exceptions Protestants, and, with the exception of Lord Inchiquin, are of English, Scotch, or Dutch descent, as such names as Vandeleur, Crowe, Stacpoole, and Burton indicate. I am not aware of the landed possessions of The O'Gorman Mahon, but I have already stated that his nephew holds only a moderate estate, let by the way at about three times the government valuation - but not, I must add, necessarily, rackrented, for Griffith's is, for reasons fully explained by a score of writers besides myself, a deceptive guide in grazing counties. The gentry of the county, however, are nearly all Protestant, and it is curious to note on Sunday at Ennis how the masters and their families go to one church and their servants to another. I am not insinuating that there is any sectarian squabbling. There is not, for the simple reason that the two classes of gentry and tradesfolk are too far apart to come into collision. On one side of a broad line stand the lords of the soil, of foreign descent, of Protestant religion, of exclusive social caste; on the other stand the people, the shopkeepers, the greater farmers and the peasants, all of whom are Irish Roman Catholics, and bound to each other by the ties of common religion, common descent, and often of actual kinship. There is, excepting perhaps a dozen professional men, no middle-class at all, through which the cultivation of the superior strata could permeate to the lower.

Probably no more difficult social condition ever presented itself. To show how completely the members of what ought to be a middle-class, I mean the large tenant-farmers, are identified with the peasant class, I may add that many of them, working with a capital of many thousands of pounds, are subscribers to the Land League, and that many are not paying their rent. Lord Inchiquin enjoys a good reputation as a landlord; but his tenants refuse to pay more than Griffith's valuation, and I hear that other great landlords in the county are not much more fortunate. What is most singular of all is that the middlemen, who are subletting and subdividing their holdings at tremendous rack-rents, are among the most prominent in refusing to pay the chief landlord. They see a great immediate advantage to themselves in the present movement, for they give but short credit to their tenants, while they enjoy the full benefit of a 'hanging gale',or owing always half a year's rent, according to the custom of this county.

Extracts taken from Bernard H. Becker, special commissioner of the 'Daily News', *Disturbed Ireland: being the letters written during the winter of 1880-81* (London 1881) , pp 153-181.

Jessie Craigen, A Visit to Bodyke, 1881

As the agitation for land reform gathered momentum in the 1880s, organisations were formed in Britain in support of Irish tenant farmers. Jessie Craigen, a Scottish lady, came to Ireland in the summer of 1881 as guest of the Lady's Land League. She was a member of a delegation of the Democratic Federation, an organisation that highlighted the plight of Irish tenants. Her purpose was to observe 'the condition of the masses of the people and to return and tell it faithfully, both at public meetings and in the less important form of a report.' Her delegation appears to have confined its activities to Munster, visiting Cork, Kerry, Limerick, Tipperary and Clare. They found many instances of rack-renting landlords. On the O'Callaghan Estate in East Clare, Michael Hussey held twenty acres. He took the land at sixteen pounds a year in 1850. The rent subsequently was raised, so that by 1872 he was paying forty pounds per year. While at Limerick Craigen took violently ill and was nursed back to health by Anna Parnell. On her return to Britain several public meetings were held as a protest at the repression of the Land League. Craigen's discourse deals with three main topics: the land question, the coercion act and the police; the booklet, *Report on a visit to Ireland in the Summer of 1881*, her only publication, is a good example of the concern the land agitation of the 1880s aroused in Britain.

I had heard of many murders done by the police in unprovoked charges upon unarmed and unresisting people in many parts of the country. One of these cases I got the full particulars of. I went to Bodyke, a remote, out-of-the way village in County Clare. I saw the parties concerned in the affair, and took their statements down in writing from their own lips. They were told that these statements were to be used in public, and would probably be tested; and they made them with great care. In the case of the Rev Mr Murphy, the parish priest of Bodyke, I may say that on the first day on which I saw him he was hurried, being at a public dinner; but on a subsequent day he came over to the hotel at Bodyke and gave me, with much solemn feeling, a statement which he signed, saying he gave it for the satisfaction of his conscience. I give it below. On the 1st of June [1881] writs were to be issued on the property of Colonel John O'Callaghan The police came into Bodyke in the morning, and I give the account which I received from [the parish priest] as to what took place further.

Statement signed by Father Murphy, parish priest of Bodyke -

On the morning of the 1st of June, on my arrival, I found the police with their bayonets fixed presented at the breasts of the people, who stood in a dense mass before them, armed with pronged forks, clubs, and sticks. With the greatest difficulty and personal danger to myself (having to take the bayonets of the police in my hands and the muzzles of the guns and turn them towards the ground to make room to stand between them in order to separate them and the people) I induced the people to give up their forks and pledge themselves not to use them again unless they were attacked by the police. This occurred about half-past ten o'clock, and was the first of the affair. The people then remained quiet until after the arrival of the county inspector, about half-past twelve o'clock, at which time the county inspector ordered his men to charge and cut right and left, the people being quite peaceful and orderly and quiet at the time, and merely laughing at the horses of the police being stung by the bees. On this order being given the people were attacked by the police, who charged and struck all before them, during which attack John Moloney was murdered. The police marched on, escorting the process-servers and Colonel O'Callaghan to serve the writs. I and Mr O'Hara, the resident magistrate, proceeded immediately after them, seated on Mr O'Hara's car, my object being to keep between the people and the police, and also to inform Mr O'Hara of the promise made by the people to keep themselves quiet if they were not attacked, as Mr O'Hara was in charge of the police forces. Behind us came a body of mounted police, with the county inspector, and after them the people who were prevented from advancing towards the process-servers by the mounted police, the county inspector threatening to cut the people up if they moved one inch further. The first body of foot police, who were with the process-server, having turned off the high road towards the first house to be served, two shots were fired from the right hand of the road at Mr O'Hara and myself (or at any rate they whistled close by us). I had promised the police to stand between them and the people, as they said it was hard to stand to be stoned, and I replied, 'They will not stone you, for I will stand between you and them.' Immediately some other shots were discharged from the heights on the left, which were directed towards the police, who immediately returned fire, and scattered all round the hill, firing at the point from which the shots came. Meantime the people who had been last in the procession and behind the horse-police, jumped into the fields to the left and ran towards the house first to be served, and from the heights behind which the shots were being fired. This proves that there was no organised and preconcerted action, for the people, if there had been, would have kept out of the range of the shots fired from the heights. The police by this time had got round the hill and fired from the height on the people as they came up, who were unarmed, having given up their sticks and pitchforks in the morning. I saw many of the people's hats with bullet holes, and one policeman afterwards showed me a bullet hole in the knee of his trousers. The county inspector swore afterwards that a rifle bullet tore the ground under his feet after we had left them. After this the police (who had been round the hill) and the people, met at the side of the hill next the village. The police seized upon the unarmed people and bandaged twenty-two of them. These were not the people who had fired the shots, but the unarmed people who had followed the police out of the village. They placed these handcuffed people in their centre and led them along with the writ-server for the protection of the police and the writ-server, and during the whole day - from two o'clock till about half past six - led them through the country serving writs on their friends. They handcuffed them hand to hand, two and two, and cut their braces and buttons off their trousers in order that they might be obliged to use their unoccupied hands in holding up their trousers, which some of them could not do so well, but that they kept tripping and stumbling as they walked; also the ties of their shoes were cut so that they might be impeded as they walked. They marched them on for six hours in this state. On the return of the police to Ennis they were again fired upon at Fortane, and one of the horses drawing the long car, on which the county inspector sat, was shot dead. Another party of police travelling at the same time towards Feakle was also fired on, and fortunately escaped unhurt.

Mr O'Hara was with this party, and his popularity protected them, all the people being unwilling to fire on him. John Malony, the man who was wounded by the police, died on the night of that day, about 12 o'clock. The inquest was held on Tuesday, the 3rd of June, and adjourned until the following Thursday, June 9th, on which a most respectable jury had been empanelled. The jury consisted of eighteen men of good repute. Neither the police nor the Crown brought forward any witnesses, nor evidence of any kind, nor aided the inquiry in any way. The coroner expressed much surprise at the inaction of the Crown, and the neglect of bringing forward evidence on its part. The verdict was wilful murder against 'Some policeman to them unknown,' with a rider condemning the action of the county inspector for ordering - 'An unprovoked and wanton attack on a peaceful and defenceless crowd of people.'. . .

P. Murphy

Our next visit was to the Widow Malony. Her farm consists of eighteen acres of stony mountain waste, of which two acres only can be put under tillage. The rent is £8, the valuation £5 10s. One son of the dead man is in America; but he has left three girls, aged sixteen, fourteen, and eight years old. The house is a rather comfortable one - its little attempts at improvement and convenience confirming, by their silent witness, the account given by the neighbours of John

Malony's character. They say that he was a good-living, industrious husband and father. I looked at the home, the fatherless children, and the widow sitting by the turf fire, and, as her eyes met mine, my heart swelled. I know how the heart bleeds when the eyes have that lonely look in them. I talked to her, but she took little heed till I happened to speak of 'justice'; then there was a sudden flashing of fire into her eyes, as she said, 'There is no justice for us.' 'But,' I said, 'if we could get the man who did it taken up, and tried and punished, would you not wish it?' 'No,' she answered, slowly and calmly; 'I forgive him for the Blessed Saviour's sake.' But I urged her still, telling her that out of regard for others, to prevent such things from being done, he should be tried in court; and I said, 'Give me your authority to ask the people in England for justice in your name.' Her face worked with an inward struggle, and she answered: 'Yes, for the sake of other people there should be justice, but I forgive him.' Before that bitter sorrow, mastered and subdued by Christian faith, I felt myself humbled and instructed. I could not say another word.

Extracts taken from Jessie Craigen, *Report on a visit to Ireland in the Summer of 1881* (Dublin 1882), pp 48-56.

William Hurlbert, Clare Under Coercion, 1888

As the land agitation in Ireland intensified, Irish affairs aroused great interest in America. Perhaps the best known American journalist to visit Ireland during these years was William Henry Hurlbert, former editor-in-chief of the *New York World*. Hurlbert was born into a staunchly Protestant family in South Carolina, 1827. He graduated from Harvard university in 1847 and in his early manhood worked for several magazines and newspapers including the *New York Times*. During the American Civil War he was arrested for his anti-slavery activities and imprisoned in Richmond, Virginia. He escaped in the summer of the following year. In 1864 he canvassed for the unsuccessful presidential candidate George B. McClellan. In 1884 he married Catherine Tracy, which perhaps explains his interest in Irish affairs. He was the author of several books including *McClellan and the Conduct of the War* (1864), *Ireland Under Coercion*, (1888) and *England Under Coercion* (1893). His two volume work on Ireland is a record of a series of visits to Ireland between January and June 1888. His purpose was to get a sense of the social and economic results of the process of 'political vivisection' to which the country had been so long subjected. Hurlbert was strongly pro-establishment and, like Bernard Becker eight years previously, lodged with Richard Stacpoole at Edenvale. County Clare was in deep turmoil as the land agitation escalated and feelings ran high on all sides. In his book Hurlbert was highly critical of Fr Patrick White, parish priest of Miltown Malbay, and future historian of County Clare, who, he claimed, had organise a boycott by publicans against the police in Miltown Malbay. He further claimed that Fr White had failed to condemn the boycott of James Connell, a former soldier of the Crimean campaign and his aged mother, who, it was alleged, had taken land from which another tenant had been evicted - a case which Mr Balfour, the prime minister, had commented upon in parliament. Fr White took grave offence at these remarks and, in a booklet written in reply, launched a ferocious attack on the American: *Hurlbert Unmasked; an exposure of the 'thumping English lies' of William Henry Hurlbert in his Ireland Under Coercion'* (1890), which for maximum effect Fr White had published in New York. Hurlbert died at Cadenabbia, Italy, 1895.

Ennis, Saturday, Feb 18 [1888]. At Ennis I was met by Colonel Turner, to whom I had written, enclosing a note of introduction to him. With him were Mr Roche, one of the local magistrates; and Mr Richard Stacpoole, a gentleman of position and estate near Ennis, about whom, through no provocation of his, a great deal has been said and written of late years. Mr Stacpoole at once insisted that I should let him take me out to stay at his house at Edenvale, which is, so to speak, at the gates of Ennis. Certainly the fame of Irish hospitality is well-founded! Meanwhile my traps were deposited at the County Club, and I went about the town. I walked up to the courthouse with

Mr Roche, in the hope of hearing a case set down for trial to-day, in which a publican named Harding, at Ennis - an Englishman, by the way - is prosecuted for boycotting. The parties were in court; and the defendant's counsel, a keen-looking Irish lawyer, Mr Leamy, once a Nationalist member, was ready for action; but for some technical reason the hearing was postponed. There were few people in court, and little interest seemed to be felt in the matter. The courthouse is a good building, not unlike the White House at Washington in style. This is natural enough, the White House having been built, I believe, by an Irish architect, who must have had the Duke of Leinster's house of Carton, in Kildare, in his mind when he planned it. Carton was thought a model mansion at the beginning of this century; and Mr Whetstone [Whitestone], a local architect of repute, built the Ennis courthouse some fifty years ago. It is of white limestone from quarries belonging to Mr Stacpoole, and cost when built about £12,000. To build it now would cost nearly three times as much. In fact, a recent and smaller courthouse at Carlow has actually cost £36,000 within the last few years.

I was struck by the extraordinary number of public-houses in Ennis. A sergeant of police said to me, 'It is so all over the country.' Mr Roche sent for the statistics, from which it appears that Ennis, with a population of 6307, rejoices in no fewer than 100 'publics'; Ennistymon, with a population of 1331, has 25; and Milltown Malbay, with a population of 1400, has 36. . . .

Only yesterday no fewer than twenty-three of these publicans from Milltown Malbay appeared at Ennis here to be tried for 'boycotting' the police. One of them was acquitted; another, a woman, was discharged. Ten of them signed, in open court, a guarantee not further to conspire, and were thereupon discharged upon their own recognisances, after having been sentenced with their companions to a month's imprisonment with hard labour. The magistrate tells me that when the ten who signed (and who were the most prosperous of the publicans) were preparing to sign, the only representative of the press who was present, a reporter for *United Ireland*, approached them in a threatening manner, with such an obvious purpose of intimidation, that he was ordered out of the court-room by the police. The eleven who refused to sign the guarantee (and who were the poorest of the publicans, with least to lose) were sent to gaol.

An important feature of this case is the conduct of Father White, the parish priest of Milltown Malbay. In the open court, Colonel Turner tells me, Father White admitted that he was the moving spirit of all this local 'boycott.' While the court was sitting yesterday all the shops in Milltown Malbay were closed, Father White having publicly ordered the people to make the town 'as a city of the dead.' After the trial was over, and the eleven who elected to be locked up had left in the train, Father White visited all their houses to encourage the families, which, from his point of view, was no doubt proper enough; but one of the sergeants reports that the Father went by mistake into the house of one of the ten who had signed the guarantee, and immediately reappeared, using rather unclerical language. All this to an American resembles a tempest in a tea-pot. But it is a serious matter to see a priest of the Church assisting laymen to put their fellow-men under a social interdict, which is obviously a parody on one of the gravest steps the Church itself can take to maintain the doctrine and the discipline of the Faith. . . .

I asked one of the sergeants how the publicans who had signed the guarantee would probably be treated by their townspeople. He replied, there was some talk of their being 'boycotted' in their turn by the butchers and bakers. 'But it's all nonsense,' he said, 'they are the snuggest (the most prosperous) publicans in this part of the country, and nobody will want to vex them. They have many friends, and the best friend they have is that they can afford to give credit to the country people. There'll be no trouble with them at all at all!'. . . .

There are some considerable shops in Ennis, but the proprietor of one of the best of them says all this agitation has 'killed the trade of the place.' I am not surprised to learn that the farmers and their families are beginning seriously to demand that the 'reduction screw' shall be applied to other things besides rent. 'A very decent farmer,' he says, 'only last week stood up in the shop and said it was 'a shame the shopkeepers were not made to reduce the tenpence muslin goods to sixpence!''

This shopkeeper finds some dreary consolation for the present state of things in standing at his deserted shop-door and watching the doors of his brethren. He finds them equally deserted. In his own he has had to dismiss a number of his attendants. 'When a man finds he is taking in ten shillings a day, and laying out three pounds ten, what can he do but pull up pretty short?' As with the shopkeepers, so it is with the mechanics. 'They are losing custom all the time. You see the tenants are expecting to come into the properties, so they spend nothing now on painting or improvements. The money goes into the bank. It don't go to the landlords, or the shopkeepers, or the mechanics; and then we that have been selling on credit, and long credit too, where are we? Formerly, from one place, Dromoland, Lord Inchiquin's house, we used regularly to make a bill of a hundred pounds at Christmas, for blankets and other things given away. Now the house is shut up and we make nothing!'

It is a short but very pleasant drive from Ennis to Edenvale - and Edenvale itself is not ill-named. The park is a true park, with fine wide spaces and views, and beautiful clumps of trees. A swift river flows beyond the lawn in front of the spacious, goodly house - a river alive with wild fowl, and overhung by lofty trees, in which many pairs of herons build. . . . Where the river widens to a lake, fine terraced gardens and espalier walls, on which nectarines, apricots, and peaches ripen in the sun, stretch along the shore. Deer come down to the further bank to drink, and in every direction the eye is charmed and the mind is soothed by the loveliest imaginable sylvan landscapes. . . .

[Edenvale, Sunday Feb 19. I asked Mr Stacpoole this morning whether the park had been invaded by trespassers since the local Nationalists declared war upon him. He said that his only experience of anything like an attack befell not very long ago, when his people came to the house on a Sunday afternoon and told him that a crowd of men from Ennis, with dogs, were coming towards the park with a loudly proclaimed intent to enter it, and go hunting upon the property. Upon this Mr Stacpoole left the house with his brother and another person, and walked down to the park entrance. Presently the men of Ennis made their appearance on the highway. A very brief parley followed. The men of Ennis announced their intention of marching across the park, and occupying it.

'I think not,' the proprietor responded quietly. 'I think you will go back the way you came. For you may be sure of one thing: the first man who crosses that park wall, or enters that gate, is a dead man.'

There was no show of weapons, but the revolvers were there, and this the men of Ennis knew. They also knew that it rested with themselves to create the right and the occasion to use the revolvers, and that if the revolvers were used they would be used to some purpose. To their credit, be it said, as men of sense, they suddenly experienced an almost Caledonian respect for the 'Sabbath-day,' and after expressing their discontent with Mr Stacpoole's inhospitable reception, turned about and went back whence they had come. . . .

In the afternoon we took a delightful walk to Killone Abbey, a pile of monastic ruins on a lovely site near a very picturesque lake. The ruins have been used as a quarry by all the country, and are now by no means extensive. But the precincts are used as a graveyard, not only by the people of Ennis, but by the farmers and villagers for many miles around. Nothing can be imagined more painful than the appearance of these precincts. The graves are, for the most part, shallow, and closely huddled together. The cemetery, in truth, is a ghastly slum, a 'tenement-house' of the dead. The dead of to-day literally elbow the dead of yesterday out of their resting-places, to be in their turn displaced by the dead of to-morrow. . . .

One exception I noted to the general slovenliness of the graves. A new and handsome monument had just been set up by a man of Ennis, living in Australia, to the memory of his father and mother, buried here twenty years ago. But this touching symbol of a heart untravelled, fondly turning to its home, had been so placed, either by accident or by design, as to block the entrance way to the vault of a family living, or rather owning property, in this neighbourhood. Until within a year or two past this family had occupied a very handsome mansion in a park adjoining the park of Edenvale. But the heir, worn out with local hostilities, and reduced in fortune by the pressure of the times and of the League, has now thrown up the sponge. His ancestral acres have been turned over for cultivation to Mr Stacpoole. His house, a large fine building, apparently of the time of James II, containing, I am told, some good pictures and old furniture, is shut up, as are the model stables, ample enough for a great stud; and so another centre of local industry and activity is made sterile.

Near the ruins of Killone is a curious ancient shrine of St John, beside a spring known as the holy well. All about the rude little altar in the open air simple votive offerings were displayed, and Mrs Stacpoole tells me pilgrims come here from Galway and Connemara to climb the hill upon their knees, and drink of the water. Last year for the first time within the memory of man the well went dry. Such was the distress caused in Ennis by this news, that on the eve of St John certain pious persons came out from the town, drew water from the lake, and poured it into the well! . . . .

It seems to be [Mr Stackpool's] impression that things look better, however, of late for law and order. On Monday of last week at Ennis an example was made of a local official, which, he thinks, will do good. This was a poor-law guardian named Grogan. He was bound over on Monday last to keep the peace for twelve months towards one George Pilkington. Pilkington, it appears, in contempt of the League, took and occupied, in 1886, a certain farm in Tarmon West. For this he was 'boycotted' from that time forth. In December last he was summoned, with others, before the board of guardians at Kilrush, to fix the rents of certain labourers' cottages. . . While he sat in the room awaiting the action of the board, Grogan, one of its members, rose up, and, looking at Pilkington, said in a loud voice, 'There's an obnoxious person here present that should not be here, a land-grabber named Pilkington.' There was a stir in the room, and Pilkington, standing up, said, 'I am here because I have had notice from the guardians. If I am asked to leave the place, I shall not come back.' The chairman of the board upon this declared that 'while the ordinary business of the board was transacting, Mr Pilkington would be there only by the courtesy of the board;' and treating the allusions of Grogan to Pilkington as a part of the business of the board, he said, 'A motion is before the board, does any one second it?' Another guardian, Collins, got up, and said 'I do.' Thereupon the chairman put it to the vote whether Pilkington should be requested to leave. The ayes had it, and the chairman of the board thereupon invited Pilkington to leave the meeting which the board had invited him to attend!. . . .

During the morning Mrs Stacpoole sent for the clerk and manager of the estate, and asked him to show me the books. He is a native of these parts, by name Considine, and has lived at Edenvale for eighteen years. In his youth he went out to America, but there found out that he had a 'liver,' an unpleasant discovery, which led him to return to the land of his birth, and to the service of Mr Stacpoole. He is perfectly familiar with the condition of the country here, and as the accounts of this estate are kept minutely and carefully from week to week, he was able this morning to show me the current prices of all kinds of farm produce and of supplies in and about Ennis - not estimated prices, but prices actually paid or received in actual transactions during the last ten years. I am surprised to see how narrow has been the range of local variations during that time; and I find Mr Considine inclined to think that the farmers here have suffered very little, if at all, from these fluctuations, making up from time to time on their reduced expenses what they have lost through lessened receipts. The expenses of the landlord have however increased, while his receipts have fallen off. In 1881 Edenvale paid out for labour £466 0s. 1½d., in 1887 £560 6s. 3½d., though less labour was employed in 1887 than in 1888. The wages of servants, where any change appears, have risen. In 1881 a gardener received £14 a year, in 1881 he receives 15s. a week, or at the rate of £39 a year. A housemaid receiving £12 a year in 1881, receives now £17 a year. A butler receiving in 1881 £26 a year, now receives £40 a year. A kitchenmaid receiving in 1881 £6, now receives £10 10s. a year. Meanwhile, the sub-commissioners are at this moment cutting down the Edenvale rents again by £190 3s. 2d., after a walk over the property in winter. Yet in July 1883 Mr Reeves, for the sub-commission, 'thought it right to say there was no estate in the County Clare so fairly rented, to their knowledge, or where the tenants had less cause for complaint.' In but one case was a reduction of any magnitude made by the commission of 1883, and in one case that commission actually increased the rent from £11 10s. to £16. In January 1883 the rental of this property was £4065 5s. 1d. The net reduction made by the commissioners in July 1883 was £296 14s. 0½d.

After luncheon a car came up to the mansion, bringing a stalwart, good-natured-looking sergeant of police, and with him the boycotted old woman Mrs Connell and her son. The sergeant helped the old woman down very tenderly, and supported her into the house. She came in with some trepidation and uneasiness, glancing furtively all about her, with the look of a hunted creature in her eyes. Her son, who followed her, was more at his ease, but he also had a worried and careworn look. . .

This was the woman of whom Mr Redmond wrote to Mr Parnell that she was 'an active strong dame of about fifty.' When Mr Balfour, in

Parliament, described her truly as a 'decrepit old woman of eighty,' Mr Redmond contradicted him, and accused her of being 'the worse for liquor' in a public court.

'How old is your mother?' I asked her son.

'I am not rightly sure, sir,' he replied, 'but she is more than eighty.'

'The man himself is about fifty,' said the sergeant; 'he volunteered to go to the Crimean War; that was more than thirty years ago!'. . . .

I questioned Connell as to his relations with Carroll, the man who brought him before the League. He was a labourer holding a bit of ground under Carroll. Carroll refused to pay his own rent to the landlord. But he compelled Connell to pay rent to him. When Carroll was evicted, the landlord offered to let Connell have half an acre more of land. He took it to better himself, and 'how did he injure Carroll by taking it?' How indeed, poor man! Was he a rent-warner? Yes; he earned something that way two or three times a year; and for that he had to ask the protection of the police — 'they would kill him else.' What with worry and fright, and the loss of his livelihood, this unfortunate labourer has evidently been broken down morally and physically. It is impossible to come into contact with such living proofs of the ineffable cowardice and brutality of this business of 'boycotting' without indignation and disgust.

While Connell was telling his pitiful tale a happy thought occurred to the charming daughter of the house. Mrs Stacpoole is a clever amateur in photography. 'Why not photograph this 'hale and hearty woman of fifty,' with her son of fifty-three?' Mrs Stacpoole clapped her hands at the idea, and went off at once to prepare her apparatus.

While she was gone the sergeant gave me an account of the trial, which Mr Redmond, M.P., witnessed. He was painfully explicit. 'Mr Redmond knew the woman was sober,' he said; 'she was lifted up on the table at Mr Redmond's express request, because she was so small and old, and spoke in such a low voice that he could not hear what she said. Connell had always been a decent industrious fellow—a fisherman. But for the lady, Mrs Moroney, [owner of the Atlantic Hotel, Miltown Malbay] he and his mother would have starved and would starve now. As for the priest, Father White, Connell went to him to ask his intercession and help, but he could get neither.'

The sergeant had heard Father White preach yesterday. 'It was a curious sermon. He counselled peace and forbearance to the people, because they might be sure the wicked Tory government would very soon fall!'. . . .

Mrs Stacpoole thinks the [photographic] operation promises a success. I suppose it would hardly be civil to send a finished proof of the group to Mr J. Redmond, M.P.

Extracts taken from William H. Hurlbert, *Ireland Under Coercion, the diary of an American*, 2 vols (Edinburgh 1888), i, pp 205-46.

Marie Anne de Bovet,
Three Months in Clare, 1891

Marie Anne de Bovet, later Marie Anne Marchioness Deschamps de Bois Hebert, French author and travel writer, is credited with some twenty five publications between the years 1888 and 1910. Some of her books were novels such as *Confessions d'une Fille de Trente Ans*, (Paris 1895) and *L'amour Triompha*, (Paris 1908), but she also published more specialised volumes like her book on the life and works of the French composer Charles Gounod in 1891. Bovet travelled in Ireland on at least two occasions. Her first journey in 1888 resulted in the publication of *Lettres d'Irland*, (Paris 1889). She made a second visit in 1890 when she spent three months touring the country. Arriving in Dublin, she completed a circuit of the island visiting fifteen of the thirty two counties. Her tour is valuable for the author's comments on food and the standard of hotel accommodation. Because she was writing in French she perhaps felt less inhibited than writers in English. In Clare she provides a most interesting account of the beleaguered Mrs Burdett Moroney of the Atlantic Hotel, Miltown Malbay, who was boycotted by her tenants because of her demand for excessive rents. The book *Trois Mois en Irlande* was an immediate success; it was quickly translated into English and a second edition appeared in 1908. An illustrator accompanied Bovet to Ireland and her book also contains many excellent illustrations of contemporary scenes.

We landed at Kilrush, on the Clare shore, a small fishing and trading port, whence one sees the Shannon, broad, majestic, peaceful and deserted, lose itself in the ocean. A car was in waiting to take us to our halting-place, nine miles across a marshy country, marked with turf cuttings, peopled by crows, herons and frogs, with a few smoky hovels at long intervals. The vegetation consisted of tufts of rushes, furze-bushes, and an abundance of those violet and yellow wild flowers which here give a little cheerfulness to barren and uncultivated parts. Soon the sight of ruins, with which this melancholy desert is strewn, shows us that once more we are in the presence of 'the Irish difficulty,' as it is called in English politics: we are on the Vandeleur property, whence people have recently been 'evicted' *en masse*. By the roadside is a house turned inside out, the thatched roof all staved in, which has undergone one of those regular sieges which I have already described. In an outhouse, in a state of indifferent repair, a whole family live, in company with the pigs and the geese. These are the evicted tenants who have been allowed to go in as 'caretakers,' not only because the others are tired of war, but also because, even with the law on their side, human beings cannot be allowed to rot in a ditch. Caretakers of what? As long as no arrangement can be come to with regard to the rent they have nothing to cultivate but two acres of potatoes - except the rushes that, twisted, dried or cut up, are used for roofing, litter and food for the cows. The traveller in Ireland must harden his heart, or else he would suffer too much at these spectacles of misery and desolation. . . .

The population of Kilkee exists a little by fishing and a great deal by the bathers. Like every other place, it is given up to pleasant indolence: at seven in the morning there is no trace of life in the one street, which follows the scarped side of the rock; donkey boys, astride on their donkeys, move about leisurely, groups of boatmen on the beach wait for a customer while smoking their pipes and talking to the drivers, who, with their whips round their necks, lean idly against the wall of the terrace; tall and well-made women, with bare legs under their short frayed-out petticoats, baskets on their heads, which they cover with a corner of their black shawl, sell their wares from door to door - gooseberries and plums so green it sets one's teeth on edge merely to look at them, little white mushrooms, big crabs, and chickens like pigeons. There are a few machines drawn up on the beach for the use of bathers. Men are forbidden to bathe after an hour so early that most prefer to go out some way along the coast, where they can enjoy themselves without infringing the regulations.

The inhabitants of Kilkee try hard to make tourists row along by the cliffs, saying that they cannot know what the celebrated coast of Clare is like if they only see it from the land. The boats they offer for these excursions are not calculated to inspire one with much confidence. They are the primitive coracles, of plaited willow-work covered with tarpaulin, which has taken the place of the cow-hide used by the ancient Celts; long, narrow, turned up in front like a gondola; they are so light that a man can easily carry them on his back, and when pulled up on shore and overturned, like large shell-fish, they have to be held down by stones lest the wind should carry them away. They behave well at sea, and are easy to manage, scudding over the waves like nut-shells, - but they are of use only to those who have a brave heart and a sailor's stomach. . . .

If one is not very particular where he sleeps, travelling in Ireland is easy, for in the smallest hole one is always able to find a lodging; and from my long and often sad experience of Irish hotels I am convinced that one is best off in the inns of remote villages. . . The English bed, whose bad reputation is fully justified, is a paradise by the side of an Irish bed. What the under-mattress is made of I have never been able to make out. One thing is certain - that it contains nothing even approaching to elasticity. On this hard basis are one or two thin mattresses, very tightly stuffed with something that resembles peach stones; over this are two calico sheets, then a huge white woollen blanket, no bolster, a large pillow, hard and flat; lastly, covering the whole, is a cotton or crotchet counterpane, so heavy that it requires the arms of a Hercules to carry it. . . As for cleanliness, one must not look too closely. Here, as in England, polished floors are unknown, and the boards are invariably covered with carpets whose equivocal colour I will leave to the imagination, and not for anything in the world would I walk on one with bare feet. The linen is fairly clean. There are never curtains to the beds, only, occasionally, to the windows; they are of white guipure or embroidered muslin, stiff with starch. The sash-windows, like those in England, rarely have shutters; if by chance there are any, it is better not to risk shutting them, for behind them will be found heaps of dust, plaster, and the dirt of ages, which the servants religiously respect. 'It is not seen; why touch it. It serves curious people right'; and they will find just as much in the fireplaces, in the drawers, in the cupboards, and in dark corners. . . .

In the second-class hotels, like those of Kilkee, there is no longer any question about cleanliness; they are decidedly dirty, to say nothing of towels in rags, and sheets with holes big enough to put you fist through. One peculiarity of this country is that they obstinately refuse to give you the *serviette* for dinner that you used at breakfast, which would be in better taste than giving you your neighbour's, or even that of the traveller who left the day before. In the same way, they give you a profusion of knives and forks, but never a clean table-cloth. Their manner of waiting is very pretentious, too. It was at this very place, Kilkee, that I remember a certain waiter, with huge red whiskers, whom we made wretched by our careless behaviour and complete want of dignity. If we helped ourselves to anything to drink he was miserable, and if we stretched out our hand to reach a plate off a table close by he rushed at it with an offended air, and looked on us as if we were not people of much account. Heaven knows the anxiety his bustling about causes us, for the antiquity of his black coat surpassed our most vivid imagination, and as for his trousers, they were rusty, threadbare, and frayed out, and seemed to be on the point of giving way: they curtailed our stay there - we fled before a certain catastrophe. . . .

You are fortunate if you have not to put up at a boycotted hotel, as happened to us at Miltown Malby, another little seaside place, twelve miles north of Kilkee. The establishment belonged to a *distressed landlady*, that is to say, a landlady ruined by agricultural troubles. As the consequence of disputes with her tenants she was subjected to a strict quarantine, mingled with constant spite and worries, which occasionally degenerated into serious personal violence. She had the greatest trouble in getting servants; and those came from afar, and rarely showed outside the hotel. The few travellers were foreigners, like ourselves; and to fill her house, Mistress Moroni lodged her whole family in it. People from Limerick, rich and of good position, who were living a little distance off for change of air, came to see us at the *Atlantic*, but they would not leave their horses by the door for fear of compromising themselves. Our *table d'hôte* was supplied by their kindness with delicacies from Dublin, bread included, for no one in the country would furnish the excommunicated house with the smallest thing. But the day we left we had a personal experience by ricochet of boycotting. There was no driver, and, consequently no omnibus to take us to the station; and our luggage was put on a rickety cart, drawn by a broken-winded mule, harnessed with ropes, and driven by a youth who was almost an idiot. We followed behind, and had to walk like this for two miles, taking short cuts through the mud to avoid the village, and our unhappy conductor, perpetually looking about him as if he was afraid of falling into some ambush; needless to say, we arrived half an hour too late. Nor were we surprised, for, on leaving the hotel, flurried, angry, and breathless, begging them to hurry, lest we should miss the train, they said, with that everlasting and good-humoured smile, 'Oh! you have already missed it!' I much doubt if Mme. Moroni, who bravely defies popular dislike, will be able to hold her own for long in this struggle, which is not only severe, but is not without danger to herself. . . .

There are no hours more peaceful than those of twilight after a stormy day. I have an exquisite recollection of a two hours' drive at nightfall from the cliffs of Moher to Lisdoonvarna. We drove over lonely moors, gently undulating and sloping towards the shore, along which our drive extended. There were no houses except a few poor huts of dry stone, sheltered from the spray by a pyramid of turf sods, the thatched roof being held in its place by a net to which huge pebbles were fastened. Thin lines of smoke rose in the now-darkening sky. On the other side of the road cows, donkeys - numerous here - and geese in rows, gravely watched us pass. Presently the moon rose, bathing the quiet sea in its silver light, and the islets in the horizon faded away in a purple mist. It was not sadness, but an infinite sweet melancholy which pervaded all things, together with the caressing warmth of an August night.

Lisdoonvarna is a watering-place - a *spa* they call it here - much frequented by the country people for its iron and sulphur waters. It is not wildly gay. A ravine, carpeted with short grass, without a bush, and from which one gets glimpses of the sea, only four miles distant, has been formed by a little stream, which flows from the top of a sandy plateau. All around are moors, where occasional cows browse among the heather. For amusements, the hotel sitting-room, and sometimes a company of comedians, bringing from Galway or Limerick a varied *répertoire*, 'arranged so as to meet all tastes without offending the most delicate susceptibilities.' So says the programme, carried about at the end of a pole by a hopelessly drunken youth.

Catholic priests, very plentiful in all seaside and watering places, seem to abound here. The *table d'hôte* is like the refectory of a seminary. It is none the less lively for that. Every one agrees that the Irish priest is irreproachable in his morals and in the performance of his religious duties. His weight is considerable in this country, where the threat of being excluded from the Holy Table would make a peasant pass through the eye of a needle. Independent of all government, the priests have placed themselves with impunity at the head of the Nationalist movement, which they make a matter of Christian Socialism; and it is nearly always the parish priest who presides over the local committee of the League. More often than not a son of the people, he thoroughly understands the character as well as the wants of his flock. Being comparatively well educated, he is their lawyer and doctor, as well as their confessor. He takes the lead in all things temporal as well as spiritual; he is the chief speaker at clubs and meetings, and presides over their athletic sports. Formerly he could get drunk with his parishioners without compromising himself; that day is over, but he still mixes so much with the laity that there is nothing clerical about his manner. Liberally supported by the piety of the faithful in the way of tithes paid in kind, money offerings, and fees for mass, marriage and burial, the priests live well, and are extremely fond of travelling, in which they employ all the leisure moments of their busy life. Everywhere one meets them, cheery and flourishing, genial and sociable, kind and fatherly - objects of the affectionate respect of all.

The plateau on which Lisdoonvarna is built crowns a huge schistose rock, which reaches to Galway Bay. This barony of Burren, which comprises the whole northern part of the county, is one of the most remarkable natural curiosities of Ireland. It is a large amphitheatre, rising by a succession of terraces from the sea, and attaining a height of 1100 feet. One might call them huge Babylonian fortifications, cut out of carboniferous sandstone of a delicate and luminous grey, with purple shadows. The descent over this stone desert by a path of the significant name of *Corkscrew* would delight the eyes of the impressionist painter. One is literally bathed in an atmosphere of that lilac-tint dear to our young artists, and which one could no longer refuse to believe in after seeing the Burren of Clare. . . .

It is worthy of remark, that in this rough and bare part of the country, of which it is said that, for want of water and trees, no one can be either drowned or hanged, people are less ragged, less dirty, and appear infinitely less poor than in other districts. At first sight it seems as if nothing grew here but stones; but between these stones is a fine and delicious grass, which fattened cows, sheep, and huge black pigs - those poor pigs whose grave is Limerick; and then, every little sheltered ravine, every valley where the winds have deposited the thinnest layer of mould, is cultivated for some purpose or other. Latterly the population of the Burren of Clare has been much reduced by emigration, as a number of deserted villages can testify. Three conclusions can be drawn from this: first, that Paddy would be less poor if he were as industrious in all other parts as he is here; secondly, that Ireland's true profit consists in the breeding and fattening of cattle; and lastly, that the principal reason of her poverty is over-population, which neither Home Rule nor any agricultural reform would be able to keep in check. At the top of the arid valley of Corcomroe are a few miserable trees. They mark the site of a farm, with whose owner I had the pleasure of making an acquaintance. He was walking about the ruins at the same time as myself. He is very proud of them, and considers himself, in a small way, their proprietor. He was delighted, too, at the interest I took in them, and we talked together in a friendly way, whilst his numerous family formed a circle round the artist who was taking a sketch of the abbey. The man had eighty acres of land (they call this land!), for which he paid 1*l.* sterling the acre. He was well satisfied with his landlord, who was a true Irish man, judging from his very Irish name of Fitzgerald. 'There are good and bad landlords, and it is unfortunate if one lights on a bad one,' said he, philosophically; 'but, anyhow, one cannot expect to get the land for nothing.' Wise words; which I commend to the notice of certain agitators, who brag a little too much about the advance of Socialism. . . .

The Irish question has so many sides and points that it is impossible to be an impartial judge. All the peasants of Burren are not as content with their fate as the farmer of Corcomroe, for agrarian crimes are not unknown there. There has been a stir in the peaceful village of Ballyvaughan lately, for judgement was given against the murderer of a policeman in a little cottage, which since then has been jokingly named 'The Court of Justice of Her Majesty the Queen.'

In the western part, and in County Clare especially, the difficulty is heightened by the national idiom, still spoken entirely by the greater part of the old people, without counting those young ones, who pretend not to understand English when they find it convenient. There is a story of a dying woman, who began her confession in Gaelic. The priest, who did not understand the language, told her to speak in English, as she was able to do so. She angrily replied, 'Does your Reverence think that I will say my last words to Almighty God in the language of the Sacsannachs?' The story does not say whether she received absolution or not.

Extracts taken from Marie Anne de Bovet, *Three Months' Tour in Ireland*, translated and condensed by Mrs Arthur Walter (London 1891), pp 184-202.

Robert Buckley, Clare as it is, 1893

Robert John Buckley, the special correspondent of the *Birmingham Daily Gazette*, a very pro-unionist newspaper, was sent to Ireland in March of 1893 to investigate the 'Irish Problem'.   Buckley spent six months travelling through the most disturbed parts of the country. He was often in personal danger and dared to go to places where even the native drivers would not venture.   He travelled extensively in Munster, Connacht and Ulster, and made telling contrasts between the prosperous north and the stagnant south. In all he covered nearly 4,000 miles and returned sixty two letters to his editor in Birmingham; it is these collected letters, unedited, that make up his book on Ireland.   After Buckley's investigations his editor could claim that the letters provided conclusive evidence that Irish nationalism was a mere 'delusive sham' and that if the land question could be settled there would be an end to the clamour for independence.   Arriving in Killaloe on 27 April 1893, Buckley proceeded to Ennis from where he fired off a dispatch to his newspaper.   The following day he drove to Bodyke, in the hope of interviewing Colonel O'Callaghan, the landlord at the centre of the Bodyke evictions; in this he was disappointed as O'Callaghan refused to meet him. Nevertheless he returned two further letters from Bodyke to his editor. It is extracts from these letters that are published here. Although clearly biased, they are full of detail and give a compelling account of the tactics used by the tenants in their struggle against the landlord.   By 1893 the power of the landlords was almost broken and there was an expectation on the part of tenants that they would soon come into ownership of the land.   Buckley appears to have written nothing more on Ireland. He is, however, credited with two further publications: one a novel called *The Master Spy* (1902) and the other a book on the composer Sir Edward Elgar.

On Friday last I had a small object-lesson in Irish affairs. Colonel O'Callaghan, of Bodyke, went to Limerick to buy cattle for grazing on his estate. The cattle were duly bought, but the gallant Colonel had to drive them through the city with his own right hand. I saw his martial form looming in the rear of a skittish column of cows, and even as the vulture scenteth the corcase afar off, even so, scenting interesting matter, did I swoop down on the unhappy Colonel, startling him severely with my sudden dash. He said, 'I'm driving cows now', and truth to tell, there was no denying it. . . .

Civil War in County Clare. [2nd. May 1893].

The name of Bodyke is famous throughout all lands, but few people know anything about the place or the particulars of the great dispute. The whole district is at present in a state of complete lawlessness. The condition of matters is almost incredible, and is such as might possibly be expected in the heart of Africa, but hardly in a civilised country, especially when that country is under the benignant British rule. The lawbreakers seem to have the upper hand, and to be almost, if not quite, masters of the situation. The whole estate is divided into three properties, Fort Ann, Milltown, and Bodyke, about five thousand acres in all, of which the first two comprise about one thousand five hundred acres, isolated from the Bodyke lands, which latter may amount to some three thousand five hundred acres. Either by reason of their superior honesty, or, as is sometimes suggested, on account of their inferior strategic position, the tenants of the Fort Ann and Milltown lands pay their rent. The men of Bodyke are in a state of open rebellion, and resist every process of law both by evasion and open force. The hilltops are manned by sentries armed with rifles. Bivouac fires blaze nightly on every commanding eminence. Colonel O'Callaghan's agent is a cock-shot from every convenient mound. His rides are made musical by the 'ping' of rifle balls, and nothing but the dread of his repeating rifle, with which he is known to be handy, prevents the marksmen from coming to close quarters. Mr Stannard McAdam seems to bear a charmed life. He is a fine athletic young man, calm and collected, modest and unassuming, and, as he declares, no talker. He has been described as a man of deeds, not words. He said, 'I am not a literary man. I have not the skill to describe incident, or to give a clear and detailed account of what has taken place. I have refused to give information to the local journalists. My business is to manage the estate, and that takes me all my time. You must get particulars elsewhere. I would rather not speak of my own affairs or those of Colonel O'Callaghan.'. . .

The road from Ennis to Bodyke is dull and dreary, and abounds with painful memories. Half-an-hour out you reach the house, or what remains of it, of Francis Hynes, who was hanged for shooting a man. A little further and you reach the place where Mr Perry was shot. A wooded spot, 'convaynient' for ambush, once screened some would-be murderers who missed their mark. Then comes the house of the Misses Brown, in which on Christmas Eve shots were fired, by way of celebrating the festive season. From a clump of trees some four hundred yards from the road the police on a car were fired upon, the horse being shot dead in his tracks. The tenantry of this sweet district are keeping up their rifle practice, and competent judges say that the Bodyke men possess not less than fifty rifles, none of which can be found by the police. Said one of the constabulary, 'They lack nerve to fire from shorter distances, as they think MacAdam is the better shot, and to miss him would be risky, as he is known to shoot rabbits with ball cartridge. . . Clare swarms with secret societies, and you never know from one moment to another what resolutions they will pass. I don't know what the end of it will be, but I should think that Home Rule, by giving the murderers a fancied security, would in this district lead to wholesale bloodshed. The whole country would rise, as they do now, to meet the landlord or his agent, but they would then do murder without the smallest hesitation.'. . .

The trouble has been alive for fifteen years or so, but it was not until 1887 that Bodyke became a regularly historic place. The tenants had paid no rent for years, and wholesale evictions were tried, but without effect. The people walked in again the next day, and as the gallant Colonel had not an army division at his back he was obliged to confess himself beaten at every point. He went in for arbitration, but before giving details let us first take a bird's eye view of his position. I will endeavour to state the case as fairly as possible, promising that nothing will be given beyond what is freely admitted by both parties to the dispute.

The Colonel, who is a powerfully-built, bronzed, and active man, seemingly over sixty years old, left the service just forty years ago. Four years before that his father had died, heavily in debt, leaving the estate encumbered by a mortgage, a jointure to the relict, Mrs O'Callaghan, now deceased (the said jointure being at that time several years in arrear), a head rent of a hundred guineas a year to Colonel Patterson, with taxes, tithe rent-charges, and heaven knows what besides. In 1846 and 1847 his father had made considerable reductions in the rents of the Bodyke holdings, but the tenants had contrived to fall into arrears to the respectable tune of £6,000, or thereabouts. Such was the state of things when the heir came into his happy possessions.

A Protestant clergyman said to me - 'Land in Ireland is like self-righteousness. The more you have, the worse off you are.' Thus was it at Bodyke.

Something had to be done. To ask the tenants for the £6,000 was mere waste of breath. The young soldier had no agent. He was determined to be the people's friend. Although a black Protestant, he was ambitious of Catholic good-will. He wanted to have the tenants blessing him. He coveted the good name which is better than rubies. He wished to make things comfortable, to be a general benefactor of his species; if a Protestant landlord and a Roman Catholic tenantry can be said to be of the same species at all, a point which, according to the nationalist press, is at least doubtful. He called the tenants together, and agreed to accept three hundred pounds for the six thousand pounds legally due, so as to make a fresh start and encourage the people to walk in the paths of righteousness. When times began to mend, the Colonel, himself a farmer, commenced to raise the rents until they reached the amount paid during his father's reign. The people stood it quietly enough until 1879, when the Colonel appointed agents. This year was one of agricultural depression. A Mr Willis succeeded the two first agents, but during the troubles he resigned his charge. The popular opinion leans to the supposition that his administration was ineffective, that is, that he was comparatively unused to field strategy, that he lacked dash and military resource, and that he entertained a constitutional objection to being shot. The rents came under the judicial arrangement, and reductions were made. Still things would not work smoothly, and it was agreed that bad years should be further considered on rent days. This agreement led to reductions on the judicial rent of 25 to 30 per cent, besides which the Colonel, in the arbitration of 1887, had accepted £1,000 in lieu of several thousand pounds of arrears then due. After November, 1891, the tenants ceased to pay rent at all, and that is practically their present position. The Colonel, who being himself an experienced farmer is a competent judge of agricultural affairs, thinks the tenants are able to pay, and even believes that they are willing, were it not for the intimidation of half-a-score village ruffians whose threatened moonlighting exploits, when considered in conjunction with the bloody deeds which have characterised the district up to recent times, are sufficient to paralyse the whole force of the British Empire, when that force is directed by the feeble fumblers now in office. . . .

New brooms sweep clean. The new agent, Mr MacAdam, began to negotiate. Pow-wows and palavers all ended in smoke, and as meanwhile the charges on the estate were going on merrily, and no money was coming in to meet them, writs were issued against six of the best-off farmers; writs, not decrees, the writ being a more effective instrument. One Malone was evicted. He was a married man, without encumbrances, owed several years' arrears, had mismanaged his farm, a really good bit of land, had been forgiven a lot of rent, and still he was not happy. A relative had lent him nearly £200 to carry on, but Malone was a bottomless pit. What he required was a gold mine and a man to shovel up the ore, but unhappily no such thing existed on the farm. The relative offered to take the land, believing that he could soon recoup himself the loan, but Malone held on with iron grip, refusing to listen to the voice of the charmer, charmed he never so wisely. The relative wished to take the place at the judicial rent, and offered to give Malone the house, grass for a cow, and the use of three acres of land. Malone declined to make any change, and as a last resort it was decided to evict him. On the auspicious day MacAdam arrived from Limerick, accompanied by two men from Dublin, whom he proposed to install as caretakers in Malone's house. The sheriff's party were late, and MacAdam, waiting at some distance, was discovered and the alarm given. Horns were blown, the chapel bell was rung, the whole country turned out in force. Anticipating seizure, the people drove away their cattle, and shortly no hoof nor horn was visible in the district. A crowd collected and, observing the caretakers, at once divined their mission, and perceived that not seizure, but eviction, was the order of the day. They rushed to Malone's house, and, with his consent and assistance, tore off the roof, smashed the windows, and demolished the doors. The place was thus rendered uninhabitable.

This having been happily effected, the sheriff's party arrived an hour or so late, in the Irish fashion. Possession was formally given to the agent, who was now free to revel in the four bare walls, and to enjoy the highly-ventilated condition of the building. . . .

At present the two caretakers hold the citadel, which is also garrisoned by a force of sixteen policemen regularly relieved by day and by night, every man armed to the teeth. Now and then the foinest pisintry in the wuruld turn out to the neighbouring hills and blaze away with rifles at the doors and windows of the little barn-like structure. . . .

Such is the state of things in Bodyke at this moment. Colonel O'Callaghan has had no penny of rent for years - that is, nothing for himself. What has been paid by the tenants of Fort Ann and Milltown has been barely sufficient to meet the charges on the estate. The Colonel thinks that the more he concedes the more his people want. He has had many narrow escapes from shooting, and rather expects to be bagged at last. He seems to be constitutionally unconscious of fear, but the police, against his wish, watch over him. In the few instances in which Mr MacAdam, his agent, has effected seizures, the people have immediately paid up - have simply walked into their houses, brought out the money, and planked down the rent with all expenses, the latter amounting to some 20 or 25 per cent. They *can* pay. The Colonel, who lives by farming, having no other source of income, knows their respective positions exactly, and declines to be humbugged. The tenants believe that they will shortly have the land for nothing, and they are content to remain in a state of siege, themselves beleaguering the investing force, lodged in the centre of the position. The fields are desolate, tillage is suspended, and the whole of the cattle are driven out of sight. Armed men watch each other by night and by day, and bloodshed may take place at any moment. The farming operations of the whole region are disorganised and out of joint. Six men have been arrested for threats and violence, but all were discharged - the jury would not convict, although the judge said the evidence for the defence was of itself sufficient to convict the gang. A ruffian sprang on MacAdam with an open knife, swearing he would disembowel him. After a terrible struggle the man was disarmed and secured, brought up before the beak, and the offence proved to the hilt. This gentleman was dismissed without a stain on his character. MacAdam asked that he should at least be bound over to keep the peace. This small boon was refused. Comment is needless.

I have not yet been able to interview Colonel O'Callaghan himself, but my information, backed by my own observation, may be relied on as accurate. The carman who drove me hither said 'The Bodyke boys are dacent fellows, but they must have their sport. 'Tis their nature to be shootin' folks, an' ye can't find fault with a snipe for havin' a long bill. An' they murther ye in sich a tinder-hearted way that no raisonable landlord could have any objection to it.'

I have the honour of again remarking that Ireland is a wonderful country.

Rent at the Root of Nationalism.

The tenants of the Bodyke property stigmatise Colonel O'Callaghan as the worst landlord in the world, and declare themselves totally unable to pay the rent demanded, and even in some cases say that they cannot pay any rent at all, a statement which is effectually contradicted by the fact that most of them pay up when fairly out-generalled by the dashing strategy of Mr Stannard MacAdam, whose experience as a racing bicyclist seems to have stood him in good stead. The country about Bodyke has an unfertile look, a stony, boggy, barren appearance. Here and there are patches of tolerable land, but the district cannot fairly be called a garden of Eden. Being desirous of hearing both sides of the question, I have conversed with several of the complaining farmers, most of whom have very small holdings, if their size be reckoned by the rent demanded. The farmers' homes are not luxurious, but the rural standard of luxury is in Ireland everywhere far below that of the English cottar, who would hold up his hands in dismay if required to accommodate himself to such surroundings. Briefly stated, the case of the tenants is based on an alleged agreement on the part of Colonel O'Callaghan to make a reduction of twenty-five per cent on judicial rents and thirty-seven and a half per cent on non-judicial rents, whenever the farming season proved unfavourable. This was duly carried out until 1891, when the question arose as to whether that was or was not a bad year. The tenants say that 1891 was abnormally bad for them, but that on attending to pay their rent, believing that the reductions which had formerly been made, and which they had come to regard as invariable, would again take place, they were told that the customary rebate would now cease and determine, and that therefore they were expected to pay their rents in full. This they profess to regard as a flagrant breach of faith, and they at once decided to pay no rent at all. The position became a deadlock, and such it still remains. They affect to believe that the last agent, Mr Willis, resigned his post out of sheer sympathy, and not because he feared sudden translation to a brighter sphere. They complain that the Colonel's stables are too handsome, and that they themselves live in cabins less luxurious than the lodgings of the landlord's horses. . . .

The Bodykers have one leading idea, to 'wait yet awhile.' Home Rule will banish the landlords, and give the people the land for nothing at all. The peasantry are mostly fine-grown men, well built and well-nourished, bearing no external trace of the hardships they claim to have endured. They are civil and obliging, and thoroughly inured to the interviewer. They have a peculiar accent, of a sing-song character, which now and then threatens to break down the stranger's gravity. That the present state of things is intolerable, and cannot last much longer, they freely admit, but they claim to have the tacit sympathy of the present government, and gleefully relate with what unwillingness police protection was granted to the agent and his men. They disclaim any intention of shooting or otherwise murdering the landlord or his officers, and assert that the fact that they still live is sufficient evidence in this direction. . . .

The Bodykers have a new grievance, one of most recent date. They had found a delightful means of evasion, which for a time worked well, but the bottom has been knocked out of it, and their legal knowledge has proved of no avail. To pay rent whenever a seizure was effected was voted a bore, a calamitous abandonment of principle, and a loss of money which might be better applied. So that when MacAdam made his latest seizures, say on the land of Brown and Jones, these out-manœuvred tenants brought forward friends named Smith and Robinson who deeply swore and filed affidavits to the effect that the cattle so seized belonged to them, Smith and Robinson to wit, and not to the afore-mentioned Brown and Jones, on whose land they were found. Here was a pretty kettle of fish. Colonel O'Callaghan, or his agent, were processed for illegal distraint, and the evidence being dead against the landlord, that fell tyrant had on several occasions to disgorge his prey, whereat there was great rejoicing in Bodyke. The new agent, however, is a tough customer, and in his quality of clerk of petty sessions dabbles in legal lore. He found an act which provides that, after due formalities, distraint may be made on any cattle found on the land in respect of which rent is due, no matter to whom the said cattle may belong. The tenants are said to have been arranging an amicable interchange of grazing land, the cows of Smith feeding on the land of Brown, and *vice versa*, so that the affidavit agreement might have some colour of decency. The ancient act discovered by the ardent MacAdam has rendered null and void this proposed fraternal reciprocity, and the order to conceal every hoof and horn pending discovery of the right answer to this last atrocity has been punctually obeyed, the local papers slanging landlord and agent, but seemingly unable to find the proper countermine. No end of details and of incident might be given, but no substantial increase could be made to the information given in this and my preceding letter. The tenants say that the landlord perversely refuses the reductions allowed in better times, and the landlord says that as a practical farmer he believes that those upon whom he has distrained or attempted to distrain are able to pay in full. He declares that he has not proceeded against those who, from any cause, are unable to meet their obligations, but only against the well-to-do men, who, having the money in hand, are deliberately withholding his just and reasonable due, taking advantage of the disturbed state of the country and the weakness of the government to benefit themselves, regardless of the suffering their selfishness entails on innocent people.

Extracts taken from R.J.B., *Ireland as it is and as it would be under Home Rule* (Birmingham 1893) pp 100-112.

Peadar Ó Hannracháin,
Mar Chonnac-sa an Clár, 1909

Bhain Peadar le ré na hAthbheochanna. Ag tús an chéid seo bhí sé ina thimire agus ina mhúinteoir taistil ag Conradh na Gaeilge. Is in aice le Sciobairín, Condae Chorcaí, sa bhliain 1873 a saolaíodh é. Bhí feirm bheag de thalamh bocht ag a athair. Trí dhuine dhéag abhí sa chlann. Cainteoirí ó dhúchas ab ea a thuismitheoirí, ach is le Béarla a tógadh Peadar. D'fhan sé ag freastal ar an mbunscoil go dtí go raibh sé ocht mbliana déag d'aois. Chuir sé suim sa Ghaeilge agus nuair nach raibh sé ach naoi mbliana d'aois, cheannaigh sé leabhar Uí Ghramhnaigh. Ní raibh aon mhúinteoir aige áfach ach a mháthair. I Samhain 1901 ceapadh ina thimire é do Chonradh na Gaelige agus bhí sé ag taisteal timpeall na tíre ag múineadh Gaeilge do dhaltaí ar feadh roinnt mhaith de bhlianta. Scríobh sé cúntas faoi na blianta sin ina leabhar *Fé Bhrat an Chonartha*. Sa bhlian 1912 caitheadh i bpriosún é i Mainistir na Féile toisc a ainm a thabhairt do phoilín i nGaeilge. Scríobh sé roinnt mhaith filíochta, tá os cionn dhá chéad de phíosaí litríochta luaite leis. Bhí sé ina eagarthóir ar an iris *An Lóchran*. Bhí baint aige le Óglaigh na hÉireann agus chaith sé an tréimhse ó Bhealtaine 1916 go Márta 1919 i bpriosúin éagsula in Éirinn agus Sasana. I ndiaidh an choghadh cathartha, cheannaigh sé feirm gar do Sciobairín. Bhí post aige mar chláraitheoir do chomhairle Chondae Chorcaí agus chaith sé tamall chomh maith ina eagarthóir ar *The Southern Star*. Tháinigh sé go Baile Átha Cliath i 1938 nuair a fuair sé post i gCoimisiún na Muc agus an Bhagúin agus is ann d'éag sé sa bhliain 1968. Scríobh sé an leabhar *Mar do Chonnac-sa Éire* le linn dó bheith ag taisteal iarthar na hÉireann ar rothar le beirt chara i ndiaidh Oireachtas na bliana 1909. Thaisteal na cairde ó Dhún na nGall go Corcaigh. Thrasnaigh siad cuan na Gaillimhe ar steamer agus shroic siad Lios Dún Bhearna. Is cosúil go raibh roinnt mhaith Gaeilge á labhairt fós i gCondae an Chláir ag an am sin agus cuireann Peadar síos faoi. Is iontach ar fad an scléip is an spórt a bhain siad amach ag snámh i gCill Chaoi sular chuaigh siad trasna na Sionainne go condae Chiarraí. Tháinig an leabhar amach an chéad uair i 1937; cuireadh athchló air sa bhliain 1944 nuair a cuireadh léarscáil agus nótaí leis toisc go raibh sé in úsáid mar théasc ag mic léinn mhéan scoile.

Ó Ghaillimh go Baile Uí Bheacháin.

Ag a cúig a chlog tráthnóna d'imigh an bád ó Ghaillimh, agus bhíomar cúpla uair a' chloig ag dul anonn go Baile Uí Bheacháin. Muna mbeadh an bháisteach do bheith ró-throm tamall, agus an ceo do bheith ag folú Sléibhte Bóirne ró-mhór, ba dheas an turas é trasna an chuain sin. . . .

Bhí dealramh na fearthainne san spéir nuair thángamar ar tír agus cé go rabhamar ar aigne dul go Lios Dún Bhearna an tráthnóna san, ní hé dheineamar ach cur fúinn i dtigh ósta Mhac Con Mara mar ar chaitheamar an oíche ar ár sástacht - cuid dí ag ithe agus ag ól: cuid dí ag léamh ar scríobh daoine eile i leabhar na n-óstaerí; cuid dí ag siúl cois imeall trá ag éisteacht le tonnuigheal na mara agus ag seancaíocht le chéile, agus a furmhór in ár sámh-chodladh.

Go Lios Dún Bheárna.

Bhí daoine ag teacht ó Lios Dún Bheárna ar maidin nuair bhogamar amach, agus iad á n-ullmhú féin chun dul go hÁra na Naomh ar an long sin do thug marcaíocht thar Chuan na Gaillimhe dhúinn tráthnóna inné. Bhí sí chun teacht ó Ghaillimh ar maidin inniu, arís, agus as san siar amach go hInis Meadhon agus thar n-ais anseo anocht agus as san anonn go Gaillimh. Ní haon ionadh í do bheith leatchiapaithe dá saol leis. Bhí na daoine go raibh fonn orthu dul tamall ar bórd loinge ag cnuasacht, agus bhí fonn ar dhuine d'ár mbuíonn-na dul ann leis, ach chuir an bheirt eile ina choinnibh agus ghéill sé dhóibh.

Is túisce d'fhág an long an áit thoir ná sinn-na, ach bhí uirthi dul i bhfad ó thuaidh amach sul ar thug sí aghaidh siar ar an muir móir. Is mire do bhíomar ag imeacht ná í dar linn féin, ach bhí orainn siúl cúpla uair agus dá laghad tiomáint do bhí fúithi sin, ba luaithe í ná sinn-na ag gluaiseacht. Chaitheamar tamall ag caínnt (mar deirid féin) le daoine anseo agus ansúid faid do bhíomar ag gabháil trí Ghleann Eidhneáin.

Is binn an teanga atá ag na sean-daoine ann. Ghabhas siar agus aniar ann cheana, agus thuigeas go maith gur fearr a thuigfidís sin - 'Cia an bhail atá ort (nó oraibh)' nó, 'Cianós a bhfuil tú (nó sibh)' ná dá mbeinn ag labhairt mo 'Chonas taoi féin' nó 'Conas tánn tú' na gCiarraigheach nó 'Cia chaoi bhfuil tú' na gConnachtach; nó 'Goid é mar tá tú' na nUltach.

Ba ghearr go raibh sé ag Seán ar bhárr a ghoib chómh maith le haon Chláiríneach, ach lean an fear eile dá, 'Cia chaoi bhfuil sibh?' ar feadh an lae nách-mór.

Rinneas moill ar lorg fraoigh bháin ag bun chnocáin agus nuair a thángas an áit ina raibh an dís eile, bhí Seán istigh i dtigh mar a raibh scata leanbh, agus é ag cómhairliú na sean-duine Gaeilge do labhairt leis na leanbhaíbh, rud ná raibh á dhéanamh, is baolach; agus bhí cochall ag teacht ar shean-duine chuige, toisc go ndúirt an cómhairlitheoir leis gur Béarla briste do bhí á labhairt acu sa tigh nuair a tháinig sé féin go doras (rud dob fhíor dó, is dócha).

Bhí Máirtín amuigh ar bharra chlaí, a dhá bhais ós cionn a rosc, a aghaidh ó thuaidh agus é ag dearcadh anonn thar cuan ar shléibhtibh Chonamara agus ar na tithe beaga bána agus ar na páirceanna.

Ba ghearr go raibh radharc againn ar Aillthe an Mhotair agus ar an gceanntar ngarbh san cois farraige go Dúlainn, agus siar amach thar ballaibh nárbh fheasach dúinn cá hainmneacha dhóibh. Nach maol an dútaigh í gan choill, gan chrann, gan sceach, gan aiteann ar a bhárr claí, ná tor le hais tí. Is maol sin.

Bhí na daoine ag suí chun boird i dtigh ósta 'Ceann Coradh' i Lios Dún Bheárna agus dinnéar maith á chur ós a gcómhair tan phreabamar d'ár rotharaibh ag doras an tí sin.

Is deas na toibreacha atá san mbaile sin taobh leis an sruthán in aice an droichid. Istigh i dtigh atáid agus daoine ag freastal ann chómh béasach agus chasfaí ort in aon bhall. Tá tobar eile ag bun leacan, in aice an teampaill, agus Gaeilgeoir binn ina fheighil. Is maith do thaithin cuid de *Chúirt an Mheadhon Oíche* leis, agus sé do thuig thar bárr é.

'Go Cill Chaoidh is fearra dhúinn dul inniu agus ansan amáireach beidh in ár gcumas dul go Cill Ruis agus trasna na Sionainne go Ciarraighe agus ó dheas go Tráigh Lí. Cad deireann sibh leis sin a chlann ó?' arsa mise leis an mbeirt óglaoch ar maidin Dé Máirt, tar éis éirí dhúinn.

'Is amhlaidh atá an scéal,' arsa duine acu, 'go bhfuil sean-eolas agat-sa ar an ndúthaigh as so ó dheas agus táim-se sásta géilleadh dhod' chómhairle'. . . .

Bhíomar ag cur 's ag cúiteamh ar an gcuma san ar aghaidh dorais ár dtí amach nuair do ghabh cara linn thar bráid a chómhairligh dúinn dul chun an Aifrinn agus gan bheith díomhaoin ansan ar thaobh sráide. . . .

Bhí cúigear sagart ag léamh Aifreann agus bhí cúpla altóir eile gan sagart ar bith ina bhfianaise. Ní fada go dtáinig beirt shagart amach agus do thosnaigh ar nithe do chur i dtreo ar an dá altóir sin. Ba ghearr gur imigh sagart eile, agus ní fada eile go raibh duine ina ionad; agus mar sin de, gan fothrom gan gleo, ach amháin monabar íseal na sagart ag léamh Laidne, agus an foth-abairt a deireadh an cléireach, agus binn-ghuth ceolmhar na mion-chlog anois agus arís. Bhí gach duine ag paidireoireacht go dúthrachtach - paidríní ag cuid acu agus leabhair ag cuid acu, agus foth-duine gan leabhar ná paidrín ach iad ag féachaint ar an gcrois ós cionn na haltórach agus ar an sagart, agus ag machnamh (is dócha) ar bhrí agus ar bhunudhas a raibh ar siul ar an altóir. Bhí na daoine saibhre ann ó na tithe ósta móra ná féachfadh ar dhaoine bochta amuigh ar an mbóthar, b'fhéidir, agus daoine bochta lena n-ais ar an suíochán gcéadna, agus na paidreacha céadna á rádh acu is dócha, agus iad ag súil leis na grástaibh ón Dia céadna, agus duine acu chómh dall leis an nduine eile ar méid na ngrásta do bhí á thuileamh aige. Bhí sagairt ag léamh Aifreann ansan ó n-a sé chlog agus bhí sé leath-uair tar éis a hocht an uair sin, agus bhí tuille acu ag fanúint san eardhamh fós. . . .

Cuireadh feabhas mór ar an séipéal san ó bhíos istigh ann cheana. Is leithne anois é ná mar a bhí, agus san áit gur ligeadh leis ar an

gcliathán thiar, do deineadh altóracha deasa i dtreo agus go bhfuil slí
ann do níos mó sagart ná mar a bhí cheana.

Turas go Cill Chaoidh.

'Seadh, chuireamar ár mbeartanna ar na rotharaibh tímpeall a deich
a chlog, agus ní fada go rabhamar ag giorrú an bhóthair go hInis
Díomáin. Ocht míle slí a bhí ann.

Lá margaidh b'eadh é agus bhí mór-chuid daoine ón dtuaith sa
tsráid do labhair Gaeilge linn agus d'innis scéalta dhúinn.   Tá
fuaimeanna san nGaeilge i gConndae an Chláir ná fuil in aon áit eile,
cé go bhfuil ana-chosúlacht idir iad féin agus na fuaimeanna atá i
bPort Láirge. 'Mhuise cia an bhail atá ort in aon chor?' an focal is
túisce deirid le duine aithníonn siad, ach bíonn 'cia nós a bhfuil tú?'
minic a ndóithin acu, freisin.

Amach an bóthar go Leacht Uí Chonchubhair linn agus ní ró-mhear
chuireamar dínn é toisc an ghaoth do bheith aniar ón bhfarraige.
Thugas súil-fhéachaint ar an gcoinbhint mar a múintear an Ghaeilge
go maith is clos dom. Bhí gearra-radharc againn ar cheanntar Leasa
Ceannúir ó thuaidh go hAillthe an Mhothair agus siar go Ceann na
Caillighe agus soir go Cill Seanaigh, agus ba bhreá an scéimh a bhí air,
mar le tír mhaol; bhí iomad tithe bána ann agus raidhse páirceanna
glasa.

Bhí cúpla lios le hais an bhóthair agus iad go féarmhar, agus dob
aoibhinn do dhuine bheith tamall ina shuí ar an gceann dob airde
dhíobh agus an scéal fiannaíochta úd *Eachtra triúr Mhac Stairn* do
chlos go slachtmhar ó sheanchaí nó é do léamh. B'shin í an dúthaigh
do bhí ag an dtriúr is dóigh liom. Agus nuair a bheadh an eachtra
cloiste ag duine d'féadfadh sé tamall do chaitheamh ag iarraidh na
hamhráin do cheap Seán Ó hUaithnín agus Aodh Buidhe Mac Cruitín
do thabhairt chun a chuimhne. Bhí filí sa dúthaigh sin tráth, a mhic ó,
ná bíodh eagal ort. Agus bheadh tamall aige ag féachaint ar na
dumhachaibh siar uaidh ar bhruach na mara, agus ar na
móinfhéarachaibh glasa, agus ar Dhroichead Uí Bhriain atá tar
Abhainn na hEidhnighe, agus ar an seanachaisleán sin thiar ar
bhruach na bhfoilleach. Ach ní dheachamar thar claí isteach, mar
b'fhada linn moilliú ann. Sráidín beag deas is eadh Leath-Ínse, nó
Leacht Uí Chonchubhair, ar bhruach an chuain, agus bíonn slua
daoine ann Domhntaí sa tSamhradh, agus sa bhFómhar. Tá foth-
dhuine ann go bhfuil Gaeilge acu, agus meas uirthi, agus bíonn
buíonn Gaeilge ann gach Geimhreadh, is dócha. . .

Ansan theas a bhí Séumas Mac Cuirtín, file, agus ní fheadar an ann
do bhí Aindrias Mac Cuirtín nó nárbh eadh, ach bhí Séumas ag
múineadh scoile ann, pé scéal é, i gCluain an Átha; agus bhí fear ann
gurbh ainm dó Peadar Ó Néill do cheap cúpla amhrán maith.

Agus anseo siar rómhainn atá an Cheathramha Chaol mar ar chonaigh Mícheál Cuimín, do chúm Laoi Oisín, agus mórán dán eile, agus sé a chúm an t-amhrán úd go bhfuil curfá mar seo leis:-

> 'Bí ag teacht, bí ag teacht, a ghrá bháin
> Bí ag teacht anois má's áil leat
> Sid í an bhliain gur gheall tú triall
> Nó fanúint siar go lá an bhráth.'

Tá fear ansan theas de mhuinntir Fhionnúcháin go bhfuil ana-chuid scríbhinní i nGaeilge aige, ach is deacair iad d'fhagháil uaidh cé gur duine galánta é. Tá filíocht na bhfear do chónaigh sa treo so ina bhosca aige. 'Moy' a tugtar ar an áit ina bhfuil a thigh, ach dar ndóigh níl sa bhfocal san ach Muighe is dócha. Ní fada uainn fó dheas ansan Sliabh Colláin mar ar thuit Conán Maol, 'fear féile na Féinne.'

Seanchas beag é sin do bhí ar siúl agam-sa tamall ag gabháil an bóthar dúinn go Sráid na Cathrach.

Is aoibhinn an radarc atá ar an bhfairraige ón gcúinne mar a gcasann duine ar a láimh chlé chun dul go Sráid na Cathrach, ach tá an áit ana-lom go deo. Puinnte nó Rinn na Spáinneach an ainm atá ar an mball deas eile thiar mar a bhfuil na tithe bána.

Ní ró-fhada d'fhanamar sa tSráid sin na Cathrach. Bia is mó do bhí in easnamh orainn ar rochtain na háite dúinn, agus d'éirigh linn é fhagháil gan ró-mhoill.

Siar go dtí na Coillte chuamar ansan. Má's coillte do bhí ag fás san áit is fada ó bhíodar ann, agus is beag dá riantaibh inniu ann. 'Quilty' an Sacs-Bhéarla tugtar ar an mball, agus is fada ó bhaile do cualathas trácht thar an ainm sin cúpla bliain ó shin nuair do dhein iascairí an bhaile gníomh fearúil chun daoine do bhí i mbaol a mbáidhte amuigh sa chuan do thabhairt slán i dtír. Casadh cuid acu orainn an tráthnóna san, agus iad i bhfeighil líontracha. Fir thréana téagartha is iad, agus raidhse den Ghaeilge acu. An fear is mó a labhair linn bhí sé ar na fearaibh ba thúisce do thug cabhair dos na daoinibh do bhí i gcontúirt a n-anma. Is fiáin na fiacla atá ar na carraigeacha san áit sin agus spící garbha dhíobh á sáthadh féin aníos tamall maith amach ón imeall ag bun na bhfoilleach.

Trí mhíle dhéag ón mbaile sin atá Cill Chaoidh, agus an bóthar díreach romhainn agus nárbh aon bhaol go raghaimís amú - an t-eolas a tugadh dúinn sul ar fhágamar an ball. Tá ainm ana-mór ar mhuinntir an bhaile bhig sin chun eascainithe do cheapadh, ach b'fhéidir gur bréag cuireadh ina leith, mar níor airigheamar-na aon ní dá shaghas uathu, cé go rabhamar tamaillín maith ag cainnt leo. Ní chualamar aon scéal fá dtaobh do theagasc na Gaeilge ins na scoileannaibh ann. Bhíodh an aindeise ar an scéal ann roimis seo toisc go raibh bainisteoir mór-chúiseach do mhuintir Chathaoir ar na scoileannaibh, agus bíodh agus go raibh Gaeilge maith aige féin, níor thaithin leis í do bheith á múineadh in aon scoil san áit, do réir dealraimh. Níor theastaigh uaidh aon teachtaire ná timthire ón gConradh do teacht isteach sa pharóiste, ach theip air iad do choimeád as...

Ag Áth na gCaorach chonaigh Séumas Mac Consaidín, file, agus bhí beirt nó triúr fear eile san gceanntar san do chúm a lán amhrán an tráth mhair Séumas. Tomás Ó Cruadhlaoich an duine b'fhearr acu, sílim; ach bhí sé sin óg nuair a fuair Séumas bás. Ní fheadar an amhlaidh do bhí breis le rádh againn, nó an amhlaidh do thit meascán mearaidhe orainn ag an Áth sin na gCaorach go ndeachamar amú, ach chuamar amú agus dhíolamar as, leis, mar chuir ár seachrán ana-thimpeall orainn. Dúirt an bheirt eile gur greannmhar an giolla do bhí acu, mar le duine do bhí ag maíomh go raibh cruinn-eolas aige ar Chonndae an Chláir. B'éigean dom éisteacht leo go foidhneach agus an tocht feirge do bhí ag borradh ionam do bhrúigh fúm. B'é ba mheasa ná go raibh an oíche ag teacht anoir in ár ndiaidh go mear agus sinn-ne ag dul amú. Ach d'aimsíomar an bóthar ceart sa deiradh, agus ghreadamar linn. Droch-bhóthar aimhréidh logánach is eadh an bóithrín sin do ghabhamar. Tá a lán bóthar dá shaghas i gClár. Thuirseodh bóithre an bhaill sin an rothaí is treise ar domhan. Ní hionadh sinn-na do bheith tuirseach mar do thuirsigh an botún do rinneamar go mór sinn, agus bhí an ghaoth agus an drochbhóthar ár dtuirsiú leis; agus ar chuma éigin bhí an dinnéar d'itheamar i Sráid na Cathrach dearmhadta ar fad againn. Ní rabhamar ró-shásta le chéile ná leis an saol ná le Conndae an Chláir ar feadh tamaill, ach nuair a shroicheamar an Dún Beag chuamar ar lorg aoíchta agus fuaramar, agus ba mhór an t-athrú do chuir sé orainn. Tháinig míneacht agus grádhmhaireacht 'nár gcainnt agus tháinig na gáirí agus an magadh ag léimridh i ndiaidh a chéile arís...

Bhailíomar linn agus bhailigh an cit (nó an múr) aniar 'nár gcoinnibh agus bhuaileamar um a chéile ar bhárr árdáin mhaoil. Siúd isteach i bpáirc sinn ar lorg fothana, mar ní raibh pioc di le fagháil ar thaobh an bhóthair. Is deacair foithin fhagháil in áiteannaibh i gClár. Níl sceacha móra tiugha ionntu, ná fiú amháin tortha an aitinn; ná tor giolcaighe; ná carraig go mbeadh lomradh fraoigh uirthi, agus crann beag cuilinn ag fás as a cliatán fé mar a chífeá i gCiarraighe. Ach bhí foithin againn nuair chromamar cois claí na páirce mar bhí páil sceach ar bhárr an chlaí agus bárr na páile sin amach ós cionn díge ná páirce. Is iontach mar chuireann an ghaoth aniar leath-cheann ar gach páil in Iarthar Cláir. Bíonn a cúl caithte go diail ag gach ceann acu agus slios ar an dtaobh eile tamall maith amach thar cliathán an chlaí....

Ní fada eile a chuamar go bhfacamar soillse Cille Caoidh agus chualamar torann na dtonn go breá ceolmhar ó thuaidh uainn. Síos le fánaidh linn agus sinn ag bualadh ár gcloigíní agus ag feadaíl agus ag screadaigh ar eagla go mbeadh éinne sa bhealach a leagfadh sinn, mar bhí iongnathiomáint fúinn....

'Túirlingidh nó béarfaidh na píléirí orainn,' arsa Máirtín nuair a shroicheamar imeall na sráide. Ní raibh lampa ar bith againn. . . .

Síos linn Sráid Uí Chómhraidhe agus timpeall an chúinne agus aníos bóthar na Trá go dtángamar 'Teach Fuineadh na Gréine.' Chuamar isteach agus chuireamar tuairisc féachaint an raibh slí d'ár leithéidí fé dhíon an tí. . . .

Ar maidin [bhí] meitheal daoine leath-lomnachta ag léimrigh i measc na dtonn mbán, nó ag snámh san doimhinn-uisce lasmuigh - cuid acu agus eagla orthu go scuabfadh tonn éigin amach chun siúl iad, agus cuid eile go neamh-eaglach ag gáirí agus ag déanamh gleoidh; seandaoine agus daoine óga ag iomaidh le chéile féachaint cia acu is fearr a shnámhfadh idir dhá thuinn árda nó do dhruim tuinne; mná agus cailíní agus gan a leath acu ag snámh ach iad ag fanúint go dtagadh na tonntacha laga isteach chúchu, agus ansan screadann siad agus beireann gach beirt acu ar a chéile chun a chéile do shábháil mar dh'eadh; foth-dhuine acu ag tabhairt géillín do charaid léi - lámh fá smig na carad san agus lámh ar chúl cinn chun gan ligint don cheann dul fá uisce. Tithe beaga adhmaid ar an dtráigh agus fir agus mná ina bhfeighil - na mná sa taobh thiar den tráigh agus na fir sa taobh eile. Istigh ionnta san cuireann ná daoine iad féin i dtreo i gcómhair an uisce, bainid díobh a gcuid éadaigh agus cuirid a mhalairt do chulaith orthu, agus ansan rithid leo síos an tráigh agus amach san uisce. Is mór an spórt bheith ag léimrigh san uisce agus na tonna ag leagadh agus is deas an radharc é bheith ag féachaint ar chúpla céad duine mar sin i measc na dtonn mar a mbrisid ar theacht 'on tráigh dóibh.

Maidin an lae do bhí chughainn bhíos páirteach san spórt úd ar an dtráigh. Ar leat-raol fuaras cead mé féin do chur i dtreo i mbosca adhmaid acu san gur thagras dóibh, agus siúd amach mé chomh maith le cách gur thomas mé féin sa tsáile. . . .

Chuamar ar lorg eolais i dtaobh na loinge a ghabhann ó Chill Ruis don Tairbeart. Ar a trí a chlog tráthnóna d'imeodh sí an lá san. Cheapamar gurbh fhearra dúinn tamall do chaitheamh ar bhruach na farraige agus gan imeacht go Cill Ruis go dtí an tráthnóna. Ghabh cáirde na hoíche aréir le n-ár gcois, agus soir amach go dtí na foillteacha árda míle ón sráid linn. Ba mheidhreach an chuideachta sinn ar bharra foille agus an ghaoth aniar go hárd ár luascadh. I bhfad síos uainn bhí na faoileáin gheala ag eitilt de dhruim na dtonn gan eagla ar bith orthu, ach iad anonn agus anall agus ansan aníos de dhruim foille agus síos arís de sciúird go barra uisce. Ó a Thiarna! dá dtitfeadh aon neach de dhruim foille acu san bheadh sé básuithe sul a mbeadh sé leath-slí go bun. Ach ba dheas é bheith ag amharc ar na héanlaithibh ag cur díobh ann, agus ar na tonntachaibh ag briseadh i gcoinnibh bun na gcarraigreacha, agus ar na curachaibh dubha tamall amach uainn agus iascairí ionnta, ba dheas san go deimhin. Ach bhí méidheagram ag teacht im cheann ó bheith ró-fhada ar fhíor-bhruach na foille sin, agus dhruideas siar tamall sa tsliabh.

Bhí cor-cheathrar á rinnce ar an mbán rómham ag mo chomrádaithe, agus foth-choisidhe eile do bhí sa treo san ag teacht ag féachaint orthu. Do canadh cúpla amhrán agus do caitheadh gal deas tobac sul ar fhágamar an áit. Bhí greas eile rinnce againn ar dhroichead adhmaid ar ár dturas abhaile 'on tsráid agus ansan bhailíomar linn.

Trasna na Sionainne. Oíche í dTráighlí.

'Ceathrú tar éis a dó! 'Seadh dar fiadh! ní díomhaoin a bheimíd ar an mbóthar go Cill Ruis agus amach go Ceapa, agus bheith ann ar a trí a chlog,' ar duine againn i gceann na sráide sul ar léimeamar ar ár rotharaibh. Ach bhí an ghaoth linn, rud dob annamh linn, agus ní raibh an bóthar go holc.

Bhí mórán daoine ar fúd na sráideanna i gCill Ruis tan thángamar [ann]. Bhí ana-chuid móna i dtrucaillíbh ann, pé scéal é. Chaitheamar tamall ag féachaint ar an leacht atá i lár na sráide is mó ann. Mar chómhartha chuimhne ar na daoine do fuair bás ar son na hÉireann le céad blian do cuireadh ar bun é. Tá Gaeilge agus Béarla scríobhtha ar a chliathánaibh, agus tháinig ceathrar seanabhan chughainn-na nuair do chualadar sinn ag léamh na Gaeilge: lucht móna do dhíol, ón dtuaith b'eadh iad, agus cé go raibh Gaeilge mhaith acu níor thuigeadar cuid d'ár léigheamar den chloich dóibh ar dtús.

'Scoláirí sibh-se,' arsa duine acu, 'agus ní foláir nó tá an Ghaeilge cheart agaibh.'

Ní ró-bhuíoch a bhíomar dá cainnt ná dá tuairim, agus dúirt-sa léi go mb'fhearr liom ná rud maith a teanga féin do bheith agam. Níor chreid sí mé.

Cheannaigh an té chaill a chaipín ceann nua, ach b'éigean dó an tríú siopa do chuardach sul a bh'fuair sé caipín Gaelach.

Bhí breis deabhaidh orainn chun dul ag seancaíocht le héinne. Agus sé rinneamar ná imeacht linn fá dheithneas go Ceapa (nó an 'Ceapach' an focal ceart? agus má's eadh ba cheart 'don Cheapaigh' a rádh, b'fheidir).

Níor ghádh dhúinn bheith chomh deitheansach san, áfach, mar cé gur ar a trí do bhí fógartha acu go n-imeodh an long, bhí sé leath-uair tar éis a ceathair sul ar chorraigh sí í féin ón áit.

Muca fá ndeara cuid den mhoill agus lucht an bhóthair iarainn fá ndeara a lán eile dhí. Bhí aonach muc i gCill Ruis an lá san, agus go Luimneach do cuireadh a lán acu. Bhí cúpla céad muc ar an long sin, cuid acu thíos ina híochtar agus cuid acu ar a huachtar mar a raibh na daoine. Ní rabhamar gan ceol - ceol na muc in ár gcluasaibh, ach níor bhinn linn é dá mhéid é ár ndúil i gceol. Ní raibh leigheas againn air, bhíodar na muca ansan agus cia chuirfeadh amach iad? Bhí scata acu in ár n-aice, agus sop féir fúthu agus iad ina gcodladh; bhí scata eile acu tamall uainn thall agus an treo céadna orthu, ach thíos a bhí an ceol agus an gleo ar fad acu. Bhí róthair agus boscaí agus málaí in áit eile agus muca mar chómharsain acu. Bhí mórán daoine iasachta ag filleadh abhaile ó Chill Chaoidh ar an long sin agus bhí scéalta deasa acu, is dócha, nuair chuadar thar n-ais abhaile mar gheall ar an onóir tugadh do mhucaibh ar bórd loinge. Sasanaigh b'eadh cuid de na daoinibh sin, agus cé go raibh málaí móra breátha acu, agus éadach maith orthu, ní raibh aon ana-dhealramh orthu féin, ach dealramh coimhtheach comónta.

Giotaí tógtha as Peadar Ó Hannracháin, *Mar Chonnac-sa Éire* (Baile Átha Cliath 1944), pp 75-100.

Robert Lynd, Rambles in Clare, 1911

The phenomenal growth in tourism in the early part of this century spawned a great number of travel books many of quite indifferent quality. One of the better ones was Robert Lynd's *Rambles in Ireland* (1912), illustrated by Jack B. Yeats. Lynd, a Belfast born journalist was educated at Queen's University, Belfast. He spent most of his life in London working as a journalist for the *Daily Mail*. He wrote the introduction to James Connolly's *Labour in Irish History* (1917). An ardent Gaelic Leaguer, he sometimes wrote under the pen name Riobard Ua Floinn. Daniel Corkery dismissed him as the 'Belfast sentimentalist' but he retained his commitment to the ideal of Irish nationhood to the end. His account of Clare is of interest for his description of the entertainments at Lisdoonvarna and the use he made of the transport services. Leaving Galway by steamer he landed at Ballyvaughan and from there travelled by horse drawn car via Lisdoonvarna to Ennistymon (the motor car had yet to make an impact). He travelled on the West Clare Railway from Ennistymon to Kilrush where he boarded the steamer for Limerick.

It was the merest accident that we went to Lisdoonvarna. Our ambition was to get from Spiddle (a little desolate village about ten miles outside Galway, where we had been attending the opening of a summer school of Irish) to Killorglin, which is in County Kerry, in time for Puck Fair. As we left Spiddle on Monday morning and the Fair (according to the railway-guide) began on Wednesday, there would be little time except for jolts on cars and other jolts in railway trains in the interval. If we made the journey by Lisdoonvarna, it was partly because this involved the passage of Galway Bay by steamer to Ballyvaughan - for who can resist these little local steamers on a holiday? - and partly because a clerk in a ticket office had expatiated on the beauties of the Cliffs of Moher, which are the wonder of County Clare as Slieve League is the wonder of county Donegal. . .

And as it involved that sea-journey across Galway Bay, car-journeys across half (or what looked like half) of the County Clare, and made possible another long voyage on a local streamer up the mouth of the Shannon from Kilrush to Limerick, we yielded as a child yields to a bribe of sweets. . . .

On the quay at Ballyvaughan a row of wagonettes and cars was standing; they could have found room for at least thirteen times as many people as the steamer had brought across. Nearly all of them seemed to come from the hotels at Lisdoonvarna, which was ten miles off by the nearest road. We had already picked our hotel at a guess from a list we had seen in a railway-guide, and after some shouting we found the car that was connected with it. Then we got up and drove off till we came to the first public-house. It seems to be a ritual with drivers of cross-country cars to stop at the first public-house, or the one after, even if it be only a few yards away. All the cars and wagonettes pulled up either here or a door or two farther on. Then we started on our journey up into the grey and gloomy hills. One of Cromwell's generals is said to have declared of this part of the county - the barony of Burren, as it is called - that it didn't contain wood enough to hang a man, water enough to drown him, or earth enough to bury him, and certainly these introductory rocks reach an extreme pitch of desolation and wildness. Grey as a dead fire, they rise in the imagination as the field of old battles of the Stone Age, when small men rushed from their hiding behind the boulders and swung their little axes with murderous cries above the heads of their enemies. Corkscrew Hill, as the road is called which winds right and left, and left and right, and right and left, till one is finally safe on the great plateau which absorbs so much of the county, is, so far as my experience goes, one of the wonderful roads of Ireland. To go along it in the dark, I imagine, would be to wander among the companies of the disembodied. The majority of people leave the cars to tug along on the round-about way, and themselves take short-cuts across the rough grassy patches that lie between bit and bit of the road up the face of the hill. Here at every step up the terraced slopes we seemed to be getting farther into a world of twilight and hilly mysteries. The greatest of the heights about us lay upon the land like the huge boss of a Titan's shield, a round of greyness.

Then, on the upper plain, we got on to the car again, and listened to the discourse of the red-whiskered driver on the demerits of the country, and foxes that creep among the unfenced hills, and the ancient stories of the County Clare. 'Did you ever hear of Maighread Ruadh?' he asked. 'She was a terrible woman. She lived - do you see the hill yonder in a line with the white house I'm showing you with the whip? Well it's near that she had her castle, and there was a cross-roads near it, and they say she kept a gate at it, and, any traveller that came that way, she wouldn't let him past till he had paid her a toll of all she asked him. And, if he wouldn't pay, she would string him up: she would give him a terrible doing, anyway. Well, for all she was cruel, there was one was crueller, and that was her husband. However it came about, one man wouldn't do her, and when the husband was away one time, what did she do but bring her lovers, twelve of them, into the castle, and had them waiting on her at the table dressed up as young girls. That went on till the husband got wind of it, and after that he hurries home and kills the twelve of them, and he takes Maighread Ruadh and - ah, he was a devil - ah, ma'am, begging your pardon, he cuts the breasts off her. Maybe it's only a story that's in it, but I always heard it told as a true story. They say it's hundreds and hundreds of years since that happened. . .'

Sudden lights appeared in the blackness, and with a sense of discovery we rattled down the hill into the settlement of hydropathics and hotels which is Lisdoonvarna, dropped into the twisted hollow of the town, and climbed a last little hill that took us to the hotel we had chosen so casually.

When we got off at the door, it was as though we had landed into the beginnings of a house-party - a house-party in which nearly every guest was a priest. The grey-haired lady in black who received us in the hall seemed more like the hostess of a country-house than the proprietor of a hotel; and, indeed, though there was business intelligence as well as the spirit of welcome marked in her face, it was as a hostess rather than a business woman that she went among her boisterous guests while we were there. We arrived just in time to get the last room in the hotel, and just in time for tea - for the arrangement of the meals here, like everything else, was in the correct Irish fashion, with tea instead of dinner in the evening. Priests were in crowds in the hall and passed one on the stairs, one humming a tune, another talking nonsense to a lot of girls, another aloof and quietly smiling and entering into the high spirits of the place by proxy, like the elderly ladies from Limerick who sat with their knitting in the corners and looked on. The two or three boys who were there were romping about among the priests' legs, tugging at sticks with them, and playing all sorts of noisy scrimmaging games. Girls in high-necked blouses chattered, not with each other, but with groups of the clergy, in every square yard of the place, and the male laity in the persons of a few young men were thrust into a wallflower loneliness. . . .

It was only weariness that kept us from going down into the village to see a travelling circus that evening. But this hive of gay priests, this black garrison of the clergy on their holidays, was, as it turned out, worth a hundred such conventional pleasures. Personally, I had long known something of the merriments of the clergy of other denominations when they gather in companies round a fire and set their pipes going. But I had never before seen the Catholic clergy disporting themselves *en masse*, as it were. Here they were like a crowd of boys on holiday. One of them walked up and down the hall flirtatiously with a girl on each arm, a challenge to the laughter of the others, who smoked him for a playboy. Others, no less flirtatious, jested and gesticulated on the crowded sofas to the immense admiration of laughing groups of girls and benign old ladies, who smiled on the fun from their corners. . .

When I got back into the hall again, the priests were still crowding about the drawing-room doors, not dancing themselves, for apparently they are not allowed to do that, but encouraging, nay, compelling, everybody else to dance. Irish priests are pictured by a good many of their modern critics as a saturine company. Perhaps there is something in the air of Lisdoonvarna which turns them jovial.

If you want to get out of Lisdoonvarna, you must do it by car - unless you have an unnatural taste for walking. If you take a direct cross-country road you will fall in with the County Clare railway system - it is far more like a steam-tram system - at Ennistymon, about nine miles away. But if you want to see the Cliffs of Moher which, says the leading guide-book, 'form some of the most sublime objects of the western coast,' you will have to go a long roundabout journey and join the train farther on at Lahinch. . . .

Here on the point of the [Moher] cliffs is a broken-down tower where red and white cows shelter in the deserted hall, and many visitors will no doubt feel a quickening of romance at the sight of it till they look at the date-stone and see that it is no older than the nineteenth century. It was built, indeed, by a neighbouring landlord, Cornelius O'Brien, M.P., in 1835, as a hostelry for visitors, and it was he, I believe, who also put up the wall of flagstones along the cliffs and the stables which now lie in ruins near the road. . . .

When one has got back to the road again and driven some way down from the heights, one comes on the showiest holy well I have yet seen. It is in a kind of grotto in a garden beside an inn, and outside the grotto-like building stands a little shrine. The walls of the grotto are thick with holy pictures, abominations of colour representing various saints, and each of them is signed with the name of some beneficiary of the blessed properties of the waters. Other visitors had made presents of rosaries, which were hung here and there from nails. If you read the inscriptions on the pictures, you will be surprised to see how many of the donors are Americans. A barefooted woman with a skin tanned like a Red Indian's and a head of glossy black hair greeted us as we went in, and asked us if we would have a drink from the well. We said we would, and she rinsed out a tin and filled it from the running water and handed it to us. And as, having given her some money, we went out, she called earnest blessings after us. The well is named after St Bridget - 'the Mary of the Gael,' as she has been called. . . .

When we drove down into Lahinch later, past the wide stretch of sandy golf-links, on which a rare knickerbockered man, his weapons borne by his page, was marching very importantly in the wake of a ball, we noticed badges of one kind and another in the buttonholes of many of the boys who loafed about the railway station.

It was only by the skin of our teeth that we caught the train. Had we missed it, we could not have reached Limerick - by the Kilrush steamer, at any rate - that night. . .

I hoped when we got on board the steamer there would be nothing to do but loosen a few ropes and speed off up the Shannon towards Limerick, and, as the captain told us there would be no food to be had till the boat started, we were especially anxious to be gone as early as possible. But, alas! we were just feeling sure that we must be on the point of going, when the advance-guard of a regiment of pigs ran grunting on to the quay. Then there was a great scene of penning in and beating with sticks and squealing, and a few pigs would be herded rebelliously into a little truck and shut in, and the pulley would begin rattling as though it were out of breath with effort, and a truck would be hoisted in the air and swung round and lowered into the hold of the steamer, a thing of terror, odour, and disharmony. It was the slowest possible business transferring the pigs from the quayside into the boat, and when one regiment of the poor dirty beasts was finished, another came down with silly ears to take its place. Ultimately, we got tired of pig, and, if it had not been for the growing smell of them, we might have enjoyed the time well enough looking over at rare Scattery Island, which lies a mile or more out in the water with a round tower rising amid its ruined churches. . . .

To steam up the Shannon on a day of wide prospects is, I am sure, a delightful experience, though even on the best of days I would rather make the voyage on a steamer that did not carry pigs. It is not that I do not like pigs: I love the shape of them, and they make a very soothing music except at times of emotional crisis. But the odour of a thousand of them is something never meant to be concentrated in the hold of a single vessel. In the hold? Alas! no, it escaped from the hold and wrapped the boat in a kind of cloud that there was no getting away from.

Extracts taken from Robert Lynd, *Rambles in Ireland* (London 1912), pp 95-128.

Seán Ó Faoláin, A Clare Journey, 1940

Seán Ó Faoláin, renowned man of letters, came from Cork where his father was a member of the Royal Irish Constabulary and his mother kept a boarding house. Educated by the Presentation Brothers, he studied English, Irish and Italian at U.C.C. He took the side of the I.R.A. in the civil war but grew disillusioned with their inability to create an Ireland in keeping with their stated vision. He became a second level school teacher and in 1924 secured employment with the Christian Brothers in Ennis. He remained in the town for a year but thereafter returned to his studies. He took an M.A. in English literature at Harvard University in 1929 and in 1933 decided to devote himself full-time to writing. He is perhaps best known for his short story collections *Midsummer Night Madness and Other Stories* (1932), and *A Purse of Coppers* (1937). He also wrote a series of historical novels *A Nest of Simple Folk* (1934), *Bird Alone* (1936) and *Come Back to Erin* (1940). In these Ó Faoláin examines the predicament of the individual torn between the revolutionary fervour of his youth and the conservative impulses of Irish society. In parallel with his fiction were his biographies of historical and political figures, *The King of the Beggars* (1938), a life of Daniel O'Connell, *Eamon de Valera* (1939) and *The Great O'Neill* (1942), a life of Hugh O'Neill of Tyrone *c.* 1550-1616. In each of these works Ó Faoláin takes a pragmatic view of leadership with a strong bias towards constitutional politics for the betterment of the people. The travel book *An Irish Journey* (1941), was written as World War II raged in Europe. Sailing down the Shannon Estuary in an old boat laden with Guinness and coal Ó Faoláin disembarked at a pier near Cahircon from where he walked to Ennis. Recalling his earlier sojourn in the town he describes the bleakness and penury of provincial towns in the 1920s without libraries or theatres that would afford a modicum of stimulation to the intellectually inclined.

When they landed me on the tiny pier opposite Foynes, on the Clare side, I looked back with regret at the great petrol-tanks, the harbour, the village, the new buildings recently built to cope with the transatlantic flights which start from there. The Shannon has been, invariably, the boundary of wildness in Irish history. 'The wild Irish across the Shannon' is a common phrase. Then I turned past Cahircon, where they train priests for the Chinese mission, and proceeded to walk along the Fergus to Ennis. It was a grand walk, for the clouds were mounting the air like soapsuds, and this is the finest possible stretch of the Shannon and the noblest and most impressive river-stretch in all Ireland. I once taught school in Ennis for a year, so

I enjoyed the prospect of revisiting old haunts, and moved in the light of my familiars.

All this region between Lough Derg and Slieve Aughty and the sea is, physically speaking, lovely in a way that no other part of Ireland is lovely - unless it be the country around Ballinrobe which George Moore has described so delicately in his autobiographies and in *The Lake*. That is the thing about Clare which gives it such attraction. It is hard, and barren, and windy, and wild, yet its power to enchant comes from the delicacy and lightness and gentleness of its lyrical moods. Clare is now a shaggy-dressed, hairy-faced, dark-eyed, rough-voiced man of the roads - a drover or a travelling man: now a girl whose natural wildness is constantly forgotten in and overlain by the softness of her temperament. (Yeats, I see, felt this double quality too: 'cold Clare rock and Galway rock and thorn. . . . That stern colour and that delicate line.') This land full of grey rocks, little lakes, large horizons, seeping dusk, clumped trees, wandering and winding roads, happy green nooks among the stones, rich deposits among the boglands, is the west without the savagery of the west, and the midlands without their sloth and ease. It is amazing that a river could make such a division. Once over that wide Shannon one is in touch with a totally different kind of life. That is why I could wish that Limerick city were Ennis city, so that Limerick richness could give to Clare at least one pocket of urban life where the nature of the county could develop into the greatest possible variety - without losing touch with its sources. Ennis is too small; and though it is a happy and cosy town, it is not fine enough for Clare.

But there is no sentimentality like the sentimentality of wishing to rewrite history. Limerick is at the head of a navigable river, and is a springboard into three counties, and Clare and Ennis pay for their isolation; even if their isolation does pay for itself in the charm of the lonely fields, the windy width of the county, its light humours, its dark streak. . . .

In the old Land League days and after, Clare had 'a bad name' - i.e. looking at it from another point of view, the Irish point of view, a good name. Clare and its capital, Ennis, have a long history of revolt behind them. O'Connell fought and won the Clare Election - the first Catholic in modern Ireland to win a seat in the British Parliament since the fall of Limerick before the Williamite guns. Long after, De Valera won Ennis for Sinn Fein. But the tradition of Clare wildness is gone, and I met, prophetically, in the Old Ground Hotel, an English painter who had perceived, rather, that other gentler side to Clare of which I have spoken. As he enthused about the shifting colours of Clare I could remember, myself, with what pleasure one evening in Miltown Malbay I looked up the long street, with its painted houses pied as Joseph's coat, and the prismatic, brittle sea-air behind them, so that the whole street was bathed in a kind of lighted spray, it then seemed to me, as in the green glare before a thunderstorm. I could not help sitting down and trying to draw it, and the man who was with me, thinking only, if naturally, of the kind of Clare discomforts that Percy French made such play with in songs like *Are you right, there, Michael, are you right?*, could not understand what on earth I saw in that ugly, long, cold street to admire. That day, I remember, there was a conference of National teachers in one of the hotels, and one particular N.T. was, as they say in Dublin, 'mouldy' with drink, and kept on blathering away in the parlour at the top of his voice. At last a colleague shouted at him to shut up.

'Look at Cassidy, there,' he pointed out. 'He's a B.A. and an M.A. and he hasn't a bloody word out of him.'

As I entered Ennis past Clarecastle I began to recall my first impressions of Ennis. The narrowest streets of any Irish town, I know, and all winding like serpents . . . one attractive Georgian terrace of houses presenting its square backside to the vulgar business street behind it . . . no library in my time - nowhere at all to get books to read, not even a shop where one could buy a book. (Now there is a first-class County Library, and when I passed the little shop where I used to order my *Times Literary Supplement*, and my *Spectator* - in the effort to keep in touch with the world outside - I realised, suddenly, what a blessing the new sixpenny books are to small towns: for there I saw a row of good books in the Penguin and Pelican series which would have been as welcome to me, in my time, as the flowers in May.) What other impressions did I recall? My little digs opposite the Franciscan church - very cosy, spotlessly clean, with my first and most kind-hearted landlady. I remember she had a great weakness for the *True Story* magazine - an American publication, I think, with real photographs as illustrations, and always a slight suggestion, not too much, just a titillation, of sex in the supposed revelations. *How I married Two Men* - a story of unconscious bigamy. *My First Wedding Night* - a ghost story with a juicy background. I used to amuse myself by stealing her magazine and putting it in the fanlight of the door whenever I thought my friend from the friary across the road, a young priest with a St Anthony face, might be coming to visit me. Once she had a slight haemorrhage. As she was very pious she took her attack as a warning from the skies, and renounced the *True Story* magazine for a whole month after.

Her brother-in-law was my colleague at the Christian Brothers School. His passion was crosswords, which had just then come into popularity. In this he was joined by all the monks in the school. 'Jezebel in six letters' once stumped them in a £1,000 competition. The next week, when the solutions came out, Brother Paul gave me the answer. 'Harlot,' he said, innocently. 'That's some queer kind of foreign woman, I believe.'

I liked that school, and I liked the brothers, and I liked the boys, and I liked Ennis. I had, I think, a salary of £150 a year. It may have been less - certainly not more. It was my first job as a teacher, and the salary was ample. I saved money on it. But, of course, if I had remained there I should have gone to seed. No books, no plays, no conversation, no stimulus. I'd have taken to drink. I would have become a bad teacher, all my freshness gone. After ten years of it I might have been earning about £250 a year. I could not have married on the salary. Being myself, I suppose I should have, in any case, turned to writing and so escaped. But not one in a thousand teachers ever does escape from these country-town jobs. Our educationalists ought to see that no teacher can be a good teacher unless he can feed himself with fresh experiences all the time. Every teacher in Ireland should get a sabbatical with salary every three years. Moreover, no teacher being paid less than £350 can possibly do justice to himself and his work.

As to country-town schooling in general, if I judge by that little school, it is quite good - granted three essential premises. There should be a chance for the promising boy to get out of the rut. For that the County Councils should provide ample scholarship money. There should be a vocational school available where a bright lad can continue his studies. And no town without a first-class free library can possibly think that it is giving its youth a fair chance in life.

In Ennis one senses the proximity of Galway, as in Galway one senses the proximity of Mayo: there is, I mean, a rising graph of astuteness as one goes north along the western side of the Shannon. A school inspector once said to me: 'In Clare you have to be alert. In Galway you have to have your eyes on pins. But in Mayo you are kept scratching your head all the time! The Ennis people are not to be fooled or flattered. Once I heard an old-time politician address the crowd there, and he let slip: 'Therefore in this great city of Ennis . . .' The crowd roared with derision. Besides, like every Irish town there is a mixture of loyalties, and of experience. There is, for example, a strong ex-British Army section in Ennis. One Armistice Day there was the devil to pay when the clergy failed or refused to hold a commemoration service. The ex-troops marched in a body to the Protestant church which did hold a service, and they were delighted with the way things were done. 'Ay,' said one of them to me, 'and cushions to kneel on, bejasus, not like the cold stone floor of the aisles in our church.' For weeks after the Catholic priests uttered fierce denunciations of the ex-soldiers, said they must go to the bishop for absolution, and threatened goodness knows what besides, short of excommunication by bell, book, and candle. The 'troops' held tough, and the matter was quietly dropped.

I find that I have nothing but good to say of my experience of Ennis and Clare. I spent there one of the happiest years of my life. And yet, I had no pastimes but to walk about Clare Abbey, and Quinn Abbey, and down by Dromoland, or even as far as Newmarket-on-Fergus and out over the bog, or swim in the river in summer, and study in the winter. But then I recall the bank-clerks in the Munster and Leinster bank whom I used to see walk out the road every evening, in a silent group of three, and I think myself back there *in perpetuum*, on a small salary.

For a year, or two - yes! After that . . . no! You need money to live in places the size of Ennis - money to be able to fish, and shoot, and play cards, and have a few drinks, and buy books, and to be able to run out to Kilkee on summer Sundays, or into Limerick to friends, or up to Galway. Above all, one should be able to take a good month's holiday out of Ireland every summer; and two or three times a year, at Easter and Christmas, say, a holiday in some other part of Ireland, such as Dublin. (Or *even* Cork.)

I should have gone across to the coast from Ennis - to Spanish Point, to Kilkee or Kilrush, or Lahinch. But as with Limerick county my heart failed me. I thought of other days when I travelled that wind-blown region behind Slieve Callan. I thought of the thorn-trees that grow at right angles to their trunks, blown into that shape by the Atlantic gales. I thought how, when I used to travel that awful West-Clare Railway, the porters at Ennistymon (where the train turns out to the edge of the coast) used lob in great four-stone weights to ballast the little carriages against the fury of the storm. When I was a commercial traveller I used do that journey about three times every winter, and I can still remember the deserted hotel at Kilkee - the season long over; the waiter in his stiff-front and tails, gazing sadly out of the glass veranda at me as I came struggling up the path with my bag - almost as if he pitied me (as well he might); even as I can remember how the boots at the old hotel in Ennistymon used light me with a blowing candle up the long, linoleumed stairs, to a back room, dark and ancient as a coffin, where, when he was gone, I would stand by the window and hear the waterfall roaring in spate below me in the darkness. As I think of it now I think of the 'B.A. and M.A.', and all the other N.T.s, in their little homes over that stony region, and I swear that whenever I hear, again, toploftical people saying that teachers are paid too much I shall say: 'What would you take to live through a Clare winter on the slopes of Callan?'

Taken from Seán Ó Faoláin, *An Irish Journey* (London 1941), pp 147-53.

Lionel Rolt, Lough Derg and The West Clare, 1946

Lionel T.C. Rolt, author and lifelong railway and inland waterway enthusiast, came to Ireland in 1946 to explore the country's canals and inland waterway system. Born in 1910, he was educated at Cheltenham College, Gloucester-shire. Qualifying in engineering, he practised as a mechanical engineer between 1926-1941. During the war years he was employed by the Ministry of Supply. Subsequently, he decided to devote himself to full time writing. His first book *Narrow Boat* was published in 1944 and was followed by *The Inland Waterways of England* (1950), *Railway Adventures* (1953), and *Pictorial History of Motoring* (1956). In a writing career spanning some thirty years he published over thirty books. His book on Ireland, *Green and Silver* (1949), is counted among his best. Rolt was co-founder of the Inland Waterways Association of England and also founding member of the Talyllyn Railway Preservation Society. He was awarded an honorary M.A. by Newcastle University in 1965 and an M.Sc. degree by the university of Bath in 1973. His hobbies included motoring in vintage cars, railways and the history of engineering. In Ireland he cruised the waterways in his boat *Le Coq*; he was among the last to travel on the Royal Canal before it fell into disuse in 1951. He provides a delightful description of the changing moods of the waters of Lough Derg and his attempt to reach Scarriff by boat. In the 1940s the first class carriages of the West Clare Railway still preserved something of their Victorian splendour; 'to do justice to such interiors' writes Rolt, 'I should, I felt, be wearing a deer-stalker and an ulster'. Arriving at Kilrush station, he found that the long-standing steamship connection with Limerick had ended and he was compelled to return by bus to Limerick.

I am glad that our first passage through Lough Derg was made in the southerly direction because it is much the better from the scenic point of view to approach the mountains which gradually converge upon the southern half of the lake. Already the heather-purpled moorlands of the Slieve Aughty Mountains were marching beside us along the Galway shore. Beyond, blue in the summer air, we could see the mountains guarding the approach to Killaloe, Slieve Bernagh - the Gapped Mountain - in the County Clare beyond Scarriff Bay, and opposite, in Tipperary, majestic Tountinna, highest point of the Arra Mounatins, with the Silvermines and Keeper Hill, highest of them all, closing the far horizon. This splendid amphitheatre of mountains looming ahead made a fitting climax to our voyage and made us realise what we should have missed had we been unable to visit Lough Derg. . . .

In the lakeside families we encountered a new stratum of Irish society, that of the Protestant Anglo-Irish or, as they are sometimes called, 'the old ascendancy'. Many of them had been resident in the district since Cromwellian times, and they represented an example, interesting to the social historian, of a community, originally colonial, which has contrived to outlive the parent stock from which it sprung. Farming, riding, fishing, shooting, or sailing, despite all the troubles with which Ireland had been rent, these people continue to follow a way of life which can have changed very little in two hundred years, but which has virtually disappeared from England as a result of our bloodless but far-reaching social revolution. In a remote and sparsely populated countryside, hospitality has not been strained by abuse as is the case in our overcrowded island; consequently their doors seem to be ever open to the traveller. To cross their thresholds was for me a bitter-sweet experience, unlocking forgotten stores of the nostalgic recollections of a childhood when vestiges of such a life still lingered in England and then seemed to me stable and assured. Spacious rooms were rich with the lovely, gracious possessions of past generations, yet there was nothing oppressive or self-conscious about them; they were no museums of a vanished past. Everything was worn and well, almost carelessly, used. . . .

While we were having tea there was a sudden change in the weather and we stepped from the wheelhouse onto the quay to find this fickle lake transformed. Though there had been no rain, the skies had hitherto been grey with hurrying clouds and the waters leaden. Now the clouds had parted, the sun was shining brightly and the wind had dropped. Lough Derg, having played us one of its capricious pranks, now lay placid, basking in the sunlight as innocent and innocuous as a village duckpond. Leaning on the weathered grey limestone of the harbour wall and gazing across to the noble shape of Tountinna Mountain I now found it impossible to believe that this same stretch of smiling, sparkling water could become a raging sea capable of battering down breakwaters and engulfing a canal boat. It was indeed a lovely prospect whichever way the eye turned. Farther to the west across the bay and beyond the grey finger of the round tower on Holy Island rose Caher Mountain and Knocknagowert, foothills of Slieve Bernagh, their green lower slopes dotted with cabins, and small farmsteads, while looking landwards the southern escarpment of the Aughty Mountains, purple with heather, lifted its long ridge above the lakeside trees. . .

Soon after the *St James* [boat] had disappeared from sight in the direction of Killaloe, the little stone quay was deserted for we had cast off and were setting out to complete our interrupted journey to Scarriff. This second stage was as languorous and idyllic as the first had been adventurous and tempest-tossed. Passing out of

Mountshannon Bay between Young's Island and Holy Island, with engine idling we drifted slowly and with scarcely perceptible motion across the blue waters of the great bay of Scarriff until searching ahead with binoculars, I picked up the navigation markers by the mouth of the little river Scarriff. The town of Scarriff lies some little distance inland from the lake, and for the one and a half tortuous miles from Lough Derg to Scarriff quay the river has been canalized. It was a curious and fascination transition to pass suddenly from the wide levels of the lake into this narrow channel which twisted bewilderingly through a bed of tall reeds, a dense swamp bordered by a belt of dark woodland.

We soon left the marsh for rich pastures and water-meadows, while at one turn we passed the disused Tuamgraney quay. The meanderings of the little river were such that it was difficult to keep a sense of direction, and as I spun *Le Coq's* [boat] wheel this way and that I was glad that I had effectively righted her steering gear. It must be as much as a loaded canal boat can do to negotiate some of these turns, and I should doubt whether the larger craft which the Grand Canal Company propose to run on the Shannon service will be able to call at Scarriff.

It was just after noon when we came in sight of Scarriff quay and Grand Canal depot at the end of a short cut which branched away from the river on our left hand. We moored against the quay wall and had our lunch before walking up to explore the town which we could see standing upon high ground about half a mile away.

Scarriff is an attractive place, curiously sited after the manner of Gloucestershire's Stow-on-the-Wold; that is to say, instead of seeking shelter as most country towns and villages do, it seems to invite the winds to do their worst. Its centre consists of a wide square perched upon a knoll to which all the radiating streets must climb. At the foot of the steep street by which we ascended we crossed a high stone bridge over a typical mountain torrent which brawled noisily in its swift descent between boulders and over shelving rocks. Looking down over the parapet it was hard to believe that this was the Scarriff river and that only a few hundred yards below this point it became navigable by boats of forty-five tons.

We found that there were some good shops in Scarriff, and after a thorough exploration we returned to the boat laden with purchases which included two pounds of most delicious butter and a pair of shoes which I am wearing as I write. We had decided that after tea we would return to our lovely berth at Mountshannon. We proposed to travel to Killaloe on the morrow and considered it advisable to take full advantage of the fair weather by returning in that direction. As there was little time left to us we could no longer afford to be unduly delayed by storms. We knew now how swiftly Lough Derg can change her moods. . . .

Killaloe, with its smaller township of Ballina just across the river bridge, occupies a magnificent situation in this narrow gorge which the Shannon has carved through the mountains. The waterfront facing the fine bridge is attractive; so is the narrow and steep main street at the foot of which stands the stately twelfth century cathedral of St Lua. Yet there seemed to me to be a slightly drab and dejected air about Killaloe for which I suspect that Ardnacrusha is at least partly responsible. For Killaloe, like O'Briensbridge and the even more celebrated Castleconnell, was a great resort of fishermen until the advent of the Shannon scheme. The dam at Parteen which diverts the river into the great headrace, or Ardnacrusha Canal as it is usually called, ruined rod fishing by altering the river levels. Upstream of the dam the level has been raised to such an extent that the Shannon spreads into a lake below Killaloe. The rapids above the bridge have ceased to exist and boats need no longer use the cut where the water makes a level at the lock. While Killaloe has too much water from the fisherman's point of view, O'Briensbridge and Castleconnell have too little, for, except in time of high flood, practically the whole flow is diverted at Parteen. Only a mere trickle is released to flow down the famous falls of Doonnass over which the mighty river once thundered like a gigantic mountain stream. It is this prodigal display of power which has now been harnessed at Ardnacrusha. By means of the Parteen dam and the titanic headrace, a fall of a hundred and ten feet has been obtained at the power station, and the water rushes down four penstocks twenty feet in diameter, each of which drives a 40,000 H.P. turbine. However much one may regret the virtual destruction of this beautiful reach of the river, or the conversion of Lough Allen into a reservoir, one must admit that, by modern standards, Ireland has paid an astonishingly small price for so much power. The waters of the river are not polluted or heated; the source of power is inexhaustible and does not therefore involve any squandering of natural capital resources and consequently none of the ugliness which such exploitation involves. No miners toil in their dim galleries, no headgears spin or spoil heaps spread to feed the turbines, while at the power station itself there is no smoke, no tall chimneys or cooling towers; only a lofty building filled with the surge of turbines as the Shannon thunders down the penstocks at the rate of four hundred tons a second. . . .

After the bleak levels of the plain, the luxuriance of this sheltered gorge of Killaloe was very striking. Great bushes of hydrangeas laden with blossom grew beside the old lock on the cut, and when we walked up a narrow valley in the Slieve Bernagh mountains on the day after our arrival we found fuschias and gladioli flourishing amidst the bracken and bell heather high up on the mountain sides. They were obviously escapes from the gardens of the ruined crofts which, alas, were all too numerous on the higher levels.

On our way back from this walk we passed along the steep flank of Crag Mountain which rises sheer from the lake, and in so doing passed by Greenanlaghua or Greenaun. This is by repute a sidh or fairy fort, and according to the annals of Lough Cé it was the home of Aeibhill, banshee of Brian Boru and his Dalcassian ancestors. From the highest point of our walk, Lough Derg had been invisible, lost in the deep gorge, and we had had a magnificent view of range beyond range of mountains, the Silvermines, Keeper Hill, Mother Mountain, Slieve Felim, and far away towards the skyline, cloud capped Galtymore. Now the more distant peaks had vanished, but as we came to Greenaun the lake suddenly came into view far below with the noble shape of Tountinna rising beyond. So steep was the declivity that it looked as though we could lob a pebble into the lake, yet such was the scale of the landscape that a Grand Canal boat, heading down the lake towards Killaloe, was dwarfed into insignificance. It resembled a minute black slug crawling slowly over a smooth surface of frosted glass and leaving in its wake a long trail of silver.

The branch railway line to Killaloe, which extends to a lakeside quay, has been closed. When we walked along the rust reddened rails down to the quay, a donkey was dozing, head a-droop, on the platform of the forlorn little station which, incidentally, is situated in Ballina on the Tipperary shore and not in Killaloe at all. For this reason we had perforce to take a bus when we decided to visit Limerick. . . .

Our slow journey back to Waterford might well have been a tedious anti-climax to this Irish tour, but I had been at some pains to ensure that this should not be so. Having explored the river and lake sections of the Shannon so thoroughly, I was anxious to catch at least a fleeting glimpse of the Shannon estuary. A careful study of train and bus time-tables had shown me that not only could I gratify this wish, but that we could combine it with a journey over what is probably the most fascinating of the surviving Irish narrow gauge railways - the West Clare Rail line.

The West Clare was built under baronial guarantee between the years 1884 and 1892. Commencing at a junction with the broad gauge Limerick-Athenry line at Ennis, the county town of Clare, it runs north and west across the county to Lahinch. Thereafter it continues almost due south along the wild Atlantic seaboard of Clare to Moyasta Junction. Here the line forks into two branches, one terminating at the seaside town of Kilkee on the west coast, and the other at the port of Kilrush on the Shannon Estuary. The total length of the line is fifty-three miles, so it promised me the longest narrow gauge journey I had ever made. Calculating that the hotels of Kilkee would be crowded at this season, and having no liking for seaside resorts, I had sent a wire from Killaloe to William's Hotel at Kilrush, reserving a room for our last night on Irish soil. Once upon a time the Limerick Steamship Company operated a passenger service to Kilrush with which the West Clare trains ran in connection. This would have been a splendid way of rounding off our journey, but, sad to relate, like many other pleasant travelling facilities, this service has long ago been discontinued, and we should have to travel by bus to Limerick on the following morning in order to catch our Waterford train. I decided, however, that a journey over the West Clare would be well worth the inconvenience of the long bus journey, and I was not disappointed. . . .

We consigned the bulk of our luggage direct to Limerick to await our arrival there next day, and booked a first class ticket to Kilrush. We might as well enjoy this protracted journey in the maximum of comfort and seclusion. The little train, the only one of the day, was standing in the bay, and we settled ourselves in a compartment that was a period piece in itself. The seats were covered with black American cloth well studded with buttons. Braided arm rests (were they ever used?) were looped on the door pillars, and the captions of the ancient and faded photographs over the seat backs were hand written in painstaking copper-plate. To do justice to such an interior I should, I felt, be wearing a deer-stalker and an ulster, for it was in such a compartment, one imagines, that Sherlock Holmes and his Watson sped down from Paddington to Devon to investigate the mystery of Silver Blaze.

Punctually at 5.30, the train drew out. For a time we ran beside the broad gauge metals, but soon we veered away westwards and almost immediately plunged into one of the wildest tracts of country I have ever seen, country calculated to break any farmer' heart. Occasionally we sighted a solitary cabin, but for the most part we saw nothing but a wilderness of grey limestone outcrop covered with a stunted but dense scrub of thorn. At Corofin, the first important station and crossing place, the prospect improved somewhat, for there seemed to be some comparatively good pasture land between the lakes and rocks. So far we had been travelling well, certainly at no 'dreamy seven miles per hour', but now there ensued a long and laborious ascent of two and a half miles at gradients of 1 in 50 and 1 in 75 onto the summit level of the line, a boggy tract of moorland two hundred and fifty feet above sea-level. Despite this modest altitude, here, and on the long descent to Ennistymon which followed, we obtained some fine extensive views over this wild country of West Clare under a stormy sky.

At Ennistymon we made our only protracted halt. What we waited for I do not know. The fire was raked out and remade, the safety valves lifted, but still we waited. I concluded that we were waiting for an Ennis bound train to cross us, but nothing had arrived when we eventually drew out. As we did so we saw the little town clinging to the steep slopes of the gorge down which the Cullenagh River rushes to the sea.

Our train had been well filled at starting, but the majority got out at the next stop at the little seaside town of Lahinch where we passed the goods train which I had expected to see at Ennistymon. It is after leaving Lahinch that, from the scenic point of view, the most dramatic section of the line commences. It ascends steeply again for two miles, and as we panted up this long climb a truly magnificent panorama of one of the most savage, storm-swept coasts in Europe unfolded before us. We were fortunate in seeing it, not merely in clear weather, but under most dramatic conditions. Although there were dark clouds overhead, the fringe had lifted from the horizon of the western sea to leave a broad band of blue sky which, as the invisible sun sank, gradually brightened from azure to gold. Looking out towards this dazzling bar of light across the vast expanse of heaving ocean spreading without check to the Americas, it was easy to understand how tales of Hy Brasil, of magic islands in the farthest west, had fired the minds of men like Brendan. We saw the golden strand of Lahinch crooked in the elbow of Liscannor Bay, a white maelstrom of surge beating beneath the cliffs of Hag's Head beyond. And as the train moved on we saw, beyond the headland, the dark shape of Aran lying far out over Galway Bay.

Our next stop was at Milltown Malbay whence we could look down towards Spanish Point where, in 1588, six proud galleons of Spain's Armada were swept to destruction on this pitiless coast. So great is the fury of the Atlantic gales that stunted trees can only grow in the more sheltered places and even so the winds have twisted and swept their branches eastwards like manes of flying hair. At Quilty village, where the line is almost at sea-level, where station and post office are combined, and where we saw black upturned curraghs like stranded porpoises upon the beach, there is a wind gauge beside the line. If the velocity on this gauge reaches sixty miles per hour a warning message is sent down the line and only rolling stock which is specially weighted down with slabs of concrete is permitted to run. All traffic is suspended if the velocity reaches eighty miles per hour. Owing to the possibility of the warning not being received on account of telephone wires being blown down, it is a rule of the line that each stationmaster shall ask by phone whether the train may proceed. Failure to receive an answer is considered as a danger signal.

At each of these lonely, windswept stations along this wild coast we drew in to find the little platform crowded. But the anticipated invasion never came, and we realized that these primitive weather-beaten people of West Clare had simply come to the station to 'meet the train'; to gaze at this one slender link of civilization and then to return to their lonely cabins until another day brings another train and with it another fleeting glimpse of strange faces and of the world beyond Clare.

After Doonbeg Station we lost sight of the sea, cutting across the long narrow peninsula that guards the Shannon mouth and which terminates in Loop Head. It was fast gathering dark now, and a prospect more desolate than this great treeless expanse of marsh and bogland I have never seen.

Soon we drew into the triangular platform of Moyasta Junction, and here we changed into the single coach of the Kilrush train which was waiting at the opposite platform face, while our train went on to Kilkee. There was little delay, both trains starting out of the station simultaneously, and fortunately it was not yet too dark for me to see my last view of the Shannon. Swinging eastwards towards Kilrush, the line drew close to the shore and I could look out over the lonely saltings, through the narrows between Kileredann Point and Beal Bar, to where the dim majestic shape of Kerry Head marked the point where this great river is finally lost in the Atlantic. As we skirted the harbour of Kilrush, I caught a glimpse of Scattery Island with its ruined monastery of St Senan and the dark finger of its round tower. Here Brendan is said to have made his first landing on his return from that momentous second voyage. But now this most interesting of railway journeys was over, and here I should like to note, for the especial benefit of the writer of 'Nightmare Trip' if he should chance to read this book, that we drew into the platform at Kilrush exactly on time.

There is little more to tell. Our hotel, which was an unknown quantity, proved to be clean and comfortable. We partook of an excellent meal followed by an equally good breakfast next morning. The bus conveyed us conveniently to the station yard at Limerick where we retrieved the rest of our luggage and entrained for Waterford. Altogether we voted our somewhat unusual choice of return route an unqualified success. I shall always remember my journey over the West Clare line. It was an experience which I should have been very sorry to miss, and one which is the more precious because I fear that before many years have passed, unless the public taste for travel changes, it may no longer be possible to repeat it.

Extracts taken from L. T. C. Rolt, *Green and Silver* (London 1949), pp 210-50.

Charles Graves, Clare Revisited, 1948

Charles Patrick Graves, journalist and author, was educated at Charterhouse, a private secondary school for boys, in Surrey, England and graduated an M.A. of St John's College, Oxford. Initially he was employed as a columnist by several newspapers including the *Sunday Express, Daily Mail* and *News of the World.* Apart from his newspaper activities, he wrote novels, travel books and some historical works. It was chiefly as a travel writer that he established his reputation, with such works as *Triptyque to Spain, Swiss Summer, Rivera Revisited, Italy Revisited, A Rich Man's Guide to Europe* etc. He wrote some forty-five books during his lifetime including *A Regimental History of the Ulster Rifles.* He resided in Guernsey in the Channel Islands where he described his recreations as golf and gin and rummy. He died in February 1971 aged seventy two. Graves came to Ireland in 1948 just as the post war tourist industry was striving to re-establish itself. He was immediately aware of the tremendous impact Shannon Airport was having on Ennis and the potential of air travel in general for the transformation of the mid-western region. American air crews stayed at the Old Ground Hotel and Dutch and Norwegian air hostesses commuted between Ennis, Shannon, Frankfort and Berlin. The scenes were light years removed from the situation that had prevailed just one hundred years previously, when hoards of half starved beggars besieged the mail coach passengers arriving in the town.

But it was now time to go on, and we drove off next day through the smiling country-side to Ennis. This took us by the same route to within two or three miles of the airport, before we branched right at the village of Bunratty. Next came Castle Clare, with more tinkers and piebald ponies and cottages, alternately thatched and corrugated.

If you look up Ennis in the guide-book you will read:

> A queer, small town with narrow streets and courts. Its modern attractions are a very good classic court-house built of grey marble, a new and handsome church, and a lunatic asylum built at a cost of £54,000.

But the guide-book is out of date, and the greatest attraction of Ennis today is Shannon Airport. From being a quiet little hamlet, Ennis has become the most prosperous place in all Ireland. Being only twelve miles away from Rineanna, it is used as an over-night village, not only by the captains, navigators, and the rest of the aircrews of American Overseas Airlines, but also by VIPs. The aircrews have a two days' break before and after flying the Atlantic. Owing to weather conditions they arrive at all hours of the day and night, and a complete staff has to be available all round the clock to greet them, cook for them, and look after them.

The Old Ground Hotel is an eighteen-century coaching hostelry with a complete new wing added for the American aircrews. The food is superb, while the proprietress is the youngest and prettiest hotel keeper I have ever met. Her name is Josette O'Reagan. She has golden hair, and celebrated her twenty-fourth birthday in May, 1948. She told me that her monthly meat bill was on average £422; her poultry bill was £200; her bill for fish was £90; general provisions were £1,200 a month; fuel and heating £100; electricity the same. The meat bill alone must have been greater than that of all the first-class hotels in London put together for the same period. And all of it was bought locally. So, too, were all the provisions and other edibles.

The inhabitants of Ennis benefit in many ways from their unique position. Every room in the little town was taken, and sixty new houses were being built. A hundred wireless operators employed at the airport has settled-in with their wives. So had the advance guard of the Flight Refuelling Department of BOAC. The local shops were doing a roaring trade in Irish tweeds, Irish shirts, Irish ties, and Irish souvenirs of every description. The bars were doing a roaring trade too. Local garages were booming, and so were the local livery stables and the local golf course.

The American aircrews certainly had a wonderful time at Ennis. They wore very colourful clothes, usually red plaid shirts over their trousers. They were very fond of saying: 'The top o' the morning to ye!' and 'Begorra!'- expressions only used by stage Irishmen. On fine days they would be sent by Miss O'Regan on picnics to Lahinch, and given their steaks to broil. When there was that strike of transatlantic pilots many of them were at Ennis, and had to live on IOUs. Then one day Denis, the hotel porter, informed them that word had just been received from Shannon Airport that they were all to go back on a cattle boat from Belfast, paying their own passage.

This hoax was a great success. In the meantime they had to wash their own shirts and socks until the strike was successful and their demand for more money was met. According to Miss O'Regan the pilots were easy to amuse and not at all rowdy. At night they would play charades, and by day I saw them hard at work trying to learn the intricacies of croquet. In spite of their desire to learn Irish words they still called cakes 'cookies,' and as a special treat would be given 'flaming Alaska.' This is ice-cream, with sherry and cake and beaten white of egg, toasted with granulated sugar, and then set alight with brandy.

There were four airhostesses - two Dutch and two Norwegian - permanently based at Ennis because they could speak German and commute between Shannon, Frankfort, and Berlin.

Miss O'Regan extracted implicit obedience from everybody with a smile and a shake of her golden head. She was the queen of 'Overnight Village,' and nobody disputed her sovereignty. She escorted us round the new wing specially built for the Americans. On some doors was the notice; 'Sleeping. Do not disturb.' On others was the notice: 'This room is ready for cleaning.' We peeped into one or two of them. They were charmingly furnished. In each was at least one pack of cards.

One of the pilots told us that we must at all costs have a special egg nog at Fanny O'Dea's on the road to Kilkee. He also said that the local urchins were as bad as the Cockneys in calling out: 'Any gum, chum?' He thought, however, that they believed that 'gum-chum' was all one word and just meant candy.

We now decided to take a look at Ennis itself. A white flag flying from the Old Ground Hotel told us that a funeral was in progress, and we were just in time to see the procession from the doorway of Denny Healy's bar. Funerals are to the Twenty-six Counties what a visit by Royalty is in England. On this occasion it was a particularly good funeral because the dead man was a publican. Two priests and a Franciscan friar led the way, followed by four carriages drawn by dark brown cobs, with the chief mourners in silk hats. Then came about two hundred people walking in column of fours. It looked as though it had been a very wet 'wake' the night before.

Ennis has the inevitable statue to Daniel O'Connell, and a main square from which several narrow streets radiate. The local surnames consist chiefly of Malones, Slatterys, Kellys, Caseys, and McNerneys, with a good sprinkling of Powers, Butlers, Quinns, Mahons, and Burkes. The best bar, somewhat late at night, is Carmody's. We did not visit the Franciscan monastery, nor the court-house, but we had a drink at Senator Honan's bar, which had fluorescent lighting.

Once again it was time to go on. The road led through orange-red ploughland, something like Devonshire, and across a green wooded country-side which soon gave place to real heather and stone walls and thatched cottages. A cemetery on a tall hill told us that we were now approaching Ennistymon, best known for the white-roofed Falls Hotel, named after a cascade on the River Collenagh. The town is full of little white cottages in rows. It is also full of garages.

Two or three miles away is Lahinch with its magnificent golf course and (in 1948) a brand-new club-house. It contains shower-baths and bathrooms, and cost nearly £10,000 to erect. The course itself has a number of famous holes - the Dell, the Klondyke, the Shore hole, the Valley hole, and the Road hole. It is only possible to go out of bounds at the seventeenth and the eighteenth, and Lahinch is regarded by many Irishmen as superior even to Portmarnock. But how these Irish love to warn you. Approaching the club-house is a large notice which says: 'Danger. Beware of golf balls in flight.' The golf club is one of the oldest in Ireland, having been laid out in 1892, and its chief character is Johnny Barrett, the caddy-master. I would have given a great deal to play a complete round at Lahinch, but time pressed once again, and we had to be on our way.

The only road out of Lahinch, as far as we could see, led back to Ennistymon, where we drove off through a pretty, green valley with rustic bridges and turf carts. A small boy was apparently practising Yoga by deliberately walking barefoot on the piles of sharp stones by the roadside.

Our next stop was Lisdoonvarna. This is a real Irish spa, with sulphur baths, ionization, massage, wax baths, and foam baths. There are eleven large hotels in the scattered little town. One of them, the State hotel, looks very smart indeed with its green and red bawneen. Lisdoonvarna is barely four miles from the Atlantic and about four hundred feet above sea-level. The mineral springs are said to be particularly good for rheumatism and glandular deficiencies, whatever those may be.

The countryside is really rocky, with hardly a bush in sight, much less a tree, and the fields look as though they had been deliberately sown with dragons' teeth. Said Mackey: 'There's scarcely room to grow a geranium.' Nor was this much of an exaggeration. It is really poverty-stricken ground, and recalls the brutality of Cromwell's instruction to the 'displaced persons' of the seventeenth century - to go to hell or Connaught.

After a few miles the countryside becomes even more desolate. It consists of nothing but miles upon miles of rocks and crags - so many of them that they look like daisies. There was not even a plover in sight, and Mackey made one of his more appalling puns. 'You could get anything at rock-bottom prices here, I should think,' he said, adding; 'imagine going barefoot at night across one of them lawns.'

There were whole terraces of rocks on the alleged fields near the road. How anybody could ever have thought it worth while to attempt cultivation was a real problem.

The road, apparently tired of the fantastic scene, now took a sudden zigzag descent to the shores of the blue Bay of Galway. It is known as the Corkscrew, and deserves its name. Even a London taxi-cab driver would find difficulty in negotiating some of the hairpin bends.

Then a charming wood came into view, surrounded though it was by these glacier stone terraces. 'Cregan's [Gregan's] Castle. Licensed,' caught the eye at the next turn of the road. The hotel itself was entirely hidden by copper beeches and chestnuts, but up to the left was a real rock mountain which looked just as if someone had poured molten stone over the green hill. Then came another, to the right, which looked even more like pure molten rock. You would not have thought that there was enough grazing for a single rabbit, and yet walls zigzagged up the slope to separate one alleged field from the next. There was, it is true, one tiny section of ploughland, but how on earth the inhabitants of Ballyvaughan live off the land was yet another problem, unless they live on the botanists who come to look for various rare plants usually found only in the Alps.

The road now follows the coast of Galway Bay; and very beautiful it is, with little old towers and carts full of seaweed, and women with sacks of fresh shorn wool over their arms trudging along the road which turns inland again to a valley with still more fantastic outcrops of rock. So it was quite astonishing to see a big new chapel which must have been erected recently. Mackey was positively angry about it. 'I am as good a Catholic as any wan,' said he, 'but many a poor man has done without his pint and his baccy for years to help pay for that.' I must say that it looked much too expensive for so poor a district.

It was just along here, at Newquay, that we were stopped for the first time by a guard, who asked for Mackey's driving licence. Mackey enjoyed himself hugely by showing him a very special licence for seven-passenger cars. The guard had evidently never seen one before and looked somewhat disgusted. There was little doubt that the only reason for his stopping us was to enjoy a nice piece of conversation, but Mackey has foiled him.

We were now running into O'Dea country, and saw not only our first swallow but our first big sow by the roadside, a surprisingly rare sight in Ireland . . . .

Kinvara is a lovely little village. It might be described as the Fowey of Clare. Many artists have painted it and its white swans, little old castle, and midget harbour. Here I saw an official differentiation between English and Irish measurements. The notice read: '14 Irish miles to Galway, or 17½ English miles.'

Taken from Charles Graves, *Ireland Revisited* (London 1949), pp 141-45.

Frank Clune, Land of Hope and Glory, 1949

A very different visitor to Clare in 1949 was the Australian writer Frank Clune. Born in Sydney, 1893, the son of George Clune, a labourer who had emigrated from Ruan, County Clare. Clune left school at the age of fourteen and after various jobs joined the United States Army in Kansas in 1911. Deserting the American army, he joined the Australian Imperial Force in 1915. Wounded in both legs at Gallipoli, he returned to Australia and was discharged from the army. He took a job as a commercial traveller and at night studied accountancy. In 1924 he established a tax consultancy firm. His first book, *Try Anything Once* (1933), an account of his adventures at sea as a trooper and as a mouse trap salesman, was an immediate success and sold tens of thousands of copies. He quickly followed with *Rolling Down the Lachan* (1935), and *Roaming Round the Darling* (1936), speedily written accounts of his travels and adventures in Australia. Clune had a rough and ready prose style and forthrightly expressed his nationalism. His combination of historical detail, narratives of explorers and contemporary political observation found a ready market. His travel books covered Europe, the Pacific, the Middle East, Asia and North America. Clune's readability and his capacity to sound like an ordinary, enthusiastic traveller brought him wide popularity. By 1952 he estimated that his twenty three books had sold over one million copies. His approach is summed up in the first number of the short lived *Frank Clune's Adventure Magazine* (1948), in which he declared 'We don't want stories of snoopy sex, written by anaemic lounge lizards and pub crawlers. Action is the password to these pages. This is reading for men with red blood in their arteries.' Although his fifty-ninth and last book appeared in 1968, he had continued to practise as a tax consultant in partnership with his eldest son. He died in March 1971 and was buried with Catholic rites at Darlinghurst, New South Wales.

At half an hour after midnight, the Constellation glided down and gently alighted at Rineanna field, on a promontory in the estuary of the Shannon. I saw the lights of the airport whirling by our windows as the monster machine taxied to a stop. The door opened, and a neatly-garbed Irish colleen entered the passenger-compartment. Her flashing dark eyes had a twinkle of merriment in them. Evidently she was a receptionist. You could have knocked me down with a feather when she spoke three words in Gaelic, and I understood her perfectly.

'*Caede mille faethe!*' she said.

'*Erin go bragh!*' was my answer to that.

The sparkling-eyed colleen continued her greetings in the Sassenach language, with a lovely brogue: 'Good evening, ladies and gentlemen. You are welcome to Ireland. The clock goes back one hour here. Will you come this way, please, to the lounge, where you have a wait of two hours, while your plane is being refuelled.'

Sleepily the passengers, kids and all, piled out to the lounge, and there I saw a sign in the convoluted Gaelic script: *Post Oifis*. That seemed to me to be Sassenach very thinly disguised. I reckoned I'd soon learn to speak Irish, if it was all as easy as that - but it wasn't.

There was a letter for me at the *post oifis*. It was from my relations, to say that they'd meet me at the Olde Grounde Hotel in Ennis town at breakfast-time.

Mick Brendan, owner of the Olde Grounde, was there at the airfield to drive me to Ennis Town, twenty miles away. Now at last I had set foot on Irish soil, and soon I was in an automobile, whizzing along a good highway, by the banks of the Fergus River, tributary of the Shannon, to bed down in Ennis in that modern hostelry, the Olde Grounde.

Just as I was dropping off to sleep, I began to wonder if there had been perchance anything peculiar about my Dad's departure from Clare, nigh on six decades previously. Had he left any debts, or done any misdeeds of which I knew naught? . . .

On the morning of my arrival, after breakfast, my relations came to the Olde Grounde Hotel to make my acquaintance, I don't know how many came, but it was a great number. The word had gone around, and they all wanted to see the 'cousin from Australia.' For the first time in my life, I realized that I was a member of a clan.

The Clune clan! My head in a whirl, I met cousins, second-cousins, cousins once or twice removed, nephews, nieces, uncles, aunts, in-laws, out-laws, friends of my father, and the children of my father's friends. It was an amazing experience for me, and the most amazing of all was the happiness, the cheerfulness, the festive atmosphere of excitement. Nearly a lifetime ago, George Clune went away to Australia, and seemingly forgot all about his relations in Clare; but they didn't forget him, and they wanted to see what his son was like, Cousin Frank, the hard-dialled, bespectacled, middle-aged stranger, come back to his father's home. Suddenly I realized the tragedy of Irish emigration - my father and four of his brothers gone away to foreign lands, leaving one brother and two sisters at home.

For those who went away, new scenes, new interests, new experiences gradually weaned them from their Irish background; but the old folks at home were still now, in heart and mind and ways, as Irish as they had been for centuries unnumbered. All over Ireland, I realized, the homecoming of exiles, and of the children of exiles, was an occasion of festivity and of thanking God. Every Irish family has relatives abroad, in foreign, faraway lands. Perhaps there are three times as many Irish people living outside Ireland as in Ireland. Yet those who have remained in Ireland are the only ones now truly Irish. All the others are subtly changed.

As the Clune clan jubilantly surrounded me, and overwhelmed me with a Hundred Thousand Welcomes, I was dazed by the sudden overnight change from England's frigid, polite, 'correct' atmosphere. The people of Ireland - my relations, anyhow - seemed one hundred percent alive and merry. Jokes and wit and the delightful 'brogue' surged around me like the sea. The men shook hands heartily, the girl cousins, aunts and nieces thought it quite the correct thing to bestow cousinly kisses on the wayfarer from Down Under. After the first shock, I realized what a great chance I had. So I kissed every colleen in sight, without fear of a reprimand - and there were many colleens.

The first excitement over, I went out by car, seven miles, to see my father's old home. Through the streets of Ennis, past Daniel O'Connell's statue and the ruined abbey, and the bridge across the Fergus, and the ruins of the round tower of Drumcliff, and all the time through a landscape of brilliant green-grassed fields, with hedgerows of white-flowering hawthorn, and white-washed cottages with brown-thatched roofs dotted about in the farm-land rectangles, undulating over the hill and dale, with mountains beyond - ah, it was Ireland, the land of fairies and leprechauns, just what Ireland is supposed to be like, and that is how it was! So after seven miles we came to the village of Ruan, and, a hundred yards beyond, to Tullyodea farm, where my father's father had tilled the soil and raised a family of six sons and two daughters.

'Tully' is pronounced to rhyme with 'fully', and is apparently derived from the name of Saint Tola, a holy hermit who lived and died in Clare twelve centuries ago. The O'Deas were one of the Clare clans, descended from King Cas, the founder of the Dalcassian dynasty. 'O'Dea' rhymes with 'break o' day' - and so you have Tullyodea, a farm with a history, every stone and every sod in it steeped in tradition.

From the door of the solid, stone-built, whitewashed, thatched farm-house emerged an elderly, motherly woman, who put her arms around me and said, 'Glory be to God! 'Tis me cousin George's boy from Australia. Welcome to your father's home. Welcome to Ireland!'

This was my cousin Bridget, daughter of my Dad's brother Jim, who had stayed on at Tullyodea farm when all his brothers emigrated. Now my Uncle Jim was dead, and his daughter Bridget, married to Michael Hogan, lived at Tullodea. They had nine children - seven girls and two boys. Four of the girls, and the two boys, lived at home, helping their parents. A healthy, happy lot of people they were, overwhelming me with the warmth of their welcome.

A wave of sentimental emotion swept over me, an upsurge of a feeling rare to me, as I heard Cousin Bridget saying, 'You can sleep in your father's bed, Francis!' She led me into a farmhouse room, simply and solidly furnished, spotlessly clean. 'Your father's room,' I heard her say, but suddenly it all seemed misted. I couldn't speak. Rudely I pushed Cousin Bridget out of the room so that she wouldn't see the tears that began running down my cheeks.

What is it that creates the upflow of emotion in the hard breast of a man? I have wandered the world, buffeted and bashed. I have seen wars, plagues, pestilence and poverty, gradually covering myself with a shield of hardness, immune to it all. Then suddenly, and to me quite unexpectedly, after I had travelled thirteen thousand miles from the Antipodes, I go to make a casual visit to relatives of whom I had heard only vaguely, and I find myself in an atmosphere of home, of friendliness, of belonging. It was too much for me altogether. Seldom in my life have I been at a loss for words. Usually I can crack back, wisely or wrongly, with a retort courteous - or otherwise - as occasion demands. But now I was dumb. . . .

Now that we're acquainted, let's go for a walk. The farm is thirty acres of splendid land, suitable for grazing or for ploughing. The fences between the fields are walls of stones, which have been picked up, dug up and heaped up for hundreds of years, to speed the plough. A few sheep, a few pigs, a dozen cows and two plough-horses comprise the livestock. My cousin, Mick Hogan, is a sound practical farmer, and every inch of his land is used to its fullest advantage. In Australia we'd think the farm small for the support of such a large family. Indeed, and it is small, too, and that's why so many of Ireland's sons and daughters have emigrated to foreign parts.

That's why my Dad and his four brothers emigrated, leaving Uncle Jim at Tullyodea. How could the five men of that family make a living and raise families of their own on thirty acres? Impossible - and there are no vacant, unoccupied waste lands awaiting development in Erin. Every acre has already been tilled for centuries. Emigrate or starve was the alternative.

The Government of the Irish Free State today is attempting, by a huge scheme of electrification from the Shannon River, to increase Ireland's population-carrying capacity. The idea is to encourage the development of industries, and so to prevent the Irish people from having to emigrate. This is a policy that is undoubtedly succeeding, to a certain extent, but Irish people are prolific breeders. There will be a human surplus for export from Eire, for a long time yet to come.

The farmhouse at Tullyodea, is spacious - stone-built, with white-washed walls and a thatched roof. It has two stories, and many rooms, and was built at least two hundred years ago. It is a house built for large families, with plenty of work for the girls of the family to do in it. For instance, the water is pumped by hand from a well outside, and carried into the kitchen in buckets. All the cooking is done at an open fireplace, in the fashion of our very forefathers from time immemorial. It has very few modern conveniences, but plenty of ancient inconveniences in its solid, enduring structure. . . .

Going into the village of Ruan, I entered the tiny *post oifis*, and met Miss Margaret O'Donnell, the postmistress, grey-haired and bent, but full of life and charm. She remembers my father as he was sixty years ago. He was a grown man then, and Margaret was only a school-kid, but she remembers him well - and indeed she remembers everybody who has lived in Ruan for the past six or seven decades, since she herself has lived in Ruan all her life. But so have most of the people who are still there! They are the stay-at-homes, and practically all of them have relations in faraway countries, particularly in America and Australia. . . .

After taking tea I went back to Ruan, and met John Leydon, the schoolmaster, who had been a teacher for fifty years, forty of them at Ruan National School. He told me that the school was built in 1831, the year that National Schools were first introduced into Ireland.

'I suppose you've seen many changes here in the last forty years,' I hazarded.

'Oh yes,' said the schoolmaster. 'In 1909, when I first came to teach here, we had ninety-one pupils. Now we have only forty-three.'

'What's the cause of the decline?'

'Emigrations, famines and wars! The number of pupils enrolled depends on conditions in the country. When there's a famine, or civil wars, and troubles, the young men emigrate, or get killed. That leaves only the girls to stay at home and work the farms. They become old maids, and naturally fewer children are born. So eventually school attendances decline. We are still suffering from the effects of the Civil War that lasted from 1916 to 1922. Many young men were killed during those troubles, others emigrated, others again were killed as volunteers in the English Army during England's two big wars against Germany. That's why the population of this district has declined - at any rate the school attendance has declined from what it was fifty years ago,' said the schoolmaster, sadly.

He showed me over the school, a solidly-built structure, with brick walls thirty inches thick. Places like that are constructed to last for centuries. 'Gaelic is the national language of Éire, and is taught to all the children in school,' said teacher John. 'We use Gaelic to impart instruction in the Three R's and other school subjects. We also teach English, as a foreign language.'

'Oh,' I said. 'So the use of Gaelic is compulsory?'

'Yes, in the same way that the use of English is compulsory in English schools, and French is compulsory in French schools! So naturally we use Irish in Irish schools - why not?'

Not feeling competent to conduct an argument on the language question (since I am mono-lingual), I later asked some of the younger people in Ruan what they thought of the Gaelic language as a medium of conversation, literary expression, and learning. They did not seem enthusiastic. It may take two or three generations before all Irish children will have learned Gaelic at school, and grown up to predominate in the country. At present, only a few of the oldsters can speak Gaelic fluently, so English is still used in the homes, while Gaelic is used at school. . . .

The policy of using Gaelic for instruction in schools will eventually make everybody in Ireland bi-lingual. After, say, another fifty years, every man, woman and child in Ireland will be able to speak and understand Gaelic. It will then be seen whether the Gaelic tongue will again become, as it used to be, the 'natural' language, spoken in the homes of the people, or whether it will remain, as it is today, a kind of poetic or scholastic achievement, like knowing Latin, useful for archaic purposes. . . .

Bidding farewell to Ruan's schoolmaster, I rambled down the village street to Saint Mary's Church, the outstanding building in Ruan, not of very great antiquity, as it was rebuilt, on the site of an old church, in July 1910. Irish and English villages appear to be built around the church, just as Burmese and Siamese villages are built around a pagoda. The church is the symbol of permanence - the place where the people are married, baptised and buried, where they ease their minds by confessing their sins, and where they go for fatherly advice, and where they meet on Sundays in their best garb, spruced up, the members of an enduring community which goes on, despite deaths and emigrations. . . .

Inside Saint Mary's Church at Ruan I read a plate on the marble altar, engraved: 'Erected by the most Reverend Patrick Clune, D.D., Archbishop of Perth, Western Australia, and the Reverend Francis Clune, C.P., of Marrickville, New South Wales, in memory of their father and mother, of Auchrim, Ruan, and of their deceased brothers and sisters. R.I.P. Pray for the donors, A.D. 1914.'

These two eminent ecclesiastics were my father's cousins who emigrated to Australia, and rose to the top of the tree, or near it; but I soon discovered that I had other cousins, or second-cousins, in Éire, and indeed in County Clare, who were priests and nuns, among them Sister Mary Colman, and the Reverends George Clune and James Clune, of Ennis. Crikey, I thought, I belong to a religious family! But there are so many Clunes in Clare that it is only reasonable to expect some clerics among them. . . .

Born at Ruan in 1863, [Patrick Clune, Archbishop of Perth, Western Australia] was educated at Saint Flannan's College, in Ennis Town, and at All Hallows' College, Dublin. Ordained priest in 1886, he was attached to the Goulburn Diocese in New South Wales until 1893, then returned to Ireland and became a Redemptorist Missionary. In the year 1899 he went out to Western Australia, at the invitation of Bishop Gibney of Perth, and became Rector of the Redemptorist Monastery there. In 1911 he was consecrated Bishop of Perth, by Cardinal Moran, and two years later his See was raised to archiepiscopal status, and he became the first Archbishop of Perth.

Great was his fame as 'the golden orator of the Golden West', and it was then, about 1913, that I met him for the first time in my life. Having deserted from a German tramp steamer in Fremantle Port, I went penniless and shirtless to the Archbishop's Palace in Perth, and told him who I was. An hour later I departed with a full belly and ten golden sovereigns in my pocket, with which I made a new start in life. So I can testify that the Archbishop was as generous as he was eloquent. . . .

Five miles from Ruan we stopped at the parish church of Dysart O'Dea where the Reverend Father Gunning, Parish Priest, went through the baptismal records, until, after turning many pages written in ink now faded and hard to decipher, he found the entry referring to my father's baptism. George, the son of Michael Clune and his wife Anne, born Anne Casey, was baptised on 17th day of November, 1861, the sponsors being Terence O'Brien and Catherine Casey. . . .

It wasn't until I visited Ireland, and mooched around among the ruins of bygone castles and abbeys in Clare, that I realized how history remains continuous for people who stay in one place. I had often heard, as a boy in Australia, of the 'sorrows of Ireland'. It was only words, words, words, as far as I was concerned. Then when I saw the ruins of proud castles, those antique sorrows became real, and lived again in the imagination, until five hundred years ago seemed only yesterday, or the day before.

One of my trips was to Inchiquin Castle, four miles from Ennis, or what's left of it now after robbers, raiders, marauders and conquerors have burned, looted, and sacked it for centuries - not much!

Inchiquin Castle was built on the shores of Inchiquin Lake. The word means 'Innis O'Quin', or the Island of the Quins. It was an ancient stronghold of that warlike tribe.

Near by is the village of Quin, where every inhabitant has the name of Clune. Yes, everybody who lives in that village has the same moniker as mine! Never in my life had I felt so deflated. Gone was an illusion of uniqueness or scarcity in my patronymic. There were Clunes galore in Quin - Clunes, Clunes everywhere. Apparently my Clune grancestors had been raiders, who wiped out the Quins, drove them from their stronghold, or else perhaps married the Quin girls and settled down happy ever after in the Quin demesnes. . . .

After spending three days at Tullyodea farm, and wandering around the ruins of Ruan's neighbourhood, I decided to fly up to Dublin, one hundred and twenty-two miles and only an hour's flying-distance from Rineanna. Yes, Dublin's now only an hour's journey from the west of Ireland, and that's another of those shocks you get nowadays, if you haven't fully realized how air-travel had folded space into concertina-compression. There once was a time - not so long ago - when the west of Ireland was a remote and inaccessible region, a full day's journey by train from Dublin. And now you can hop right across Ireland in two shakes of a lamb's tail like a flea with Saint Vitus's Dance, and the good old days of dawdle and loiter have gone for ever . . . .

Twelve noon, and I was waiting at Tullyodea for the taxi-driver from Ennis who had been engaged to drive me the twenty-six miles to Rineanna airport.

Twelve-thirty, and I was still waiting, so we telephoned to inquire. Pat's missus answered the phone, and said that Pat must have forgotten me, but she'd send somebody else. At 1.30 p.m., the substitute arrived in a rattling Ford and said, with a broad grin and a broader brogue, that sure he'd get me to the airport in time.

Hasty hugs and cousinly kisses to the colleens, and off I was rattled at crazy speed along a narrow lane-road that was designed, two or three thousand years ago, for jaunting cars driven by drunks, to dodge trees, castles and fairy forts. Now we dodged donkey-carts, fowls, pigs in pokes, and cursing pedestrians as my driver stepped on the throttle for the honour of Éire, to get me to Rineanna on time, or die in the attempt. . . .

Along a tarred road, between white-thorn hedges, in flower and fragrant, or anon between stone-heaped walls we sped, and, rolling around the turns, reached Newmarket on Fergus, then, with a final dash along a concreted stretch for five miles in five minutes, we arrived at Rineanna, glory be to God, alive and with four minutes to spare, weighed in, paid out and climbed aboard the D.C.3 aircraft bound for Dublin, per Aer Lingus, just as the gangway was being wheeled clear.

Extracts taken from Frank Clune, *Land of Hope and Glory* (Sydney 1949), pp 82-110.

Frank O'Connor, A Tour of Clare, 1950

Frank O'Connor (pseudonym of Michael O'Donovan), was a short story writer, translator and novelist. Born in Cork, he was raised in poverty by a devoted mother largely in the absence of his father who was in the British Army. He left school at the age of twelve but read voraciously and came under the influence of Daniel Corkery who directed him to Gaelic poetry and nationalism. O'Connor took the republican side in the civil war and was interned in Gormanstown in 1923. His first volume of short stories *Guest of the Nation* drew on his wartime experiences and contrasted the romantic idealism of the struggle and the barbarism of warfare. After his release O'Connor became a librarian and established himself in Dublin literary circles. In the 1940s much of his best work was banned under the Censorship Act, notably in 1945 his translation of Brian Merriman's *Cuirt An Mhean-Oiche*, which his opponents rightly saw as a criticism of contemporary Ireland. In his book *Leinster, Munster and Connaught*, written towards the end of the 1940s, O'Connor is clearly bitter towards those who, though unable to read Merriman, condemned his translation out of hand. He is particularly harsh in his criticism of Clare County Council who refused to raise a memorial in the poet's honour. Increasingly frustrated with life in Ireland, and finding it difficult to make a living, O'Connor contemplated leaving. The breakdown of his marriage finally decided him and in 1951 he emigrated to the United States where he lectured on the university circuit and wrote three critical works on Irish literature. Returning to Ireland in 1960, he became an inspiration to Ireland's younger writers and when he died in 1966 his graveside oration was delivered by Brendan Kennelly.

The main road from Limerick to Ennis follows first the Shannon and then its tributary, the Fergus, passing on its way the fine old castle of Bunratty, which guards the bridge over its little river in perilous juxtaposition to Shannon Airport. I have no doubt that already some engineer has drawn up plans involving the demolition of this charming old bridge, which, with its ruined castle, its Georgian manor-house and a few bits of ruined chapel, is all that remains of an Irish attempt at a village. The castle contains some interesting plasterwork.

The back road, a little before you come to Bunratty, runs through Sixmilebridge and Quin. Sixmilebridge is a nice eighteenth-century village intended for a prosperous future it never attained, and it contains one of the most beautiful of Irish houses of Queen Anne date, Mount Ivers. This is a very tall house, more like a tower than a house, with tall steps, tall, narrow doorways and tall windows, all with the original heavy sashes. It replaced a fortified house, of which the main chimney piece is in the hall, and it contains a number of fine mantelpieces by Bossi. There is also a painting of the house as it was intended to be and never became, with gardens like those of a French château. A tall house with tall notions, for you have only to mount the stairs to see where the money gave out on the first landing, and the windows are still unpanelled, and in the attics you can see the plaster centre-pieces all ready to be fixed up, and can visualise that sad morning when carpenters and plasterers realised that they would never be paid and set off on the journey back to Limerick.

Quin, which also lies on this back road, is the completest of the Irish Franciscan monasteries, and in a country where so many things are incomplete it would be interesting on that account alone. . . .

The Franciscan monastery at Ennis, built a hundred and fifty years earlier, is a far finer building, though the tower was badly knocked about by some nineteenth century restorer who didn't think the battlementing austere enough and changed it for spikes. . . .

Ennis must have been a very wealthy monastery. It has a mass of carved work - a St Francis, a Christ, a Virgin and Child; none very good, though all deeply interesting - as well as some fine tombs, or the remains of them. One is in smithereens, though a couple of labourers could put it together in a few days. The other, a nineteenth-century monstrosity, has been eked out with five beautiful panels of the Passion, imitated from English alabaster work of the period. These are rotting away in the open air, and Ennis should be ashamed of the fact. A town with three first-rate hotels should know better. . . .

But the whole county is rich in peculiar little churches with fascinating decorative detail. Take, for instance, Dysert O'Dea, off the road to Corofin, about seven miles out of Ennis. This was apparently a rich monastery, because the east window of the little church was put together, apparently by the village idiot, with bits and pieces of carved stone in half a dozen different styles. The south doorway, though it, too seems to have been badly mucked about, is a splendid bit of work, with noble jambs and soffits carved in the boldest of decorated chevron patterns, and among the archstones is an outer row of mingled beakheads and human heads of a distinctly Mongolian cast. This ranks with the best Romanesque carving in Ireland, and one would dearly love to know something about the masons who were responsible for it and about their patrons. . . .

The ideal time to see Killaloe is after dark on a wet and stormy night, as a few friends and myself last saw it. Once inside the door, nothing whatever could be discerned but the three tall, pale pencils of light from the east window, so narrow that one could scarcely imagine them giving light at all, while those along the quire might just as well not have been there. Finally, after we had let this sink in, I managed to find the lighting switches in the transept, and the splendid lighting system picked out the whole decorated expanse of the east wall, leaving the rest of the church almost in darkness. Outside, the rain fell, the wind whistled, but we stood there entranced. Rarely have I experienced anything in Ireland so satisfyingly beautiful.

That matter of the Romanesque work built into an Early Gothic building can be pursued farther up the lake in the nasty little hamlet of Tomgraney. Tomgraney Church was here when Brian Boru was a boy; he must have frequently visited it, and he presented it with a belfry which had disappeared (I only wish the present one would do the same, for it is a ponderous little Victorian structure which has caused the high gable of the old church to be lowered). It is the only tenth-century Irish church still in use. . .

Up the hills over the Shannon, just off the road between Tomgraney and Quin, is the little village of Feakle. This locality is doubly famous, principally as the headquarters of Biddy Early, whom all readers of Yeats rapidly tire of hearing about. Biddy was a witch, and she had the second sight, and the greatest praise Yeats has for any old woman is that she resembled Biddy Early. Like other wise women, she had her bottles of medicine, and with these she also had a bottle, which served her as a crystal and told her whether or not she could help the patient. If the patient had any doubts about her powers, the bottle registered the fact. If he hadn't, she gave him a bottle of medicine and a warning as to the occult powers which would try to deprive him of the bottle; it might be no more than the shying of his horse, or the slipperiness of the road, or frogs crossing the road between Kilbarron Cross and Hayes' Forge, but whatever it was she warned him against, it was bound to happen. The priest threatened to put a curse on anyone going to her himself or showing others the way to her house. On her death-bed she is supposed to have handed over the crystal to the priest, who thereupon threw it into Kilbarron Lake. It is there still, so I am told, and ever since there have been no fish in the lake. I haven't tried: if I did I should probably find millions, I am that unsusceptible to charms and spells.

The second great figure is Bryan Merryman, the poet. He is one of the most curious figures in Irish literary history. For the usual five or ten pounds a year he taught in the hedge school at Knocknageeha, eked it out with a little farming, and somehow or other managed to read and assimilate a great deal of contemporary literature. Local tradition describes him as a master of Greek, Latin and English. Even with compulsory education, the English language and county libraries, you would be hard set today to find a Clareman of Merryman's class. . .

After [*The Midnight Court*] Merryman never wrote again. If, as tradition says, he was a United Irishman, the very urge to write must have been destroyed by the failure of the '98. About 1799 he went to live in Limerick with his daughter and her husband, Michael Ryan, a tailor, and died suddenly in 1805 in a house in Clare Street, which you still can see. He was brought back to Feakle for burial.

Why did he go there? Probably because what Professor Corkery sneers at as 'his much-enlightened soul' longed for some sort of intellectual society. To say that the man was 150 years before his time would be mere optimism. When my translation of the poem appeared it was immediately banned by the Southern Irish Government. My publisher appealed against the ban, but the appeal was rejected without hearing witnesses or counsel for the defence. Professor James Hogan, well known to all who know Cork well, wrote to the papers to say it was an immoral poem, though he admitted that he couldn't read it. Neither, apparently, could any other member of the Board, but somebody had told them that two lines were inaccurately translated. I regret to say there were at least twenty.

But then began the comedy of the memorial. In my translation I had pointed out that Merryman had none and was never likely to get it. This was admittedly a try-on, and it produced instant results. A fund was started to erect a memorial over his grave in Feakle, and Mr de Valera, whose Government had banned the translation of the poem, was the first subscriber. Then followed a long correspondence in a Clare paper denouncing the proposal to erect a monument in a decent Clare graveyard to a dirty ruffian the likes of that. One public man declared that if such an infamous thing was permitted he would tear the thing down with his own hands. Another suggested that Merryman was really a decent Clareman, and anything that was wrong in the poem had been introduced by someone else - a Corkman, no doubt. The damage is always done by the boys from another parish. Even Merryman's good national record availed him nothing. The Clare County Council refused to permit the erection of the monument, and the money collected is now being spent on a new edition of the poem, which will probably be immediately banned.

It is understood that the Clare County Council is proposing to erect a monument to Biddy Early instead. Witches are more in their line.

Extracts taken from Frank O'Connor, *Leinster, Munster and Connaught* (London n.d.) [1950], pp 219-33.

Bibliography

Hereunder is a list of books of Clare interest that have not been included in the anthology because (a) lack of space (b) the accounts were not the result of direct observation but were derived from other sources (c) the material was lacking in quality or (d) the information was available in better and more accessible sources. However, the bibliography will be of interest to those who wish to engage in further research.

Addison, Robert, *Recollections of an Irish Police Magistrate* (Dublin 1862).

Arensberg, Conrad M. *The Irish Countryman* (London 1937).

Arensberg, Conrad M. and Kimball, S.T. *Family and Community in Ireland* (Cambridge, Massachusetts 1940).

Barrow, John, *Tour of the Sea Counties of Ireland* (London 1836).

Balch, William S. *Ireland as I Saw it* (New York 1850).

Blood, Sir General Bindon, *Four Score Years and Ten* (London 1933).

Butler, Elizabeth, *From Sketch Book and Diary* (London 1909).

Connor, John, *County of Clare Election* (Cork 1828).

Coppard, A.L. & Gibbings Robert, *Rummy* (London 1932).

Cooper, Austin, *Visit to Lough Derg*, ed. Liam Price (Dublin 1940).

Creagh, Sir O'More, *Autobiography of Sir O'More Creagh* (London 1924).

Day, Ella, *Diary of Mr Justice Day of Kerry, 1745-1841*, ed. Ella B. Day (Dublin 1938).

Dickson, M.F., *Scenes on the Shores of the Atlantic*, 2 vols (Dublin 1845).

Doyle, Lynn, *The Spirit of Ireland* (London 1935).

Dwyer, Rev. Canon Philip, *A Handbook to Lisdoonvarna* (Dublin 1876, reprint Ennis, 1998).

Dutton, Hely, *Statistical Survey of the County of Clare* (Dublin 1808).

Edmunson, William, *A Journal of the Life, Travels. . . of William Edmunson 1627-1712* (London 1829).

Fanshawe, Lady, *The Memoirs of Anne, Lady Halkett and Anne, Lady Fanshawe* ed. J. Loftis (Oxford 1979).

Ferguson, Mary Catherine, *Sir Samuel Ferguson in the Ireland of his Day* (Edinburg 1896).

Foster, Thomas Campbell, *Letters on the Condition of the People of Ireland* (London 1841)

Forbes, Sir John, *Memorandums of a Tour in Ireland in 1852*, 2 vols (London 1853).

Fraser, James, *Handbook for Travellers in Ireland* (Dublin 1838, new edition 1843).

Gauci, Paul, *Select Views of Lough Derg and the River Shannon* (London 1831).

Grancey, Baron de E. Mandat, *Paddy at Home* (London 1887).

Hall, W.H. Bullock, *Gleanings in Ireland after the Land Acts (London 1883)*.

Hall, Mr. & Mrs. S.C., *Ireland: its Scenery and Character etc.*, 3 vols (London 1843).

Ham, Elizabeth, *Elizabeth Ham by Herself*, ed. Eric Gillet (London 1930).

Hoare, Sir Richard Colt, *A Tour in Ireland, 1806* (London 1807).

Holmes, George, *Sketch of Some of the Southern Counties of Ireland during a Tour in the Autumn of 1797*, (London 1801).

Howell, Charles, *An Irish Ramble*, (New York 1930).

Kennedy, Barth, *The Green Sphinx*, (London 1905).

Knott, Mary John, *Two Months at Kilkee* (Dublin 1836, reprint Ennis, 1997).

Lewin, Harry Ross, *With the 32nd in the Penninsular and Other Campaigns* ed. John Wardell (Dublin 1904).

Lloyd, John, *A Short Tour in the County Clare* (Ennis 1780, reprint Cambridge 1893).

McMahon, John T., *Ramblers from Clare* (Dublin 1936).

Mason, W. Shaw, *A Statistical Account, or Parocial Survey of Ireland*, 3 vols (Dublin 1814-17)

Molony, J. Chartres, *The Riddle of the Irish* (London 1927).

O'Donnell, George, *Reminiscences of a Country Boy*, (Dublin 1949).

Pellew, George, *In Castles and Cabin, Ireland 1887* (New York 1888).

Rodenberg, Julius, *A Pilgrimage Through Ireland* (London 1860).

Shand, Alexander, *Letters from the West of Ireland* (London 1885).

Sheil, Richard Lalor, *The Speeches of Richard Lalor Sheil* ed. T. MacNevin (Dublin 1845).

Speakman, Harold, *Here's Ireland*, (New York 1927).

Stokes, William C.E. *A Pictorial Survey and Tourist's Guide to Lough Derg and the River Shannon* (London 1842).

Tocqueville, Alexis de, *Journey in Ireland in 1835* trans. and ed. Emmet Larkin (Dublin 1990).

Wilkinson, G., *Practical Geology and Ancient Architecture of Ireland* (London 1845).

Wilson, W., *The Post Chaise Companion Through Ireland* (Dublin 1783, new editions 1805, 1815).

Young, Canon A.B.R., *Reminiscences of an Irish Priest, 1845-1920* (Dundalk 1932).

Index

Page numbers referring to authors of extracts appear in bold type.
References to text in Irish are given in italics.

From ENNIS to Innistymond and to Kilfenora.

Ennis to Innistymond   M. F.   Ennis to Kilfenora   M. F.
Corrofin to Innistymond   12 4   14 0
                           8 6